*Dionysus Reborn*

# DIONYSUS REBORN
*Play and the Aesthetic Dimension
in Modern Philosophical and
Scientific Discourse*

## MIHAI I. SPARIOSU

Cornell University Press
ITHACA AND LONDON

International Standard Book Number 0-8014-2327-9
Library of Congress Catalog Card Number 89-923
Printed in the United States of America
*Librarians: Library of Congress cataloging information appears on the last page of the book.*

*The paper in this book is acid-free and meets the guidelines for permanence and durability of the Committee on Production Guidelines for Book Longevity of the Council on Library Resources.*

*For Janis and Hilary*

# Contents

# *Preface*

Despite the widely recognized importance of the play concept for modern thought and the impressive number of cultural-anthropological and literary studies devoted to play, we still lack a critical historical perspective on the topic. This book, outlining a history of the concept of play in philosophy and science since the end of the eighteenth century, constitutes a first step in contemporary Anglo-American scholarship. The only extensive study related to it (but not available in English) is Ingeborg Heidemann's *Der Begriff des Spieles und das aesthetische Weltbild in der Philosophie der Gegenwart* (Berlin, 1968). Heidemann, however, confines herself to the phenomenological tradition, adopting mainly a systematic approach, whereas I attempt to provide a historical theoretical model for a much-needed interdisciplinary survey of the field.

The book has three sections. The introduction, "Play, Power, and the Western Mentality," addresses some of the theoretical issues confronting any historical investigation of play in Western thought. I relate my history of the play concept to a history of the Western mentality as a whole, suggesting that this mentality has always fluctuated between various rational and prerational sets of values. Consequently, I draw a distinction between a rational and a prerational group of play concepts, briefly tracing their origins in archaic and classical Hellenic thought. Part I, "Play and Modern Philosophical Discourse," examines the various returns of the play concept in Continental philosophy since the end of the eighteenth century. Initially this concept, which was pushed into the background by the dominant Cartesian tradition of the seventeenth century, finds its way back into metaphysics at the end of the Age of

Reason, especially through Kant, and then becomes central through Schiller. This first return of the play concept in German idealism, however, restages the repression of prerational play, initiated by Plato and Aristotle and perpetuated by the Neoclassical rationalist tradition. Then, in the wake of Schopenhauer, prerational play itself returns to the philosophical center stage, both through Nietzsche and through such twentieth-century "artist-metaphysicians" as Heidegger, Fink, Gadamer, Deleuze, and Derrida. Part II, "Play and Modern Scientific Discourse," examines, on the one hand, some of the play concepts that surface in modern science in connection with the Darwinian theory of evolution and, on the other hand, the play of scientific discourse itself, as exemplified by the New Physics and the "anarchistic epistemology" in the contemporary philosophy of science. Although the prerational play concepts resurface in modern science as well, here they remain subordinated to their rational counterparts; thus, the play of contemporary scientific discourse, unlike that of contemporary philosophical discourse, remains a predominantly rational one.

Another modern intellectual development closely linked to the return of the play concept(s) in philosophical and scientific discourse is aestheticism. A history of the modern concept of play will have to run parallel to a history of modern aestheticism, and my book attempts to sketch the broad outlines of such a history. Revising the accepted view, I argue that actually there have been not one, but two aesthetic turns in modern thought: one is related to a rational mentality and is initiated by Schiller in the wake of Kant; the other is related to a prerational mentality and is inaugurated by Nietzsche in the wake of Schopenhauer. I also emphasize the radical difference between artistic and philosophical-scientific aestheticism: whereas the first often arises in response to the attempts of philosophy and science to impose their standards on art, the second is an effective way of dealing with the epistemological crises that periodically shake these disciplines, and therefore plays an important role in safeguarding their cultural prestige.

In our methodologically self-conscious age, one can no longer write history from an unbiased, objective, or factual point of view, not least because this point of view has itself become part of yet another methodological model, commonly referred to as "positivism." Thus, history has returned to its hermeneutical roots, and any cultural historical inquiry needs to show itself aware of a dialectic of logical and ideological exigencies, conditioned by the historian's own historicity or relative position vis-à-vis his object of study. The historical approach that I use here may be called "interpretive-configurative," and should not be confused with the common hermeneutical approach that nowadays bears the name of "critical rationalism" in philosophy and science and *Rezeptionsgeschichte* in literary studies. According to the latter historical-hermeneutical model, which can be seen as the latest attempt at reconciling metaphysics with history, the play concept(s) appear, in evolutionary fashion, as a series of interpretations that cumulatively constitute their object ad infinitum. By contrast, in an interpretive-configurative model, the play concept no longer appears as the sum total of its interpretations or as a dialectic of temporality and permanence, but as an incommensurable, discontinuous series of interpretations engaged in a supremacy contest. The history of what we call "play" in the Western world is, then, a history of conflict, of competing play concepts that become dominant, lose ground, and then reemerge, according to the needs of various groups or individuals contending for cultural authority in a given historical period. Therefore, my intention here is not to offer yet another definition of play as "universal" phenomenon, but to show how any definition of play functions in the concrete, historical context of our culture.

Although my book takes into account a fairly large variety of play concepts, it by no means claims to be a comprehensive history of the modern concept of play. Such a history, if it were ever written, would not only reach monumental proportions but could also easily miss its mark. Play is one of those elusive phenomena that can never be contained within a systematic scholarly treatise; indeed, play transcends all disciplines, if not all discipline. Consequently, this volume should be read less as a systematic survey than as a series of loosely connected essays or case studies, combining broad historical theoretical considerations with concrete textual analyses of individual works or key passages within these works. I have chosen to discuss well-known texts because their authors are among the most articulate and persuasive spokesmen for the modern Western mentality. And in addition to such familiar thinkers as Kant, Schiller, Nietzsche, Heidegger, Gadamer, Deleuze, Derrida, Spencer, Freud, Piaget, Bateson, Monod, Planck, Einstein, Heisenberg, Schrödinger, Kuhn, and Feyerabend, my case studies include less familiar figures who have also substantially contributed to the shaping of contemporary consciousness—Eugen Fink, Karl Groos, D. W. Winnicott, Richard Dawkins, Manfred Eigen, René Thom, David Bohm, Hans Vaihinger, and others. I have, moreover, attempted to see all these authors both from within their imaginative worlds and from a distance, as key figures who are symptomatic of a whole cultural trend or a whole set of values and beliefs. Thus, even where I deal with familiar works, I believe my interpretations of these works often diverge sufficiently from those currently circulating in the Anglo-American academic community to warrant careful and relatively extensive development.

Finally, because my book attempts to relate the modern concept of play to a history of the Western mentality as a whole, it addresses itself not only to the "play specialist" but also to a considerably wider audience. Through a detailed examination of several Western concepts of play I attempt to offer not so much a critique as a diagnosis of a basic mentality we all share. This diagnosis will perhaps enhance our understanding of ourselves, which may in turn broaden the range of our intellectual and existential choices.

I am deeply indebted to several institutions and to a great number of individuals for having assisted me during the various stages of this project, and I regret that I cannot properly acknowledge all of them here. I am particularly grateful to the Alexander von Humboldt Foundation for its generous support through two crucial years of research and scholarly interaction at the universities of Konstanz and Hamburg. Special thanks are also due to the Andrew W. Mellon Postdoctoral Fellowship Program at Cornell University and its director, Anna Geske, as well as to professors W. Wolfgang Holdheim and William Kennedy for their equally generous support during my tenure as a Mellon Fellow in Comparative Literature at Cornell.

I am no less grateful to Matei Calinescu of Indiana University, Herbert S. Lindenberger of Stanford University, and Virgil Nemoianu of Catholic University, teachers, colleagues, and friends who have closely followed my intellectual development over the years and have critically commented on my work both privately and in print; to Giuseppe Mazzotta of Yale University, for our long and passionate debates about the exiled soul, in wintry Ithaca; to Wolfgang Iser of the University of Konstanz, Karl Robert Mandelkow of the University of Hamburg, and Steven Rendall of the University of Oregon for many delightful and rewarding conversations during my tenure as a Humboldt Fellow; to Joel Black of the University of Georgia and Michael Cahn of the University of Konstanz, for their perceptive critiques of my work; to Albert J. Guerard, René Girard, and David Halliburton of Stanford University for their enlightened and inspiring presence during my years at Stanford; to Stanley Fish, Murray Krieger, Edward Said, and Barbara Herrnstein Smith, whose lectures at the School of Theory and Criticism, University of California at Irvine, first led me to thinking about some of the theoretical issues raised in this book; to my colleagues and friends at the University of Georgia, Ronald Bogue, Linda Brooks, Betty Jean Craige, Kent Kraft, Tonglin Lu, and the greatly mourned Frank Warnke, whose genial, cosmopolitan, and witty personality we all miss, as well as to Brian Sutton-Smith of the University of Pennsylvania and Richard Brown of the University of Maryland, for their sympathetic and substantial support during various stages of this project; to the two anonymous readers of my manuscript for Cornell University Press who have offered many useful suggestions and have initiated a spirited debate, helping me further to clarify and sharpen my arguments; to Penny Nichols, Marigene Banks, and Deana Howard for patiently and painstakingly processing several drafts of the manuscript; to Janis Brennan for her generous help with the manuscript, and her loyal friendship through the years; to Jennifer Forbragd, Robert McNamara, and Lisa and Tim O'Brien for their timely assistance at critical moments in the revision of the manuscript; to Alexa Selph for preparing the index; and to Anne Lunt, my copyeditor, and Kay Scheuer of Cornell University Press for their invaluable editorial suggestions.

MIHAI I. SPARIOSU

*Athens, Georgia*

*Dionysus Reborn*

# Introduction:

# Play, Power, and the Western Mentality

Whereas play has always had an important, if sometimes unthematized, role in Western literary discourse, in modern philosophical and scientific discourse its revival begins with the German idealists at the end of the eighteenth century. During the last few decades of the nineteenth century, with Nietzsche, the Neo-Kantians, and the Darwinian evolutionists, play steadily moves toward the center not only of theoretical discourse but also of scientific research, gradually spreading in our century to the majority of the newer as well as the older disciplines such as biology, ethology, zoology, anthropology, sociology, psychology, education, economics, political science, modern warfare, cybernetics, statistics, physics, mathematics, and philosophy of science.

Despite an ever-growing interest in play and countless attempts to explain its nature and function, the play concept remains today as elusive as it was two thousand years ago. We all seem to know what play is and can recognize it as such, but find ourselves at a loss when confronted with the task of conceptualizing this knowledge. In other words, play seems to belong to what the Germans call *das stumme Wissen* (tacit knowledge), involving intuition rather than the rational faculty. There are hundreds of definitions of play, but none seems satisfactory. This situation has led certain contemporary theorists, especially in the sciences, either to deny the possibility of defining play altogether or to classify it as a paradox.[1] Other scholars, particularly in

1. See, e.g., Corinne Hutt, "Exploration and Play in Children," *Symposium of the Zoological Society* 18 (London, 1966): 61–81. Hutt argues that the activities and behaviors associated with play are too heterogeneous to be included in a single category. On the other hand, Gregory Bateson, in "A Theory of Play and Fantasy"

the fields of cultural theory and cultural anthropology, prefer drawing a distinction between play and games, or *paidia* and *ludus*, with the former remaining undefinable and the latter being defined as freedom limited by rules, or institutionalized play.[2]

In contemporary philosophy, play has been described as having an ambivalent ontological status, being both phenomenon and subjectivity or both behavior and intentionality. When encountered by those who are not "in the know," playing is no different from other human and animal behavior. In order to be recognized as such, play has somehow to reveal its intention. Both animals and men, for example, use sound or body signals to indicate that "this is play."[3] This double nature of play has been formulated not only phenomenologically, as a confluence of phenomenon and subjectivity, but also epistemologically, as a mixture of reality and irreality, of truth and illusion. On this view, play appears as a contingency-free, self-enclosed realm that nevertheless manifests itself only in and through the phenomenal world.[4] And it may be precisely this amphibolous nature of play that accounts for its centrality

---

(1955), later published in *Steps to an Ecology of Mind* (San Francisco, 1972), applies to play Bertrand Russell's concept of logical paradox as a "class of classes which are not members of themselves." For a detailed discussion of Bateson's theory of play, see Part II, sec. 1.3.

2. This is, for example, the position of Johan Huizinga in *Homo Ludens* (Leyden, 1938) and, after him, that of a host of theorists of cultural play, among whom Roger Caillois is the best known, especially through *Les jeux et les hommes* (Paris, 1958). For comprehensive surveys of game and play concepts in contemporary literary and cultural theory, see the special issue of the *Yale French Studies* 41 (1968), *Game, Play, Literature*; and, more recently, the special issue of the *Canadian Review of Comparative Literature* 12 (June 1985), *Game and the Theories of Game/Jeu et théories des jeux*. For a recent view of this topic in French theory, see Michel Picard, *La lecture comme jeu* (Paris, 1986). I discuss Huizinga's, Caillois's, and other cultural theorists' views on play in *Literature, Mimesis, and Play* (Tübingen, 1982), particularly in chap. 1, "Literature and Play: History, Principles, Method."

3. See, for example, Bateson, *Ecology of Mind*, pp. 179–181.

4. See, e.g., Eugen Fink, *Spiel als Weltsymbol* (Stuttgart, 1960), especially chap. 2, sec. 6, "Der Unwirklichkeits-Character des Spiels." I examine Fink's theory of play in some detail in Part I, sec. 3.1. For an excellent account of the various modern onto-epistemological approaches to play in general, see Ingeborg Heidemann, *Der Begriff des Spieles und das aesthetische Weltbild in der Philosophie der Gegenwart* (Berlin, 1968), especially book 1, "Die Ontologische Bestimmung des Spieles," pp. 3–116. Heidemann's pioneering study is absolutely indispensable to any student of the modern philosophical concept of play. Although its interpretation of the aesthetic tradition in modern philosophical discourse differs from mine, I am deeply indebted to it for its many valuable insights.

in contemporary thought, where it has become an expedient way of mending the age-old split between subject and object, if not a universal remedy for all our metaphysical and practical problems. From a different onto-phenomenological perspective, however, even this sophisticated attempt to enlist play in the service of Western metaphysics may be doomed to failure, because play is ultimately "unthinkable" in terms of our logical or illogical categories. This utopian, or rather *atopian*, quality of play as the Other of Western metaphysics cannot be approached with critical or analytical tools, implying a mode of being that remains inaccessible to either rational thought or intuition.[5]

Although onto-phenomenological description has nowadays become the standard philosophical approach to play, there are other theoretical avenues for approaching this topic. In fact, any onto-phenomenological description of play may appear rather suspect, precisely because of its implicit ahistorical and universal claims, through the so-called phenomenological reduction or bracketing, which is itself a play concept. Upon close scrutiny, all these supposedly value-free or neutral descriptions may turn out to be historical products of our culture. For instance, I shall argue that the contemporary philosophical views of play as ambivalent and paradoxical may simply be the consequence of our established notions of reality and being, deriving from the split nature of all Western values. One should therefore consider play not in a universal light—this would soon lead to paradox and aporia—but in the concrete historical context of our world. To this end one could adopt a "historical-descriptive" method in studying play, combining Susanna Millar's suggestion that "perhaps play is best used as an adverb; not as a name of a class of activities, nor as distinguished by the accompanying mood, but to describe how and under what conditions an action is performed"[6] with Ludwig Wittgenstein's notion of "family resemblances," interpreted historically. In this regard, one can "define" play by what it does, by its function, rather than by what it means. Indeed, Wittgenstein would argue that a word's meaning coincides with its use; this is to say, one can examine play as a concept or as a speculative tool that has been put to certain uses and has fulfilled certain functions in Western thought.

5. This is essentially the position of Heidegger and Fink, as well as that of Deleuze, Derrida, and other French and Anglo-American poststructuralist thinkers. For a full examination of this position, see Part I, secs. 2.2, 3.1, 3.2, and 3.4.

6. Susanna Millar, *The Psychology of Play* (Harmondsworth, Middlesex, 1968), p. 21.

In *Philosophical Investigations* Wittgenstein introduces the notion of family resemblances in order to elucidate his functionalist theory of language as an infinite network of crisscrossing games. Since this notion will play a crucial role in my book as well, it might be useful to let Wittgenstein speak here at some length:

> 65. Here we come up against the great question. . . . For someone may object against me: "You take the easy way out! You talk about all sorts of language-games, but have nowhere said what the essence of a language-game, and hence of language is: what is common to all these activities, and what makes them into language. . . ."
> And this is true. —Instead of producing something common to all that we call language, I am saying that these phenomena have no one thing in common which makes us use the same word for all, —but that they are *related* to one another in many different ways. . . .
> 66. Consider, for example, the proceedings that we call "games" (*Spiele*). I mean board-games, ball-games, Olympic games, and so on. . . . For if you look at them you will not see something that is common to *all*, but similarities, relationships, and a whole series of them at that. . . . We see a complicated network of similarities overlapping and criss-crossing. . . .
> 67. I can think of no better expression to characterize the similarities than "family resemblances"; for the various resemblances between members of a family: build, features, color of eyes, gait, temperament . . . overlap and criss-cross in the same way. And I shall say: "games" form a family.[7]

7. Ludwig Wittgenstein, *Philosophical Investigations*, trans. G. E. M. Anscombe (New York, 1953), pp. 31e–32e. A detailed consideration of Wittgenstein's theory of language-games will have to be reserved for another occasion: in order to remain within manageable size, I have made the hard choice of forgoing an examination of play and contemporary analytic philosophy in general. However, Part I, secs. 2.2 and 3, do contain brief discussions of language and play in Heidegger, Gadamer, and other contemporary artist-metaphysicians.

It will also become apparent that this book attempts in part to do for the concept of play what Richard Rorty's *Philosophy and the Mirror of Nature* (Princeton, N.J., 1979) has done for the concept of representation in modern philosophical discourse. Even though we share the same Wittgensteinian approach to the history of philosophical concepts, our basic premises differ considerably. For example, faithful to his analytical philosophical background, Rorty rejects the various representational views of language and the world that have, according to him, dominated Western thought since Descartes if not since the Greeks, in favor of a nonrepresentational or performative view that he associates with contemporary German hermeneutics and Anglo-American philosophy of language. For me, on the other hand,

Like Wittgenstein, I shall say that play forms a family of play concepts, to which his "language-games" equally belong. Moreover, this family can be viewed not only synchronically, but also diachronically or historically; in this sense, the family of play concepts is a very old and respectable one, whose genealogical line goes back all the way to the beginnings of Western thought, in archaic Greece.

A quick look at the history of play in Western thought, however, will reveal that this thought has not only operated with a large number of play concepts, but has also subordinated these concepts to a power principle, which has in turn controlled the Western mentality as a whole. Like play, power is hard to define and can also be regarded as belonging to the realm of "tacit knowledge" and that of "family resemblances." The notorious philosophical difficulty of defining power may also be due to its all-pervasiveness, which makes its "definition" coincide with a description of the Western mentality in general.[8] But, as in the case of play, one can proceed historically and examine the various concepts of power that have arisen in Western thought, particularly at its dawn, in the Hellenic world. Even a very superficial glance at the history of the Hellenic notions of power will show that the most complicated philosophical concept may originate in the simplest and most concrete word-notion, and power is precisely this kind of word-

---

this nonrepresentational or performative view is certainly not a fresh point of departure in Western thought; rather, I see it as a "return" to an archaic, prerational mentality that does not differ fundamentally from its representational, rational competitor, belonging to the same power-oriented conceptual world.

8. Although from a philosophical point of view power largely remains undefinable, there have been countless analyses of its political and institutional aspects throughout the Western tradition. Among the most prominent thinkers who have focused on these aspects in the past few centuries are Machiavelli, Hobbes, Grotius, Montesquieu, Vico, Locke, Burke, Rousseau, Thomas Jefferson, Alexander Hamilton, James Madison, Proudhon, Marx, Stirner, Mommsen, Jacob Burckhardt, Nietzsche, J. S. Mill, Bentham, Bakunin, Kropotkin, and Tocqueville. Contemporary authors include Hannah Arendt, Theodor Adorno, Karl Mannheim, Antonio Gramsci, George Orwell, Karl Popper, Victor Ehrenberg, Elias Canetti, Milovan Djilas, Michael Oakeshott, John Rawls, Robert Nozick, Georges Bataille, Michel Foucault, Gilles Deleuze, Louis Marin, Edward Said, and Michael Mann. This book, on the other hand, emphasizes less the political and institutional aspects of power than its conceptual aspects or its *mentality*. In this respect, my approach is closer to that of Nietzsche, Freud, and Foucault than to that of Vico, Marx, and Gramsci, not least because I share the assumption that discourse analysis or *diagnosis* is a most effective instrument of understanding power and its mode of operation. Finally, however, I can no longer share any of these thinkers' power-oriented values.

notion turned philosophical. In the Homeric epic, for instance such words as *menos, sthenos, bia, is, kratos, alke,* and *dunamis* denote concrete, physical, mostly violent forms of power. Later, however, these words turn increasingly abstract and metaphorical until some of them come to denote impersonal symbols of force, for example, *dunamis* and *energeia* in physics. Their semantic development coincides with the development of an abstract philosophical-scientific vocabulary that gradually transforms power from an immediate, personal, and spontaneous physical attribute into a transcendental principle. Whereas in such Presocratic thinkers as Heraclitus power may still be conceived of as "that which arises spontaneously" (*phusis*), as the violent, arbitrary, and ceaseless movement or *play* of physical Becoming, in Plato and his followers it largely turns into "that which is," or the abstract, ideal, and immutable order of transcendental Being. In turn, the Hellenic notion of play—which originally (for instance in the Homeric epic and in Hesiod) is inextricably linked to the notion of immediate physical force, as in such words as *agon* and *athlon* (competition, contest)—gradually loses this link until it becomes *paidia*, a word that initially denotes only the harmless play of children and then becomes, in Plato, a philosophical term for nonviolent cultural play in general. From the very beginning the divided Hellenic notions of power, as well as their divided counterparts, the Hellenic notions of play, engage in a contest for cultural authority that has intermittently been carried on to the present day.

A proper historical understanding of the concepts of power and play in their interrelation must therefore also take into account the divided nature of the Western mentality which, since its birth in ancient Greece, has periodically swayed between a prerational and a rational pole. As I shall constantly operate with this distinction, it may be useful to list some of the main features that give a certain historical period or a certain ethnic-geographical area a predominantly rational or prerational orientation.[9]

9. My model here draws freely upon a great number of studies, most of them classical or cultural anthropological in nature. Among those of particular relevance are Arthur W. H. Adkins, *Merit and Responsibility. A Study in Greek Values* (Oxford, 1960); Ruth Benedict, *Patterns of Culture* (Boston, 1934); Walter Burkert, *Homo Necans* (English trans. Berkeley, 1983) and *Structure and History in Greek Mythology and Ritual* (Berkeley, 1979); F. M. Cornford, *Principium Sapientiae* (Cambridge, Eng., 1952); Marcel Detienne, *Les maîtres de vérité dans la Grèce archaïque* (Paris, 1967); E. R. Dodds, *The Greeks and the Irrational* (Berkeley, 1951); M. I. Finley, *The World of Odysseus* (Harmondsworth, Middlesex, 1954); Sigmund Freud, *Civilization and Its Discontents* (English trans. London, 1961); Hartvig Frisch, *Might and*

1. *Power*. In a prerational mentality, power conceives of itself as physical, naked, and immediate. Authority largely depends on physical strength or cunning intelligence, and is often imposed and maintained by violence. Competitive values prevail over cooperative values, and violence or threat thereof is commonly employed in resolving conflicts; a prerational mentality as a rule creates highly unstable, authoritarian, and hierarchical forms of government.

In a predominantly rational mentality, by contrast, power does not *present* but rather *re-presents* itself, being increasingly mediated and shared. Authority depends less on strength than on intellectual ability or on knowledge and truth. Cooperative values and social consensus are increasingly emphasized, although they remain subordinated to competition. Violence is less commonly employed in resolving conflicts and becomes strictly regulated by the social body at large. A rational mentality may create a variety of forms of government, ranging from the more centralized and hierarchical kinds, with a king or an autocrat representing the gods or the people, to more democratic kinds in which power is shared by an elected body of citizens, delegated to represent the will of the majority.

2. *Law*. In a prerational mentality, customary law prevails according to the principle of might makes right. Justice is largely a private matter that concerns the community only indirectly. Right is restored by violent means, according to the principle of blood revenge or retribution. The ethics of the victimizer prevails over that of the victim. Shame rather than guilt is the most effective social censor.

In a predominantly rational mentality, written law often replaces or coexists with customary law, according to the principle of might *and*

---

*Right in Antiquity* (Copenhagen, 1949); René Girard, *La violence et le sacré* (Paris, 1972) and *Le bouc émissaire* (Paris, 1982); Jack Goody, *The Domestication of the Savage Mind* (Cambridge, Eng., 1977); Eric A. Havelock, *Preface to Plato* (Oxford, 1963), *The Literate Revolution in Greece and Its Cultural Consequences* (Princeton, N.J., 1982), and *The Muse Learns to Write* (New Haven, Conn., 1986); Julian Jaynes, *The Origin of Consciousness in the Breakdown of the Bicameral Mind* (Boston, 1976); Claude Lévi-Strauss, *La pensée sauvage* (Paris, 1962); Lucien Lévy-Bruhl, *Les fonctions mentales dans les sociétés inferieurs* (Paris, 1910); Albert Lord, *A Singer of Tales* (Cambridge, Mass., 1960); Alasdair MacIntyre, *After Virtue* (Notre Dame, Ind., 1981); Friedrich Nietzsche, *The Genealogy of Morals: An Attack*, trans. F. Golffing (New York, 1956); Walter J. Ong, *Orality and Literacy* (London, 1982); R. B. Onians, *Origins of European Thought* (Cambridge, Eng., 1951); Bruno Snell, *The Discovery of the Mind: The Greek Origins of European Thought* (English trans. Cambridge, Mass., 1950); and Jean-Pierre Vernant, *The Origins of Greek Thought* (English trans. Ithaca, N.Y., 1982). I extensively discuss this model in relation to Hellenic culture in *God of Many Names: Play, Art and Power in Hellenic Thought: From Homer to Aristotle* (forthcoming).

right. Rational mentality effects a conscious separation between power and justice: right becomes independent of might, but remains nevertheless protected by the latter. Justice turns from a largely private matter into a public one. Moral responsibility toward the community is emphasized over individual merit. Although right is still restored by violent means, violence is strictly regulated by the community and the principle of reciprocity is emphasized over the principle of retribution. The ethics of the victim takes precedence over that of the victimizer, and guilt, rather than shame, becomes the most effective social censor.

3. *Religion.* In a prerational mentality, religion is as a rule animistic and/or anthropomorphic, with centralized, hierarchical, and violent societies of gods, conceived as extensions of human societies: the difference between men and gods resides in the degree of power they have rather than in the kind. Gods communicate directly with men, especially through voices, and they are amoral, violent, and irrational. Sacrificial rituals are the most effective mechanism of appeasing vengeful gods and purging human communities of violence.

In a predominantly rational mentality, gods become increasingly abstract and removed, until they are replaced by an impersonal, impenetrable power, in monotheism. They hide from and no longer communicate directly with men, appearing only to a privileged few, indirectly, in portents and visions or in oracular states of possession-madness. Religious cults remain sacrificial, although scapegoat rituals become increasingly abstract and symbolic; human sacrifice becomes "unnatural" and real scapegoats are replaced by surrogates. Religion turns increasingly rational and the gods increasingly moral and nonviolent.

4. *Consciousness.* A prerational mentality is often also a preconscious one, with the auditory taking precedence over the visual. In many cases a prerational mentality is a predominantly oral one as well. The voice is an important source of authority: to hear is to obey. Speech is "thought" whose seat is not in the brain but in the lungs or diaphragm. A prerational mentality does not distinguish between speech and action, cognition and emotion. Language is concrete and practical, having poetical, that is, *performative* power and being structured according to mnemonic rather than visual or logical principles.

By contrast, a rational mentality is largely a conscious one (with the preconscious mentality becoming incorporated into it as its "unconscious" or "subconscious.") The visual replaces the auditory as the main seat of perception. Whereas emotions remain located in the lungs or diaphragm, understanding moves to the brain, and consciousness is born as a result of this split. Language becomes increasingly abstract and logical, whereas thought becomes dialectical, or antithetical. Writing emerges and spreads to an increasingly broader section of the community, and a rational mentality is also largely a literate one.

5. *Education and Knowledge.* In a prerational culture education consists mainly of physical and professional training, as well as of what the archaic Greeks understand by *mousike*, that is, an amalgam of poetry reciting, music making, and dancing. Although prerational communities practice a division of labor, their idea of knowledge (as distinguished from that of individual skills) is holistic. *Mousike* is "wisdom" (*sophia*, in its archaic sense), that is, a mechanism both of preservation and transmission of the dominant cultural values and of ethnic and social cohesion. Poetic performance is carried out by the singer of tales or the rhapsode, who is the mouth of tradition rather than an individual "author." There is a complete identification between the rhapsode and his audience through what one can call mimesis-play.

In predominantly rational cultures there occurs a division of knowledge, with philosophy, history, rhetoric, and natural science replacing *mousike* as main cultural authority. *Mousike* itself breaks up into individual "arts" (poetry, music, dancing, etc.), while poetry is written down and becomes literature. The science of interpretation (hermeneutics) develops from the old art of divination and becomes the most important *critical* instrument of producing texts. History as written documentation replaces oral tradition or *muthos* (which a literate mentality translates as "fiction") in its function of preserving and transmitting the dominant cultural values. The singer of tales becomes separated from his audience and turns into a "poet" (a maker of literary texts) or into an individual author-authority.

If one examines the history of the West in terms of this admittedly oversimplified model, one can readily see that archaic Greece and early Rome, for example, are mostly prerational, whereas Hellenistic Greece and imperial Rome are predominantly rational. Other largely prerational communities can be found in early medieval Europe, for instance, in Anglo-Saxon, Germanic, or Slavic ethnic-geographical areas (as opposed to, say, the Byzantine world), with Christianity acting as the most important cultural instrument for spreading a rational mentality to the majority of the Western world. Since the early Renaissance most of Western Europe has steadily moved toward a rational mentality, which becomes predominant in the seventeenth century and prevails to the present day. One can also associate the two kinds of mentality with various dominant social groups. For instance, many aristocratic, agrarian, or feudal cultures are predominantly oral and prerational, whereas middle-class, industrialized cultures are predominantly literate and rational. Likewise, the transition from a prerational to a rational culture may affect only certain segments of a population, with the two mentalities either coexisting or engaging in an active conflict. Thus, there are ethnic-geographical areas within the Western world (remote, rural communities within several modern European states, the early American "Wild West," etc.) where a prerational mentality has remained dominant until quite recently. Furthermore, even when it becomes submerged within a predominantly rational culture, prerational mentality will often resurface, in one form or another, during periods of sociocultural crisis, such as wars, invasions, revolutions, and so forth.

Freud's description of the "evolution of the mind" is helpful in understanding the interplay of rational and prerational mentality:

> For the evolution of the mind shows a pecularity which is present in no other process of development. When a village grows into a town, a child into a man, the village and the child become submerged in the town and the man. Memory alone can trace the earlier features in the new image; in reality the old materials or forms have been superseded and replaced by new ones. It is otherwise with the development of the mind. Here one can describe the state of affairs which is a quite peculiar one, only by saying that in this case every earlier stage of development persists alongside the later stage which has developed from it; the successive stages condition a co-existence, although it is in reference to the same materials that the whole series of transformations has been fashioned. The earlier mental state may not have manifested itself for years, but nonetheless it is so far present that it may at any time again become the mode of expression of the forces in the mind, and that exclusively, as though all later developments had been annulled, undone. This extraordinary plasticity of the evolution that takes place in the mind is not unlimited in its scope; it might be described as a special capacity for retroversion for regression—since it may well happen that a later and higher stage of evolution, once abandoned, cannot be reached again. But the primitive stages can always be reestablished; the primitive mind is, in the fullest meaning of the word, imperishable.[10]

Freud's model of the coexistence of the two stages of mental evolution can also describe the relationship between a prerational and a rational mentality, but not without first undergoing certain modifications. For instance, one can include in this model not only the mental history of Western man but also the history of his behavioral patterns,

10. Sigmund Freud, "Reflections upon War and Death," in Philip Rieff, ed., *Character and Culture* (New York, 1963), pp. 118–119.

with their underlying sets of values and beliefs. One can further introduce a dynamic element in Freud's model by seeing the two mentalities
as engaging in a ceaseless agon, constantly trying to supersede one
another. A modified version of this model will no longer share Freud's
essentially rational and evolutionary bias (see Part II, sec. 1.2), or his
view of mental development as a history of progress and regress; rather,
it asssumes that the two mentalities are equally agonistic and that their
contest has little to do with what a rational mentality calls "progress" or
"evolution." In this sense, the concept of evolution itself is a product of
this mentality, which in turn employs it as an ideological weapon
against its chief rival, prerational mentality. One can also point out that
what Freud understands by the "unconscious" (or Jung, by the "collective unconscious") can in part be seen as the prerational mind that
becomes repressed and then *interpreted* by its rational counterpart. In
this regard, such antipsychoanalytical works as Deleuze and Guattari's
*L'anti-Oedipe*, for example, with their emphasis on the impossibility of
interpreting the unconscious (or, indeed, denying its existence altogether), should be seen as a Nietzschean attempt to free prerational
mentality of its rational bonds and therefore as a reaffirmation of prerational values in modern culture.

The various shifts from a prerational to a rational mentality (and vice
versa) bring about deep psychological changes in both the individual
and the community at large, changes that have been described, for
example, in epic and tragic poetry, which as a rule flourishes during such
shifts. The metamorphosis of immediate power configurations into
mediated, representational ones often results in both a repression of and
a nostalgia for origins. On the one hand, rational mentality represses its
prerational counterpart, labeling it "savage," "barbarian," and "primitive," precisely because prerational power presents itself in a naked,
unashamed, and violent form. On the other hand, rational mentality
experiences the transition to mediated forms of power as a loss of
presence and a yearning for (absolute) authority. The prerational historical past becomes idealized either in the sentimental notion of a
"golden age" or in the philosophical notion of a "totality of Being," of a
"unity of world and self."

The reversals to a prerational mentality produce equally profound,
and often traumatic, psychological changes, and such influential authors as Sade, Nietzsche, Orwell, and Deleuze have partially attempted
to document these changes. Becoming as an arbitrary and violent play
of forces, the melting of the self into the ecstatic play of the world,

necessity as affirmation of pure chance, the overcoming of the Christian guilt mentality through joyful forgetfulness, the "beyond-good-and-evil" ethics of the Overman—these are some of the modern philosophical themes that promote prerational values.

The split nature of the Western mentality also reflects itself in the split nature of the various play concepts with which Western thought has operated over the centuries. For example, prerational thought generally conceives of play as a manifestation of power in its "natural," unashamed, unmediated form, ranging from the sheer delight of emotional release to raw and arbitrary violence. Power can be experienced both as ecstatic, exuberant, and violent play and as a pleasurable welling up and gushing forth of strong emotion. Rational thought, in contrast, generally separates play from both unmediated or "innocent" power and raw violence. Indeed, it sees play as a form of mediation between what it now represses as the "irrational" (the chaotic conflict of physical forces, the disorderly eruption of violent emotion, the unashamed gratification of the physical senses, etc.) and controlling Reason, or the universal Will to Order. Given the wide gulf between these play concepts, a good course is to follow the dividing line between them and to regard them as forming two distinct camps: a prerational and a rational one. The major prerational play concepts include play as prerational agon, play as the arbitrary and violent conflict of physical forces or as a manifestation of ceaseless physical Becoming, play as chance-necessity, mimesis-play, play as an *as if* prerational mode of being, and play as unrestrained freedom. Among the major rational play concepts are play as nonviolent, rational agon, play as the rational order of Being, play as the rule-determined interaction of chance and necessity, play as mimesis-imitation, play as an *as if* rational mode of being, and play as rational or limited freedom. As some of these rational and prerational play concepts are obvious symmetrical opposites, it would be useful to review them briefly in relation to their historical origins in Hellenic thought.

Prerational agon is the single most important concept of play in archaic thought, determining the nature of all the other play concepts with which this thought operates. For example, it permeates Homeric epic poetry, and can conveniently be examined in terms of the Homeric concept of *arete*. This concept points to the ethical standards of the *aristoi* (aristocrats)—significantly, *arete* and *aristos* have a common etymological root—emphasizing the predominantly competitive nature of these standards. Although it is usually translated as "virtue" or "excellence," Homeric *arete* can more accurately be rendered as "prowess in battle" and is geared toward those qualities which are most needed in a warlike society, such as physical strength, valor, endurance, and the like. It also has a second meaning, describing intellectual rather than physical abilities, but again in a competitive context: Odysseus, for example, is praised as being *aristos* in counsel because of his ability to bring about, through skillful manipulation or cunning (*metis*), his own party's success in war or peace. Throughout Homeric society—and this is true of the early medieval heroic worlds as well—power presents itself in the form of (predominantly violent) agonistic play. This means not only that competition has a crucial function in Homeric life, but also that the Greek hero sees his relationship to other heroes and to the gods, as well as to existence in general, in terms of a huge power game. Peleus's famous counsel to his son Achilles, "Always be best and excel others" (*Iliad*, 11.783), epitomizes the Greek aristocratic ideal of life, based on contest, and will constitute one of the major topoi of Hellenic thought from the Presocratics to Plato.

In Presocratic thought the prerational notion of agon is used to describe the natural world as a ceaseless play of forces or Becoming, assuming a somewhat more impersonal and abstract form than it has in Homeric thought. The world gradually becomes less "full of gods" (Thales) than of warring, impersonal physical forces, of what Aristotle will later call "elements" or "principles." For example, in Heraclitus prerational strife (*eris*) or war (*polemos*) becomes a cosmic principle, accounting for both stability and change: "It is necessary to know that war is common or shared and right [*dike*] is strife, and that all things happen by strife and necessity [*ananke*]."[11] Or, again: "War is the father and king of all, and some he shows as gods, others as men; some he makes slaves, others free" (frag. 53). Heraclitus still imagines the agonistic play of physical forces in concrete and personal terms as the arbitrary violent and innocent play of a child: "Lifetime [*aion*] is a child at play, moving pieces in a game, the kingship belongs to the child" (frag. 52). Later on, however (for instance, in Greek scientific thought), the notion of the physical world as a network of powers (*dunameis*) at play is increasingly separated from its anthropomorphic context and turns into scientific abstraction. Accordingly, the agonistic play of physical forces becomes increasingly abstract, impersonal, and objective.

Likewise, with the rise of a rational and literate mentality in archaic

11. All the fragments from Heraclitus cited here are from G. S. Kirk and J. E. Raven, *The Presocratic Philosophers: A Critical History with a Selection of Texts* (Cambridge, Eng., 1957), following the numerotation of Diels-Kranz.

Greece, prerational agon slowly gives way to good and bad eris. One can see the first signs of this development in Hesiod. In *Works and Days*, for instance, Hesiod draws a distinction between bad eris, associated with violent aristocratic values, and good eris, associated with the peaceful contest between members of various trades and crafts, including poets:

> Strife is no only child. Upon the earth
> two strifes exist; the one is praised by those
> who come to know her, and the other blamed.
> Their natures differ: for the cruel one
> makes battles thrive, and war;
>
> . . .
>
> The other, first-born child of blackest night,
> Was set by Zeus, who lives in air, on high,
> Set in the roots of earth, an aid to men.
> She urges even lazy men to work:
> A man grows eager, seeing another rich
> From ploughing, planting, ordering his house;
> So neighbor vies with neighbor in the rush
> For wealth: this Strife is good for mortal men—
> Potter hates potter, carpenters compete,
> And beggar strives with beggar, bard with bard.[12]

Hesiod contrasts the heroic values of the aristocracy with the relatively peaceful values of the middle class, by relating eris to work (*ergon, ponos*) rather than to agon. Thus, we discern in Hesiod the dim beginnings of a dialectic of play and work, which has its origins in the contest between aristocratic, prerational and middle-class, rational values, and which will resurface throughout the history of Western thought. Hesiod also begins the long process of separating play from unmediated power and violence, a process that will be completed by Plato and Aristotle. Although it remains competitive, play as good eris or rational contest emphasizes the nonviolent and productive side of competition, repressing its violent and destructive side. The philosophical process by which prerational eris is subordinated to rational competition parallels the similar process by which the arbitrary and violent play of physical forces (Becoming) is subordinated to the rational play of Being. The latter process is already discernible in Parmenides and is completed by

12. Hesiod, *Works and Days,* trans. D. Wender (Harmondsworth, Middlesex, 1973), lines 21–29.

Plato through his concept of physical Becoming as a bad imitation (*mimesis*) of the eternal, spiritual world of Being.

The prerational notion of play as chance-necessity is closely related to the archaic notion of the world order (*kosmos*) as the varying outcomes of a huge power game, in which myriad divine, human, and physical forces ceaselessly contend for supremacy; in other words, play as chance-necessity is closely related to play as prerational agon. One can understand this notion by tracing the genealogy of such Greek words as *moira* and *aisa* in their relation to *ananke* and *tuche*. Archaic *moira* or *aisa*, which can be translated as "share" or "lot," has little to do with its later, rational meaning of immutable Fate that binds man from his birth. Rather, it designates the share of power for which man competes not just with other men but with the gods as well. Defeat and/or death are the only measure or limit of this power game. In Homer, for example, the hero takes ever greater risks against the celestial bank and his *moira* becomes "fate" only after he loses or comes to grief. Competition, therefore, creates *moira* or *aisa*, just as it creates and dissolves all human and divine hierarchies. The gods themselves have their *moirai*, portions, which are the limits of their power. But because their portions both encompass and supersede those of the mortals, from the latter's point of view the cosmos appears as a divine lottery in which misery and happiness are indifferently alloted; they are distributed not according to merit but according to arbitrary will or "chance." As Achilles points out to Priam: "There are two urns that stand on the door-sill of Zeus. They are unlike / For the gifts they bestow: an urn of evils and an urn of blessings / If Zeus who delights in thunder mingles these and bestows them / On man, he shifts, and moves now in evil, again in good fortune."[13]

In other words, Zeus scatters good and evil fates or lots among men not according to any principle of fair play, let alone divine justice, but according to his own whims. This belief also explains why casting lots or dice is a common way of administering justice in archaic societies. The fall of the dice has little to do with chance in our sense of the word: it simply reveals the arbitrary will of the gods to which men must submit because of their inferior power. Archaic necessity and chance are therefore interchangeable, being human ways of experiencing the cosmic power game, in which men have a subordinate and limited role. In this sense, Homeric cosmos is "not so much like a piece of clockwork as it is

13. *Iliad*, 24.527–530, trans. R. Lattimore (Chicago, 1951). Further citations refer to this edition.

like a game of celestial snakes and ladders. Most moves are free; but should one alight at the foot of one's particular ladder, or at the head of one's particular snake, the next move is determined."[14] The interchangeability of archaic necessity and chance as well as their inextricable link to the cosmic power game can also be traced in their closely related etymologies: both *ananke* and *tuche* orginally seem to have conveyed the idea of "binding." *Ananke* (necessity) is seen by some as an etymological relative of *anchein*, to strangle. Likewise, its Latin equivalent *necesse* is "almost naturally related to *necto*, *nexus*, with an original reference to binding or being bound."[15] *Ananke* is thus connected to the threads of the Moirae, who spin their nets around mortals. In turn, *tuche* (chance) is conceived as tying cords around men, which they may loosen after death.[16] In any case, the agonistic play of chance-necessity is far removed from what a later rational and teleological mode of thinking will call *predetermination*, reflecting the chaotic and arbitrary play of physical forces, which transforms men into both players and playthings.

With the advent of a rational mentality, the notion of play as chance-necessity becomes severed from the concept of play as violent agon and assumes an abstract, philosophical-scientific guise, in Plato and Aristotle, for instance, and in modern theology and modern science. Since the cosmos is now conceived of as an eternal, immutable order of Being, chance becomes separated from and subordinated to necessity. Moira as Necessity or Fate, rather than the chance-necessity of an individual's portion in an ever-shifting cosmic power game, transforms competition into a rational principle, that is, it transforms the arbitrary, violent, and reckless contest of physical forces into a cultural game, subject to rules. Thus, power in its rational, mediated guise presents itself as an interplay of necessity and chance: necessity becomes the limit or the rule of the (power) game, whereas chance becomes both that which the game attempts to limit and that which makes the game possible. In turn, Moira assumes a theological and teleological guise, becoming an all-powerful divine providence: fashioned after the model of a giant clock-

14. Adkins, *Merit and Responsibility*, p. 19.

15. Onians, *Origins of European Thought*, p. 332. For a semantic history of *ananke* see also Heinz Schreckenberg, *Ananke: Untersuchungen zur Geschichte des Wortgebrauchs*, Zetemata 36 (Munich, 1964).

16. Onians, *Origins of European Thought*, pp. 450–451. For the interchangeability of chance and necessity in early Greek thought, see also W. K. C. Guthrie, *A History of Greek Philosophy*, 3 vols. (Cambridge, Eng., 1962–1969), vol. 2, pp. 414–419.

work, it regulates all competition according to the principle of universal justice or fair play, and guides chance with an iron hand.

Along with the notion of play as agon, mimesis-play is one of the most important play concepts in prerational thought, pointing to the fact that a history of the Western concept of play ought to go hand in hand with a history of the concept of mimesis. The Greek word *mimesis* (as well as its older relatives, *mimos, mimeisthai,* and *mimema*) is as a rule associated with the modern concepts of imitation and representation, but this connection is by no means certain before Plato. What does seem certain is that the *mimesis* semantic group was employed in a ritualistic-dramatic context, designating a performative function that we moderns associate with play. Consequently, this semantic group, at least before Plato, should not be understood as conveying the idea of imitation in the sense of "representation or reproduction of an original or a model," but rather the idea of "miming," "simulating," or even "presencing" (invoking, calling something forth). This interpretation of non-Platonic mimesis is far from being generally accepted, especially by the Anglo-American scholarly community, and further clarification would perhaps be useful.

In *Die Mimesis in der Antike* (Bern, 1954), Hermann Koller suggests that *mimesis* and *mimeisthai* were originally used exclusively in connection with music and dancing, and that Plato later extends these terms to poetry and painting, or to the fine arts in general. According to Koller, *mimesis* needs consequently to be translated as "Darstellung" or "Vorstellung" rather than "Nachahmung," a view that comes close to my own interpretation. In his critique of Koller's book, Gerald Else suggests, on the contrary, that the *mimesis* semantic group may mean:

1) "Miming": direct representation of the looks, actions, and/or utterances of animals or men through speech, song, and/or dancing (dramatic or proto-dramatic sense). . . .

2) "Imitation" of the actions of one person by another, in a general sense without actual miming (ethical sense). . . .

3) "Replication": an image or effigy of a person or thing in material form (*mimema* only).[17]

While Else seems to me right in pointing out that the *mimesis* and *mimeisthai* group may also be used outside the context of music and dancing before Plato, I find it hard to agree with his definition of

17. Gerald Else, "Imitation in the Fifth Century," *Classical Philology* 53 (April 1958): 71–90.

miming as "direct representation," which seems to me an interpretation of ritualistic-dramatic mimesis from a Platonic and Aristotelian point of view. Furthermore, the leap from miming to imitating or replicating may not be an easy one, because it may indicate a transition from an archaic to a rational mentality. Plato attempts to redefine *mimesis* as imitation or duplication against archaic miming, present in both *mousike* and ritual, thus separating mythopoeic language in general from its central cultural function within a prerational mentality. He "modernizes" poetry, turning it into "literature" and assigning it a new function: to aid philosophy in supporting the new rational values.

Although Koller's hypothesis may be hard to verify historically because of the scant evidence available, theoretically it is justifiable: He attempts to find evidence for a mimetic theory of music and dancing in the archaic period, based on the archaic performative function of *mimesis*. Even though it remains debatable whether such a theory was ever fully developed, its usefulness would have been obvious: music, poetry, and dancing were originally part of the holistic, mythopoeic complex, and as they became increasingly separated, the Greek thinkers must certainly have felt the need to reflect upon them. Koller seems inconsistent, however, when he argues that Plato extends the meaning of *mimesis* to poetry, for the simple reason that Plato already finds it there. What Plato does do is attempt to redefine its meaning and function in rational terms. With the advent of philosophical thinking, characteristic of a rational mentality, the abstract notion of likeness (*homoiosis*), which was certainly implicit all along in *mimeisthai*, prevails over the performative sense of "bringing something forth"; in fact, the word *mimesis* itself may well be a coinage of the Ionian philosophers, along with similar abstract terms ending in *-is*. Consequently, this book will operate with a distinction between the archaic, prerational and the modern, rational meanings of *mimesis*, or indeed with two different concepts of mimesis altogether: a prerational one, which can be called "mimesis-play," and a rational one, which can be called "mimesis-imitation." Yet one should always bear in mind that even in Plato the two can never be completely separated: "simulation" and "role playing," for example, may imply both imitation and pretense, or an *as if* mode of being that is usually associated with play.

We have a partial glimpse into the nature of mimesis-play, for instance, in Plato's account of the rhapsode's performance and its impact on the audience in the *Ion*. In that dialogue, Socrates employs the analogy of the lodestone in order to describe (disparagingly) the mimetic "frenzy" that spreads from the bard to the audience. The archaic audience totally identifies with the performer through mimetic participation (*methexis*), which is a kind of hypnotic trance eventually leading to catharsis or a pleasurable relief of pent-up emotions. As Eric Havelock points out: "The regularity of the performance had a certain effect of hypnosis which relaxed the body's physical tensions and so also relaxed mental tensions, the fears, anxieties and uncertainties which are the normal lot of our mortal existence. Fatigue was temporarily forgotten and perhaps the erotic impulses, no longer blocked by anxiety, were stimulated. . . . It is therefore to be concluded that the recital of the tribal encyclopaedia, because of the technology of the recital, was also a tribal recreation. In more familiar terms the Muse, the voice of instruction, was also the voice of pleasure."[18]

Although Havelock does not call it play, the performative function of the singer of tales which he describes has been identified as such by most modern psychologists from Spencer to Groos to Freud. Because it combines the auditory-visual with emotion-action and collective participation, mimesis-play gives the bard considerable power over his audience, which he can move at will to laughter or tears, to pleasurable composure or violent emotion. This power, which in the archaic period perhaps remains unconscious, being attributed to the gods and shared collectively, later comes to be used consciously and self-servingly by politicians, rhetoricians, priests, and teachers, as well as by the new breed of professional rhapsodes who are organized in guilds (such as the Homeridae) and who, like Ion, make a living out of performing at religious festivals. And it is precisely this power that to Plato's age, when mimesis-play has already largely lost its central cultural function, appears arbitrary and "irrational."

It is Plato himself who contributes decisively to the transformation of mimesis-play into mimesis-imitation, by separating it from immediate power and violent emotion and subordinating it to the rational, mediated, and nonviolent pleasure of philosophical contemplation. The semantic shift from mimesis-play to mimesis-imitation, then, reflects the larger cultural shift from a prerational to a rational mentality in the Hellenic world. Through mimesis-play, power presents itself as the free, spontaneous, and violent play of physical Becoming; through mimesis-imitation it re-presents itself as Being, Reason, and immutable Order. But both these concepts remain operative in Western thought, and

18. Havelock, *Preface to Plato*, p. 152.

mimesis-play resurfaces with renewed vigor in modern philosophical discourse. Kant and German idealism in general unwittingly initiate the long, uneven, and by no means irreversible process of restoring mimesis-play to its high pre-Platonic cultural status. This process culminates in Nietzsche and is carried on in the twentieth century in the thought of Heidegger and Fink in Germany, and of Deleuze and Derrida in France. From a suppressed epistemological prop of philosophy (controlled and regulated by mimesis-imitation), mimesis-play turns once more into an indispensable cognitive tool, a fundamental way of understanding the world of Becoming. In this context, mimesis-imitation also reverses its function: it is no longer an instrument for subordinating mimesis-play to knowledge and truth (as it was in Plato and Aristotle) but is on the contrary an instrument for subordinating knowledge and truth to mimesis-play. Plato's nightmare of bad mimesis, associated with immediate power and violence finally comes true. In such contemporary thinkers as Deleuze, Derrida, and their followers play is no longer good mimesis, installing Being and Truth; rather, mimesis is (Platonic) bad play, replacing Being and Truth with the eternal play of simulacra. In terms of our premises, however, this simply points to the fact that the internal movement of philosophical discourse has seen a partial reversal of what Adorno and Horkheimer call the dialectic of Myth and Reason,[19] or a "return" to prerational concepts of play as a means of perpetuating certain discursive power configurations.

Another play concept that reflects the shift from a prerational to a rational mentality in Hellenic thought is that of play as an *as if* activity or mode of being. This concept is related both to mimesis-play and to mimesis-imitation through the idea of *homoiosis* (likeness), which is an implicit component of *mimeisthai*, *mimema*, and *mimesis*. Originally, play as an *as if* mode of being or human activity is inextricably bound with ritualistic simulation and role playing (e.g., in archaic ritual practices involving masks), but later on, notably in philosophy, it will also involve an abstract, rational operation that can be termed an *as if* approach to knowledge. This approach is based on the philosophical premise that whereas man can never attain absolute truth or knowledge, he can at least act *as if* truth or knowledge were accessible. Xenophanes was one of the first Greek thinkers to use the *as if* play concept in its rational guise, as part of his critique of Homeric, prerational values. After he points out the violence and amorality of the Homeric gods,

19. See Theodor W. Adorno and Max Horkheimer, *Die Dialektik der Aufklärung* (Amsterdam, 1947).

Xenophanes dismisses the Homeric concept of divinity as a projectional fallacy (or what, in modern times, Kant will call *symbolischer Anthropomorphismus*):

> But mortals consider that the gods are born, and that they have clothes and speech and bodies like our own. (Frag. 14)

> But if cattle and horses or lions had hands, or were able to draw with their hands and do the works that men can do, horses would draw the forms of the gods like horses, and cattle like cattle, and they would make their bodies such as they had themselves. (Frag. 16)[20]

Next Xenophanes denies that man can ever know truth, which means that he can hardly know anything about the gods either: "No man knows, or ever will know, the truth about the gods and about everything I speak of: for even if one chanced to say the complete truth, yet oneself knows it not; but seeming is wrought over all things [or: fancy is wrought in the case of all men]" (frag. 34).

But then Xenophanes reintroduces symbolical projection in his argument, only now in its refined, rational form of the good analogy, or good symbolical anthropomorphism: "Let these things be stated as conjectural only, resembling truth [or reality]" (frag. 35, my translation). On this conjectural basis, Xenophanes postulates divinity to be not many but one, "greatest among gods and men, in no way similar to mortals either in body or in thought" (frag. 25–26). Thus, he seems to be among the first to introduce what Vaihinger calls a "useful philosophical fiction" in epistemology. Xenophanes transforms the archaic notion of play as an *as if* mode of being into a rational analogical principle, later on associated by Plato with *mimesis* (in the sense of imitation), through which inaccessible truth becomes at least partly accessible in the *as if* play of Reason. In modern philosophical and scientific discourse the concept of play as an *as if* rational activity will become not only a major instrument of cognition from Kant to Vaihinger, but also an indispensable approach to the problem of knowledge and truth in the theoretical and applied sciences.

The last play concept to be briefly reviewed here is play as freedom, in both its prerational and its rational guises. In the Homeric corpus, play as freedom implies the arbitrary, exuberant, and unconstrained play of physical forces and is inextricably linked to play as prerational agon.

---

20. As in the case of Heraclitus, and unless otherwise specified, all the fragments from Xenophanes cited here are from Kirk and Raven, *The Presocratic Philosophers*.

One can easily trace this link in the Homeric notions of *aristeia* and *charme*: while engaged in *aristeia*, a warrior's single-handed tour de force in combat, the hero becomes possessed by *charme*, battle lust, which makes fighting "sweeter" than returning home (*Iliad*, 2.354–355). He joyfully "sweeps over the field with instincts and energies free," experiencing the "supreme realization of the pride of power."[21] Hector is "forever avid of battle" (*Iliad*, 13.80), while the two Aiantes are "joyful in the delight of battle the god had put in their spirits" (*Iliad*, 13.81–82). In other words, for the Homeric mind, the feeling of power is interchangeable with both the feeling of pleasure and the feeling of freedom. Because the gods are more powerful than men, moreover, their feelings of pleasure or freedom are much more intense than those of the mortals. Apollo's *aristeia*, for instance, is explicitly described in terms of free, delightful, and effortless play: "As when a little boy piles sand by the sea shores when in his innocent play he / makes sand towers to amuse him and then, still playing, with hands and feet ruins them and wrecks them / So you, lord Apollo, piled in confusion much hard work and painful done by the / Argives and drove terror among them" (*Iliad*, 15.362–366).

Thus, the analogy of divine and child play in an agonistic context is as old as Homer, pointing to the innocence, spontaneity, and exuberance or the *freedom* of power. The gods go on killing sprees as lustily as mortals do and the extent of their freedom coincides with the extent of their power. This Homeric passage also contrasts play as an effortless, pleasurable, and free movement to work as painful constraint. In this sense, any prerational, aristocratic mentality will invariably favor play over work, regarding the latter as a severe limitation of power-freedom. On the other hand, a predominantly rational, middle-class mentality will tend to favor work over play, an attitude we have already discerned in Hesiod. Modern play theorists will often be torn between these conflicting valuations of play, attempting both to reaffirm its primacy over work on the ground of its "freedom" and to separate it from its violent, agonistic, prerational context. Hence, they will often replace the archaic notion of free play as unbounded risk taking with the rational notion of free play as calculated risk, or play as freedom *within reason*. The modern concept of play as freedom will therefore share the split character of all the other play concepts: In its prerational guise it will relate to the violent, unconstrained, and arbitrary play of the will and of physical forces, while in its rational guise it will relate to the

21. Onians, *Origins of European Thought*, p. 20.

limited, orderly, and rule-determined game of social conventions or the cosmic game of necessity and chance.

It has perhaps become clear that all these play concepts are loosely interrelated, bearing a family resemblance and recurring throughout the history of Western thought. At times they may go hand in hand, and at other times they may enter a dialectical relationship, or turn into binary oppositions. They may become submerged, joining the ranks of tacit assumptions, then resurface with renewed force, becoming once more explicit or self-reflective. Some of these play concepts are closer relatives than others and they may finally diverge into two separate branches of the same family tree, according to their relative proximity to power. In turn, these two branches may engage in a relentless feud, each seeking to subdue or repress the other, but their victory or defeat always proves to be temporary and inconclusive: the vanquished may often stage a strong comeback, retipping the scales in its favor.

This study will trace the vagaries of the feud between the prerational and the rational branch of the family tree of play concepts along several stretches of philosophical and scientific discourse since the end of the eighteenth century. This does not mean, however, that before that time there were no play concepts operative in post-Hellenic thought. On the contrary, the Middle Ages, the Renaissance, and the Baroque can be seen as some of the most playful ages in Western history, and only obvious time and space limitations prevent me from giving these periods the attention they deserve.[22] Whereas most of the rational and the prerational play concepts reviewed here return either implicitly or explicitly throughout the post-Hellenic Western tradition, the last quarter

22. To my knowledge, no comprehensive history of the play concepts in any of these periods exists, and most of the specialized studies have largely confined themselves to literary play. For partial views of play as a general concept in the Middle Ages, the Renaissance, and the Baroque, see Huizinga, *The Waning of the Middle Ages* (1924; New York, 1985), and the brief historical surveys in *Homo Ludens* (e.g., chap. 11, "Western Civilization Sub Specie Ludi"); V. A. Kolve, *The Play Called Corpus Christi* (Stanford, Calif., 1966); Giuseppe Mazzotta, *The World at Play in Boccaccio's* Decameron (Princeton, N.J., 1986); M. Bakhtin, *Rabelais and His World* (English trans. Cambridge, Mass., 1968); Richard A. Lanham, *The Motives of Eloquence: Literary Rhetoric in the Renaissance* (New Haven, Conn., 1976); Anne Righter, *Shakespeare and the Idea of Play* (London, 1962); Eileen J. Allman, *Player King and Adversary: Two Faces of Play in Shakespeare* (Baton Rouge, La., 1980); and Frank Warnke, *Versions of Baroque: European Literature in the Seventeenth Century* (New Haven, Conn., 1972). One might also consult Gerald Guinness and Andrew Hurley, eds., *Auctor Ludens: Essays on Play in Literature* (Philadelphia/Amsterdam, 1985).

of the eighteenth century is a convenient starting point for a discussion of the modern concepts of play. The choice is not arbitrary. Rather, it follows the historical principle according to which attempts at conceptualization or introspection appear at times when implicit governing assumptions begin to lose their authority and undergo a crisis, in other words, when they are no longer automatically accepted and require (re)definition. The end of the Age of Reason and the dawn of Romanticism is precisely such a period of crisis in Western values, when both philosophy and fine art become again introspective; only the recently established modern science preserves a relative stability, which a century later will in turn be shaken through the theories of evolution and relativity. (Other such periods of crisis, of transition from one cultural paradigm to another, can be placed at the end of the Middle Ages and the beginning of the Renaissance, or at the end of the Baroque and the dawn of the Age of Reason.)[23] During this period, the play concept as a whole comes again to the foreground of Western consciousness, partly in its prerational guise, as a challenge to the largely rational, middle-class values of the Enlightenment, and partly in its rational guise as a response to this challenge.

One must also constantly bear in mind that the return of the play concept(s) examined here is never a "return of the same." It is only one of an infinite number of returns occurring throughout the history of Western thought, each having its individual or unique features. In this regard, the notion of "family resemblance" is crucial in understanding the present historical model, which attempts to deal with a wide variety of historical, ethnical-linguistic, and disciplinary contexts. Each play concept may share certain general recognizable features with its forefathers from past ages or with its siblings from other stretches of discourse, but it also has its own unmistakable individuality, given by its specific historical, ethnical-linguistic, and disciplinary habitat. For example, a "return" of the Hellenic play concepts in modern thought may signify a return *to* them, through a conscious historical program of

23. It would be rewarding, for instance, to explore the dynamic of the rational and prerational play concepts in the context of the Italian and the English Renaissance, whose mentalities seem to have had a great deal in common with that of the Greek polis during the fourth and fifth centuries B.C. For some of the issues involved in studying the shift in cultural paradigms that occurred during the Renaissance see, for example, Thomas Kuhn, *The Copernican Revolution* (Cambridge, Eng., 1967); P. O. Kristeller, *Renaissance Thought*, 2 vols. (New York, 1979); and Paul Feyerabend, *Against Method* (London, 1975).

"imitation," which in turn may imply various perceptions of Antiquity that are themselves filtered through and mediated by previous perceptions. Or it may signify an unconscious historical process—conceptual or intellectual problems arising in kindred power-oriented cultures suggest kindred solutions. More often than not, it may signify both: An excellent example of the latter kind of return is offered by Nietzsche, who gives up classical scholarship only to develop an anti-Platonic, "Presocratic" mode of thought, thus reintroducing certain Hellenic prerational play concepts in modern philosophy. Furthermore, any individual play concept belonging to a certain branch of the family can be put to various uses and will receive its full meaning or value only in the concrete historical context of its use. For example, the concept of play as an *as if* rational activity may assume widely different functions not only in philosophy, science, or fine art but within the various contexts of these fields themselves. Likewise, the Hellenic concept of mimesis-play will be employed in philosophical and literary contexts that could not have occurred in a predominantly oral and prerational culture, where it operated mostly at the level of tacit assumptions before it was "identified" and "repressed" by Plato and his followers.

Since my book concentrates on the internal movement of the history of the play concept(s) in both philosophical and scientific discourse, it will soon become apparent that the dynamic of this history follows a different course in each field, not least because these fields are in turn engaged in a contest for cultural authority; in other words, it will become apparent that one needs to take into consideration not only the intraspecific but also the extraspecific competition among play concepts. In the course of this competition, the play concepts deliberately withdraw from or attack each other, form and dissolve alliances, claim and reject kinships, and so forth. In this regard, their identity is constituted in the play of their differences, rather than the other way around, and therefore the historical model that would account for their agon must also be understood in agonistic terms: rather than being a Hegelian model in which the differences between various play concepts would be understood in terms of their identity, it is a Viconian or a Nietzschean model, in which their identity is understood in terms of their (functional) differences.

Although this book concentrates principally on the play concepts of philosophy and science, one should never lose sight of their siblings from other stretches of discourse that have proven to be equally strong contestants in the ongoing power game of Western culture. A particularly important role in this power game is held by what has, at least since Plato and Aristotle, been known as artistic or fictional discourse, which for the sake of expedience is given the generic name of "literature." Literature is born out of the "ancient quarrel between philosophy and poetry" (Socrates in Plato's *Republic*), and has from the very beginning been associated with play, sharing its value fluctuations on the metaphysical stock market. Despite its repeated repression at the hands of philosophy and science, literature has proven a powerful antagonist—indeed, it has proven an indispensable element of the cultural power game as a whole. I regard literature, therefore, both as a major form of play and as a mediated form of power, characteristic of a rational mentality, to be distinguished from sung poetry (or music), which is a vestige of an older, unmediated form of power play, characteristic of a prerational, oral mentality. Ever since its birth in Plato and Aristotle, literature has acted as a differential principle for other stretches of discourse. By openly displaying its fictionality, it allows other linguistic constructs (scientific, philosophical, historical, ethical, political, juridical, and religious) to be invested with the authority of knowledge and truth. Furthermore, literature has often stepped in and filled the power vacuum during periods of so-called cognitive nihilism or axiological relativism in our culture. For instance, in Romanticism and more recently in Postmodernism, it may reassert its claim to supreme cultural authority by exposing all truth as fiction. In response, philosophy-science would again attempt to replace literature as authority-truth. In this regard, the so-called self-conscious moments in literary history are far from being flights from reality—on the contrary, they can be seen as last-ditch attempts to reinforce a certain reality or truth. Each discursive power configuration has its own official texts or truths (interpretations) that attempt to exclude, repress, or subordinate the others, but they can in turn be challenged and replaced by any of the others. What is treated as literature or fiction in one age may become philosophy and science in another, while certain stretches of philosophical and scientific discourse may in turn come to be regarded as literature.

Viewed in this functional light, literature is neither illusion nor higher truth but a linguistic construct like any other, participating in the creation, perpetuation, and destruction of a certain discursive power configuration. This view clearly differs from that of modern literary aestheticism (as distinguished from modern philosophical or scientific aestheticism), which proclaims the absolute independence of literature, as well as of all art, from other cultural phenomena. But one can argue that literary aestheticism itself is only a strategy in the ceaseless agon that literature carries on with other stretches of discourse, and therefore is only a necessary moment in the history of cultural play. Without being relatively independent, literature could never fulfill its differential cultural function: its effectiveness depends upon its being able to create a free, self-enclosed space or *neutral* play ground, where certain models for or alternatives to reality can be proposed, tested, adopted, and rejected at will. By insisting upon this freedom requirement, literary aestheticism actually guarantees the proper functioning of the discursive power mechanism as a whole.[24]

Although I define the Western discursive practices, and the Western mentality in general, as power oriented, I do not mean to draw an invidious comparison between the Western world and other cultural-geographical areas, based on the criterion of power. Employing this criterion would lead to a distorted view of both other worlds and our own, distortion that has become all too obvious in the twentieth century and has been diagnosed variously as ethnocentrism, primitivism, Orientalism, and so forth.[25] Other cultural-geographical areas such as

24. My views on literary and aesthetic phenomena in general are to a certain extent sympathetic to those of the contemporary literary and cultural historians who, in the wake of the older *Ideologie-* and *Kulturkritik*, again turn their attention to the relation between aesthetic discourse and power or to the institutional aspects of art, theory, and criticism. See, for example, Jürgen Habermas, *Knowledge and Human Interests*, trans. J. Shapiro (Boston, 1971) and *Communication and the Evolution of Society*, trans T. McCarthy (Boston, 1976); Karl-Otto Apel, *Towards a Transformation of Philosophy*, trans. G. Adley and D. Frisby (London, 1980) and his collective volume on *Hermeneutik und Ideologiekritik* (Frankfurt, 1973); Karl Robert Mandelkow, *Goethe in Deutschland: Rezeptionsgeschichte eines Klassikers* I (Munich, 1980); Herbert Lindenberger, *Historical Drama: The Relation of Literature and Reality* (Chicago, 1975); Peter Uwe Hohendahl, *The Institution of Criticism* (Ithaca, N.Y., 1982); Matei Calinescu, *Five Faces of Modernity* (Durham, N.C., 1987); Timothy Reiss, *The Discourse of Modernism* (Ithaca, N.Y., 1982); Dominick LaCapra, *Rethinking Intellectual History: Texts, Contexts, Language* (Ithaca, N.Y., 1983); Roy Strong, *Art and Power: Renaissance Festivals, 1450–1650* (Berkeley/Los Angeles, 1984); W. J. T. Mitchell, ed., *The Politics of Interpretation* (Chicago, 1983); and Paul Bové, *Intellectuals in Power: A Genealogy of Critical Humanism* (New York, 1986). My approach is also especially sympathetic to that of Louis Marin, e.g., in *Utopiques: Jeux d'espaces* (Paris, 1973) and *Le portrait du roi* (Paris, 1981).

25. A relatively early critique of Eurocentrism can be found in René Guénon, *East and West* (Eng. trans. London, 1941). For recent discussions of primitivism and/or orientalism see, among others, Jack Goody, *The Domestication of the Savage*

the Orient, the Middle East, Africa, South America, and Polynesia may contain human communities that are equally power oriented, although an examination of their history would undoubtedly show that their power-oriented mentalities or sets of values and beliefs differ considerably from ours. My definition of the Western world should therefore not be regarded as contrastive or oppositional (like that of Spengler or Toynbee, for instance), but rather as somewhat idiosyncratic and subjective, as describing a set of basic values in which I have been immersed and of which I have become a part, first as an Eastern European and then as an American. In this respect, I could indeed claim with some justification that my experience encompasses two extremes of the Western world, not only from a geographical but also from a spiritual point of view. Yet even though in one sense the cultural distance between Eastern Europe and America seems enormous, in another sense they are part of the same world, sharing the same basic values, which can in turn be traced back to our common spiritual ancestors, the ancient Greeks.

But if the Western world with its predominant mentality can be viewed as a recognizable whole, it can also be viewed as a multiplicity of smaller worlds, throughout which different spatial (geographical), temporal (historical), and linguistic (ethnic) coordinates allow for infinite diversity. Thus, many other definitions of the Western world are possible, and they would not necessarily invalidate the one with which this volume operates. Indeed, the (playful) notion of a plurality of worlds ought to be kept in mind throughout. One can imagine a pluriverse inhabited by an infinity of worlds, small or large, intersecting or incommensurable, appearing or disappearing. Of these worlds, the power-oriented ones may well constitute only a tiny fraction. Moreover, a power-oriented world such as ours does not necessarily exclude nonpowerful sets of values; rather, it employs these values for its own ends. Finally, this world may conceivably change or shift its orientation, despite the fact that as long as it holds its course it may appear incompatible or incommensurable with other worlds. While hoping to cast further light on the nature of this course, I shall implicitly stress the need to open ourselves to other courses and therefore to other worlds as well.

---

*Mind*, and Edward Said, *Orientalism* (London, 1979). Finally, the cultural anthropological work of Arnold van Gennep, Sir James Frazer, Ruth Benedict, Claude Lévi-Strauss, Mircea Eliade, and, more recently, René Girard, Victor Turner, and Clifford Geertz has contributed to a revision of our ethnocentric notions of other cultures.

# PART I

# Play and Modern Philosophical Discourse

In Western metaphysics, play has often been employed in the form of a game metaphor that imagines the relationship between divinity and man as one between a player and a plaything. In ancient Greek thought this game metaphor originates in Homer, is used for the first time in a philosophical context by Heraclitus, and is then transformed into a rational principle by Plato. It is, however, much older than the Hellenic world, and can be traced back to the ancient thought of the Sumerians, Hebrews, Hindus, and the Chinese.[1] In the Western world it has also constituted the foundation of a *theologia ludens*, recurring in such religious figures as St. Augustine, St. Thomas Aquinas, Cornelius à Lapide, Gregory Nazianzus, Maximus Confessor, Clement of Alexandria, the Venerable Bede, Bernhardt, Meister Eckhart, Jerome, and Luther and in such lay figures as Pascal, Leibniz, Kant, Fichte, Schelling, Hegel, Schopenhauer, Nietzsche, and Heidegger.[2]

In addition to this game metaphor (which recurs consistently

1. For partial discussions of play and non-Western traditions, see Huizinga, *Homo Ludens*, especially chap. 2, "The Play-Concept as Expressed in Language"; Ananda Coomaraswamy, *The Dance of Shiva* (New York, 1957); and David Miller, *Gods and Games: Toward a Theology of Play* (New York, 1973), chap. 3, "The Origins of Ideas about Games and Play."

2. The most important contemporary advocates of *theologia ludens* are Hugo Rahner in *Der spielende Mensch* (Einsiedeln, 1954); Romano Guardini in *Vom Geist der Liturgie* (Freiburg, 1957); and Hans Urs von Balthasar in *Theodramatik*, 4 vols. (Einsiedeln, 1973–1983). A recent American advocate is Robert Neale in his Ph.D. dissertation, "Play and the Sacred: Toward a Theory of Religion as Play" (Ann Arbor, Mich., 1964), later revised and published as *In Praise of Play* (New York, 1970).

throughout Western thought and deserves separate study), play as a major *explicit* philosophical topic resurfaces with the rise of German idealism and may be connected with the aesthetic turn in Western metaphysics.[3] This turn occurs in the wake of the cognitive crisis accompanying the loss of faith in the ideas of the Enlightenment, and has the ultimate effect of restoring the authority of precisely these ideas, chiefly through an *as if* mode of knowledge whose playful origins can be traced back to Greek thought, particularly to Xenophanes, the older Sophists, and, later on, to Plato and Aristotle. The rise of aesthetics as a branch of philosophy during the Age of Reason facilitates the introduction in metaphysics of consciously simulative or fictional procedures that were previously connected primarily with the fine arts (see Bacon's definition of epic as "feigned history" in the *Advancement of Learning* or Defoe's narrative principle of "lying like truth"). During the eighteenth and the nineteenth centuries, major philosophical figures again speak openly of "conscious illusion" and "necessary fictions," not only in regard to literature or art but in regard to metaphysical thought as well (for example, Berkeley, Hume, Kant, Schelling, Fichte, Hegel, Schopenhauer, Nietzsche, and certain Neo-Kantians such as Lange and Vaihinger).

Since metaphysics has always regarded art as a form of (serious or nonserious) play, its aesthetic turn in Germany will also bring about extensive reflection upon the idea of play in general, and this idea will be invoked by virtually every major idealist philosopher, beginning with Leibniz. But it is Schiller who for the first time explicitly calls the heuristic fictions of philosophy "play," relinking art and aesthetics with the nonviolent, rational play concepts in their Platonic version. Thereafter, these concepts will frequently be employed by his contemporaries and successors, notably by Fichte, Schelling, and Hegel, who will attempt to ground their metaphysical speculations not only ontologically and ethically, but also aesthetically. Like Schiller, however, they will always subordinate aesthetics and play to morality, seriousness, and rationality. A few decades later, in the wake of Schopenhauer, Nietzsche

3. For the standard view on the aesthetic turn in German philosophy, see Wilhelm Windelband, *A History of Philosophy*, trans. J. H. Tufts (New York, 1901). For a more recent discussion, see Heidemann, *Begriff des Spieles*, which explicitly links aestheticism and play in modern philosophy. The most recent Anglo-American treatment of aestheticism (without relating it to play) can be found in Alan Megill, *Prophets of Extremity* (Berkeley/Los Angeles, 1985), pp. 2–25. See, however, my critique in sec. 2.1 of Megill's views on modern aestheticism. Of particular interest to the present argument is Arthur C. Danto, *The Philosophical Disenfranchisement of Art* (New York, 1986).

will break with this Schillerian tradition: although he will also attempt to ground his thought aesthetically, he will no longer subordinate aesthetics to ethics and rationality but vice versa. Nietzsche effects this reversal by going back, beyond Plato, to the archaic origins of art in the violent, exuberant, and innocent play of power, thereby reintroducing the prerational notions of play in modern philosophy. Once they resurface in modern thought, the philosophical concepts of play reengage in an authority contest and, in the past hundred years or so, the rational play group has slowly but steadily lost ground to the prerational play group, although the outcome of this agon remains inconclusive. Part I of this book will therefore sketch a brief outline of the contest between rational and prerational play in modern philosophical discourse on the example of Kant, Schiller, Nietzsche, and Heidegger, examining its far-reaching consequences in the contemporary period, particularly in the thought of Fink, Gadamer, Deleuze, and Derrida.

## SECTION 1

# Play and the Aesthetic Turn in German Idealism

In its essentially Romantic aesthetics, German idealist philosophy combines the Cartesian rationalist tradition with its English empiricist counterpart. With the victory of Cartesianism in seventeenth-century Continental thought, art becomes largely subordinated to Reason. Although Descartes himself does not formulate an aesthetic theory, such Cartesian followers as Malebranche and Boileau take this task upon themselves, and the result is the well-known Neoclassical doctrine of art as an imitation of nature according to rational rules. Because art has always had close ties to the world of the senses and the imagination, Cartesian thought looks upon it with suspicion and attempts to "rationalize" it, imposing upon it the rigorous and rigid laws of logic and mathematics. For instance, in Malebranche's *De la recherche de la vérité* (*Inquiry Concerning Truth*, 1675), imagination, as opposed to the rational faculty, does not lead to truth but to all kinds of delusions and errors in the realm of metaphysics and ethics. Consequently, as Ernst Cassirer points out, to "keep the imagination in check and to regulate it deliberately is the highest goal of all philosophical criticism."[4] These severe rational restrictions apply not only to art but to all play, which

---

4. Ernst Cassirer, *The Philosophy of the Enlightenment*, trans. F. C. A. Koelln and J. P. Pettegrove (Princeton, N.J., 1951), p. 283.

the Neoclassical mentality generally condemns as frivolous, devoid of cognitive value, and conducive to error.

Rebelling against the more dogmatic forms of Neoclassical rationalism, German idealist aesthetics turns to the English empiricists, such as Hobbes, Locke, and Hume, for a less rigid view of sensory perception and imagination. Consequently, the English doctrines of artistic taste, especially as expounded by Shaftesbury, Hutcheson, Hume, and Burke, will figure prominently in eighteenth-century German aesthetics from Baumgarten to Meier to Mendelssohn to Kant and Schiller. However, the eighteenth-century aestheticians, German or English, and their nineteenth-century followers do not mean to reassess art's subordinate role in relation to metaphysics when they make it a serious object of metaphysical study. On the contrary, even as they attempt to enlist art in the service of metaphysics, they mean to separate it further from such traditional philosophical disciplines as logic, ethics, and metaphysics by emphasizing its lack of rationality and cognitive value. In this respect, the German Romantic philosophical tradition largely remains a rationalist one, as opposed to a certain Romantic literary tradition, which exhibits definite prerational features and in which one may include, among others, Hölderlin, Hoffmann, Jean Paul, and, to an extent, Friedrich Schlegel.[5] Nevertheless, by inaugurating the aesthetic turn in modern philosophy, the eighteenth-century metaphysicians facilitate the task of a poet-philosopher like Schiller, who extends the word *aesthetisch* from a single faculty (in Baumgarten and Kant) to a whole mode of awareness or a whole mode of being. Thus, Schiller paves the way for such idealist thinkers as Schelling, Fichte, and Hegel, who will build entire metaphysical systems on aesthetic foundations.

Like art, play in general becomes useful to Romantic metaphysics, which attempts to mediate between Reason and Desire or Will, that is, between the ideal world of the spirit and the material world of the senses. Because of its amphibolous nature, play, like art, is ideally suited for such a mediating role, and will be employed to this purpose throughout nineteenth-century idealist thought. Although it is at first regarded with as much suspicion as art (and precisely for the same reason—its all-too-obvious connection to a prerational mentality), play is gradually stripped of its irrational, violent, and arbitrary connota-

5. For a perceptive appraisal of this early (or what I would call "prerational") Romantic literary tradition in Germany, see Ernst Behler's work, e.g., *Friedrich Schlegel* (Hamburg, 1966) and *Klassische Ironie—Romantische Ironie—Tragische Ironie: Zum Ursprung dieser Begriffe* (Darmstadt, 1972).

tions, becoming a useful instrument in supporting the ontological and ethical fictions of philosophy. It is again Schiller who establishes play in its Platonic and Neoplatonic guise as a serious philosophical topic, and its metaphysical status rises so rapidly that young Hegel is led to affirm that, even at its lightest, play is "the noblest and the only true seriousness" (*der erhabenste und der einzig wahre Ernst*)[6]—a phrase that play theorists have never tired of repeating. But a brief look at the uses of play in German idealist philosophy, as exemplified by Kant and Schiller, shows that this notion is far from free of contradictions and ambiguities, and that these contradictions and ambiguities arise because the concept of play, like many other major concepts operative in Western thought, remains split between a rational and a prerational mentality.

## 1·1   Immanuel Kant: Philosophy and/or Play?

Kant is one of the first idealist thinkers to return to the play concept, especially as it appears in classical Hellenic thought. But this return is hardly explicit, and direct references to the Sophists or to Plato and Aristotle are infrequent in his texts. The word *Spiel* (play, game), though it appears much more often, is seldom defined beyond a specific, immediate context, and is frequently used in an ordinary rather than a philosophical sense. Thus, in Kant, play cannot even be properly called a "concept" (*Begriff*); rather, it is an anticoncept, or that which resists all conceptualization and which renders the critiques of pure Reason and the power of judgment necessary. Nevertheless, we can discern in Kant, at the level of tacit assumptions, most of the uses of play that we find in classical Greek philosophy. Moreover, these uses exhibit the same ethical polarization that we encounter in Hesiod, some of the Sophists, and Plato and Aristotle. It would be impossible, in this short space, to discuss all the Kantian uses of play, so I shall limit myself only to a few moments in the *Critique of Pure Reason* (*Kritik der reinen Vernunft*), and then concentrate mainly on the *Critique of [the Power of] Judgment* (*Kritik der Urteilskraft*) and the *Anthropology from a Pragmatic Point of View* (*Anthropologie in pragmatischer Hinsicht*), with occasional references to the posthumous "Reflexionen zur Anthropologie."[7]

6. See Hegel, *Erste Druckschriften*, Lassonausgabe (1928), p. 128.

7. For a detailed discussion of the philosophical and anthropological uses of play in Kant, see Heidemann, *Begriff des Spieles*, "Der Spielbegriff bei Kant," pp. 125–216. In addition to this study, I have found helpful Hans Vaihinger, *Philosophie des Als Ob* (Berlin, 1911), sec. 3, A, "Kants Gebrauch der Als-Ob Betrachtung,"

In the *Critique of Pure Reason*, as Heidemann points out, play and knowledge are separated (*Begriff des Spieles*, p. 125). In fact, the explicit goal of the first *Critique* is to replace the "mere play" (*blosses Spiel*) of the imagination and thought, in which, according to Kant, philosophy has indulged all too often, with the seriousness of scientific investigation. In the wake of Plato and Aristotle, Kant believes that competitive play among its practitioners has prevented philosophy from reaching a *consensus omnium*, the necessary condition of scientific knowledge: "So far, too, are the students of metaphysics from exhibiting any kind of unanimity in their contentions, that metaphysics has rather to be regarded as a battle-ground quite peculiarly suited for those who desire to exercise themselves in mock combats, and in which no participant has ever yet succeeded in gaining even so much as an inch of territory, not at least in such manner as to secure its permanent possession."[8]

In the manner of the Academy and the Lyceum, Kant rejects the *agones logon* of the Sophistic in favor of a "spirit of thoroughness," or an "orderly establishment of principles, clear determination of concepts, insistence upon strict proof, and avoidance of venturesome, non-consecutive steps in our inferences." Those who ignore these requirements can have "no other aim than to shake off the fetters of *science* altogether, and thus to change work into play, certainty into opinion, philosophy into philodoxy" (Bxxxvii).[9]

---

pp. 613–733; Heinrich W. Cassirer, *Commentary on Kant's Critique of Judgement* (1938; rpt. London, 1970); Ernst Cassirer, *Kant's Life and Thought*, trans. James Haden (New Haven, Conn., 1981); Eva Schaper, "The Kantian 'as if' and Its Relevance for Aesthetics," *Proceedings of the Aristotelian Society* 65 (1964–1965): 219–234; Donald W. Crawford, *Kant's Aesthetic Theory* (Madison, Wisc., 1974); T. Cohen and P. Guyer, eds., *Essays in Kant's Aesthetics* (Chicago, 1982); and Paul Guyer, *Kant and the Claims of Taste* (Cambridge, Mass., 1979). A useful critical commentary on Kant's third *Critique* can be found in Derrida, "Economimésis," in *Mimésis/des articulations* (Paris, 1975), which I discuss in my essay "Six Authors in Search of a Shadow," *Literature, Mimesis, and Play*, pp. 53–74.

8. Immanuel Kant, *Critique of Pure Reason*, trans. Norman Kemp Smith (New York, 1929; rpt. 1950), preface to 2d ed., Bxiv. I have used in parallel the German texts in *Kants gesammelte Schriften*, Königlich Preussische Akademieausgabe (Berlin, 1900). Further citations refer to this edition. In the case of the first *Critique*, there are two standard texts: the first edition of 1781, referred to as A, and the second edition of 1787, referred to as B; accordingly, quotations in the text may entail two different page references.

9. Cf. "the game played by idealism" in B276; or "the empty play upon words and the merely sophistical subterfuge" in A257/B313; or, toward the end of the work, "The Discipline of Pure Reason," all of sec. 2 (chap. I), "The Discipline of Pure Reason in Respect of Its Polemical Employment," A739/B767 and *passim*. Kant's complaint echoes that of Aristotle in *De Caelo*, 297b7.

A critique of pure Reason also implies distinguishing between empty Sophistic "pseudo-rational" contentions and the "skeptical method" in terms of good and bad eris. The Sophistic contentions disclose a dialectical battlefield (*Kampfplatz*), where whoever opens the attack is permitted to win, no matter whether he supports a good cause or a bad one. The skeptical method, in contrast, provokes a conflict of assertions not in order to win or to lose, but in order to see whether the object of the controversy is not simply a deceptive appearance. As opposed to skepticism, which undermines the foundations of all knowledge, the skeptical method aims at certainty (A422/B450).[10] It seeks to overcome the natural and unavoidable delusions of the rational faculty by relating the transcendental employment of a concept to its empirical employment, and it is this relation that distinguishes mere fiction (*Erdichtung*) from the objective validity of experience (*Erfahrung*), mere playing with concepts from true knowledge: "Therefore all concepts, and with them all principles, even such as are possible *a priori*, relate to empirical intuitions, that is, to the data for a possible experience. Apart from this relation they have no objective validity, and in respect of their representations are a mere play of imagination or of understanding" (A239/B299).

Whereas experience itself is a play of appearances, because the objects can never be known in themselves but only as they arise in the intuition (*Anschauung*), Kant distinguishes between appearance (*Erscheinung*) and mere illusion (*blosses Schein*): Appearance is the only possible way to knowledge, illusion results precisely from confusing the object in itself with its appearance, that is, from ascribing objective reality to this appearance—Bishop Berkeley's "error" (B69–71). But the play of appearances remains empty and can yield no knowledge (A101) unless it can be reproduced in the imagination (*Einbildungskraft*). In the imagination the play of appearances becomes a play of representations (*Vorstellungen*) that in turn need to be ordered, connected, and brought into relation through the categories of understanding (*Verstand*), notably through time and space. Any cognitive moment must therefore contain

10. Cf. earlier, A298/B355: "There exists, then, a natural and unavoidable dialectic of pure Reason—not one in which a bungler might entangle himself through lack of knowledge or one which some sophist has artifically invented to confuse thinking people, but one inseparable from human reason, and which, even after its deceptiveness has been exposed, will not cease to play tricks with Reason and continually entrap it into momentary aberrations ever and again calling for correction." Its pseudorational (*vernünftelnde*) assertions must nevertheless be distinguished from Sophistic ones, because they "are sophistications not of men but of pure reason itself" (A339/B397).

a threefold synthesis of apprehension (through the intuition), reproduction (through the imagination), and apperception or recognition
(through the understanding).

Note the decisive role of understanding, without which appearances
and representations remain a "mere play" of our intuition and our
imagination (A96–A120). Yet understanding engages in its own play,
which in turn is subordinated to the play of pure Reason, for instance in
what Kant calls the transcendental ideas, such as God, Totality of Being,
Immortality, Freedom, and so forth. For Kant these transcendental
ideas are heuristic fictions, "over-stepping the limits of all experience"
(A327/B384). They are regulative rather than constitutive principles of
pure Reason and do not allow for the possibility of objective knowledge, having merely internal coherence. Even the "highest" Idea, that of
the Totality of Reason, leads to the fiction of the "absolute beginning,"
according to which Reason itself should be regarded as the determining
cause (*bestimmende Ursache*). In this case "we have to proceed as if we
had before us an object not of the senses, but of the pure Understanding . . . and the series of states [*Reihe der Zustände*] can therefore be
regarded *as if* it had an absolute beginning (through an intelligible
cause)" (A685/B713). Likewise, the idea of God is a regulative principle of pure Reason and has the same *as if* or simulative character that
we encounter in, for example, Xenophanes' notion of divinity (A686/
B714).

Although he refrains from calling it "play," here Kant employs the *als
ob* approach indispensable to any philosophy that denies an absolute
character to human knowledge. If the thing-in-itself (*Ding an sich*) is
unknowable, then cognition becomes possible only in the *as if* mode,
and can manifest itself, at least at the primary sensorial level, only as play
of appearances. Hence the necessity in the Kantian thought, just as in
the Platonic one, of distinguishing between good and bad appearances,
good and bad illusions, good and bad representations, good and bad
play, good and bad analogies, good and bad symbolical anthropomorphism, and so on; in other words, the necessity for moral fictions.

That Kant is fully conscious of the Platonic source of his *as if* approach to knowledge is apparent in his references to the Platonic doctrine of eternal Ideas (which is the model for his own doctrine of
transcendental ideas). For him, Plato's Republic is not a mere fiction
but an *analogon*, having the value of a moral imperative: "This perfect
state may never indeed come into being; none the less this does not
affect the rightfulness of the idea, which, in order to bring the legal
organisation of mankind ever nearer to its greatest possible perfection,

advances this maximum as an archetype" (A317/B374). According to Kant, the domain in which Plato's enterprise most "calls for respect and imitation" is the moral sphere, "in regard to the principles of morality, legislation, and religion, where the experience, in this case of the good, is itself made possible only by the ideas—incomplete as their empirical expression must always remain" (A318/B375). And it is this moral sphere that constitutes the *telos* of Kant's own system and in the name of which play is ultimately dismissed as mere trifling.

Even from this brief and schematic discussion of the word *Spiel* in the first *Critique* it is perhaps clear that Kant uses this word in a polarized and ambiguous way. On the one hand, he employs it in the everyday sense of a nonserious, unproductive activity, and on the other hand as a technical term in his philosophy. In the first sense, play is still connected with agon or contest, for example in the interminable and inconclusive mock combats of metaphysics, but this contest is declared to be detrimental to knowledge and to the privileged status of philosophy as a master science. This negative use of the word recalls Hesiod's bad eris and the Platonic and Aristotelian dismissal of the agonistic intellectual play of the Sophists in favor of serious, scientific, *authoritative* procedures. (This association is reinforced by Kant's repeated references to the Sophistic play of "pseudo-rational assertions.") In the second sense, play is connected, on the one hand, with the empirical and the irrational, for example in the arbitrary play of appearances and representations before they are sifted through, ordered, and given meaning by the understanding; and, on the other hand, with the "unavoidable delusion" of pure Reason when it does *not* take into account the empirical and the irrational, in the antinomy of pure Reason, for example, or in the transcendental dialectic of ideas. Most of these Kantian uses of play have negative rational and moral implications; when it could be valued positively, for example in the description of the *as if* activity of the transcendental ideas, play is never identified as such, but is instead linked with a serious moral imperative demanded by Reason.

Whereas in the first *Critique* play is treated largely as a negative activity which, left to itself, yields no knowledge and therefore requires the serious criticism of Reason, in the third *Critique* it is called upon, under the name of aesthetic judgment, to mediate between Reason and understanding, or between the realm of the concept of nature and that of the concept of freedom. Even in the third *Critique*, however, play is only partially identified with the aesthetic judgment, and Kant's use of the term remains highly ambiguous.

Before examining the relationship between Kantian aesthetics and play, it would be useful to give a brief account of the use of the term *aesthetic* in Kant's work. As is well known, between the first and the third *Critique* Kant changes his mind about the proper use of this term. In the first *Critique*, he employs (transcendental) aesthetic to mean the "science of all principles of *a priori* sensibility," particularly of two pure forms of sensible intuition, space and time (A21/B35). Thus, he points out in a footnote: "The Germans are the only people who currently make use of the word 'aesthetic' in order to signify what others call the critique of taste. This usage originated in the abortive attempt made by Baumgarten, that admirable analytical thinker, to bring the critical treatment of the beautiful under rational principles, and so to raise its rules to the rank of a science. But such endeavors are fruitless" (B36).

In this passage Kant refers to the eighteenth-century English theories of the beautiful as the subjective experience of the percipient or as "taste." The "critique of taste" and not "aesthetics" should be concerned with the beautiful and the fine arts, therefore, and in this sense Kant demands only the proper imitation of the English models (especially Shaftesbury, Hutcheson, Home, Addison, Hume, and Burke). In the third *Critique*, however, he adopts Baumgarten's use of *aesthetic* (in *Aesthetica*, 1750–1758) in connection with fine art, thus reviving the latter's "abortive attempt . . . to bring the critical treatment of the beautiful under rational principles." Baumgarten had attempted to develop a "science" of what he calls (in keeping with a long metaphysical tradition) the "inferior" faculties of the imagination and the intuition, and Kant, as we shall see, does not challenge this value judgment.

In addition to the terms *aesthetic* and *aesthetic judgment*, Kant adopts and develops from Baumgarten and his colleagues G. F. Meier (e.g., in *Anfangsgründe aller schönen Künste und Wissenschaften*, 1757) and Moses Mendelssohn (e.g., in *Betrachtungen über die Quellen und die Verbindungen der schönen Künste und Wissenschaften*, 1757) several other concepts that form the cornerstone of the newly invented "science" of aesthetics: the concept of the beautiful as disinterested pleasure in an object (pleasure that is not bound to the utility of the object or to the viewer's desire to possess it); the concept of the sublime; the notion of art as the imitation of the processes, rather than the products, of Nature; and the theory of the artist as *ingenium* or genius. All these Kantian concepts, particularly as mediated by Schiller, will later be taken over by Romantic aesthetics. This Romantic takeover in turn will involve a reinterpretation of the Neoclassical foundations of Kantian aesthetics, a reinterpretation that up to the present remains the standard view on Kant's philosophy of art. Paul Guyer and Ted Cohen reaffirm this Romantic view when they argue that "in its actual content Kant's critical theory of aesthetic judgment substantially departed from its early roots in rationalism, and it was not irremediably distorted by Kant's late decision to connect it with his attempt to solve outstanding problems in his theory of natural science by a half-hearted resurrection of teleological reasoning."[11] Guyer and Cohen further argue that Kant's analytic of the beautiful and the sublime, while implying a rejection of both the "Platonic conception of the desirable subordination of feeling to reason" and the "Humean conception of the necessary submission of reason to passion," also makes the "revolutionary suggestion that a full understanding of the rational development of human capacities requires not the subordination of all feelings to understanding—or to reason—but interaction between these two capacities" (p. 7). Yet a brief reexamination of Kant's aesthetics in the light of his notion of play will reveal that, as in the case of the first *Critique*, he is far from valuing reason and imagination equally; on the contrary, he consistently subordinates imagination to reason, art to philosophy and science, and play to morality and seriousness.

One can begin by reexamining Kant's concept of aesthetic judgment in relation to play. Whereas understanding belongs to the realm of the cognitive faculty and reason to that of the faculty of desire, the "judgment" of the *Kritik der Urteilskraft* belongs to the feeling of pleasure and pain. Therefore the judgment, at least in its aesthetic form, concerning "the Beautiful and the Sublime of Nature or of Art" or the feeling of pleasure would seem to fall within the realm of play. This does not mean, however, that in the third *Critique* play is restricted to the aesthetic judgment, and even less that the aesthetic judgment is restricted to play.

The aesthetic judgment seems to share with play a "purposiveness without purpose" (*Zweckmässigkeit ohne Zweck*) and a "disinterestedness" (*Interesselosigkeit*) in regard to the object of cognition. Here the aesthetic judgment as play is again separated from knowledge because, within its domain, understanding and imagination exercise their functions merely for their own sake, as it were, rather than for a definite cognitive purpose. Since no definite concept limits the aesthetic judgment to any specific rule of cognition, this judgment "can refer to

---

11. See Paul Guyer and Ted Cohen, *Esssays in Kant's Aesthetics*, introduction, p. 2. Further citations are in the text.

nothing else than the state of mind in the free play of the Imagination and the Understanding."[12]

Kant again emphasizes the separation between the aesthetic judgment as play and cognition when he draws a distinction between the good and the beautiful on the grounds that the first implies a concept, whereas the second does not. He defines the beautiful as "that which pleases universally without a concept" (§10), and this definition may also apply to the pleasure produced by and in play. Thus the aesthetic judgment and play share, besides a lack of cognitive value, a certain freedom from empirical constraints as well as a certain delightful spontaneity. Beyond this point, however, they seem to part ways, and Kant distinguishes between them, paradoxically, precisely in terms of freedom, spontaneity, and pleasure. In regard to freedom, for instance, imagination does and does not have "free play" in the judgment of taste, or, as Kant puts it, imagination is free to conform to law. On the one hand, imagination must be considered in its freedom, that is, not in its reproductive or repetitive role of arresting the play of representations for the benefit of the understanding, but in its productive and spontaneous role as "the author of arbitrary forms of possible intuitions," in other words in its *play* role. On the other hand, however, imagination still follows the law of understanding, of its own accord. Kant himself points out the apparent contradiction: "But that the *imaginative power* should be *free* and yet *of itself conformed to law*, i.e., bringing autonomy with it, is a contradition" (§22). The way out of this contradiction is again the *as if* approach, which Kant had also employed in the case of the judgment of taste as purposiveness without purpose: "Although in the apprehension of a given object of sense it [the Imagination] is tied to a definite form of this Object, and so far has no free play (such as that of poetry), yet it may readily be conceived that the object can furnish it with such a form containing a collection of the manifold, as the Imagination itself, if it were left free, would project in accordance with the *conformity to law of the understanding* in general. . . . Hence it is a conformity to law without a law" (§22).

The paradoxical character of Kant's statement disappears when we realize that he again operates with two different concepts of play: the arbitrary play of the senses and the orderly play of the imagination under the guidance of the understanding. This amphibolous use of play becomes clear in Kant's distinction between a pure and a confused

12. Kant, *Critique of the Power of Judgment*, trans. J. H. Bernard, 2d rev. ed. (London, 1931), §9. Further citations refer to this edition.

judgment of taste (a notion he also borrows from Baumgarten), which in turn is based on a distinction between what is beautiful (the proper object of a pure judgment of taste) and what is merely pleasant or charming: "Every form of the objects of sense . . . is either figure [*Gestalt*] or *play*. In the latter case it is either play of figures (in space, viz. pantomime and dancing) or the mere play of sensations (in time). The *charm* of colours or of the pleasant tones of an instrument may be added; but the *delineation* in the first case and the composition in the second constitute the proper object of the pure judgment of taste" (§14).

Kant first opposes play to *Gestalt*, figure, but then introduces a further distinction between the play of figures, such as pantomime and dancing, and the *mere* play of sensations; in other words, he introduces a distinction between good and bad play, the first connected to order or form and the second to disorder or formlessness. The charming and the pleasant have little to do with the pure judgment of taste because they are grounded in sensation and therefore are only incidental to beauty. What *is* essential to beauty is "delineation," or form, that is, what arrests the mere play of sensations and representations. Here the notion of *Gestalt* turns out to be similar to Aristotle's notion of form, for instance, in tragedy as *plot* or the ordering of events in a coherent whole. Just as in Aristotle's case, what pertains to the senses, such as *opsis* and *melopoiia*, being charming and pleasant, is relegated to a secondary function of aiding form as mere ornament (*parergon*). The "sensuous attractions" are distrusted because they may arouse strong emotions, in other words, because they come too close to (unrestrained) power and violence: "*Emotion*, i.e., a sensation in which pleasantness is produced by means of a momentary checking and a consequent more powerful overflow of the vital force, does not belong at all to beauty. . . . Thus a pure judgment of taste has for its determining ground neither charm nor emotion, in a word, no sensation as the material of the aesthetical judgment" (§14). Just as in the case of Plato and Aristotle, then, what Kant wants to dismiss as *blosses Spiel* is the irrational, ecstatic play of power in its immediate form, whose media are the senses, emancipated from the strict control and guidance of Reason; in turn, Reason can be defined as that mediated form of power which represses its violent origins, (re)presenting itself as contemplative beauty and eternal law and order.

The ambiguous nature of the Kantian relation of play to power, which derives from the ambiguous nature of power itself, becomes especially evident in the "analytic of the sublime," to which the passage from §14, quoted above, belongs. Whereas the beautiful and the sublime share such characteristics as lack of cognitive value, purposiveness without purpose, and disinterestedness, they differ just as the beautiful and the pleasant do, in terms of *Gestalt*: beauty (in Nature) is connected with the form of the object, which consists in having boundaries. The sublime, on the other hand, resides in a formless object, "so far as in it or by occasion of it *boundlessness* is represented, and yet its totality is also present to thought" (§23). Through its involvement with totality, the sublime is connected to Reason (whereas beauty is connected only to understanding), but through its boundlessness it is connected to the bad play of the senses and of representations.

The beautiful brings with it a "furtherance of life, and thus it is compatible with charms and with the [good] play of the Imagination"; the sublime, on the other hand, is a pleasure that arises only indirectly, because it is produced by "a feeling of momentary checking of the vital powers and a consequent stronger overflow of them, so that it seems to be regarded as emotion—not play [here in the sense of a free, disinterested activity], but earnest in the exercise of the Imagination" (§23). Thus, the sublime is "incompatible with charms" and experiencing it does not entail so much positive as negative pleasure, involving feelings of admiration and respect. Whereas beauty is the result of the harmony between imagination and understanding, the sublime resides in the conflict between imagination and Reason. This conflict produces "a feeling that we possess pure self-subsistent Reason, or a faculty for the estimation of magnitude, whose pre-eminence can be made intuitively evident only by the inadequacy of that faculty [Imagination] which is itself unbounded in the presentation of magnitudes" (§27). In this conflict, then, imagination has to fail in order to secure the triumph of Reason.

The feeling of respect inherent in the sublime is directed toward what is "mighty" and holds "dominion" over us (Kant defines dominion as a "might" that is "superior to the resistance of that which itself possesses might" [§28]). We should not, however, look for this might in Nature, which is a purposeless mechanism the irrationality of which "excites the Ideas of the sublime in its chaos or in its wildest and most irregular disorder and desolation, provided might and size are perceived" (§24). Rather, we should look for it in culture, in the law and order of moral Ideas, dictated by Reason. Without a proper development of moral Ideas, what the cultivated man calls sublime appears to the uneducated one merely terrible. In fact, one cannot think of the sublime in Nature without "combining therewith a mental disposition which is akin to the moral" (§29). In this regard, the highest proper feeling of sublimity is also the highest moral idea, that is, the Idea of God as an all-powerful yet rational Being (§28).

The Kantian notion of sublimity, therefore, is ultimately a highly rational one (in the tradition of the eighteenth-century thinking on the sublime, from Addison to Burke).[13] Power as the irrational, violent play of Becoming can be experienced in it only indirectly, from a safe distance, within the rule-governed and well-marked play ground of culture. Within this play ground even war and human violence appear as safe and proper objects of sublimity, productive of high cultural values: "War itself, if it is carried on with order and with a sacred respect for the rights of citizens, has something sublime in it, and makes the disposition of the people who carry it on thus, only the more sublime, the more numerous are the dangers to which they are exposed, and in respect of which they behave with courage. On the other hand, a long peace generally brings about a predominant commercial spirit, and along with it, low selfishness, cowardice, and effeminacy, and debases the disposition of the people" (§28).

Here Kant praises the modern equivalent of the old Homeric ideal of *arete* which, however, now assumes tame, bourgeois features. War is presented in its positive aspect, as a creator rather than a destroyer of civilization. It is noble, indeed sublime, agon, but (ironically) only as long as it is conducted with "order and with a sacred respect for the rights of citizens." Peace, on the other hand, leads to cultural effeminacy

13. Kant inherited and developed his ideas of the sublime both directly from the English writers mentioned above and through the mediation of Moses Mendelssohn, who speaks of *vermischte Empfindung*, a combination of pleasure and pain in experiencing the sublime, and who was himself strongly influenced by Burke's *Philosophical Inquiry into the Origins of Our Ideas of the Sublime and the Beautiful* (1756). Kant draws a rather unclear distinction between a "mathematical" and a "dynamic" sublime, which seems to be based on a distinction between spatial-temporal extensions as pure forms of sensible intuition and the raw and arbitrary play of physical forces (for a full discussion of the two kinds of Kantian sublime, see Guyer, *The Claims of Taste, passim*, and Crawford, *Kant's Aesthetic Theory passim*). From the point of view of the present discussion, however, this distinction reinforces Kant's deliberate separation, in the notion of the sublime, of unmediated, prerational power from its rational counterpart. For a recent analysis of the Romantic concept of the sublime, especially in the English tradition, see Thomas Weiskel, *The Romantic Sublime: Studies in the Structure and Psychology of Transcendence* (Baltimore, 1976).

and to the degeneration of high civic "virtues" that obviously remain competitive and violent, despite their thin, rational disguise. This passage, then, shows Kant's ambiguous attitude toward play as prerational agon, typical of any cultural mentality where aristocratic values are still prevalent but need to accommodate the commercial spirit of the middle classes. On the one hand play is dismissed, when opposed to work, as a nonserious, unproductive activity, and on the other hand it is praised, in its agonistic, military guise, as an indispensable generator of high cultural values.

Kant exhibits the same ambiguous attitude toward aesthetics and play in his view of fine art and the creative activity of the genius. For instance, he makes a distinction between art and handicraft, which he in turn bases on a distinction between play and work: "*Art* also differs from *handicraft*; the first is called *free*, the other may be called mercenary. We regard the first as if it could only prove purposive as play, i.e. as occupation that is pleasant in itself. But the second is regarded as if it could only be compulsorily imposed upon one as work, i.e. as occupation which is unpleasant (a trouble) in itself, and which it is only attractive on account of its effect (e.g. the wage)" (§43).

Thus, art and play (as well as the aesthetic judgment) share those elements of pleasure, spontaneity, and freedom that have been part of traditional definitions of play since Homer. But Kant proceeds to further distinguish between art and play on no other criterion than work, which for him is also the opposite of freedom:

> But it is not inexpedient to recall that in all free arts there is yet requisite something compulsory . . . without which the *spirit*, which must be free in art and which alone inspires the work, would have no body and would evaporate altogether. . . .
> It is not inexpedient, I say, to recall this, for many modern educators believe that the best way to produce a free art is to remove it from all constraint, and thus to change it from work into mere play. (§43)

In the end, for Kant, art turns out to be a higher kind of work because it serves the higher purpose of moral Nature, to which it is indirectly subordinated. "Fine art," he states, "is an art, in so far as it seems like Nature" (§45). This view bears a strong family resemblance to the Platonic and Aristotelian view of art as *mimesis* (in the sense of simulation), although it is couched in the aesthetic vocabulary of the eighteenth century: "In a product of fine art we must become conscious that it is Art and not Nature; but yet the purposiveness in its form must seem to be as free from all constraint of arbitrary rules as if it were a product of mere nature. On this feeling of freedom in the play of our cognitive faculties, which must at the same time be purposive, rests that pleasure which alone is universally communicable, without being based on concepts. Nature is beautiful because it looks like Art; and Art can only be called beautiful if we are conscious of it as Art while yet it looks like Nature" (§45).

In Kant, Aristotelian mimesis becomes the *as if* interplay of simulation on the part of the artist and conscious self-deception on the part of the reader or viewer. This notion of art as self-conscious illusion (*bewusste Selbsttäuschung*) will run through nineteenth-century aesthetics (and nineteenth-century theories of play), enjoying considerable critical authority even today, in the form of Coleridge's "willing suspension of disbelief."[14] Artistic simulation itself can be defined in Kant as a playful imitation, whose end is not knowledge but pleasure, and in this it closely resembles Aristotelian and Neoclassical versions of mimesis. Where it does differ from these versions, however, is in its object and manner of imitation.

The object of art's imitation is indeed nature but, in Kant, the latter is as ambiguous a notion as that of play. In the preceding quotation, for instance, we can see that he distinguishes between "mere nature" and Nature: the first is merely a purposeless mechanism, the second is the product of the moral ideas that infuse it with purposiveness and practicality; nature may lead to bad symbolical anthropomorphism, which needs to be dismissed as mere play of appearances and sensations, Nature is a prime example of good symbolical anthropomorphism, which "concerns only language and not the Object itself," and is a higher or purified form of moral fiction.[15] The nature that art is supposed to simulate is an ethical construct of the teleological judgment, under the direct guidance of pure Reason, and in a certain sense is *almost* interchangeable with art. Thus, in the second part of the third *Critique*,

14. Cf. the discussion of play and art as self-conscious illusion in Part II, sec. 1.2.

15. For the notion of symbolical anthropomorphism see especially *Prolegomena*, §58, from which the short quotations were taken. Its *als ob* character derives, as in the case of human knowledge in general, from the Kantian distinction between the *Ding an sich* and the *Ding für mich*: "Wenn ich sage, wir sind genötigt, die Welt so anzusehen, als ob sie das Werk eines höchsten Verstandes und Willens sei, so sage ich nichts mehr, als: wie sich verhält eine Uhr, ein Schiff, ein Regiment zum Künstler, Baumeister, Befehlshaber, so die Sinneswelt . . . zu dem Unbekannten, das ich also hierdurch zwar nicht nach dem, was es an sich selbst ist . . . aber doch nach dem, was es für mich ist . . . erkenne."

the "Critique of the Teleological Judgment," it is not only art that needs to be viewed *as if* it were nature, but also nature that needs to be viewed *as if* it were art.

In turn, in the teleological perspective, art becomes as much a moral category as nature does, and the beautiful is seen as a "symbol of morality" (*ein Symbol der Sittlichkeit* [§59]). Kant does, however, preserve the distinction between art and nature, which is the same as the distinction between the aesthetic and teleological judgment or that between play and seriousness: One concerns the pleasure of purposiveness without purpose, while the other concerns the utility of purposiveness; one is the "mere play, without a concept," of the cognitive faculties, the other is their serious employment for a practical purpose. In this sense, Kant ultimately reenacts the Platonic and Aristotelian subordination of art to philosophy or to the "serious business" of life, subordination that he justifies, just like Plato and Aristotle, on both cognitive and ethical grounds.

But, as opposed to Classical and Neoclassical views of art as mimesis, for Kant, as for all subsequent Romantic theorists, art is a simulation of *natura naturans* rather than *natura naturata*; in other words, art simulates nature's processes rather than its products. Imitation recedes into the background, and the work of art is no longer a copy of nature but the "original product of a Genius," who receives his rules from nature spontaneously, upon his birth. Because genius is a "gift" and not merely an "aptitude for what can be learned by rule," *originality* must be its first property (§46). Nevertheless, imitation does not disappear completely: because genius "also can produce original nonsense," its products must in turn "become models, i.e., *exemplary*." Although these products must not arise from imitation themselves, they must serve as a standard or rule of judgment for others, and it is also in this sense that they are *like* nature.[16] Not only imitation, but originality itself turns out to be an ambiguous notion. On the one hand, Kant sees it as a necessary condition of genius, but on the other hand, he sees it as being irrational, and

16. For a detailed discussion of the artist-genius as imitator of natural process, see Derrida, "Economimésis," especially pp. 68–72. Derrida, however, seems to attribute to Kant a concept that has a long pre-Kantian history, from Shaftesbury to Baumgarten. For the relationship between the early German aestheticians and their English models, see Cassirer, *Philosophy of Enlightenment*, pp. 297–330. For a fine discussion of the relation between genius, wit, and judgment in eighteenth-century aesthetics, see Stanley Corngold, "Wit and Judgment in the Eighteenth Century: Lessing and Kant," *MLN* 102 (April 1987): 461–482.

here he comes close to Socrates' definition of the rhapsode-poet in the *Ion*: "The author of a product for which he is indebted to his genius does not himself know how he has come by his ideas; and he has not the power to devise the like at pleasure or in accordance with a plan, and to communicate it to others in precepts that will enable them to produce similar products" (§46).

Because of his irrationality the genius is, predictably, inferior to the man of learning or the scientist. But the genius is also inferior to the scientist, less predictably, because he is "entirely opposed to the spirit of imitation," and Kant supports his argument by offering an Aristotelian definition of learning: "Now since learning is nothing but imitation, it follows that the greatest ability and teachableness [capacity] regarded *qua* teachableness, cannot avail for genius" (§46). It is true that in science "the greatest discoverer only differs in degree from his laborious imitator and pupil," but this by no means detracts from his greatness. In fact, the scientist is greatly superior to the genius precisely because his talent is directed not only to the "ever-advancing greater perfection of knowledge and every advantage depending on it," but also to imparting this knowledge to others. Whereas the scientist's products can be communicated through imitation, the gift of the genius remains untransmittable (although it does inspire good eris in other artists, who attempt to surpass it), and dies with him.[17]

Because it is innate, rather than acquired, the genius needs moreover to be cultivated and polished. Hence it involves both a great deal of effort (work) and taste, which is dictated by judgment in general, that is, by a cognitive faculty. In short, the genius needs to be disciplined by science and in this respect Kant's view remains within the confines of the rationalist Neoclassical tradition: "Taste, like the Judgment in general, is the discipline (or training) of Genius; it clips its wings closely, and makes it cultured and polished; but, at the same time, it gives guidance as to where and how far it may extend itself, if it is to remain purposive. . . . If, then, in the conflict of these two properties in a

17. Similar statements can be found in the *Anthropology*, §57. This Kantian view of the scientist as a Neoclassical imitator persists in the sciences long after the Romantic view of the artist as genius replaces, in the fine arts, the Neoclassical concept of the artist as imitator of traditional models. For a combination of the Neoclassical and Romantic views of artistic creation in a theory of "scientific revolutions" see Thomas Kuhn, *The Structure of Scientific Revolutions* (Chicago, 1962). Cf. my introductory remarks to sec. 3 and my discussion of Kuhn's philosophy of science in Part II, sec. 3.3.

product something must be sacrificed, it should be rather on the side of genius; and the Judgment, which in the things of fine art gives its decision from its own proper principles, will rather sacrifice the freedom and wealth of the Imagination than permit anything prejudicial to the Understanding" (§50).

If in the contest between the scientist and the genius Kant gives the palm to the former, ranking science above art, in the contest between the arts he awards the first prize to poetry. He tentatively sets up a hierarchy among the arts on the basis of thought, intuition, and sensation, recalling Aristotle's ranking of the six elements in tragedy according to object, manner, and means of imitation.[18] There are three kinds of arts, corresponding to the three epistemological divisions in Kant's system: the arts of speech, concerned with thought; the formative arts, concerned with intuition; and the arts of the play of sensations. Not surprisingly, the arts of speech are ranked first. But Kant does depart from Aristotle when he reverses the hierarchy in regard to poetry and rhetoric, favoring the former. The criterion of this reversal is, ironically, a Platonic one, and involves simulation and play or the *as if* approach: "*Rhetoric* is the art of carrying on a serious business of the Understanding as if it were a free play of the Imagination; *poetry*, the art of conducting a free play of the Imagination as if it were a serious business of the Understanding" (§51). The key to these definitions lies in the opposition between play and seriousness or frivolity and utility. Though he formulates the distinction between poetry and rhetoric as a playful paradox, which is itself, consciously or unconsciously, modeled upon a favored Sophistic rhetorical trick—the antithesis—Kant ends up judging them according to their degree of seriousness. The orator promises a "serious business" but, because he wants to sweeten his pill by entertaining the audience, he presents this serious business "as if it were a mere *play* with Ideas." Thus, he gives something that he does not promise, which is "an entertaining play of the Imagination," but he also fails to deliver what he has promised, which is the "purposive occupation of the understanding." The poet, on the other hand, promises little, announcing a "mere play with Ideas." In the process, however, he "supplies something which is worth occupying ourselves with, because he provides in this play food for the Understanding, and by the aid of the Imagination gives life to his concepts" (§51). The criteria of judging the relative value of these arts are utilitarian and dictated by the pure practical Reason. Rhetoric has little value for the understanding be-

18. I examine in detail Aristotle's *Poetics* in terms of the rational values that metaphysics imposes on fine art, in *God of Many Names*, chap. 5.

cause it provides, as Socrates had already argued, (for example, in the *Phaedrus*), a mere Sophistic play with concepts or only an appearance of knowledge. Although poetry is also a mere play with concepts, it is of much more value for the understanding, first because it does not pretend to be more than play and therefore implicitly recognizes the superiority of understanding, deferring to its judgments; second, because it acts as a mediator, in the service of Reason, between the abstract ideas and the senses.

The other arts are also ranked according to their relative value for the understanding, and just as in Aristotle, form and intellectual pleasure rather than the "sensual attractions" are the positive standards of evaluation: "Yet in all beautiful art the essential thing is the form, which is purposive as regards our observation and judgment, where the pleasure is at the same time cultivation and disposes the spirit to Ideas. . . . The essential element is not the matter of sensation (charm or emotion), which has only to do with enjoyment" (§52).

Moreover, the fine arts are ultimately to be judged in terms of their relevance to moral ideas, "which alone brings with them a self-sufficing satisfaction." When they fail to conform to these ideas, and are merely designed to gratify the senses, they can only serve as useless distractions and can never produce a lasting and satisfying enjoyment. If music occupies the last place in the hierarchy of the fine arts, it is because, like Aristotelian *melopoiia*, it "merely plays with sensations"; conversely, such formative arts as sculpture, painting, and landscaping rank far above music because, by "putting the imagination in a free play, which is also accordant with the Understanding, they at the same time carry on a serious business" (§53).

In the two *Critiques* considered so far, play appears mainly in relation to cognition, and although it is itself devoid of cognitive value, it may serve, in its good, rational guise, either to provide food for imagination and understanding in the form of the play of sensations, appearances, and representations, or to help the pure practical Reason enforce its moral and beautiful fictions in the form of fine art. Though play as a tool of the cognitive faculties also figures prominently in the *Anthropology from a Pragmatic Point of View*, the emphasis shifts onto its unwieldy, irrational guises when Kant places it in an anthropological perspective.[19] To be sure, the functions of play as an anthropological phenomenon are not all negative. When it is opposed to work, play has the

19. The English translation of the *Anthropology* I have used here is by V. L. Dowdell, ed. and rev. H. H. Rudnick (Carbondale, Ill., 1978). Further citations refer to this English edition.

compensatory role of recovering the energy spent during active hours (§§31, 33, 87). Children's play reminds the teacher of the "best time of all" in his childhood, and he vicariously enjoys its pleasures once more (§1); athletic games are "daring enterprises deliberately spurred on by the wisdom of Nature so that they all test [men's] strength in a competition with others" (§86); social role playing or pretense has a civilizing function, for "even the appearance of the good in others must have value for us, because in the long run something serious can come from such a play with pretenses" (§14). In the form of a "hobbyhorse," play preserves the vitality of the old and offers a harmless pastime to the young (§45); in party games, play fosters sociability and amiable feelings (§88).

In all of these cases, however, the potential harm inherent in play offsets its benefits. Play as recreation may turn into laziness (§§14, 87). The mind may "amuse itself by dallying with the fine arts" (§14), but its overindulging in the free play of the imagination leads to a "bad habit," causing the weakening of the mental powers (§33). The teacher may take pleasure in a child's play, but this pleasure is empty, because his memory cannot reach back to his own childhood, which is not a "time of experiences" but one of "mere sporadic perceptions," not yet unified by "any real concept of an object" (§1); in other words, childhood is a mere play of sensations, without a concept, and the teacher's temporary relapse into it should not detain him long from his serious pursuits. Competition among human beings may answer nature's purpose of making us strong, but it also fosters the illusion (e.g., in certain games of chance) that we are in control, when in fact we are mere toys in the hands of nature (§86). Even though role playing may lead to true virtue which, by reiteration, may become "part of the actor's disposition," (cf. Socrates' similar argument in the *Republic*, 3.395d) the play of appearances will always remain deceptive, especially in the "cases of conscience" (§14). And whereas the hobbyhorse reflects a relatively harmless "fondness for the occupation with objects of the imagination, with which the understanding only plays for amusement," it nevertheless is a deviation "across the borderline of sound understanding" (§45). Finally, although sociablity is a "virtue," the inclination to be sociable "often becomes a passion," for example, in gambling. Music, dance, and play may have a certain social value as recreation, but they "are conducive to company without conversation," because the few words that are needed for play do not encourage a "mutual exchange of thought." And although play should serve only to "fill out the emptiness of conversation after dinner," it is often turned into the "principal affair," and thus it does not "further the union of social good living with virtue" (§88).

Because of its potential harm, which is all the more fatal because it is often disguised as sensuous pleasure, play needs to be subordinated to work, utility, and serious business: "What is in itself nothing but play is suitable for the relaxation of powers expended during the day, but what is business is suitable for a man strengthened as well as reborn, as it were, through a good night's rest" (§33). Unless it is checked and bridled, play leads to passion and mental disorder. Even such apparently harmless pursuits as daydreaming and poetry may lead to a "delusion of the senses," to mental weaknesses, and eventually to madness (§§47–52). The reading of novels, for example, "in addition to causing many other mental disorders . . . makes distraction habitual." In a distracted state, we "blindly follow the free play of our imagination," instead of "checking it by reason," and thus become "useless for society" (§47). Delirium, on the other hand, is the illness in which the mental patient most resembles a poet: "*Delirium* (*insania*) is disordered faculty of judgment in which the mind is deceived by analogies, which are being confused with concepts of similar things, so that the imagination offers dissimilar objects as similar and universal ones in a process resembling that of the understanding. . . . The delirious person of this type cannot be cured because he is creative and entertaining through diversity, like poetry in general" (§52).

Unbridled and unruly imagination (see definition in §33) plays tricks upon Reason, which no longer operates on the basis of the harmony of the cognitive faculties. To surrender oneself to the "play of the un-premeditatedly creative imagination" means to "reverse the natural order of the cognitive powers, since then the rational elements do not take the lead (as they should) but instead follow behind" (§4). It also means, paradoxically, that one loses one's freedom and turns from a player into a toy: "We play with the imagination frequently and gladly, but . . . the imagination just as often plays with us" (§31). Likewise, we often play with obscure ideas, but then we ourselves "become an object of obscure ideas, and our understanding is unable to rescue itself from absurdities which were caused by those ideas, although we recognize them as an illusion" (§5). In short, once we give up the rules of Reason, we become the helpless toys of the irrational. It is this arbitrary, chaotic, and uncontrollable play of the irrational that Kant constantly runs up against and attempts to come to terms with throughout his philosophical thought. The irrational relentlessly haunts him, in the *Ding an sich*, in the free, spontaneous, and unruly play of the intuition and the imagination, in the disjunctive play between the similar and the dissimilar, in the disparity between the beautiful and the sublime, in the divided moral nature of man, in the cosmic interplay of necessity and chance, in the inscrutable designs of Nature. In a remarkable note to §31 of the *Anthropology*, for instance, Kant observes in regard to the irreconcilable heterogeneity of sensibility and understanding:

> The play of powers in inanimate Nature, as well as in the animate, in the soul as well as in the body, is based on separating and uniting the dissimilar. We reach cognition of the play of powers by experiencing the effects; the ultimate cause and the most basic ingredients into which their substance can be analyzed, cannot be found by us. What is the reason for the fact that all known organic beings are propagated through the union of the two sexes . . . ? We cannot very well assume that the Creator was merely amusing himself out of eccentricity and just making on this earth-globe an arrangement that pleased him. . . . In what obscurity does the human reason lose itself when it seeks to establish the reason for our lineage, or when it only tries to make a guess of it? (§31)

This passage, which could have been written, with slight alterations, by Heraclitus or Schopenhauer, clearly shows the ethical polarization not only of play but of power, which Kant calls both "Nature" and "the Creator." In turn, "nature" here is no less amphibolous than it is in his *Critiques*, having at least three different meanings. Kant employs it in the "common" sense of an objective and subjective world, around and within man, which is perhaps endowed with a higher, all-encompassing intelligence. He also understands it as a purposeless mechanism, which cannot be known in itself, but only as it arises in the intuition. Then, again, he uses it in the sense of a moral construct or fiction that is demanded by Reason and concerns the teleological judgment (a specific Kantian version of the first, "common" usage). The second concept of nature is the modern version of the archaic idea of power as the arbitrary, irrational play of divine or tellurian forces, while the first and the third concepts correspond to the Parmenidean and Platonic idea of power as an abstract, rational, and essentially benevolent supreme Being. In all three cases, Kant no longer sees man as a master player or a master manipulator, but only as a puppet of unfathomable forces within and without. Sensibility is the human faculty that is in closest contact with these frightening forces and through which they often manifest themselves. Hence, one can understand why Kant, like Plato and a host of other metaphysicians before and after him, distrusts the senses and attempts to discipline them through the understanding, which in turn is disciplined by Reason.

One can also understand why Kant is forced to operate with highly ambiguous and polarized concepts of power, play, freedom, art, nature, and so forth. Although he seems fully convinced of the hypothetical foundation of human knowledge, temperamentally he does not seem able to accept a relativist stand, and therefore he seeks certainty in the conscious delusion (or in what Nietzsche will later call "joyful forgetfulness") of the moral ideas. Because the *als ob* character of these ideas and of pure Reason in general closely resembles the *als ob* character of play, Kant takes great pains to distinguish between the two not only in moral-practical but also in logical terms (and in this he also follows Plato, who carries on his agon with the Sophists on similar grounds). A critique of pure Reason is therefore necessary not because of Reason's excessive cognitive claims, but because of its disciplinarian mission. As its "proper duty" is to "prescribe a discipline for all other endeavors" (*Critique of Pure Reason*, A710/B738), Reason needs in turn to be subjected to a rigorous discipline, "a system of precautions and self-examination . . . in face of which no pseudo-rational illusion will be able to stand, will at once betray itself, no matter what claims it may advance for exceptional treatment" (A711/B739). Play is both that which most needs discipline and that which escapes all discipline: hence its elusive and amphibolous character in Kant's philosophical system.

## 1·2   Friedrich Schiller: The Play of Reason

In *Über die ästhetische Erziehung des Menschen in einer Reihe von Briefen* (1795), Schiller sets out, under the immediate impact of Kant—and that of the French revolution—to investigate the relationship between the moral and the aesthetic realms, or between education and fine art, with a view to establishing the conditions of the possibility of what he calls the "aesthetic State." This State would replace not only the traditional European states but also the newly formed, "enlightened" State of the French people, which has just drowned itself in a blood bath. Schiller's project can, then, be described as Platonic in intent and Kantian in method. Its most important result, from our point of view, is the firm reestablishment of play as a legitimate topic of serious philosophical discourse, thereby bringing about a revolution in the modern history of the play concept(s). Here "revolution" should be understood both in the sense of radical change and in the sense of return. The radical change occurs in relation to Kant: although Kant reintroduces play in modern philosophical thought, he sees it only as a sort of negative condition of the possibility of this thought. Schiller, on the other hand, frankly designates the *als ob* activity of Reason as play, and thus can be seen as completing the aesthetic turn of transcendental philosophy. Schiller's return to play as a useful philosophical concept occurs in relation to Plato, who, after purging it of irrationality and violence, acknowledges it as the "noblest" activity of Reason.

Although he starts from the Kantian (and Platonic) distinction between the realm of the senses or necessity and that of Reason or freedom, Schiller radicalizes this distinction in at least two ways: following Fichte, he recasts it in the form of a dialectic of equal terms, which he then attempts to transcend by positing a third mediating term.[20] Thus, in a preliminary stage Schiller distinguishes between a sense-drive *(Stofftrieb, sinnlicher Trieb)*, and a form-drive or rational drive *(Formtrieb, vernünftiger Trieb)*. The sense-drive proceeds from the physical existence of man, or his sensuous nature, and it requires that "there shall be change, that time shall have a content." Its realm encompasses man's finite being, ruling over humanity's phenomenal aspect *(die ganze Erscheinung der Menschheit)*. The form-drive proceeds from man's rational nature, and is "intent on giving him freedom to bring harmony into the diversity of his manifestations, and to affirm his Person among all his changes of Condition."[21] It embraces the "whole sequence of time,"

20. Schiller himself acknowledges his indebtedness to Fichte in the footnotes to letters IV, sec. 2, and XIII, sec. 2. For the problematic personal relationship between Schiller and Fichte, as well as the former's philosophical sources, see Hermand Meyer, "Schillers philosophische Rhetorik," in *Zarte Empirie: Studien zur Literaturgeschichte* (Stuttgart, 1963). Because of the triadic character of his dialectic, Schiller is credited with having anticipated Hegel, who held his theory of art as play in high esteem. In Hegel, however, play becomes subordinated to reason and to work to such an extent that it loses its mediating position between freedom and necessity. For Schiller's influence on Hegel, see, e.g., I. Kowatzki, *Der Begriff des Spiels als ästhetisches Phänomen. Von Schiller bis Benn* (Bern, 1972), pp. 11–38.

21. Friedrich Schiller, *On the Aesthetic Education of Man, in a Series of Letters*, ed. and trans. Elizabeth M. Wilkinson and L. A. Willoughby (Oxford, 1967), letter XII, sec. 4. Further citations refer to this edition; unless otherwise specified, italics are in the original. Wilkinson and Willoughby's lengthy critical introduction to their edition is the most exhaustive English discussion of the *Aesthetic Education*. Other relevant studies are W. Bohm, *Schillers Briefe über die ästhetische Erziehung* (Halle, 1927); H. Lutz, *Schillers Anschauungen von Kultur und Natur* (Berlin,

which amounts to saying that it annuls (*aufhebt*) time and change. The form-drive wants the "real to be necessary and eternal, and the eternal and the necessary to be real," insisting on "truth and on the right." If the sense-drive furnishes individual cases (*Fälle*), the form-drive gives laws (XII, 5).

Schiller sees these two drives as opposing forces, engaged in an agonistic relationship, but he warns against merely subordinating the sensuous to the rational drive, as so often happens in eighteenth-century philosophy, including that of Kant: the interaction between them should be reciprocal (XIII, fn. 1). For Schiller, however, this reciprocity is not so much a fact of experience as a desideratum belonging to the realm of transcendental Ideas demanded by Reason. The Idea of his humanity requires that man "feel himself as matter and come to know himself as mind." If such an Idea could materialize, then it would give rise, in man, to a third drive, both opposed to and reconciling the other two: "That drive . . . in which both the others work in concert . . . the play-drive, therefore, would be directed towards annulling time *within time*, reconciling becoming with absolute being and change with identity" (XIV, 3).

The play-drive would thus arise only as a result of the *als ob* activity of Reason and is, in turn, a play concept or a fiction devised by Reason in order to mediate between itself and experience. The play-drive occupies the same middle position in Schiller that the aesthetic judgment does in Kant, and for the same reason: while it is itself devoid of any cognitive value, it nevertheless helps Reason mediate between the realm of the concept of nature and that of the concept of freedom. But whereas in Kant these two realms ultimately remain heterogeneous, in Schiller they

---

1928); Kowatzki, *Der Begriff des Spiels als ästhetisches Phänomen*; and D. Henrich, "Beauty and Freedom: Schiller's Struggle with Kant's Aesthetics," in Cohen and Guyer, *Essays in Kant's Aesthetics*, pp. 237–257. Another is Benjamin Bennett's brief discussion of Schiller and Nietzsche in "Nietzsche's Idea of Myth: The Birth of Tragedy from the Spirit of Eighteenth-Century Aesthetics," *PMLA* 94 (1979). Whereas Bennett acknowledges Nietzsche's antimoralistic stance as a crucial difference between his and Schiller's aesthetics, he ignores the fundamentally different concepts of play underlying these two aesthetics. See, e.g., n. 16, where Bennett remarks: "The idea of 'Spiel,' which in *Über die aesthetische Erziehung* is the mediating force, is prominent in 'Die dionysische Weltanschauung,' but is almost entirely eliminated in the developed thought of *The Birth of Tragedy*" (p. 433). What is almost entirely eliminated from the latter is not the idea of *Spiel*, but its Schillerian, teleological overtones. Cf. my discussion of Schiller's and Nietzsche's concepts of play and aesthetics in sec. 2.1.

may become reconciled in the *as if* modality of the aesthetic State demanded by the play-drive. The explicit *als ob* character of this State allows Schiller to use it both as an ideal standard of evaluation of the historical States and as a moral imperative, or a utopian model, to be actualized by future generations. According to Schiller, the historical States have proven inadequate precisely because they fail to reconcile the sense-drive and the moral-drive in a harmonious manner. He distinguishes between a natural State (*Naturstaat*) and a moral State, according to the degree to which one of the drives prevails over the other. He defines the *Naturstaat* as the political body the organization of which "derives originally from forces and not from laws" (III, 3). These "blind forces" that rule physical man are at variance with man as moral being. So when "out of the long slumber of the senses he awakens to consciousness and knows himself for a human being," man cannot rest content with his *Naturstaat*, because of the demands made upon him by his rational drive. He therefore opposes another State to it, a moral one, based on a "state of nature" (*Naturstand*), not in Hobbes's but in Rousseau's sense of a heuristic fiction through which Reason would retrieve the "childhood of the race": "[Man] conceives, as idea, a *state of nature*, a state not indeed given to him by experience, but a necessary result of what Reason destined him to be; attributes to himself in this idealized natural state a purpose of which in his actual natural state he was entirely ignorant, and a power of free choice of which he was at that time wholly incapable; and now proceeds exactly as if he were starting from scratch, and were, from sheer insight and free resolve, exchanging a state of complete independence for a state of social contracts" (III, 2).

Schiller employs the typical modern equivalent of the *phusis-nomos* dichotomy, with its various conflicting concepts of nature, *phusis*, out of which two seem to be especially at work in the present passage: nature as a battlefield of blind, chaotic forces (Kant) and nature as the lost unity of sense and intellect (Rousseau). *Nomos*, in the sense of both law and culture, is the necessary substitute of nature in the second sense, and is demanded by the awakening of mankind from its sensuous slumber. Later on, Schiller also employs the ancient antithesis of Greek and barbarian, which he turns into an opposition between the savage-barbarian and the man of culture, linking it to the kind of States that the interplay of the sense-drive, form-drive, and play-drive may engender (IV, 6). The savage obeys the sense-drive, or Nature as "arbitrary play of the senses," leading to the *Naturstaat*; the barbarian only *pretends* to obey the form-drive, while in fact obeying the sensuous one, thus being an unworthy citizen of the moral State; and the *gebildete Mensch* obeys the form-drive, thus belonging to the moral State but also having the potential, through the play-drive, of founding the aesthetic State.[22] Schiller thereby operates with an enlightened, rational version of human history, which resembles that offered by Protagoras, Plato, and Rousseau: the age of arbitrary violence and savagery is, or ought to be, superseded by one of law and order under the guidance of Reason. Ironically, the agonistic nature of the Greek *polis* is no longer perceived as such, and now functions in turn as a "golden age," or the perfect expression of the unity between sense and intellect, to be contrasted to the dissociation of sensibility that plagues the modern age: "At that first fair awakening of the powers of the mind, sense and intellect did not as yet rule over strictly separate domains; for no dissension had as yet provoked them into hostile partition and mutual demarcation of their frontiers. Poetry had not as yet coquetted with wit, nor speculation prostituted itself to sophistry! . . . Both of them could, when need arose, exchange function, since each in its own fashion paid honor to truth" (VI, 3). By contrast, the modern age suffers from the wounds inflicted upon it by an "all-dividing Intellect," which has managed to suppress an "all-unifying Nature" (VI, 6).

Whereas Schiller's sharp critique of the modern division of knowledge is still relevant today, the archaic agonistic roots of this division are ignored in favor of an idealized, sentimental vision of classical Greece—a "golden age fiction" (Vaihinger) unusually persistent in European culture up to the present.[23] On the other hand, the contest between the ancients and the moderns remains a major concern in Schiller's age as

22. Cf. letter XXVIII, where the three States are now called "dynamic," "ethical," and "aesthetic": "If in the *dynamic* State of rights it is as force that one man encounters another, and imposes limits upon his activities; if in the *ethical* State of duties Man sets himself over against man with all the majesty of law, and puts a curb to his desires; in those circles where conduct is governed by beauty, in the *aesthetic* State, none may appear to the other except as form, or confront him except as an object of free play" (XXVII, 9). For an extensive commentary on Rousseau's political ideas, see Cassirer, *Enlightenment*, pp. 253–274.

23. In Germany, J. J. Winckelmann, especially through *Gedanken über die Nachahmung der griechischen Werke in der Malerei und Bildhauerkunst* (1775), was largely responsible for establishing this golden-age fiction about Greece. For a discussion of Winckelmann's influence on Schiller's view of ancient Greece, see, e.g., H. Hatfield, "Schiller, Winckelmann, and the Myth of Greece," in J. R. Frey, ed., *Schiller, 1759/1959* (Urbana, Ill., 1959). For the idea of ancient Greece in nineteenth-century German culture in general, see, e.g., M. S. Silk and J. P. Stern, *Nietzsche on Tragedy* (Cambridge, Eng., 1981), chap. 1, "Germany and Greece."

well: in the quotation above he seems to take the side of the ancients, but later on (VI, 11), he also gives the moderns their due.[24] Characteristically, he situates himself on both sides of an argument, eventually attempting to overcome it through a third, mediating position. In this case he grants that the development of the intellect at the expense of the senses was historically inevitable and that the modern period contains within itself the potentiality of a return to the Greeks on a higher level. And now we are given a first inkling of the play-drive and the aesthetic State, in the form of an apology for Fine Art: the latter is to carry out the task of Reason where both Science and Morality have failed. In this respect Schiller departs from Kant and raises Art to the same level as Science, arguing that "both rejoice in absolute immunity from human arbitrariness"; despite contingent political or utilitarian obstructions, "Truth and Beauty will always struggle to the surface" (IX, 3).

Art can carry out the task of Reason precisely because of its double nature as semblance and reality, play and seriousness, entertainment and morality. Employing Platonic arguments, Schiller urges his brethren to educate their contemporaries by combining the *dulce* and the *utile*: "The seriousness of your principles will frighten them [the artists' contemporaries] away, but in the play of your semblance they will be prepared to tolerate them. . . . In vain will you assail their precepts, in vain condemn their practice; but on their leisure hours you can try your shaping hand. Banish from their pleasures caprice, frivolity, and coarseness, and imperceptibly you will banish these from their actions and, eventually, from their inclinations too" (IX, 7).

Art shares the amphibolous nature of play which troubled Kant, but which Schiller sees positively as "the happy medium between the realm of law and the sphere of physical exigency . . . removed from the constraint of the one as of the other" (XV, 5). Art's goal is Beauty, which also shares the double nature of play, being a perfect balance between the sense-drive and the form-drive, that is, *lebende Gestalt*, living form. Although Schiller's polemic with Kant remains implicit, it is nevertheless unmistakable:

> But . . . is beauty not degraded by being made to consist of mere play and reduced to the level of those frivolous things which have always

24. Here my reference is, of course, to the famous "Querelle des anciens et des modernes," which began in the early Renaissance and raged with great fury and inkshed all the way into the early nineteenth century. H. Rigault's *Histoire de la querelle des anciens et des modernes* (1859; rpt. New York, 1965) still remains one of the more readable accounts of this "battle of the books" in Western culture.

borne this name? Does it not belie the rational concept as well as the dignity of beauty—which is, after all, here considered as an instrument of culture—if we limit it to *mere play*? . . .

But how can we speak of *mere play* [*blosses Spiel*], when we know it is precisely play and play *alone*, which of all man's states and conditions is the one which makes him whole and unfolds both sides of his nature at once? (xv, 6, 7)

Schiller clearly challenges Kant's underestimation of play as a legitimate and productive rational activity. Whereas the latter had painstakingly avoided designating the *als ob* employment of Reason as play, Schiller takes the opposite path: for him the play-drive is a rational fiction that operates in the realm of *als ob*, having the force of a moral imperative in the practical realm, just like any other transcendental Idea. He takes up the dichotomy between play and seriousness employed by Kant and attempts to reconcile it on a higher plane. In the process of carrying out this task, ironically he returns to Plato, who dissolves seriousness into play and play into seriousness when he declares man to be the "plaything of the gods" (*Laws* 7.803c). In this instance, Schiller argues that the form-drive and the sense-drive lose their earnestness (*Ernst*), with salutary effects for both, when they come under the dispensation of the play-drive (xv, 5).

Schiller goes even farther and declares that man is human only insofar as he plays, thereby replacing *homo sapiens* and *homo politicus* with *homo ludens*: "For, to mince matters no longer, man only plays when he is in the fullest sense of the word a human being, and *he is only fully a human being when he plays*" (xv, 9). This proposition would, according to him, be a paradox only in the eyes of philosophy (read: Kant), because "it was long ago operative in the art and in the feeling of the Greeks." The latter "banished from the brow of the blessed gods all the earnestness and effort which furrow the cheeks of the mortals." They released the gods, "those ever-contented beings, from the bonds inseparable from every purpose, every duty, every care, and made *idleness* and *indifferency* [*Müssiggang* and *Gleichgültigkeit*] the enviable portion of divinity—merely a more human name for the freest, most sublime state of being" (xv, 9). Schiller seems to reverse the polarity of not only seriousness and play but also work and play, ostensibly turning against the Protestant work ethic which, we have seen, lay at the foundation of Kant's anthropology. He thereby sets the pattern for all modern discussions of play, which will always involve a polarity of play and seriousness, play and work, play and morality, play and necessity, and so forth, in which one term will invariably take precedence over the other.

Despite his reversal and dynamization of the Kantian dichotomies, however, Schiller never manages to wrestle himself free of these dichotomies; like Kant, moreover, he operates with polarized notions of play. For instance, he reintroduces the distinction between play and mere play in the form of an opposition between transcendental and material (or physical) play. When we speak of play, he cautions, "we must not think . . . of the various forms of play which are in vogue [*im Gange*] in actual life, and are usually directed to very material objects"; rather, "with the ideal of Beauty that is set up by Reason, an ideal of the play-drive, too, is enjoined upon man, which he must keep before his eyes in all his forms of play" (xv, 7). The distinguishing factor between the ideal or transcendental play-drive and the material one is (non)violence. Schiller again offers a Greek example, in which the Olympic games become the embodiment of the nonviolent, rational Idea of play and act in turn as a critical norm for the play activity of other nations: "We shall not go far wrong when trying to discover a man's ideal of beauty if we inquire how he satisfies his play-drive. If at the Olympic games the peoples of Greece delighted in the bloodless combats of strength, speed, and agility, and in the nobler rivalry of talents, and if the Roman people regaled themselves with the death throes of a vanquished gladiator or of his Libyan opponent, we can, from this single trait, understand why we have to seek the ideal forms of a Venus, a Juno, an Apollo, not in Rome but in Greece" (xv, 8).

Although Schiller seems to depart from Kant when he favors play over work or utility on the basis of its freedom, a closer look at his definition of these terms will reveal that for him, just as for Kant, play is essentially only a higher kind of work or utility. The question of the relationship between play as freedom and utility comes up precisely when Schiller attempts to bridge the gap between material and transcendental play. He employs such Kantian concepts as purposiveness without purpose and disinterestedness when he defines animal and human (physical) play in terms of limited freedom: "Nature has given even to creatures without reason more than the bare necessities of existence, and shed a glimmer of freedom even into the darkness of animal life. When the lion is not gnawed by hunger, nor provoked to battle by any beast of prey, his idle strength creates an object for itself: he fills the echoing desert with a roaring defiance, and his exuberant energy enjoys its *self* in purposeless display" (xxvii, 3). For Schiller, work is the outside compulsion of want, while material play is the inner compulsion of superabundance or superfluity (*Überfluss*) which demands release: "An animal may be said *to be at work*, when the stimulus to activity is some lack; it may be said *to be at play*, when the stimulus is sheer plenitude of vitality, when superabundance of life is its own incentive to action. Even inanimate nature exhibits a similar luxuriance of forces, coupled with a laxity of determination [*Bestimmung*] which, in that material sense, might well be called play" (XXVII, 3).

Material play is "squandering in carefree joy," and Schiller sees the freedom from utility and from outside compulsion (or from what he calls, employing another anthropomorphic metaphor, "physical earnestness") as the common denominator of material and aesthetic play: "Thus does Nature, even in her material kingdom, offer us a prelude in the Illimitable, and even here remove *in part* the chains which, in the realm of form, she casts away entirely. From the compulsion of want, or *physical earnestness*, she makes the transition via the compulsion of superfluity, or physical play, to aesthetic play" (XXVII, 3).

Just like the animal and human bodily organs, imagination has its own material play, which is none other than Kant's free play of representations, with an added element of "delight in its own activity." And what imagination delights in, as in the case of the lion, is "its absolute and unfettered power." Here we seem to come very close to the archaic concept of play as the violent, arbitrary, and exuberant movement of power, which is later repressed by the rational mentality of Postsocratic philosophy. But the same repression remains operative in Schiller as well, for example when he acknowledges that in reality no bridge is possible between the free and arbitrary play of imagination and aesthetic play; what is needed instead is a *leap*: "A leap it must be called, since a completely new power goes into action; for here, for the first time, mind takes a hand as law-giver in the operations of blind instinct, subjects the arbitrary activity of the imagination to its own immutable and eternal unity. . . . The aesthetic play-drive, therefore, will in its first attempts be scarcely recognizable, since the physical play-drive, with its willful moods and its unruly appetites, constantly gets in the way" (XXVII, 4).

The physical or material play-drive, which for Schiller apparently is more than a heuristic fiction, stands in the way of the aesthetic and transcendental play-drive, which is *only* a heuristic fiction; in other words, in Schiller, as in Plato and in Kant, the world of the senses turns out again to be the archenemy of Reason. The "powerful" and "dynamic" intellect is thus called upon to do battle with the senses. Its mission is a double one: on the one hand, it is supposed to defeat the "passivity" of matter by energizing it into form; on the other hand, it is supposed to control, or keep within the bonds of this form, the chaotic and violent forces that purportedly make up matter. Although he presents the material and the rational drives as equal forces, Schiller loads the dice in favor of Reason through the transcendental play-drive: "Reason on transcendental grounds, makes the following demand: Let there be a bond of union between the form-drive and the material drive; that is to say, let there be a play-drive, since only the union of reality with form, contingency with necessity, passivity with freedom, makes the concept of human nature complete" (XV, 4).

Whereas feeling may have "no say whatsoever" in the realm of truth and morality, in the sphere of the senses form has "every right to exist, and the aesthetic play-drive every right to command." In fact, it is in the physical sphere that man must begin his moral life: "He must, if you will permit the expression, *play* the war against Matter into the very territory of Matter itself, so that he may be spared to fight this dread foe on the sacred soil of freedom" (XXIII, 8). Forgetting the "leap" from the material to the transcendental play-drive, Schiller describes the transition as an orderly process carried out by Form, which "gradually comes upon man from without, transforming at first only the outer, but ultimately the inner man, too." He illustrates his argument by another agonistic analogy, this time taken from the *Iliad* and dramatizing the contrast between the rational and the material play-drive (might we have to leap again?): "[Under the shaping power of Form] uncoordinated leaps of joy turn into dance, the unformed movements of the body into the graceful and harmonious language of gesture. . . . If the Trojan host storms on to the battlefield with piercing shrieks like a flock of cranes, the Greek army approaches in silence, with noble and measured tread. In the former case we see only the exuberance of blind forces; in the latter, the triumph of form and the simple majesty of law" (XXVII, 6).

Although an enlightened, rational mentality must always repudiate violence and conflict, and the transcendental play-drive must accordingly be defined by nonviolence, the violent, power-oriented nature of rationality comes to the surface when Reason's commands are to be carried out in practice: "Reason has accomplished all that she can accomplish by discovering the law and establishing it. Its execution demands a resolute will and ardour of feeling. If Truth is to be victorious in her conflict with forces, she must herself first become a *force* and appoint some *drive* to be her champion in the realm of phenomena; for drives are the only motive forces in the sensible world" (VIII, 3).

In other words, Reason must employ unreason or force to wage war on its behalf in the realm of forces that is the material world (cf. the Athenian's argument in *Laws*, 1.645a). Schiller's favored metaphor here is also of Greek origin, and this time it is appropriate enough, for it discloses the agonistic origin of rational values, as embodied in the Horatian motto, *sapere aude*: "Dare to be wise! . . . Not for nothing does the ancient myth make the goddess of wisdom [Athena] emerge fully armed from the head of Jupiter. For her very first action is a warlike one. Even at birth she has to fight a hard battle with the senses, which are loath to be snatched from their sweet repose" (VIII, 6).

It is not for nothing, as Schiller says, that Pallas-Athena, the goddess of wisdom in classical Greece, is also one of the most warlike gods in the Pantheon and the first lieutenant of Zeus, the supreme power in the Greek world. She carries over her violent, agonistic features from the archaic period, when she was second in strength only to Zeus and second in cunning only to Metis. With the advent of rational and literate values, her cunning turns into wisdom and her force into justice—a historical transformation that Schiller ignores.

The transcendental play-drive as instrument of Reason proves to be useful not only in waging war against the senses, but also in educating the moral drive in man, through the medium of aesthetic semblance. Schiller's theory of art may differ from Kant's as far as terminology and nuances go, but ultimately it does not depart from the latter's view of art as *bewusste Selbsttäuschung* and as mimesis of natural process, rather than product. For instance, Schiller draws a distinction between aesthetic and logical illusion on the same Kantian grounds that he had employed in his distinction between play and work: "It goes without saying that the only kind of semblance I am here concerned with is aesthetic semblance [*Schein*, illusion] (which we distinguish from actuality and truth) and not logical semblance (which we confuse with it). It has been expressly proved that beauty can produce no result, neither for the understanding nor for the will; that it does not meddle in the business of either thinking or deciding; that it merely imparts the power to do both, but has no say whatsoever in the actual use of that power" (XXIII, 3).

The question may be asked why Schiller who, unlike Kant, is an artist himself, insists on the separation between Art-Beauty and power-knowledge, especially when some of his Romantic colleagues insist on their indissoluble link. A possible answer can be found precisely in the notion of art as an *als ob* activity, which Schiller borrows from Kant. By openly admitting art's fictionality and forfeiting its claims to power and truth, Schiller actually changes its dubious status as a pretty lie to a morally neutral position between lie and truth. This allows art to become a mediator between philosophical-scientific discourse and unknowable reality, between the arbitrary and chaotic physical world and human morality. In Schiller, then, art occupies a middle position between play and seriousness, sensuousness and rationality, utility and superfluity, and so forth. In other words, in Schiller, art opts out of the power struggle among disciplines, but only in order to avail itself of the most advantageous position among them—that of arbitrator.

Art as self-conscious illusion remains at all times in the service of Reason, which is in turn an "enlightened" mediated form of power. Although Schiller's letters are presumably concerned with the aesthetic education of *all* men, they are in effect concerned only with the aesthetic education of the ruling class (one must not forget that they were addressed to an "enlightened" potentate, the duke of Augustenburg). Schiller distinguishes between the majority of human beings (whose behavior is analogous to that of the sense-drive) and an elect few: "The majority of men are far too wearied and exhausted by the struggle for existence to gird themselves for a new and harder struggle against error. Happy to escape the hard labour of thinking for themselves, they are only too glad to resign to others the guardianship of their thoughts" (VIII, 6).

It is toward these guardians of thought that Schiller directs his educational efforts. As in Plato's case, Schiller's audience is the upper classes, who would share his views of play and leisure as a higher kind of work ("the hard labor of thinking"). The aesthetic State that Reason is to bring about with the aid of Art-Beauty is a new Platonic Republic, which implies a consensus between the rulers and the ruled, based on a rational decision, rather than on force. In principle, all citizens are equal, but some are willing to serve and others to be served (a social arrangement that is a modified, modern version of Solon's aristocratic notion of *eunomia*): "In the aesthetic State everything—even the tool which serves—is a free citizen, having equal rights with the noblest; and the mind, which would force the patient mass beneath the yoke of its purposes, must here first obtain its assent" (XXVII, 11).

We are never told how this consent is to be obtained, and the gap between the majority and the elect is clearly that between the material and the transcendental play-drive (presumably to be overcome via a leap): the aesthetic State is possible only "in the proximity of thrones, [where] fine breeding comes most quickly and most perfectly to maturity" (cf. the Athenian's remarks on philosophy and power in *Laws*, 4.711c–712a). As a desideratum, this State "exists in every finely attuned soul." As actual fact, we may find it, "like the pure Church and the pure Republic, only in some few chosen circles, where conduct is governed not by some soulless imitation of the manners and morals of others, but by the aesthetic nature we have made our own" (XXVII, 12).

In conclusion, in Schiller, aesthetic play is the orderly *als ob* activity of the imagination under the direct guidance of Reason, and in this he remains the spiritual heir of Plato and Kant. Yet he is the first modern thinker, as far as I know, to call rational heuristic procedures "play," thus paving the way for the rehabilitation of the play concept in twentieth-century theories of cognition. Moreover, by a not-infrequent historical irony, his revisionary version of Kantian aesthetics and play will become the "true Kant" not only for the Romantics but also for such Neo-Kantians as F. A. Lange and Hans Vaihinger, according to whom Schiller, "with the insight of the diviner, grasps the innermost kernel of the Kantian doctrines."[25] It also remains the "authoritative" view of many present-day Anglo-American and Continental scholars. Finally, Schiller's theory of play and aesthetics will provide an important link not only between literature and philosophy, but also between literature and modern science, and in Part II we shall see that several of his casual statements on play have over the years attained the status of scientific hypotheses.

## SECTION 2

# Return of the Repressed: Play and *Machtphilosophie*

In the wake of Kant, Schiller inaugurates a *metaphysica ludens* in close relation to a Romantic idealist aesthetics which, like its Neoclassical counterpart, continues to subordinate art and play to Reason. Moreover, this Schillerian concept of aesthetics and play lingers on virtually unchanged in many contemporary interpretations of Romanticism. Schiller's rational aesthetics, however, stands in direct opposition to a whole Romantic "irrational" literary practice (both in Germany and in

25. See Hans Vaihinger, *The Philosophy of "As If,"* trans. C. K. Ogden (London, 1924), p. xliv. For an elaboration of this point, see Part II, sec. 3.

England), and it is partially upon this literary practice that such anti-idealist and antimetaphysical thinkers as Schopenhauer, Nietzsche, and Heidegger draw when they turn Schiller's aesthetic theories upside down, subordinating Reason to art and play. In the process, they radically change the meaning of these terms, relinking them to a pre-rational mentality, in which reason is only an instrument of the Will, rather than its master and legislator. With Schopenhauer and his heirs, one can speak of a second aesthetic turn in modern philosophy, in which the orderly and telos-bound play of Reason is replaced by the arbitrary and violent play of physical forces, or the unmediated play of power.

In his major work, *The World as Will and Representation* (*Die Welt als Wille und Vorstellung*, 1819), Arthur Schopenhauer starts from the Kantian (and Platonic) distinction between the noumenal and the phenomenal world, describing the former as "Will," whose manifestation one can know only indirectly, through the latter. For Schopenhauer, however, as opposed to Kant and German idealism in general, the Will is not of a subjective, conscious, or spiritual nature; on the contrary, it is the restless movement of physical forces. The Will as noumenon is "blind," purposeless, and arbitrary, without consciousness or knowledge, and its essential nature is "endless striving." In the phenomenal world the Will appears as "representation," that is, it becomes objectified and then conscious of itself (in man); as such, but only as such, the Will becomes knowable, largely through introspection or inner experience. In this regard, Schopenhauer also erases the Cartesian distinction between subject and object, returning to a prerational holistic view of the world, based on the unity of the Will as primal force: "Without the object, without the representation, I am not knowing subject but mere, blind will; in just the same way, without me as subject of knowledge, the thing known is not object, but mere will, blind impulse. In itself, that is to say outside the representation, this will is one and the same with mine; only in the world as representation, the form of which is always at least subject and object, are we separated out as known and knowing individual. As soon as knowledge, the world as representation, is abolished, nothing in general is left but mere will, blind impulse."[26]

26. Arthur Schopenhauer, *The World as Will and Representation*, 2 vols., trans. E. T. J. Payne (New York, 1966), vol. 1, p. 180. For an illuminating discussion of Schopenhauer's concept of Will as primal energy or force see Bryan Magee, *The Philosophy of Schopenhauer* (Oxford, 1983), especially chap. 7, "The World as Will."

Reason itself is only part of the world as representation or conscious manifestation of the Will, and Schopenhauer is far from regarding it as a metaphysical principle or Universal Spirit. On the contrary, he discloses its physical nature, describing it under the name of the "principle of sufficient reason" (*der Satz vom Grund*), first mentioned as such by Leibniz but adopted under various names by rationalist thinkers through the ages. This principle also lies at the foundation of all science, which therefore does not concern the essence of the world (the Will), but only its appearance. For Schopenhauer it is only art, especially music, that touches this essence, and in his thought art becomes a privileged mode of cognition through which the truth of the world as Will may reveal itself. As we shall see, this position regarding art and aesthetics (and therefore also play) is adopted partially by Nietzsche, especially in *The Birth of Tragedy*, and wholeheartedly by Heidegger in his concept of the artwork as ontic truth.

Through his concept of Will as the "endless striving" of physical forces, Schopenhauer also shows power to be the hidden source of Western metaphysics and inaugurates a *Machtphilosophie* that will find its culmination in such modern thinkers as Nietzsche, Heidegger, and the twentieth-century artist-metaphysicians. Nietzsche, for example, adopts this Schopenhauerian concept at the same time that he dispenses with the Kantian distinction between the noumenal and the phenomenal world as being secondary in relation to power, the essential problematic of Western thought. Furthermore, whereas for Schopenhauer the Will is ultimately something to be "denied" and "overcome"— hence his interest in Buddhist thought—for Nietzsche this Will (which he no longer calls *der Wille zum Leben* but *der Wille zur Macht*) is something to be accepted and joyfully affirmed even in its violent guises. Going beyond Schopenhauer, and thereby also returning to the Presocratics, Nietzsche conceives of the Will to Power as prerational play, as an exuberant and violent cosmic movement, beyond good and evil, which engenders and destroys entire worlds. In turn, Heidegger attempts to go beyond what he sees as Nietzsche's "subjectivist" and "metaphysical" interpretation of the Will to Power (an understandable misprision, given the subjectivist and voluntaristic overtones of the term "Will," which Nietzsche inherits from Schopenhauer). For Hei-

---

For the relation of Schopenhauer's thought to that of Nietzsche, see Magee, *Philosophy of Schopenhauer*, app. 2, "Schopenhauer and Later Thinkers"; and Georg Simmel, *Schopenhauer and Nietzsche*, trans. H. Loiskandle, D. Weinsten, and M. Weistein (Amherst, Mass., 1986).

degger, the play of Being or the play of the world is also a play of physical forces or a play of Becoming, in which man is both player and plaything. In this section, then, while tracing the link between play and power in Postromantic *Machtphilosophie* as exemplified by Nietzsche and Heidegger, I shall also examine the role of art and aesthetics within this philosophy. Here my interpretation of the history of modern philosophical aestheticism will again diverge substantially from that of other contemporary scholars. For many of them, Nietzsche's or Heidegger's aestheticism is a more-or-less sophisticated version of art for art's sake. For me, this aestheticism differs both in nature and in function not only from the literary but also from the metaphysical kinds, and the difference stems again from that between a prerational and a rational mentality. Nevertheless, there *is* a sense in which both the rational and the prerational brands of philosophical aestheticism form a common front, and that is precisely when they are confronted with literary aestheticism. In the manner of Plato, Kant, and other philosophers, both Nietzsche and Heidegger employ poetry, and fine art in general, as a *philosophical* tool, and thus do not seriously challenge philosophy's own status as a master discipline.

## 2·1  Play and Nietzsche's Will to Power

Nietzsche's philosophical project can be seen as a return to Hellenic prerational values, and his critique of modern culture as being carried out from the point of view of these values. In *Ecce Homo* (1888, published 1908), Nietzsche himself points to this shift in philosophical perspective. While claiming that he is the "first tragic philosopher," Nietzsche nevertheless acknowledges his debt to Heraclitus: "I still retained a doubt about Heraclitus, in whose presence, in general, I felt warmer and more at ease than anywhere else. The yea-saying to the flux and destruction of all things, the decisive element in any Dionysian philosophy; the yea-saying to contradiction and strife, the idea of Becoming, together with the radical rejection even of the concept of Being—these things, at all events, force me to recognize him who has hitherto had the closest affinity to my thought. The doctrine of 'Eternal Recurrence'—that is, of the absolute and eternal cyclical repetition of all things—this doctrine of Zarathustra's might also have been taught by Heraclitus."[27]

27. Friedrich Nietzsche, *Ecce Homo*, in *The Philosophy of Nietzsche* (Modern Library edition; New York, 1954), pp. 868–869. In addition to the Modern Library

If Nietzsche's doctrine of eternal return can be traced back to Heraclitus, that of the Will to Power can be traced back to the archaic principle of might makes right, and that of the *Übermensch* to the epic and tragic hero. Furthermore, Nietzsche's oracular, gnomic, and dithyrambic style bears a strong family resemblance to that of lyric and tragic poetry, suggesting a reversion to a prerational mentality. Consequently, to a predominantly rational mode of thinking Nietzsche will appear as a paradoxical, ambiguous, multidimensional thinker. But viewed from a prerational perspective, his philosophical project loses its paradoxical and ambiguous quality, offering instead a far-ranging critique of modern rational values.[28] I shall attempt to assess the role of play within this project by briefly examining selected passages from the early academic essays, *The Birth of Tragedy*, *Thus Spake Zarathustra*, and the collection of notes known as *The Will to Power*.[29]

edition, I have used several other English editions of Nietzsche's works, as well as two German editions: *Gesammelte Werke*, 23 vols., Musarionausgabe (Munich, 1920); and *Werke: Kritische Gesammtausgabe*, 8 vols., ed. G. Colli and M. Montinari (Berlin, 1967–1978), especially for *Der Wille zur Macht* (vol. 8).

In *Ecce Homo*, one also finds Nietzsche's often-quoted remark regarding the importance of play in his thought: "I know of no other manner of dealing with great tasks, than as *play*; this, as a sign of greatness, is an essential prerequisite" (p. 853). This remark should again be understood in terms of Nietzsche's return to archaic values, however; otherwise, one runs the danger of equating it with Schiller's or Hegel's rational view of play.

28. Of course, one can argue that Nietzsche eventually leaves the prerational perspective behind as well. In this sense, a full examination of the "case of Nietzsche" would have to deal with two incommensurable thinkers: the Nietzsche of the Will to Power and the gentle, "mad," and silent Nietzsche who, as legend would have it, throws his arms around a helpless carthorse in the streets of Turin in order to shield it from the whip of its master. This second Nietzsche seemingly turns away from the Will to Power and its fateful mission (although he will have relapses, and his periods of serenity and gentleness will occasionally be troubled by violent fits). Indeed, one can argue that he turns away from metaphysics and writing altogether—perhaps his final, radical way of renouncing power? But it is the first Nietzsche who, for better or worse, has had a tremendous impact on modernity and whose views on play and power must be examined here.

29. Among the great number of critical commentaries on Nietzsche are Georg Brandes, *Friedrich Nietzsche* (English trans. London, 1914); Martin Heidegger, *Nietzsche*, 2 vols. (Pfullingen, 1958); Karl Löwith, *Von Hegel zu Nietzsche: Der revolutionäre Bruch im Denken des neunzehnten Jahrhunderts* (Stuttgart, 1964); Karl Jaspers, *Nietzsche: Einführung in das Verständnis seines Philosophierens* (Berlin, 1947); H. M. Wolff, *Friedrich Nietzsche: Der Weg zum Nichts* (Bern, 1956); E. F. Podach, *Nietzsches Zusammenbruch* (Heidelberg, 1930); *Nietzsche*, Cahiers de Royaumont, Philosophie no. 6, 7 Colloque, 1964 (Paris, 1967), especially the essays by Löwith, Foucault, Deleuze, and Klossowski; *Nietzsche Aujourd'hui?* vol. 1,

Among the early works that are directly concerned with Hellenic topics and show a preoccupation with archaic mentality are Nietzsche's scholarly projects, related to his academic career as professor of classical philology at the University of Basel.[30] Judging from the forewords

*Intensités* (Cerisy-La-Salle/Paris, 1973), especially the essays by Deleuze, Derrida, and Vuarnet; Georges Bataille, *Sur Nietzsche, volonté de chance* (Paris, 1945); Gilles Deleuze, *Nietzsche et la philosophie* (Paris, 1962); A. Danto, *Nietzsche as Philosopher* (New York, 1965); Walter Kaufmann, *Nietzsche: Philosopher, Psychologist, Antichrist* (Princeton, N.J., 1974); Erich Heller, *The Disinherited Mind* (Cambridge, Eng., 1952); F. A. Lea, *The Tragic Philosopher: A Study of Friedrich Nietzsche* (London, 1973); David B. Allison, ed., *The New Nietzsche: Contemporary Styles of Interpretation* (New York, 1977); J. P. Stern, *A Study of Nietzsche* (Cambridge, Eng., 1979) and, with M. S. Silk, *Nietzsche on Tragedy* (Cambridge, Eng., 1981); Paul de Man, *Allegories of Reading: Figural Language in Rousseau, Nietzsche, Rilke, and Proust* (New Haven, Conn., 1979); A. Megill, *Prophets of Extremity* (Berkeley/Los Angeles, 1985); Daniel O'Hara, ed., *Why Nietzsche Now?* (Bloomington, Indiana, 1985); Alexander Nehamas, *Nietzsche, Life as Literature* (Cambridge, Mass., 1985); Stanley Corngold, *The Fate of the Self: German Writers and French Theory* (New York, 1986), esp. chaps. 3 and 4. Among the studies that pay special attention to Nietzsche's concept of play are E. Fink, *Nietzsches Philosophie* (Stuttgart, 1960); I. Heidemann, "Nietzsches Kritik der Metaphysik," in *Kant-Studien* 53 (1961/1962): 507–543; John Sallis, "Nietzsche's Homecoming," *Man and World* 2 (1969): 108–116; Rose Pfeffer, *Nietzsche: Disciple of Dionysus* (Lewisburg, Pa., 1972); Lawrence M. Hinman, "Nietzsche's Philosophy of Play," in *Philosophy Today* 18 (Summer 1974): 106–124; and Stephen Byrum, "The Concept of Child's Play in Nietzsche's 'Of the Three Metamorphoses,'" *Kinesis* 7 (1974): 127–135. One can also mention Ernst Behler's essay "Nietzsche und die frühromantische Schule," *Nietzsche-Studien* 7 (1978): 59–96; even though Behler does not distinguish between a rational and a prerational mentality, in places he seems to parallel my own argument that Nietzsche (in the wake of Schopenhauer) partially draws upon a prerational Romantic artistic practice in order to reverse the rational Romantic aesthetics of German Idealism. Behler also acknowledges the crucial importance that ancient Greek thought played in the development of Nietzsche's own, quoting Friedrich Schlegel's profound hermeneutic insight that "jeder hat noch in den Alten gefunden, was er brauchte und wünschte; vorzüglich sich selbst" (p. 72).

30. I hope it is clear that here I am not interested in evaluating Nietzsche as a classicist, although his influence in this field has been great, if not always readily acknowledged. For studies on this topic, see, e.g., J. C. O'Flaherty, T. F. Sellner, and R. M. Helen, eds., *Studies in Nietzsche and the Classical Tradition* (Chapel Hill, N.C., 1976); and Silk and Stern, *Nietzsche on Tragedy*. Neither am I presenting a *Quellenkritik* in the usual sense. I am less interested in the precise archaic sources of Nietzsche's philosophy than in the "archaic" nature of Nietzsche's thought. This, however, is not to deny that his close familiarity with archaic Hellenic culture played an important role in shaping his mentality (cf. Behler, "Nietzsche und die frühromantische Schule, esp. 77–80), and a close study of this process would be extremely helpful in further understanding Nietzsche's philosophy. Here I can hope only to sketch the broad guidelines that such a study might follow.

(*Vorreden*), which appear to be the only extant parts of these projects, Nietzsche seems to have attempted to replace certain dominant idealized images of the Greek world—such as were shared, in the wake of Winckelmann, by Kant, Schelling, Schiller, Goethe, Hegel, and the majority of the eighteenth- and nineteenth-century *Grezisten*—with his own more "naturalistic" image of Greek culture as the most direct and candid expression of the Will to Power. Ironically, perhaps even paradoxically, Nietzsche's Greeks still soar high above the "decadent" moderns, but for reasons that are exactly the opposite of the traditional ones: it is almost as if he delights in standing the famous *Querelle* on its head. He praises the Ancients neither for their Periclean golden age nor for their urbane rationality, Olympian serenity, and consummate mores, but, on the contrary, for their excessive political factionalism, envy, contentiousness, lust for power, pride, and violence. He admires them not for their sublime poetry and immortal works of art but for their courage in staring the stark truth of existence in the face—a grotesque, shattering, yet exhilarating experience. This truth is the truth of tragedy, which goes beyond all (Schopenhauerian) pessimism and accepts, indeed welcomes, life in its full horror.

Nietzsche begins the foreword to his projected book on the Greek State (*Der griechische Staat*) by rejecting what he sees as two sacred beliefs of modern liberalism: the dignity of labor (*Würde der Arbeit*) and the dignity of man (*Würde des Menschen*). He argues that the Greeks did not need such *Begriffshalluzinationen* because they could openly declare that work is a disgrace (*Schmach*), worthy only of slaves. Not that the slaves did not have an indispensable function in the Greek world: their misery and suffering enabled a few "Olympian men" to create the Greek "artistic world" (*Kunstwelt*). This artistic world, however, is not what we understand by the world of fine art today, but the totality of culture, and in this sense the greatest *Künstler* or genius is the military leader, whereas the greatest work of art is the State itself. Its creation justifies not only the miserable condition of the slaves but also the excesses of the conquerors.

Nietzsche puts Hobbes's concept of *bellum omnium contra omnes* to uses different from those of Rousseau and Schiller. His *Naturstaat* coincides with Schiller's aesthetic State, but "aesthetic" here no longer implies the mediating and harmonizing play of Reason; on the contrary, it implies the violent, chaotic play of antagonistic forces, which leads to the Apolline creations of the (military and political) genius: "Under this mysterious connection, which we here divine between State and art, political greed and artistic creation, battlefield and work of art, we understand by the State, as already remarked, only the cramp-iron, which compels the Social process; whereas without the State, in the natural *bellum omnium contra omnes* Society cannot strike root at all on a larger scale and beyond the reach of the family."[31]

The *bellum omnium contra omnes* does not disappear in Nietzsche's aesthetic State as it does in Schiller's; rather, as in Plato's ideal Republic, it becomes a congealing factor for the contending forces within the community, channeling their violence outside it, toward a common enemy. It also becomes a rare, if an ever-more-devastating, occurrence, thus allowing culture to thrive in the interim period (pp. 12–13).

The rest of the foreword is an extended apology of war as the supreme agon, and of the military genius as its highest product. Nietzsche argues that war arbitrarily sets up and destroys all values and hierarchies and that the warrior is, like the slave, only an instrument in the hands of the military genius, who uses it cold-bloodedly for his own purposes. In his conclusion he points out that the Platonic republic itself is based on this elitist principle. The fact that Plato does not favor *all* genius, discriminating against the poets, is only a minor consequence of the Socratic agon with poetry that Plato makes his own, and should not detract from his basic intuition that the majority exists for the benefit and purpose of the few.

In the foreword to "Homer's Contest" (*Homers Wettkampf*), another academic book that was never completed, Nietzsche continues his discussion of archaic values, now concentrating on competition, especially as expressed in Hesiod's notion of eris. He contrasts the ancients and the moderns again, criticizing the modern concept of *Humanität* (humanity, humaneness, humanitarianism) from the perspective of the *phusis-nomos* dichotomy. Modern civilization tends to separate nature

---

31. See Nietzsche, "The Greek State," in *Early Greek Philosophy and Other Essays*, trans. M. A. Mügge (London, 1911), p. 8 (vol. 2 of *Complete Works*, ed. O. Levy, 18 vols.). Further citations from the early academic essays refer to this edition. In these early essays, Nietzsche was indebted for his view of the agonistic character of Hellenic culture not only to Friedrich Schlegel (see Behler, "Nietzsche und die frühromantische Schule," 79), but also to Jacob Burckhardt—see, for example, the latter's *Griechische Kulturgeschichte*, Kroner-Ausgabe, 3 vols. (Stuttgart, 1941). Although Burckhardt's book came out after Nietzsche's death, as his young colleague and friend at the University of Basel Nietzsche had plenty of opportunities to acquaint himself with Burckhardt's thought. For a (hostile) discussion of Nietzsche's concept of Hellenic agon, see Ingomar Weiler, "*Aien aristeyein*. Ideologie-kritische Bemerkungen zu einem vielzitierten Homerwort," in *Stadion* 1 (1975): 205–208.

from culture, whereas in effect such a separation is impossible, and here Nietzsche gives a new twist to the old arguments of Callicles and Thrasymachus. Man in his "highest and noblest capacities is completely Nature," carrying within him the latter's "awful twofold character" (p. 51). Those attributes usually considered inhuman and dreadful are precisely the ones that have proven most fruitful for humanity. Witness the Greeks, who are generally seen as the most humanitarian people of the ancient world but often reveal ferocious, tigerish traits. Nietzsche offers several famous historical examples of Hellenic cruelty, attempting to dispel the traditional classical image of an urbane Hellas (pp. 55–56).

Nothing separates the ancient and the modern worlds so much as their respective attitude toward certain ethical concepts, for instance toward eris and envy, which for the Greeks were altogether positive values. Nietzsche proceeds to examine good and bad eris in Hesiod's *Works and Days*, arguing that the bad one leads, as *Vernichtungslust*, to pure destruction, whereas the good one leads, as *Wettkampf* (contest, competition), to cultural healthiness and creativity. He further reveals the agonistic mechanism that lies not only behind "ostracism," which expels the individuals who arrest the competitive flow by rising too high above the others, but also behind the artistic creative process. He uses again the example of Plato:

> That, which by way of example in Plato is of special artistic importance in his dialogues, is usually the result of an emulation with the art of the orators, of the sophists, of the dramatists of his time, invented deliberately in order that at the end he could say: "Behold, I can also do what my great rivals can; yea I can do it even better than they. No Protagoras has composed such beautiful myths as I, no dramatist such a spirited and fascinating whole as the Symposion, no orator penned such an oration as I put up in the Gorgias—and now I reject all that together and condemn all imitative art! Only the contest made me a poet, a sophist, an orator!" What a problem unfolds itself there before us, if we ask about the relationship between the contest and the conception of the work of art! (pp. 59–60)

For Nietzsche, then, the contest, like war (which for him is indeed the noblest form of agon), creates the highest Hellenic cultural values. Its absence has disastrous social and moral consequences, with the Hellenic world relapsing into pre-Olympian chaos and self-destructive violence. The fall of Athens and then Sparta proves, paradoxically, that "without

envy, jealousy, and contesting ambition the Hellenic State like the
Hellenic man degenerates." Once these states give up "the noblest
Hellenic fundamental thought, the contest," they betray Hellenism as a
whole (pp. 61–62).

In *Philosophy in the Tragic Age of the Greeks* (*Die Philosophie im tra-
gischen Zeitalter der Griechen*), another unfinished piece dating from his
Basel period, Nietzsche carries his thesis of the agonistic character of
culture into philosophy proper. In this book, he examines the birth of
philosophical thought in the Presocratics in terms of their agon with
each other, this same agon finding a cosmic projection in their *Weltanschauung*. Of particular interest for the history of the play concept are
Nietzsche's discussions of Heraclitus and Anaxagoras. According to
Nietzsche, Heraclitus—whose vivid psychological portrait sounds very
much like both Nietzsche's own and that of an *Übermensch*—thought
intuitively, rather than logically, so much so that Aristotle "accused him
of the highest crime before the tribunal of reason: to have sinned against
the law of contradiction."[32] One of Heraclitus's radical intuitions is the
"strife of the opposites," which creates the world of Becoming, and here
again Nietzsche points out the inseparable bond between Hellenic
philosophy and the Hellenic mode of life based on play as agon: "Only a
Greek was capable of finding such an idea [strife] to be the fundament
of a cosmology; it is the contest-idea of the Greek individual and the
Greek state, taken from the gymnasium and the palaestra, from the
artists' *agon*, from the contest between political parties and between
cities—all transformed into universal application so that now the
wheels of the cosmos turn on it" (p. 55).

Another radical intuition is Heraclitus's "aesthetic" view of the
world: the Ephesian becomes an "artist-metaphysician" and a forerun-
ner of Schopenhauer. In the Heraclitean-Nietzschean aesthetic perspective, the cosmos is a divine game, played by Zeus or by the eternal Fire,
on the analogy of a child's or an artist's innocent play. Commenting on
the famous fragment 52 (Diels-Kranz), Nietzsche writes:

> In this world only play, play as artists and children engage in it,
> exhibits coming-to-be and passing away [*Werden und Vergehen*],
> structuring and destroying, without any moral additive [*moralische
> Zurechnung*], in forever equal innocence [*in ewig gleicher Unschuld*].
> And as children and artists play, so plays the ever-living fire. It con-
> structs and destroys, all in innocence. Such is the game that the aeon

32. Nietzsche, *Philosophy in the Tragic Age of the Greeks*, trans. M. Cowen (Chicago, 1962), p. 54. Further citations refer to this edition.

plays with itself. Transforming itself into water and earth, it builds towers of sand like a child at the sea-shore, piles them up and tramples them down. . . . Not hybris but the ever self-renewing impulse to play calls new worlds into being. The child throws its toys away from time to time—and starts again in innocent caprice. (p. 62)

The "aesthetic" perspective that Nietzsche has in mind in this passage is exactly the opposite of that of Kant and Schiller, because it concerns the world of the senses and Becoming, rather than that of Reason and Being. This aesthetic view goes back to the original, etymological sense of *aisthesis* (in its traditional opposition to *noesis*, as Kant himself points out in the first *Kritik*, B36), and thereby reverses the Platonic-Kantian hierarchy of metaphysical values: the play of the senses and the imagination gains priority over the play of understanding and reason. It is true that aesthetic man conforms to the "inner laws" of his creation, standing "contemplatively above and at the same time actively within his work." Moreover, "necessity and random play, oppositional tension and harmony, must pair to create a work of art" (p. 62), and therefore aesthetic play obeys its own rational rules. In other words, the world, like the work of art, is not so much pure play as it is a game (the German *Spiel* cannot make this distinction), and here Schiller and Nietzsche are certainly in agreement. But Nietzsche implicitly criticizes both Schiller and Kant when he charges that the Stoics reinterpret Heraclitus "on a shallow level, dragging down his basically esthetic perception of cosmic play to signify a vulgar consideration for the world's useful ends, especially those which benefit the human race" (p. 65). Unlike Schiller or, ultimately, Kant, Nietzsche sees play as cosmic, rather than human *disinterestedness*, this phrase now meaning "beyond all rationality and ethics." Chance overrides necessity, just as willfulness and arbitrariness override largely self-imposed rules: "The child throws its toys away from time to time—and starts again in innocent caprice." Nietzsche returns to this prerational view of play when he speaks of Anaxagoras's notion of *nous* as the random cosmic creative force: "At this point we might well ask what notion possessed the *nous* to impel a random material particle, chosen from that enormous number of points, and to revolve it in whirling dance. And why this notion did not possess it earlier! To this Anaxagoras would say, '. . . *Nous* has no duty and hence no purpose or goal which it would be forced to pursue. Having once started with its motion, and thus having set itself a goal, it would be . . .' To complete this sentence is difficult. Heraclitus did; he said, '. . . a game'" (p. 112).

As opposed to Plato, Anaxagoras believes that *nous* has "free, arbitrary choice," and it is because of this belief that he has to introduce the play concept: "Absolute free will can only be imagined as purposeless, roughly like a child's game or an artist's creative play impulse" (p. 116). This Schopenhauerian "absolute free will," emancipated from teleology, which Nietzsche attributes to Anaxagoras and which can express itself only as purposeless, arbitrary play, reappears in later works as the *Wille zur Macht*, being the normative principle of Nietzsche's critique of metaphysics.

*The Birth of Tragedy from the Spirit of Music* (*Die Geburt der Tragödie aus dem Geiste der Musik*, 1870–1871), which was written about the same time as, or perhaps only shortly before, *Philosophy in the Tragic Age*, is a much richer but also a much more ambiguous and confusing work. Nietzsche's project of "transvaluating" classicist values is fully present here as well, but is rather awkwardly combined with both an apology for Wagner's music and an attempt at harmonizing the latter with Schopenhauer's view of the world as *Wille und Vorstellung*. The main thesis of the book is that Greek tragedy is a product of the reconciliation between the Dionysiac and the Apolline impulses in Hellenic art and culture. These two impulses are hostile to each other, engaging in a contest similar to those inspired by Hesiod's good eris in "Der griechische Staat" and "Homers Wettkampf": "The two creative tendencies [the Apolline and the Dionysiac] developed alongside one another, usually in fierce opposition, each by its taunts forcing the other to more energetic production, both perpetuating in a discordant concord that *agon* which the term art [*Kunst*] but feebly denominates: until at last, by the thaumaturgy of an Hellenic act of will, the pair accepted the yoke of marriage and, in this condition, begot Attic tragedy, which exhibits the salient features of both parents."[33]

The most salient feature of the Apolline "formative force" is the *principium individuationis* (the principle of individuation), which operates in the realm of Schopenhauerian "representation" or illusion (*Schein*) and is the will to order, symmetry, and beauty, creating the laws of causation, time, and space. It is this realm of illusion that gives the Apolline world that dreamlike, serene quality to be discerned, for example, in Greek plastic art. If the Apolline has the most affinity with the world of dreams, the Dionysiac finds its physical equivalent in intoxication (*Rausch*). It is by far the oldest and the most basic impulse, surging

33. Nietzsche, *The Birth of Tragedy from the Spirit of Music*, trans. Francis Golffing (New York, 1956), p. 19. Further citations refer to this edition.

from the very ground of Being, the "mystical Oneness." Under its spell, the laws of causation are suspended and the *principium individuationis* shattered. Seized by Dionysiac rapture, the individual forgets himself and becomes at one with other individuals and the world. In the Dionysiac state, man is no longer an artist, shaping and giving form, as he was in the Apolline state, but becomes himself a work of art, shaped and given form by the "productive power of the whole universe . . . to the glorious satisfaction of the primordial One" (p. 24). This primordial One is the Schopenhauerian Will playing with itself the game of individuation and integration, in which men are spectators, players, and toys, all at the same time and in one movement. Thus, the Apolline and the Dionysiac forces turn out to be the two playful sides of the same entity, which in *The Birth of Tragedy* is not yet called the Will to Power, although it possesses most of the latter's attributes.

The Apolline impulse to order and harmony should not be confused with Socratic rationalism or, by extension, with the Kantian and Schillerian moral-aesthetic imperative. For Nietzsche, the first is the strong and healthy will to illusion, whereas the latter two are the chronic symptoms of a decaying culture whose will is weakened and whose instincts are "caught in anarchic dissolution." One can also readily see the difference between Nietzsche's and Schiller's dialectical pairs. Whereas in Schiller the *Stofftrieb* and the *Formtrieb* are reconciled by the *Spieltrieb* under the aegis of Reason, in Nietzsche both the Apolline and the Dionysiac (whose "marriage" is by no means harmonious, but "forced") are already part of the eternal game of individuation and integration that the Will plays with itself. In Nietzsche, then, Reason loses its centrality and becomes merely a toy of the Will, which replaces it as the *magister ludi*.

For Nietzsche, art is also a counterplay of the Apolline and the Dionysiac forces, but all in the realm of appearance, and here his argument becomes rather confusing and tautological. He describes art as an imitation (*Nachahmung*) of the Apolline and the Dionysiac, the two "immediate creative conditions of nature" (p. 24). The artist can accordingly be an Apolline "dream artist," a Dionysiac "ecstatic" one, or a "dream and ecstatic artist in one" (p. 24). In Hellenic culture, the musician and the lyrical poet are predominantly Dionysiac, the epic poet and the plastic artist are predominantly Apolline, and the tragic poet strikes an equal balance between the two impulses. But problems start cropping up when Nietzsche, faithful to his models, Schopenhauer and Wagner, attempts to establish both a distinction between art and reality (the Will) and a hierarchy among the arts according to their relative proximity to this reality. Arguing that lyric poetry arises out of music by translating, through a mimetic process, an imageless reality into images and ideas, he goes on to say that music manifests itself in "that mirror of images and ideas . . . as *will*, using the term in the Schopenhauerian sense, that is to say as the opposite of the esthetic, contemplative, unwilling disposition" (p. 45). But then he hastens to qualify his statement: "At this point it becomes necessary to discriminate very clearly between essence and appearance—for it is obviously impossible for music to represent the essential nature of the will; if it did, we would have to banish it from the realm of art altogether, seeing that the will is the non-esthetic element *par excellence*. Rather we should say that music *appears* as the will" (p. 45).

Music appears as (or "imitates") reality, although this reality is no longer the Platonic rational Being but the arbitrary, violent, and playful Will. In turn, lyrical poetry imitates not reality but music, presumably because it can apprehend the Will only indirectly, through an intermediary. In other words, despite its Dionysiac nature, lyrical poetry is a copy of a copy just as in the Platonic mimetic doctrine, albeit that in Nietzsche it copies a different model. Music is raised above all the other arts, because "it is not a copy of the phenomenon, or more accurately, the adequate objectivity of the will, but it is a direct copy of the will itself, and therefore represents the metaphysical of everything physical in the world, and the thing-in-itself of every phenomenon" (p. 99). In this sense, "we might just as well call the world embodied music as embodied will" (p. 99). If in the Kantian hierarchy of the arts music occupies the last place because it is too far from rational language, and too close to the play of Becoming, in Nietzsche it occupies the first place for precisely the same reason (p. 46).

Music is and is not appearance, or, rather, it is privileged appearance, but why it should be a more direct copy of the Will than lyrical and tragic poetry remains a question, especially if we do not share the belief that language is the "organ and symbol of appearance" (p. 46). Nor is it very clear why poetry should imitate music, unless it is for the sake of emulation, and indeed, in *The Birth of Tragedy*, *Nachahmung* acquires the prerational performative sense of competition, which is conspicuously absent in Plato's, Aristotle's, and Schiller's notion of art as mimetic play. But, finally, one cannot help suspecting that poetry imitates music for no other reason than because Nietzsche, faithful to Schopenhauer and Wagner, *wills* it to be so. In this sense his use of mimesis-imitation is no different from that of his predecessors, denoting a power relationship between model and copy.

Whereas the Dionysiac-Apolline dichotomy may work in the real world, it seems to break down in the realm of art: if all art, including music, is appearance, than all art *has* to be Apolline, because it deals with illusion and, therefore, attempts by definition to tame the Dionysiac to the extent that the latter may become at least graspable, if not representable. Furthermore, Nietzsche conceives the play of the Dionysiac-Apolline artist on the analogy of the play of the Will, and the play of the Will on the analogy of a child's or an artist's play: "Only as an esthetic product can the world be justified to all eternity—although our consciousness of our own significance does scarcely exceed the consciousness a painted soldier might have of the battle in which he takes part. Thus our whole knowledge of art is at bottom illusory, seeing that as mere *knowers* we can never be fused with that essential spirit [the Will], at the same time creator and spectator, who has prepared the comedy of art for his own edification. . . . He is at once subject and object, poet, actor, and audience" (p. 42).

Here Nietzsche's argument becomes tautological, implying that art "imitates" art. What makes the play of the Will more real than the play of the artist, or the play of the artist more illusory than the play of the Will? One is certainly contained within the other, which turns the artist into both player and toy, but this says nothing about the reality of either the artist or the Will, *unless* one discards Kantian ontology altogether and equates reality with power, in the form of Becoming and appearance. But Nietzsche is not yet completely ready for this move, and in *The Birth of Tragedy* the problem remains unsolvable, because he is still wavering between the Platonic (and Kantian) dichotomies of Being and Becoming, essence and appearance, art and reality.

Nietzsche's notion of mimesis also remains ambiguous, fluctuating between its prerational and its Platonic-Aristotelian meanings. On the one hand, the distinction between art and reality (the Will) demands, as we have seen, a Platonic-Aristotelian interpretation of mimesis as imitation (*Nachahmung*). In this sense, for Nietzsche, artistic mimesis may denote both the direct manifestation of the Will as appearance (*Erscheinung*) in music, and its representation (*Vorstellung*) in the other arts. On the other hand, mimesis may also denote miming or becoming one with the object or the Other, "with the individual effacing himself through entering a strange being"; that is, it may denote what I have called "mimesis-play." Nietzsche, however, does not see this mimesis-play as operating in the case of epic and lyrical poetry, but only in the case of drama or the "dithyramb." In the latter, "we see a community of unconscious actors all of whom see one another as enchanted"—this mimetic phenomenon, moreover, is "not singular but epidemic: a whole crowd becomes rapt in this manner" (pp. 55–56). Outside the realm of art proper, mimesis may again have the pre-Platonic sense of the ecstatic, innocent play of the Will, aimlessly and exuberantly creating and destroying worlds, on the analogy of the child and the artist. Finally, the dramatic, ecstatic, and violent aspects of mimesis come together in the Dionysiac scapegoat ritual, where "in his existence as dismembered god, Dionysos shows the double nature of a cruel, savage daemon and a mild, gentle ruler" (p. 66).

Fifteen years later, in the final edition of *The Birth of Tragedy*, Nietzsche shows himself fully aware of the problematic character of some of his arguments. First of all he drops music (and Wagner) from the title of the book, which now reads simply *Die Geburt der Tragödie*: the implication is that music is no longer the master art but has an equal status with the other arts. He also adds a polemical subtitle, *Griechentum und Pessimismus*, by which he attempts to distance himself from Schopenhauer. In the "Versuch einer Selbstkritik" (An attempt at self-criticism), which serves as a foreword to this last edition, he explains that what separates him from Schopenhauer is their conflicting notions of pessimism: his own is "strong," welcoming what is "hard, terrible, evil, and dubious in existence," whereas Schopenhauer's is "weak," repudiating these painful attributes of existence in Buddhist, if not Christian, fashion (see the last chapters of *The World as Will* and *Representation*, especially chapter 48, "On the Doctrine of the Denial of the Will to Live"). Observing that he, Nietzsche, had originally made the claim that "art, rather than ethics, constituted the essential metaphysical activity of man" and that existence can be "justified only in aesthetic terms," he adds: "That whole esthetic metaphysics might be rejected out of hand as so much prattle or rant. Yet in its essential traits it already prefigured that spirit of deep distrust and defiance which, later on, was to resist to the bitter end any moral interpretation of existence whatsoever. . . . Morality, on this view, became a mere fabrication for purposes of gulling: at best, an artistic fiction; at worst, an outrageous imposture" (p. 10).

What Nietzsche points out in this key passage is the function of aesthetics and play in his later philosophical project: to provide a strong antidote to the poisonous effect of ethics on modern mentality. As opposed to Kant, Schiller, Schelling, Hegel, and even Schopenhauer, he sees the aesthetic as a playful manifestation of power which can never be reconciled with morality. The latter, by which Nietzsche now understands "Christian, absolute ethics," is the opposite of free play (i.e., the free play of power), evincing a "hatred of the 'world,' a curse on the affective urges, a fear of beauty and sensuality, a yearning for extinction" (p. 11). Nietzsche reverses the hierarchical polarity of seriousness and play, or ethics and aesthetics, favoring the second term over the first. To the "moroseness, exhaustion, and biological etiolation" of Christian ethics he opposes a "radical counterdoctrine, slanted esthetically," christening it with "the name of a Greek God, Dionysos."[34] This counterdoctrine is imbued with the spirit of play, which one day will "send all metaphysical palliatives packing, metaphysics herself leading the great exodus" (p. 15). And here, appropriately, Nietzsche assumes the mask of "that Dionysiac monster," Zarathustra, exhorting his readers to mime him and put on their crowns of Dionysiac revelry (p. 15). Nietzsche's reference to Zarathustra transforms his "Versuch" from a simple critique of his youthful work into a bridge linking this work with his mature thought, and reveals a remarkable continuity between the two. In fact, as we have seen, all the early works discussed so far contain the seeds of Nietzsche's major philosophical themes, developed in his later books: the will to power, the Overman, the eternal return, the transvaluation of all values. And what remains constant throughout his philosophical project is precisely a concept of power as play, beyond

34. As is well known, in his later work Nietzsche all but drops the opposition between the Apolline and the Dionysiac and instead employs the opposition of "Dionysus versus the Crucified." For a good account of the latter opposition see Nietzsche's own words in *The Will to Power*, trans. W. Kaufmann and R. J. Hollingdale (New York, 1968), sec. 1052, pp. 542–543. (Further citations refer to this edition.) Critics seem, however, to make too much of this conceptual shift: one should take seriously Nietzsche's contention in the "Versuch zur Selbstkritik" that throughout *The Birth of Tragedy* he had maintained a "hostile silence" toward Christianity. The Dionysiac, as a shorthand for Greek archaic values, bespeaks a prerational mentality, which conducts itself according to the principle of might is right, and shows no unhappy consciousness about violent power, as Christianity presumably does. Therefore, it would be only logical for Nietzsche to employ the Dionysiac as a counterdoctrine to the Christian notions of guilt and humility. Consider also that the Dionysiac already contains the Apolline, whose nature is as openly power oriented and violent as the former's and is therefore equally inimical to Christian values.

good and evil, or beyond a morality based on guilt, a concept that can be traced back to Greek archaic mentality.[35]

*Thus Spake Zarathustra* (*Also sprach Zarathustra*, 1884) is not only a book that turns play and aesthetics into a major philosophical topic, but is itself a brilliant example of aesthetic play. It is playful, first of all, in the agonistic sense of a literary *Wettkampf* with its great predecessors, such as the Bible in Luther's translation and the German classical tradition, especially the work of Goethe and Schiller. As Nietzsche himself points out in *Ecce Homo* and in some of his letters, he attempts, in *Zarathustra*, to surpass these German models. In this respect his comments on Plato's literary agon with the Sophists cited earlier apply word for word to his own book—indeed, Plato and his master Socrates are not the least competitors against whom Nietzsche tries to measure himself. But *Zarathustra* is also playful in its cavalier, carefree, and innocently destructive attitude toward its philosophical subject matter, its frequent reversal of positions, its "joyful leaps and tangents," its incessant donning and doffing of masks, its gleeful, impudent flight in the face of all reason and logic. If his worthy opponent, Plato, can be said to have converted poetry into philosophy, one can say with equal reason that, in *Zarathustra*, Nietzsche converted philosophy back into poetry, thus seeking the gloat of victory over his antagonist.

In *The Birth of Tragedy* the *Wille zur Macht* is not yet called by its true name, and wears the mask of the Schopenhauerian Will; in *Zarathustra* the mask is dropped. But here, too, the link between the Will to Power and play remains firm—indeed, one can understand power only as play, specifically as agon and as risk taking or chance. Nietzsche introduces the Will to Power as a counterdoctrine to the traditional metaphysical Will to Truth, arguing that the latter is only a disguised form of the former, and so are all value judgments and estimates of good and evil that go with it:

> "Will to Truth" do you call it, ye wisest ones, that which impelleth you and maketh you ardent? Will for the thinkableness of all being: thus do I call your will!. . .

35. The present view would therefore require yet another division of Nietzsche's work, although it also offers, through the concept of play, a principle of continuity between the early and the mature Nietzsche. It assumes that the Will to Power is Nietzsche's central concern from the very beginning (as his early academic essays testify) and that a shift occurs only with his *Zusammenbruch*, in 1889. For this shift, however, we have no supporting texts, but only the unreliable testimony of a few friends and psychiatrists.

Your will and your valuations have ye put on the river of becoming; it betrayeth unto me an old Will to Power, what is believed by the people as good and evil.[36]

What this passage expresses in a poetic, almost formulaic, manner is the old Sophistic doctrine of might is right which, in turn, had been the tacit assumption of archaic Greece. One should also note the argument that metaphysical thinking itself has a violent origin, being a manifestation of power, the "will for the thinkableness of all being," which assumes a full philosophical form for the first time in Parmenides.[37] Zarathustra-Nietzsche proceeds to demonstrate, in Parmenidean fashion, that (Schopenhauer's) Will to Life (*Wille zum Leben*, or *zum Sein*) cannot exist any more than the Will to Truth: "For what is not, cannot will; that, however, which is in existence—how can it strive for existence?" (p. 125). Only where "there is life, is there also a will . . . not, however, the Will to Life, but . . . the Will to Power" (p. 125). Power, then, is not interchangeable with life, for life itself "may sacrifice itself for power" (p. 125).[38] But, like life, the Will to Power "must surpass itself," that is, it can never attain its object. In this sense power has no "reality" and can be understood only as a mirage, an infinite mirror, or a contest with windmills.[39] Zarathustra had already introduced this Ho-

36. Nietzsche, *Thus Spake Zarathustra*, trans. W. Kaufmann, in *The Portable Nietzsche* (New York, 1954), p. 123.

37. Cf. Nietzsche, *The Will to Power*: "To impose upon becoming the character of being—that is the supreme will to power. Twofold falsification, on the part of the senses and of the spirit to preserve a world of that which is, which abides, which is equivalent, etc." (sec. 617, p. 330). Here I have used Walter Kaufmann's numbering of Nietzsche's notes, which Kaufmann calls "sections."

38. Cf. Nietzsche, *The Will to Power*: "Life is merely a special case of the will to power" (sec. 692, p. 369). In other words, Nietzsche implies that the Will to Power includes, but also goes beyond what Schopenhauer calls the Will to Life: it may, for instance, manifest itself in the realm of inorganic matter. Yet cf. Schopenhauer's similar statements about the Will as an "objectified" form of all that is, in *Die Welt als Wille*, e.g., vol. 2, pp. 18–19; 214–215; 259–260; 278; and 642–643.

39. Here René Girard's theory of imitation may be helpful in a critique of the Nietzschean Will to Power. In his essay "Strategies of Madness: Nietzsche, Wagner, Dostoevski," in *To Double Business Bound* (Baltimore, 1978), Girard presents a case history of conflictual mimesis, especially in regard to the relationship between Nietzsche and Wagner, evaluating the *Wille zur Macht* as the "ideology of mimetic desire." Once we see that Nietzsche's "feeling of power" is in part mimetic desire, we begin to understand the meta-physical, empty character of power—this emptiness may also be a reason why power is so difficult to define. On the other hand, by completely identifying power with mimetic desire, Girard downplays the immedi-

meric agonistic notion of power a few paragraphs earlier: "Wherever I found a living thing, there found I Will to Power. . . . And as the lesser surrendereth himself to the greater that he may have delight and power over the least of all, so doth even the greatest surrender himself, and staketh—life, for the sake of power. It is the surrender of the greatest to run risk and danger, and play dice for death" (p. 124).

The dice metaphor accurately describes the power-oriented mentality, which "must ever surpass itself" and must therefore ever defeat itself. As in the case of the Homeric and tragic hero, the "living thing" takes ever more reckless risks against the celestial bank, but the outcome is invariably the same. The negative justice operating in Greek tragedy operates here as well: What lives by the sword must die by the sword. Or as Zarathustra puts it: "Whenever it commandeth, the living thing risketh itself thereby . . . even when it commandeth itself, then also must it atone for its commanding. Of its own law must it become the judge and avenger and victim" (p. 124). This is the famous principle of the *amor fati*, the Nietzschean version of Greek moira and of Anaximander's and Heraclitus's agonistic notions of cosmic justice.[40] But Fate and Chance go hand in hand: if the Will to Power must always surpass itself then it must also always surrender itself to chance or to the throw of the dice. Chance, like death ("Fate"), is the logical outcome of pure, unregulated competition. Zarathustra is fully aware of this fact and is as eager to embrace chance as he is to embrace Fate.[41] In a later passage,

---

ate, physical quality of archaic power, or power in its premetaphysical stages. Furthermore, Girard is unable to deal with the playful dimensions of Nietzsche's Will to Power, drawing no distinction between an imitative and an *as if* mode of being, or between imitation and simulacrum. For power as play of simulacra see sec. 3.3 and 3.4. For a general critique of Girard's work see the second section of my essay "Mimesis and Contemporary French Theory," in M. Spariosu, ed., *Mimesis in Contemporary Theory* (Philadelphia/Amsterdam, 1984), vol. 1, pp. 79–101.

40. Cf. *The Will of Power*, where the term *amor fati* (love of fate) is applied not to the warrior, but to the philosopher-hero: "a Dionysian affirmation of the world as it is, without subtraction, exception or selection—it wants the eternal circulation:— the same things, the same logic and illogic of entanglements. The highest state a philosopher can attain: to stand in a Dionysian relationship to existence—my formula for this is *amor fati*" (sec. 1041, p. 536). Nietzsche first introduces the term in *The Gay Science*, sec. 276, and also uses it in *Ecce Homo*, sec. 10, "Why I Am So Clever," and *The Case of Wagner*, sec. 4, as well as in the epilogue of *Nietzsche contra Wagner*. In all these contexts, *amor fati* implies the joyful acceptance of the agonistic, "fatal" character of existence.

41. Cf. *The Will to Power*, where Nietzsche points out the conceptual link between power as agon and chance: "To recognize the active force, the creative

Zarathustra again employs the dice metaphor in order to affirm the priority of chance over (rational) necessity or predetermination:

> "Of Hazard"—that is the oldest nobility in the world; that gave I back to all things; I emancipated them from bondage under purpose. . . .
> This wantonness and folly did I put in place of that Will, when I taught that "In everything there is one thing impossible—rationality!"
> . . . A little wisdom is indeed possible; but this blessed security have I found in all things, that they prefer—*to dance* on the feet of chance.
> O heaven above me! thou pure, thou lofty heaven! This is now thy purity unto me, that there is no eternal reason-spider and reason-cobweb:
> That thou art to me a dancing floor for divine chances, that thou art to me a table of the Gods, for divine dice and dice-players! (pp. 183–184)

This passage can certainly be read as a parody of church language and a critique of the theological notion of divine providence, but one also needs to understand the point of view from which this critique is carried out—Zarathustra's critical standard again finds its source in Hellenic archaic values, specifically in the notion of power as violent contest and as chance-necessity. A concept of rational absolute power—such as was developed, for example, by an eighteenth-century "enlightened" theology—is essentially totalitarian and conservative, aspiring to consolidate and preserve the same power configurations ad infinitum. The view of the universe as an immense clockwork, wound up once and for all by a divine and almighty watchmaker, is designed to curb the contest among forces and to eliminate chance from human affairs. God as Reason (or Reason as God) offers "blessed security" to the mediocre, that golden mean or measure (the Greek *metron*, and the Latin *ratio*) whereby risk taking or chance is minimized, or at least given the appearance of being regulated and therefore under control.

To this static concept of absolute power (which Nietzsche would say

---

force in the chance event:—chance itself is only the clash of creative impulses" (sec. 673, p. 355). For a different interpretation of Nietzsche's notion of chance-necessity, see my discussion below of Deleuze. Unlike Nietzsche, however, Deleuze seems unaware of the inseparable link between *agon*, *tuche*, and *ananke* in archaic thought; instead, he attempts to relate Nietzschean "chance" directly to the "eternal return," which he then interprets positively as a return of active forces (cf. also Heidegger and Fink, n. 76, below).

is the secret dream of every petit bourgeois) Zarathustra opposes the "nobility of hazard," a concept of power as eternal play of forces, with no ultimate judge or absolute ruler, but only an infinite number of players, losers and winners indifferently. From the point of view of this relativistic, agonistic notion of power, what can be more appropriate than the image of heaven as an immense casino, complete with a "dancing floor for divine chances" and a "table of the Gods for divine dice and dice-players"? Here Zarathustra invokes the archaic metaphor of the world as the varying outcome of a divine cast of dice, a metaphor that is present not only in Greek but also in Germanic mythology.[42] This concept of power as the play of chance-necessity is literally the "oldest nobility in the [Western] world": it is the aristocratic agonistic mentality raised to cosmic dimension, it is the "language of command" transformed into the "language of obedience," or the "surrender of the greatest to run risk and danger and play dice for death." Conversely, reason with its attendant play-it-safe morality—the end of all "noble" play—is plebeian and mediocre, it belongs to the lower classes and their need for "blessed security."[43]

But there *is* a "little reason in everything" (p. 183), because all power play, including the play of chance, must abide by rules if it is to continue at all. On a cosmic plane these rules assume the guise of "iron-handed" Necessity or Fate which is the other face of power—one should not forget that for the Greeks *tuche*, *ananke*, and *moira* were originally interchangeable. Thus, Zarathustra's doctrine of the *amor fati* and the eternal return of the same (*die ewige Wiederkunft des Gleichen*)[44] are the

42. Nietzsche again uses this dice metaphor in *Menschliches—Allzumenschliches* in order to characterize, in no less poetic terms, teleological thinking as "acts of Will": "Jene eisernen Hände der Nothwendigkeit, welche den Würfelbecher des Zufalls schütteln, spielen ihr Spiel unendliche Zeit. . . . *Vielleicht* sind unsre Willensakte, unsre Zwecke nichts Anderes, als eben solche Würfe" (Musarion, vol. 4, p. 130).

43. Cf. *The Will to Power*: "The instinct of the herd considers the middle and the mean as the highest and the most valuable: the place where the majority finds itself. It is therefore an opponent of all orders of rank, it sees an ascent from beneath to above as descent from the majority to the minority. The herd feels the exception, whether it be below or above it, as something opposed and harmful to it. . . . Fear ceases in the middle: here one is never alone; here there is little room for misunderstanding; here there is equality; here one's own form of being is not felt as a reproach but as the right form of being; here contentment rules. Mistrust is felt toward the exceptions; to be an exception is experienced as guilt" (sec. 280, p. 159).

44. Critics have perceived slightly different nuances in Nietzsche's terms *ewige Wiederkehr* and *ewige Wiederkunft*, but for my purposes here they can be used interchangeably.

other faces of the doctrine of chance, and in this, as Nietzsche himself points out, he again follows his Hellenic archaic models, particularly Heraclitus. The eternal return is operative only in a power-oriented world conceived as play, where an endless host of contestants, winners and losers, come and go, but where the game remains the same.

Zarathustra again employs a play metaphor in his account of the *ewige Wiederkunft*, this time taken from the races in the arena (and perhaps from Parmenides and Zeno):

> "Observe," continued I, "This Moment! From the gateway, This Moment, there runneth a long eternal lane *backwards*: behind us lieth an eternity.
>
> Must not whatever *can* run its course of all things, have already run along that lane? Must not whatever *can* happen of all things have already happened, resulted and gone by? . . .
>
> And must we not return and run in that other lane out before us, that long weird lane—must we not eternally return? (p. 174)

The simile is that of contestants running endlessly around the arena with no goal, only endless striving, with victory no longer the object of the race. Although in most other contexts the thought of the eternal return is associated with joyful forgetfulness and ecstatic participation in the endless cycle of Becoming, here the impression is one of weariness: the never-ending race is joyless. The other, negative name for the eternal return is the Freudian "compulsion to repeat," and its source can be traced back, paradoxically, beyond the pleasure principle, to the death wish—the secret wish of every "commander" to "obey."

On the other hand, the dreamlike yet negative vision of the eternal return is immediately followed by the nightmarish yet positive enigma of the shepherd who frees himself of the serpent fastened in his throat. Awakened from his reveries about eternity by the howling of a dog, Zarathustra sees a shepherd lying on the ground with a heavy black snake hanging out of his mouth. Attempting in vain to pull the snake out of the shepherd's mouth, Zarathustra admonishes him to free himself by biting off the snake's head:

> The shepherd . . . bit with a strong bite! Far away did he spit the head of the serpent:—and sprang up.—
>
> No longer shepherd, no longer man—a transfigured being, a light-surrounded being, that *laughed*! Never on earth laughed a man as *he* laughed! (pp. 175–176)

The shepherd's Dionysiac laughter and his "transfigured," "light-surrounded being" identify him as the *Übermensch*, whereas Zarathustra-Nietzsche becomes the prophet of the latter's advent. The good shepherd (Christ) turns into the Overman when he cuts himself off from the black, heavy guilt that seeks to choke him. The shepherd's parable becomes a joyful, affirmative version of the joyless, negative vision of the eternal return. The shepherd bites off the head of the Ouroboros, the serpent of infinity (before it closes itself around him, biting its own tail), and thus frees himself of the negative circle of eternity, creating himself anew. He becomes light and innocence, his laughter the laughter of joyful forgetfulness. The "praying lion" in him which had the strength to bite off the snake's head gives way to the child Dionysus.

As Zarathustra teaches somewhere else, "Innocence is the child, and forgetfulness, a new beginning, a game, a self-rolling wheel, a first movement [*Bewegung*, stirring], a holy Yea. . . . Aye, for the game of creating which is at the same time a game of destroying there is needed a holy Yea unto life: *its* own *will*, willeth now the spirit; *his own* world winneth the world's outcast" (p. 15). Here, too, the Overman is supposed to cast away the "camel's burden"—which, like the heavy black serpent in the other parable, stands for the "life-strangling" Christian guilt mentality and "ethics of pity"—assuming the guise of the "praying lion" only to become, eventually, an innocent child. And this child is the child not of Christ, but of Heraclitus. It is the *aion*, or innocent power as eternity, beginning its game of creation and destruction each time anew, without remorse, in blissful self-forgetfulness. The Overman, then, shares the ambivalent features of the "child" Dionysus, who embodies the heroic world of tragedy, showing the "double nature of a cruel, savage daemon and a mild, gentle, ruler."[45]

Play has a crucial role in a prerational, aristocratic mentality, being the primary way in which power conceives of itself. With the advent of a rational, middle-class mentality, play becomes separated from immediate power, which now begins to present itself as reason, knowledge, morality, and truth. Consequently, play loses its centrality in culture, being tamed and repressed alongside all the other archaic values. A

45. The "Dionysiac" character of the Overman in the two parables is reinforced by the fact that Dionysus's favored animal incarnations are the lion and the serpent. In the *Bacchae*, Pentheus is torn apart by the bacchantes under the hallucinated form of a lion. For a distinction between the Overman and the "highest man," see Deleuze, *Nietzsche and Philosophy*, pp. 187–191.

philosophical "return" to these values, therefore, also presupposes a revaluation of play by reinstating its connection to power, and this is precisely what Nietzsche does in much of his work. A brief look at the collection of notes published posthumously as *The Will to Power* (*Der Wille zur Macht*, 1901) confirms the fact that Nietzsche conceives of his Will to Power in terms of prerational play.[46] In a famous aphorism, included at the very end of the collection, he offers a remarkable formulation of his Presocratic view of the world as eternal conflict and *Spiel der Kräfte*:

> And do you know what "the world" is to me? Shall I show it to you in my mirror? This world: a monster of energy, without beginning, without end; . . . a sea of forces flowing and rushing together, eternally changing, eternally flooding back, with tremendous years of recurrence, with an ebb and a flood of its forms; . . . still affirming itself in this uniformity of its courses and its years, blessing itself as that which must return eternally, as a becoming that knows no satiety, no disgust, no weariness: this, my *Dionysian* world of the eternally self-creating, the eternally self-destroying, this mystery world of the twofold voluptuous delight, my "beyond good and evil," without goal . . . without will . . . —do you want a *name* for this world? A *solution* for all its riddles? . . . —*This world is the will to power—and nothing besides*! And you yourselves are also this will to power—and nothing besides! (sec. 1067, pp. 549–550)

46. A good number of Nietzsche's critics refuse a serious consideration of his collected notebooks, either because they contain material that Nietzsche himself omitted from his published books or because they were presumably tampered with by their editors, Peter Gast and Nietzsche's sister, Elisabeth Förster. An added inhibition is the great popularity *The Will to Power* enjoyed during the Nazi period. My position is that the notebooks contain important clarifications of Nietzsche's general philosophical project and should be treated with the same care as any other writer's "work in progress" (such as Dostoevski's or Gide's notebooks). As to the "unethical" attitude of Nietzsche's editors, even such a mainstream scholar as Walter Kaufmann remarks: "Some unkind comments on Frau Förster-Nietzsche, Richard Wagner, anti-semitism, the German *Reich*, and Christianity were suppressed by the editors; but there is no reason whatever for believing that the hitherto withheld material includes anything of significance that would have corroborated Frau Förster-Nietzsche's version of her brother's thought. It is therefore quite unlikely that future editions of Nietzsche's works will necessitate any radical revision of an interpretation which does justice to the material so far published" (bibliography, *Nietzsche* [Princeton, N.J., 1950]; quoted in appendix, *The Will to Power*, p. 551). This judgment remains sound even in the wake of the recent Colli-Montinari revised edition of *Der Wille zur Macht*.

Here Nietzsche brings together the main strands of his cosmogonical thought in the terse, oracular, *poetic* style of an Anaximander or a Heraclitus. In fact most of these strands are already present in the Presocratic thinkers: the world as the ecstatic play of the *aion*, as the "play of contradictions" and the "joy of concord," as a Becoming which "must return eternally," but "knows no satiety, no disgust, no weariness." Above all, the world is conceived as an enormous play of forces, beyond good and evil, both creative and destructive, on the analogy of the heroic agon of epic and tragic poetry. Dionysus is again the symbol of this "mystery world of the twofold voluptuous delight," where pleasure and pain, joy and sorrow commingle ecstatically.

Now one can also understand why Nietzsche saw his idea of eternal return anticipated in archaic thought: if Becoming is eternal and can never resolve itself either into Being or into Nothingness, then the world as an incessant play of forces will repeat itself endlessly, producing the same combinations over an infinite time span, as in an enormous numbers game.[47] Nietzsche points out, however, that this view of the world as an eternally recurring play of forces is not a mechanistic one. The mechanistic view presupposes not an "infinite recurrence of identical cases" but, on the contrary, a final state that it calls "eternal repose," "immutability," or "Being." Thus, as in the case of Anaxagoras's creative *nous*, Nietzsche's world at play (or as a manifestation of the Will to Power) is free of the "pitfalls of teleology" and can only be imagined as "purposeless, roughly like a child's game or an artist's creative play impulse."

The Will to Power and its play finally remain undefinable and groundless—or, in positive terms, constitute their own justification—at the same time that they ground or justify Nietzsche's entire philosophical project. He himself indirectly suggests this fact, in a different context, when he defines pleasure and displeasure in terms of the Will to Power: "If the innermost essence of being is will to power, if pleasure is every increase of power, displeasure every feeling of not being able to

47. Cf. sec. 1066: "If the world may be thought of as a certain definite quantity of force and as a certain number of centers of force . . . it follows that, in the great game of existence, it must pass through a calculable number of combinations. In infinite time, every possible combination would at some time or another be realized; more: it would be realized an infinite number of times . . . The world as a circular movement that has already repeated itself infinitely often and played its game *in infinitum*" (sec. 1066, p. 549). Nietzsche's game analogy will reappear in game theory and in the statistical notions of chance and necessity in contemporary science. See Part II, secs. 2, 3.

resist or dominate; may we not then posit pleasure and displeasure as cardinal facts? Is will possible without these two oscillations of Yes and No?—But *who* feels pleasure?—But *who* wants power?—Absurd question, if the essence itself is power-will and consequently feelings of pleasure and displeasure!" (sec. 693, p. 369).

Whereas in Nietzsche both play and the Will to Power remain undefinable, they are partly describable in terms of each other: play is a manifestation of power just as power is a manifestation of play, and here both terms should be understood in their archaic sense, as "Dionysian," ecstatic and violent play of physical Becoming, as aristocratic agon, and as chance-necessity. In this respect Nietzsche's grounding philosophical premises can best be described as neither rational nor irrational, but as *prerational*. From this point of view, the familiar labels of cognitive nihilism, axiological relativism, perspectivism, irrationality, and aestheticism commonly attached to Nietzsche's thought will appear in a new light.

One hears much, especially today, about Nietzsche's denial of the possibility of knowing reality or his contention that truth is only an older, more persistent form of lie. These statements, however, make sense only in terms of Nietzsche's critique of the rational definition of these words, and to call him a cognitive nihilist (as he sometimes calls himself, for polemical reasons) is to apply to him criteria that he has set out to challenge. For example, he says: "*The new world-conception.*—The world exists; it is not something that becomes, not something that passes away. Or rather: it becomes, it passes away, but it has never begun to become and never ceased from passing away—it maintains itself in both.—It lives on itself: its excrements are its food" (sec. 1066, p. 548).

Here Nietzsche does not deny the existence of the world or its cognibility, he simply changes the meaning of these words. To the Kantian notion of the world as the "thing-in-itself" and to the theological notion of the world as a created object he opposes the notion of the world as an endless entity, made up of a "certain definite number of centers of force," engaged in a "great dice game [where] all events, all motion, all becoming [appear] as a determination of degrees and relations of force, as a *struggle*" (sec. 552, p. 299). This world which "does not expend itself, but only transforms itself," having an unalterable size and a circular movement, is perfectly knowable. But knowledge for Nietzsche no longer means the dispassionate pursuit of universal truth for its own sake; on the contrary, it means the direct manifestation of the Will to Power:

The so-called drive to knowledge can be traced back to a drive to appropriate and conquer: the senses, the memory, the instincts, etc., have developed as a consequence of this drive. (sec. 423, p. 227)

Knowledge works as a tool of power. Hence it is plain that it increases with every increase of power. . . .

In order for a particular species to maintain itself and increase its power, its conception of reality must comprehend enough of the calculable and the constant for it to base a scheme of behavior on it. . . . In other words: the measure of the desire for knowledge depends upon the measure to which the will to power grows in a species, grasps a certain amount of reality in order to become master of it, in order to press it into service. (sec. 480, pp. 266–267)

It follows, then, that there are not one but many "realities" that are the result of the agent's *interpretation*. For Nietzsche, however, interpretation is no longer the process of cognition through which the agent (or the "player") discovers the world as it is already constituted; on the contrary, it is the process through which he creates the world as he goes along. In this respect Nietzsche challenges the positivist assumption of the existence of "facts" independent of interpretation:

Against positivism which halts at phenomena—"There are only *facts*"—I would say: No, facts is precisely what there is not, only interpretations. . . .

In so far as the word "knowledge" has any meaning, the world is knowable; but it is *interpretable* otherwise, it has no meaning behind it, but countless meanings.—"Perspectivism." (sec. 481, p. 267)

Furthermore, it is the Will to Power that interprets, that is, "defines limits, determines degrees, and variations of power." Therefore, interpretation is "itself a means of becoming master of something" (sec. 643, p. 342).[48]

One can also understand Nietzsche's famous perspectivism as a multiplicity of "interpretations" where truth and fiction, taken in their tradi-

---

48. In sec. 604, Nietzsche draws a distinction between "interpretation" and "explanation": " 'Interpretation,' the introduction of meaning—not 'explanation' (in most cases a new interpretation over an old interpretation that has become incomprehensible, that is now itself only a sign). There are no facts, everything is in flux, incomprehensible, elusive; what is relatively most enduring is—our opinions" (p. 327). For similar statements on the relation of truth and untruth to interpretation, see sec. 605, 606, pp. 327–328.

tional epistemological and ethical sense, are relative and interchangeable. Indeed, from a traditional point of view, Nietzsche argues that human existence is guided not by the will to truth, but by the will to illusion (*Wille zur Täuschung* or *zum Schein*), which is the foundation not only of art, as in eighteenth- and nineteenth-century aesthetics, but also of metaphysics. In Nietzsche's *als ob* perspective, later taken up by such Neo-Kantians as Lange and Vaihinger, truth has no more value for "life" than falsehood; indeed, truth is not the opposite of error, but an older, more deeply ingrained error, without which we cannot live.[49] Yet if we remember that the Will to Truth, no less than life in general, is "merely a special case of the will to power," then we realize that Nietzsche's critique of traditional epistemology, unlike that of the Neo-Kantians, needs to be placed in direct relation to this Will to Power. Consequently, his perspectivism is far from meaning something like our contemporary "pluralism" or benign acceptance of the other's point of view, nor does it lead to axiological or epistemological relativism; on the contrary, as in the case of Hellenic *isomoiria*, its context is strictly agonistic: "Perspectivism is only a complex form of specificity. My idea is that every specific body strives to become master over all space and to extend its force (its will to power) and to thrust back all that resists its extension. But it continually encounters similar efforts on the part of other bodies and ends by coming to an arrangement ("union") with those of them that are sufficiently related to it: thus they then conspire together for power. And the process goes on—" (sec. 636, p. 339).

Likewise, it is not enough to see Nietzsche's view of truth and fiction from a purely epistemological and ethical perspective. Just as for the

---

49. "Auf welchen Standpunkt der Philosophie man sich heute stellen mag: von jeder Stelle ausgesehen, ist die Irrthumlichkeit der Welt, in der wir zu leben glauben, das Sicherste und Festeste. . . . Ja, was zwingt uns überhaupt zur Annahme, dass es einen wesenhaften Gegensatz von 'wahr' und 'falsch' giebt? . . . Warum dürfte die Welt, *die uns etwas angeht*, —nicht eine Fiktion sein?" (Musarion, vol. 15, pp. 49–50). Nietzsche regards science itself as nothing but a lie for the sake of living: "Die beste Wissenschaft, die uns am besten in dieser *vereinfachten*, durch und durch künstlichen, zurecht gedichteten, zurecht gefalschten Welt festhalten will, wie sie unfreiwillig willig den Irrthum liebt, weil sie die Lebendige, das Leben liebt!" (Musarion, vol. 15, pp. 37–38). An early text on the performative character of truth and lie bears the self-explanatory title of "On Truth and Lie in an Extra-moral Sense" (1873). A recent discussion of this text can be found in Megill, *Prophets of Extremity*, pp. 47–54. Megill, however, gives an art-for-art's-sake slant to this essay, ignoring the functional character of Nietzsche's terms, that is, their link to the Will to Power. See n. 52, below.

archaic Greeks, for Nietzsche truth and lie are not moral categories but
have a *performative* value, and can be used indifferently as long as they
further the goals of life (i.e., power; we recall, for instance, that Odysseus is quite proud of his "lies," which have the full approval of Pallas-
Athena as a brilliant evidence of his *metis*, cunning). Epistemologically
speaking, truth is not something to be found or discovered in the nature
of things, but rather "something that must be created and that gives a
name to a process." It is a *"processus in infinitum*, an active determining—not a becoming-conscious of something that is in itself firm and
determined." Nietzschean truth, then, is also an agonistic notion, indeed it is a "word for the 'will to power'" (sec. 552, p. 298), and its
criterion "resides in the enhancement of the feeling of power" (sec. 534,
p. 290).

   Nietzsche himself points out his debt to the Sophists for a performative, extramoral notion of truth, tracing back his own epistemological
roots to Presocratic prerational thought: "The Sophists verge upon
the first *critique of morality*, the first *insight* into morality: —they jux-
tapose the multiplicity (the geographical relativity) of the moral value
judgments; —they let it be known that every morality can be dialectically justified; i.e., they divine that all attempts to give reasons for
morality are necessarily *sophistical* . . . they postulate the first truth that a
'morality-in-itself,' a 'good-in-itself' do not exist, that it is a swindle to
talk of 'truth' in this field" (sec. 428, p. 233). Finally, Nietzsche has
good words even for Plato, because he "wanted to have *taught* as
absolute truth what he himself did not regard as even conditionally true:
namely, the separate existence and separate immortality of souls" (sec.
428, p. 233).

   Despite his seemingly radical statements about the fictional nature of
truth (and one should not forget that all radicalism is positional or
relative to the dominant values that precede it), Nietzsche is far from
being an "axiological relativist." On the contrary, like the Sophists, he
believes that power and competition are the determining factors in
establishing a "true hierarchy of values." His political thought also
comes close to that of the Sophists, who were training a small aristocratic elite to become the rulers of the *polis*. Like these Sophists, and not
unlike Plato and Schiller, Nietzsche does not favor democracy (or the
rule of the "herd"), but an oligarchical, tyrannical, or monarchical
system, based on an aristocratic elite; for him, as for Plato, the Spartan
model is the best form of government mankind has ever known.[50] He

   50. Nietzsche would be the first to agree with this characterization of his
thought. As Stern points out, he praises the Danish critic Georg Brandes for

also shares with Plato the latter's educational concerns, envisaging the development of a "higher" or a "sovereign" type of man. Out of his many statements about what this kind of man would be like, one in particular has proven to be the most ironically prophetic for our own age: "The possibility has been established for the production of international racial unions whose task will be to rear a master-race, the future 'masters of the earth';—a new tremendous aristocracy, based on the severest self-legislation, in which the will of philosophical men of power and artist-tyrants will be made to endure for millennia—a higher kind of men who, thanks to their superiority in will, knowledge, riches, and influence, employ democratic Europe as their most pliant and supple instrument for getting hold of the destinies of the earth, so as to work as artists upon 'man' himself" (sec. 960, p. 504).[51]

This passage reveals the striking similarity between Plato's "philosopher-king" and Nietzsche's "philosophical man of power" and "artist-tyrant." For Nietzsche, as for Plato, the philosopher "must be a legislator," charged with creating the "new values" (sec. 979, p. 512). Like Plato's legislator he possesses "uncanny privileges," he is "beyond good and evil . . . but no one must know it." He never says what he himself thinks, but "always only what he thinks of a thing in relation to the requirements of those he educates." In order to be effective, he must not be "detected in this dissimulation; it is part of his mastery that one believes in his honesty" (sec. 980, p. 512). Again, the question is not one of moral relativism, but one of performance in relation to the goals to be reached (Nietzsche's favored example of good modern educators is the Jesuits).

The foregoing discussion has shown that Nietzsche's "transvaluation of all values" also presupposes a reversion to an aristocratic, prerational mentality. From a strictly philosophical point of view, this means a reversal of Platonic metaphysical values. Now semblance, illusion, appearance, simulacrum, the world of the senses and Becoming are valued over Being, Truth, reality, essence, and the world of the spirit. Violent play, the aesthetic, and "art" in general are again valued over science, seriousness, and morality. As I have suggested, however, play and the aesthetic are originally manifestations of immediate power which then become repressed by a rational mentality as irrational, inauthentic, and culturally harmful. By returning to prerational values, Nietzsche returns to the world of immediate power, to which he subordinates the world

describing his writings as "*aristocratic radicalism*—with respect, the most intelligent thing I have so far read about myself" (quoted by Stern, in *Nietzsche*, p. 24).

51. For other statements on the Overman, see *The Will to Power*, pp. 457–509.

of mediated, disguised power. In this light, therefore, one also needs to reconsider the meaning of Nietzsche's aestheticism.

Especially in recent years, Nietzsche has been portrayed as a promoter of art for art's sake and as a champion of art against philosophy and science. Allan Megill states: "In short, Nietzsche envisages not the destruction of the conceptual world but rather (to borrow Derrida's terminology) its deconstruction . . . that is, its transformation into a realm of aesthetic illusion and play" (*Prophets of Extremity*, p. 53). Many of Nietzsche's statements can be construed in this manner, particularly his pronouncements on art in *The Birth of Tragedy*. Yet if we turn to his other works, to *The Will to Power* in particular, a much more complex attitude toward art emerges than the one implied in Megill's version of contemporary aestheticism.[52] Consider a passage that appears as an

52. In his introduction to *Prophets of Extremity* Megill states: "As it is usually employed, the word *aestheticism* denotes an enclosure within a self-contained realm of aesthetic objects and sensations, hence also denotes a separation from the 'real world' of nonaesthetic objects. Here, however, I am using the word in a sense that is almost diametrically opposed to its usual sense. I am using it to refer not to the condition of being enclosed within the limited territory of the aesthetic, but rather to an attempt to expand the aesthetic to embrace the whole of reality. To put it in another way, I am using it to refer to a tendency to see 'art' or 'language' or 'discourse' or 'text' as constituting the primary realm of human experience" (p. 2). Although Megill does distinguish between various kinds of aestheticisms and admits the possibility that Nietzsche might not have been "unequivocally an aes-theticist" (in Megill's sense), his general definition remains purely epistemological and therefore misses the functional nature of Nietzsche's categories. He quotes most of the Nietzschean passages relevant to art out of their context—the modus operandi of the Will to Power—and thus obscures the relationship of the aesthetic (and play) to this Will. Megill's critique of aestheticism from the point of view of what he calls an "intelligent empiricism" (which turns out to be based on the old definition of reality as a "truck coming down the road," p. 34) never questions the assumptions behind the dichotomy of the "aesthetic" and the "nonaesthetic"; it simply requires that "art" and "life" remain separate, without considering the possibility that these two terms may be engaged in a functional dialectic of shifting or even interchangeable meanings. Consequently, for Megill thinkers like Nietzsche and Heidegger become New Critical "intellectual aesthetes," and their *Fragestellung* is completely distorted into some superficial tenet of art for art's sake. In turn, Megill's definition of "aestheticism" comes full circle to the one he wants to distance himself from in the first place, that is, aestheticism as "a self-contained realm of aesthetic objects and sensations," and so forth.

It seems to me that one should begin where Megill leaves off: the time has come not for a critique of the aesthetic from the point of view of "reality" (we have been engaged in this kind of critique for over two thousand years now), but for a critique of aestheticism and play as power. In other words, we should finally work out the consequences of the realization that art and play are not a subversion of or an alternative to power, but an older, more immediate form of it.

unqualified valuation of art and artists: "Our religion, morality and philosophy are decadence forms of man. The *countermovement*: art" (sec. 794, p. 419).

Even in this lapidary formulation, it seems clear that Nietzsche does not have in mind *all* art (most of which he also considers decadent), but only the one that is a direct manifestation of the Will to Power. For him (a certain kind of) art represents a valuable vestige of archaic mentality. In turn, the true artist is a most "transparent phenomenon," a window to the "basic instincts of power, nature, etc." He is like an innocent child whose vitality, strength, and exuberance are unashamed and uninhibited. A child's and an artist's play can in this respect be compared to that of God, and the reference is again to Heraclitus: "The 'childlikeness' of God, *pais paizon* a child at play" (sec. 797, p. 419).[53] Nietzsche commends art for both its uselessness and its violence (thereby going against a powerful philosophical tradition that condemns it precisely for the same reasons), qualities that he associates with an aristocratic mentality.[54] At their best, artists resemble archaic aristocrats: they are "strong, full of surplus energy, powerful animals, sensual" (sec. 800, p. 421). The early artist is first and foremost defined by his "sexuality, intoxication, cruelty—all belonging to the oldest *festal joys* of mankind"

53. The question may be asked why Nietzsche often describes the Will to Power as "a child at play"—the fact that the same metaphor was employed by Heraclitus in a similar context makes this question only more intriguing. As I have suggested in the introduction, a prerational mentality does not disappear with the advent of a rational one, but simply becomes submerged or repressed. Anyone who has the slightest experience with children will perhaps agree that their behavior, especially at an early age, seems a clear indication of the survival of archaic mentality. Some of the archaic traits observable in children are: unashamed pleasure in power and manipulation (e.g., in torturing, maiming, and killing insects and small animals; in getting their way with adults), immediacy of feeling, *insouciance* about "moral" standards or the Other, lack of self-image or self-consciousness and therefore also of guilt, preference for oral art forms, such as nursery rhymes, narrative, songs, etc. Nietzsche seems fully aware of the recurrence of archaic mentality in children, for instance when he gives an ironical twist to Wordsworth's line "The child is father to the man" by remarking: "One would make a fit little boy stare if one asked him: 'Would you like to become virtuous?'—but he will open his eyes wide if asked: 'Would you like to become stronger than your friends?'" (918, p. 485) In this light, education would be precisely the means through which archaic mentality is repressed again, and the child is inculcated with rational values.

54. See, for example, sec. 943, "What is Noble?" where the "ability for *otium*," leisure, is favored over "industriousness in the bourgeois sense" (p. 497). Here Nietzsche points to the social origins of the distinction between work and play, which most play theorists tend to ignore—see, e.g., Fink, *Nietzsches Philosophie*, and Josef Pieper, *Leisure, The Basis of Culture*, trans. A. Dru (New York, 1952).

(sec. 801, p. 421). The aesthetic state appears "only in natures capable of that bestowing and overflowing fullness of bodily vigor" (sec. 803, p. 422), and beauty itself is not a disinterested feeling, but the "highest sign of power, namely power over opposites . . . that everything flows, obeys, so easily, so pleasantly—that is what delights the artist's will to power" (sec. 803, p. 422). Unlike the men of knowledge who "leave everything as it is," the artists are "productive, to the extent that they actually alter and transform" the world (sec. 585, p. 318). They are superior even to the (post-Platonic) philosophers insofar as they have not lost their "scent for life" and have "loved the things of 'this world' . . . have loved their senses" (sec. 820, p. 434). They can be contrasted with the decadent moderns in general, who have lost their will to power, the "sober, the weary, the exhausted, the dried up (e.g., scholars)," who cannot receive anything from art because they "do not possess the primary artistic power, the pressure of riches" (sec. 801, p. 422).

Although Nietzsche praises art and artists for their exuberance and energy and for having stayed in touch with the world of the senses and immediate power, he ultimately sees them only as an intermediary stage within his philosophical program. They are a useful tactical weapon in overcoming metaphysics "through the destruction of the world of being," during an intermediary period of nihilism, that is, "before there is yet present the strength to reverse values and to deify becoming and the apparent world as the only world, and to call them good" (sec. 585A, p. 319). The artist is to be replaced by the "artist-metaphysician" (and the artist-tyrant): "The *artist*-metaphysician (*Artistenmetaphysiker*). Higher concept of art. Whether a man can place himself so far distant from other men that he can form them? (—Preliminary exercises: (1) he who forms himself, the hermit; (2) the artist hitherto, as a perfecter on a small scale, working on material)" (sec. 795, p. 419).

Through his notion of philosophy as a "higher concept of art" Nietzsche again comes very close to Plato's ideal Republic, where philosophy replaces poetry as the true *mousike*. In this respect, at the very moment that he argues for an "aesthetic metaphysics" and an "aesthetic justification of existence," Nietzsche reenacts the Platonic and the philosophical exclusion of the artist from the realm of power, from what really "matters." But Nietzsche goes even farther than Plato because he manages, in the process, to take the work of art itself away from the artist, who is, "after all, only the condition of the work, the soil from which it grows, perhaps only the manure on that soil" (*Genealogy of Morals*, p.

235). Nietzsche envisages his brave new world as a self-creating work of art for which the artist is responsible only in an incidental way:

> The work of art where it appears without an artist, e.g., as body, as organization (Prussian officer corps, Jesuit order). To what extent the artist is only a preliminary stage.
> The world as a work of art that gives birth to itself [*Die Welt als ein sich selbst gebärendes Kunstwerk*]—. (sec. 796, p. 417)

If the world is a "work of art that gives birth to itself," or is "nothing other than art," then the professional artist becomes superfluous; his function is taken over by the strong personality, the Overman, who is a (self-)creator in the realm of existence. He builds his "artworks" not with pen and paper, brush and canvas, or chisel and stone, but with human material; he creates the world itself. This Overman bears the names of "artist-metaphysician" and "artist-tyrant," which makes the Nietzschean scapegoating of art complete: we remember the Socratic scapegoating of poetry in the *Republic*, which also entails assuming the name of the victim. Nietzsche's artist-metaphysician, just like his artist-tyrant or his "philosophical man of power," bears a strong family resemblance to Plato's philosopher-king: although in some ways they situate themselves at opposite philosophical poles, ultimately they share the same power-oriented objectives, different versions of the same cultural ideal.

By going back to the Presocratics Nietzsche reintroduces archaic values in modern philosophy. Thus he is instrumental in creating the cultural *episteme* that later on comes to be known as Postmodernism. The aesthetic perspective which he introduces in modern thought is at the opposite pole from that of Kant and Schiller, or even from that of the various contemporary versions of the art-for-art's-sake movement. The essential difference lies in the opposite concepts of play these aesthetic perspectives employ. The Nietzschean kind of aestheticism is based on an archaic, prerational concept of play as power or as the violent, exuberant, and arbitrary movement of Becoming, whereas the Kantian or the Schillerian kind stems from a rational concept of play as the rule-determined, orderly, and predictable manifestation of Being.

## 2·2 After Nietzsche: Martin Heidegger and the Play of Being

Heidegger is undoubtedly the most influential and the most difficult of the contemporary thinkers who, following Nietzsche, turn to play

and art in an attempt to find a new grounding for philosophical speculation. His dense, oracular, poetic style is reminiscent not only of *Also
sprach Zarathustra* but also of the inscrutable paradoxes of Heraclitus,
whose proverbial obscurity he may have succeeded in equaling. Like
any other influential figure in the Western tradition, including Heraclitus and Nietzsche, Heidegger engages in his own agon with this
tradition. He attempts both to distance himself from his predecessors
and to appropriate them for his own thought.

Arguing for a distinction between Being (*Sein*) and the being (*das
Seiende*, or *das Seiende im Ganzen*), which he calls the "ontic-ontological
difference" (hereafter referred to, for brevity's sake, as the ontological
difference), Heidegger claims that Western thought has forgotten this
distinction, losing sight of Being and concentrating exclusively on the
being. Although the question of Being is posed at the beginning of
metaphysics, in Anaximander, Heraclitus, and Parmenides, it gradually
becomes obscured.[55] According to Heidegger, the obscuring of Being
in the being culminates with Nietzsche: the latter conceives *Sein* as the
*Seiende im Ganzen* in terms of the Will to Power, which Heidegger
interprets as the "Will to Will" (*der Wille zum Willen*), thus revealing
and thereby bringing to an end the metaphysics of subjectivity that has
dominated Western thought since Descartes.

The history of Heidegger's relation to Nietzsche is as complex and
ambivalent as (and to a large extent parallels) the history of Heidegger's

55. Heidegger argues that this obscuring of Being in the being is already commented upon by Plato, for example, in the *Sophist*: "For manifestly you have long
been aware of what you mean when you use the expression 'being.' We, however,
who used to think we understood it, have now become perplexed" (quoted as
epigraph to *Sein und Zeit*, 1927; hereafter *SZ*). F. M. Cornford, however, translates
this Platonic passage as follows: "Stranger: 'We are completely puzzled, then, and
you must clear up the question for us, what you do intend to signify when you use
the word "real." Obviously you must be quite familiar with what you mean, whereas
we, who formerly imagined we knew, are now at a loss'" (*Sophist*, 244b, in *Collected
Dialogues*, ed. E. Hamilton and H. Cairns [Princeton, N.J., 1963]). Clearly, Heidegger uses the passage out of its context (the Stranger's imagined *agones logon* with
his predecessors, the Presocratics), reversing its meaning. It would also be useful to
recall that *onta* (things that are), or what Heidegger translates as "being" and
Cornford as "real," are equated by Plato with *power*: "Stranger: 'I suggest that
anything has real being that is so constituted as to possess any sort of power either to
affect anything else or to be affected, in however small a degree, by the most
insignificant agent, though it be only once. I am proposing as a mark to distinguish
real things that they are nothing but power'" (*Sophist*, 247e). I examine the Platonic
concepts of Being and power in more detail in *God of Many Names*, chap. 4.

working out the relation of the being to Being. On the one hand, he sees Nietzsche as the end of metaphysics; on the other, he sees himself as "bringing Nietzsche's accomplishment to a full unfolding." This means both (re)turning, like Nietzsche, to the origins of metaphysics in early Greek thinking, and carrying out Nietzsche's radical questioning of the being when, for example, he proclaims the demise of God.

Heidegger assumes the same ambivalent attitude toward Nietzsche's notion of play. Although he himself will eventually conceive of Being as power play, he pays little *explicit* attention, in his published work, to Nietzsche's *Wille zur Macht* and *ewige Wiederkunft* as play. It is not until the end of his monumental study of Nietzsche, in the section on "Nihilism and the History of Being," that he briefly addresses this question, and then only in the context of the *Seinsvergessenheit*. There he shortly considers Nietzsche's poem "An Goethe" (To Goethe), a light-hearted parody of certain leitmotifs from *Faust* that is part of "The Songs of the Outlaw Prince," usually included as an appendix to *The Gay Science*. The last two stanzas of Nietzsche's poem concern "world-play" (*Welt-Spiel*), and Heidegger comments: "All being as such could occur essentially as a game in which everything is at stake, and that being itself is such 'world-play.'"[56] In Nietzsche, the world-play gains meaning, according to Heidegger, only in relation to the Will to Power (interpreted as Will to Will) and the eternal return: "The unity of will to power and eternal recurrence signifies that the will to power is in truth the will-to-will, a determination in which the metaphysics of subjecticity attains the peak of its development, its fulfillment. The metaphysical concept of "world-play" identifies the affinity in the history of Being between what Goethe experienced as 'nature' and Heraclitus as *kosmos* (see Fragment 30)" (p. 237).

It is clear that Heidegger realizes the essential link between power and play (as risk taking) in Nietzsche's thought, but he attributes it to the latter's unawareness of the ontological difference (cf., for example, pp. 237–238). In a certain sense Heidegger's own project might appear as an attempt, contra Nietzsche, to sever the link between power and Being-Play by showing that the power-oriented mentality of Dasein—

---

56. See Heidegger, *Nietzsche*, 4 vols., trans. Frank A. Capuzzi (New York, 1982), vol. 4, p. 236. Further citations refer to this edition. I have used in parallel the German edition, *Nietzsche*, 2 vols. (Pfullingen, 1961). In German, the last two stanzas of Nietzsche's poem read: "Welt-Rad, das rollende / Streift Ziel auf Ziel: / Not—nennt's der Grollende, / Der Narr nennt's—Spiel. / Welt-Spiel, das herrische, / Mischt Sein und Schein:— / Das ewig-Närrische / Mischt *uns*—hinein!"

as it manifests itself, for instance, in modern man's representational thinking and technological quest—is only one mode of the (un)concealment of Being, that it belongs to the being, rather than to Being. This view of Heidegger as an anti-Nietzschean uncritically adopts Heidegger's own critique of the Will to Power as subjectivity, and is shared by many Anglo-American scholars who focus on Heidegger's later work.

It can, however, be argued that by interpreting the Will to Power as the Will to Will Heidegger does not sufficiently meditate on Nietzsche's notion of *Weltspiel* as arbitrary and violent play of forces; this would in turn mean that Heidegger never sufficiently reflects on his own notion of the Play of Being, never gives it the kind of thoughtful attention that the *Vollendung der Metaphysik* would require. And if this were the case, then the question would arise whether his thought could ever reach to the bottom of Western metaphysics, let alone go beyond it. I shall attempt to approach this question through a reexamination of the various notions of play that Heidegger employs in his later work in relation to what he calls his "one thought," the thought of Being.[57]

In Heidegger one can find most of the play concepts that have been discussed so far in Kant, Schiller, and Nietzsche. To be sure, the context of their use may be widely different and in this case one should again speak of family kinship, rather than of exact correspondences or identity. The play concept is by no means inoperative in *Being and Time*, notably in the form of Dasein's *Spielraum* (leeway, play-space) and *Geworfenheit* (throwness), which implies a dangerous existential game of risk taking, whose limits are circumscribed by Death (perhaps Heidegger's own existentialist-phenomenological version of "tragic" or agonistic moira?). But Heidegger's philosophical use of play becomes more and more frequent in his later thought. In the passages examined below from *Woodpaths* (*Holzwege*, 1950), *Lectures and Essays* (*Vorträge und Aufsätze*, 1954), *On the Way to Language* (*Unterwegs zur Sprache*, 1959), and *The Principle of Ground* (*Der Satz vom Grund*, 1957), play invariably crops up whenever the author attempts to describe Being, so much so that the thought-endeavors of the later Heidegger can rightly be gathered under the name of *Sein und Spiel*.[58]

57. Heidegger, *Was heisst Denken?* (Tübingen, 1954), p. 20; hereafter *WD*.
58. Among the general studies on the later Heidegger I have found particularly helpful Otto Pöggeler, *Der Denkweg Martin Heideggers* (Pfullingen, 1963); Walter Biemel, *Martin Heidegger in Selbstzeugnissen und Bilddokumenten* (Hamburg, 1973); Thomas Langan, *The Meaning of Heidegger* (London, 1959); William

In "Hölderlin and the Essence of Poetry" (*Hölderlin und das Wesen der Dichtung*, 1936, published 1937), Heidegger goes out of his way to separate the essence of art from play, which he still understands in a Kantian, negative fashion. Examining Hölderlin's statement that the writing of poetry is the "most innocent of all occupations," Heidegger comments: "Writing poetry appears in the modest guise of *play* [*Spiel*]. Unfettered, it invents its world of images and remains immersed in the realm of the imagined. This play thus avoids the seriousness of decisions, which always in one way or another create guilt [*Schuld*; also obligation, debt]. . . . Poetry is harmless and ineffectual. For what can be less dangerous than mere speech? But in taking poetry to be the 'most innocent of all occupations,' we have not yet comprehended its essence."[59]

In this passage, Heidegger seems to share the widely accepted view of play as nonseriousness, as a harmless, ineffectual, and innocent occupation, which he is at pains to distinguish from serious poetry writing. Although our existence is "fundamentally poetic," this cannot ultimately mean that it "is really only a harmless game [*Spiel*]" (p. 35). Heidegger further draws a distinction between poetry and play loosely based on the Kantian notion of play as a pleasurable activity that fosters a feeling of community among participants, but also "emptiness of thought":[60] "Poetry looks like a game [*Spiel*] and yet it is not. A game does indeed bring men together, but in such a way that each forgets

Richardson, *Heidegger: Through Phenomenology to Thought* (The Hague, 1963); G. J. Seidel, *Martin Heidegger and the Presocratics: An Introduction to His Thought* (Lincoln, Neb., 1967); J. Kockelmans, ed., *On Heidegger and Language* (Evanston, Ill., 1972); J. L. Mehta, *Martin Heidegger: The Way and the Vision* (Honolulu, 1976); David White, *Heidegger and the Language of Poetry* (Lincoln, Neb., 1978); M. Murray, ed., *Heidegger and Modern Philosophy* (New Haven, Conn., 1978); and Reiner Schürmann, *Le principe d'anarchie: Heidegger et la question de l'agir* (Paris, 1982). Among the studies dealing specifically with Heidegger's concept of play are Heidemann, *Begriff des Spieles*, pp. 278–372; John Caputo, "Being, Ground, and Play in Heidegger," *Man and World* 3 (1970): 26–48, and *The Mystical Element in Heidegger's Thought* (Athens, Ohio, 1978), especially "The Play of Being," pp. 80–89; and David Halliburton, *Poetic Thinking: An Approach to Heidegger* (Chicago, 1982), especially chap. 7, "Poetic Thinking and the World," and chap. 8, "The Play of the World."

59. Heidegger, "Hölderlin and the Essence of Poetry," trans. D. Scott, in V. W. Grass, ed., *European Literary Theory and Practice* (New York, 1973), pp. 28–29. Further citations refer to this edition.

60. Cf. Kant, *Anthropology from a Pragmatical Point of View*, §88.

himself in the process. In poetry, on the other hand, man is reunited on the foundation of his existence" (pp. 37–38).

Heidegger certainly goes against Kant's view of the aesthetic as a mere bridge between intuition and understanding, seeing poetry as an act of "firm foundation [*feste Gründung*]" or as the "establishment of Being [*Stiftung des Seins*]" (p. 38). Nevertheless he does retain Kant's notion of poetic creation as a *freie Gabe* (which is now granted not so much by the genius as by Language or Being itself), as well as Kant's notion of play as the uncontrolled creative overflow of the imagination: "Yet every inaugural act remains a free gift [*freie Gabe*], and Hölderlin hears it said: "Let poets be free as swallows." . . . But this freedom is not undisciplined arbitrariness and capricious desire, but supreme necessity" (p. 38).

Poetry as the *Stiftung des Seins* is not the unrestrained play of the imagination; rather, it is subject to a "twofold control," the signs of the gods (*Winke der Götter*) and the voice of the people (*Stimme des Volkes*) (pp. 38–39). Although Heidegger rejects Kant's subordination of poetry to Reason and to metaphysics, his redemption of poetic language still depends on the separation of this language from play. This separation is demanded precisely by Kant's undervaluation of poetic discourse as "mere play" and therefore it remains well within the limits of that Western metaphysics which Heidegger attempts to overcome.

If in the "Essence of Poetry" this essence has little to do with play or, rather, can be defined only in an act of separation from play, in "The Origin of the Art Work" ("Der Ursprung des Kunstwerkes," 1935–1936, published in *Holzwege*, 1950) a dramatic shift seems to occur: the essence of the artwork, and therefore of poetry as well, can be defined *only* as play. This play, however, is not yet called simply *Spiel* but *Widerspiel* or *Urstreit*, and therefore can be traced back directly to the Nietzschean and the Presocratic notions of agon. Thus, Heidegger's shift is perhaps not so dramatic after all: since he wrote the "Origin" about the same time that he wrote the "Essence," could he still have been operating with both Kantian and Nietzschean (divided) notions of play?

The concept of play as agon appears relatively late in the essay, in connection with Heidegger's attempt to describe the essence of the artwork in relation to the essence of art and to that of truth (*Wahrheit*), that is, in its essential relation to Being. After he reviews the prevalent notions regarding the artwork and distances himself from both the aestheticist and the mimetic (imitative and representational) views of art, Heidegger suggests that the artwork is the locus (*Spielraum*) of the counterplay (*Widerspiel*) of world and earth. The work of art sets up (*aufstellt*) a world and sets forth (*herstellt*) the earth. By "world" Heidegger understands "the self-disclosing openness of the broad paths of the simple and essential decisions in the destiny of an historical people";[61] by "earth" he understands "the spontaneous forthcoming of that which is continually self-secluding and to that extent sheltering and concealing" (p. 48). World and earth are opposites that engage in an agon within the play ground of the work: "In setting up a world and setting forth the earth, the work is an instigating of this striving. This does not happen so that the work should at the same time settle and put an end to the conflict in an insipid agreement [pace Schiller], but so that the strife [*Streit*] may remain a strife. . . . It is because the struggle arrives at its high point in the simplicity of the intimacy that the unity of the work comes about in the fighting of the battle" (pp. 49–50).

Here, then, Heidegger employs the Hellenic notion of play as agon among equal forces resulting in *isomoiria*, or a balance of power. His choice of images suggests either wrestling or sexual intercourse, or perhaps both, and throughout his essay he resorts to poetical and mythical wording that imparts an unmistakably archaic flavor to his thought. Furthermore, Heidegger insists that the striving (*Streit*) between world and earth should not be confused with "discord" and "dispute" and thus be seen simply as disorder and destruction. In other words, he invokes, following Nietzsche, the Hesiodic distinction between good and bad eris. In what he calls "essential striving" (*wesenhafter Streit*), an obvious kin of good eris, the opponents "raise each other into the self-assertion of their natures" at the same time that they "let themselves go into the intimacy of simple belonging to one another."

Truth itself, according to Heidegger, happens in the primal conflict (*Urstreit*) between world and earth, which is also the conflict between the self-concealment and the self-revelation of beings (*das Seiende im Ganzen*) in the Open (*das Offene*) of Being. He no longer interprets truth simply as "an agreement or conformity of knowledge with fact" (p. 51), but as the Greek *aletheia*, (un)concealment. His description of

61. Heidegger, "The Origin of the Art Work," in *Poetry, Language, Thought*, trans. A. Hofstadter (New York, 1971), p. 48. Further citations refer to this edition. I have used in parallel the German text, included in *Holzwege, Gesamtausgabe*, Klostermann edition (Frankfurt, 1977), vol. 5; hereafter *HW*. Quotations from "What Are Poets For?" ("Wozu Dichter?" *HW*), which I discuss shortly, also refer to Hofstadter's translation in *Poetry, Language, Thought*.

*aletheia* as taking place in the primal conflict of the clearing (*Lichtung*) and the concealing (*Verbergung*) of the Open in the midst of beings (cf. p. 53) reminds us of the poetic, oracular language of Heraclitus and Parmenides. It is as if Heidegger confronts Parmenides' "allegory of Truth" and the description of Being (*eon*) in fragment 8 (Diels-Kranz) with Anaximander's notion of *to apeiron* (the boundless) and with Heraclitus's question, "How can one hide himself before that which never sets?" (frag. 16). Although Heideggerian *aletheia* shares the ago-nistic, hermeneutical quality of truth present in Parmenides, it is no longer tied to an authoritarian notion of Being that attempts to do away with chaos, chance, indeterminacy, obscurity, and concealment. On the contrary, it brings into play Anaximander's *to apeiron* and, perhaps, the Pythagorean "void," challenging the securedness and rigidity of Par-menidean Being which, Heidegger would say, has already begun to turn toward the metaphysics of the Will to Power.[62]

The nature of truth is unconcealment, but at the same time, in true Heraclitean fashion, it is denial and withdrawal; in other words, "truth in its nature is also un-truth" (p. 54). This, however, does not mean that truth "is at bottom falsehood," nor that, viewed dialectically, it "is always also its opposite." Rather, the concealing denial present in truth is "intended to denote that opposition in the nature of truth which subsists between clearing, or lighting [*Lichtung*] and concealing. . . . The nature of truth is, in itself, the primal conflict in which that open center is won within which what is, stands, and from which it sets itself back into itself [*der Urstreit, in dem jene offene Mitte erstritten wird, in die das Seiende hereinsteht und aus der es sich in sich selbst zurückstellt*]" (p. 55). It is highly significant that, in the last revised edition of his essay (1960), Heidegger replaced the word *Urstreit* with *Ereignis*, (event, but also "disclosure of appropriation"). This seems to be an indication that the later Heidegger attempts to think the play of Being in less agonistic terms. In the initial version of "The Origin of the Art Work," however, he is clearly still too close to the Presocratics and to Nietzsche to be able to distance himself effectively from their agonistic notion of *Weltspiel*.

62. Heidegger discusses these questions at length in "Der Spruch des Anaxi-mander," in *HW*, as well as in "Logos," "Moira," and "Aletheia," in *Vorträge und Aufsätze* (Pfullingen, 1954), vol. 3. The English versions of these essays are col-lected under the title *Early Greek Thinking*, trans. D. F. Krell and F. A. Capuzzi (New York, 1975). For discussions of the relationship between the thought of Heidegger and that of the Presocratics, see Seidel, *Martin Heidegger and the Pre-Socratics*, and Krell's introduction to *Early Greek Thinking*.

At the end of his essay, Heidegger introduces and interprets in his own manner two other interrelated notions of play that are familiar to us from Nietzsche and also from Plato, Kant, and Schiller: play as *Überfluss* or *Schenkung*, gratuitious expenditure or bestowal—here he takes over and elaborates his notion of art as *freie Gabe* from the "Essence of Poetry"—and play as *Ur-sprung*, primal leap. Both concepts appear in connection with Heidegger's rejection of the mimetic (imitative and representational) theories of art and his reinterpretation of the Romantic concept of creative process, *poiesis*, as "founding" (*Stiftung*) in the triple sense of grounding, bestowing, and beginning.

Poetry as the setting-into-work (*Ins-Werk-Setzen*) of truth is *original* in the sense of founding and preserving, which means first of all the bringing and holding forth of what has never before appeared in the clearing (and the concealing) of the Open in the midst of beings. What art founds can "never be compensated and made up for by what is already present and available," because founding is "an overflow, an endowing, a bestowal [*ein Überfluss, eine Schenkung*]" (p. 75).

Poetry is also origin-al in the sense of having the immediacy (*das Unvermittelte*) of any beginning. But the unmediated nature of a beginning or the particularity of a leap (*Sprung*) out of immediacy should not be confused with the primitive, and Heidegger attempts to distance himself from the Romantic notions of "naive" poetry as elaborated, for instance, by Schiller. The primitive lacks the bestowing and grounding leap as well as the "fore-leap" (*Vorsprung*). A genuine beginning always prepares itself for a long time and unperceived, it is always a *Vorsprung*, in which "everything to come is already leaped over, even if as something disguised. The beginning always contains the end latent within itself [*der Anfang hält schon verborgen das Ende*]" (p. 76). The primitive, on the other hand, is futureless, and "contains nothing more than that in which it is caught" (p. 76). Poetry (and, by extension, all true art) lets truth originate (*lässt die Wahrheit entspringen*), it is the leap (*Sprung*) that springs to the truth of the being in the work. "To originate something by a leap, to bring something into being from out of the source of its nature in a founding leap—this is what the word origin [*Ur-sprung*, primal leap] means" (pp. 77–78). Thus, the origin of art for Heidegger is the same as the origin of art and play for Plato, and is to be found in man's excess of energy, spontaneous exuberance, or in his urge to leap (*Laws*, 2.653d–e). Although in "The Origin of the Art Work" Heidegger never calls the *Ur-sprung* and the *Überfluss* "play," viewed from the perspective of his later work (and of Plato's own definition of art-as-play) they can hardly be anything else: he attempts to think them out of the essence of Being, which later on (in *Der Satz vom Grund*, for example) can be thought only out of the essence of play.

At first sight, "What Are Poets For?" ("Wozu Dichter?" 1946, published in *HW*, 1950) does not seem to go beyond the notions of play that are already present in "The Origin of the Art Work." Superficially, at least, one can discern the same Presocratic and Nietzschean descriptions of Being in terms of play as agon and in addition as risk taking, the latter notion being "retrieved" (*wiederholt*) from *Sein und Zeit*. And yet, in the intervening years, Heidegger has thoroughly studied Nietzsche and the Presocratics (to whom Nietzsche no doubt led him), developing a critical distance toward them that is lacking in "Der Ursprung." Play as agon and as risk taking are still seen as ways of the manifestation of the Being of beings but—and this is a crucial point—interpreted *metaphysically* as Heraclitus's Cosmos, Leibniz's Nature, Hegel's Absolute Spirit, and Nietzsche's Will to Power. Here, again, a poet (Rilke) is taken as a pre-text for Heidegger's thought-endeavors, being compared unfavorably to another poet (Hölderlin).

Rilke's poetry, according to Heidegger, can be understood only in the context of the realm from which it speaks, and this realm turns out to be "the truth of particular beings, as it has developed since the completion of Western metaphysics by Nietzsche." In his own way, Rilke poetically experiences and endures "the unconcealedness of beings [*Unverborgenheit des Seienden*; *Unverborgenheit* here meaning also *exposure, unshieldedness*] which was shaped by that completion" (p. 98). Consequently, his poetry is spoken in a time that is even more destitute (*dürftig*) than the one to which Hölderlin belonged because now Being, through increasing *Seinsvergessenheit*, has withdrawn or concealed itself even further from Dasein, and beings have become even more unconcealed-unshielded. This poetry, nevertheless, goes as far as it *can*— Hölderlin's poetry was able to go farther—which is only as far as thinking Being, with Nietzsche, in terms of the Will to Power. Thus, it turns out that through his reading of Rilke Heidegger again addresses Nietzsche. On a certain level, and *mutatis mutandis*, the confrontation between Rilke and Hölderlin is also the confrontation between Nietzsche and Heidegger, between the Being of beings interpreted "metaphysically," as the *Wille zum Willen*, and the Being of beings interpreted "post-metaphysically," as *das Gevirt* and *das Ereignis*; or, closer to our concerns, it is the confrontation between the Nietzschean *Weltspiel* of the Will to Power and the Heideggerian *Weltspiel* of the fourfold.

Quoting from a titleless poem in the *Späte Gedichte*, Heidegger argues that the word *nature* employed by Rilke in that poem in effect means the Being of beings, but interpreted metaphysically, as the Will to Power: "We must here think of Nature in the broad and essential sense in which Leibniz uses the word *Natura* capitalized. It means the Being of beings. Being occurs as the *vis primitiva activa*. This is the incipient power gathering everything to itself, which in this manner releases every being to its own self. The Being of beings is the will" (pp. 100–101).

This passage corresponds to and further illuminates Heidegger's rather elliptical references to Goethe's Nature and Heraclitus's Cosmos in his discussion of Nietzsche's *Weltspiel* in "Nihilism and the History of Being"—a chapter in his Nietzsche book that he wrote approximately during the same period that he wrote the Rilke essay; it now becomes clear that Goethe's and Heraclitus's concepts should also be read, like Leibniz's Nature, in terms of the Being of beings as the *vis primitiva activa*, that is, as power. Consequently, the metaphysically interpreted relationship of Being and the being is a power relationship, and Heidegger describes it in terms of play as risk taking or venture. In the game that Being plays with the being, the former "gives" particular beings "over to venture," as Rilke puts it. Being flings beings loose or ventures them out into unconcealedness-unshieldedness. Venture (*das Wagnis*) means flinging into danger (*das Loswerfen in die Gefahr*), whereas daring (*das Wagen*) means "to risk the game" (*auf das Spiel setzen*; to place your bets). Heidegger then establishes the connection between venture, power, and will, reiterating the argument from his book on Nietzsche that the Will to Power is only a disguised form of the Will to Will, the true "subject" of Metaphysics (cf. p. 102). He implicitly contrasts Rilke's Nature, which he argues remains interpreted metaphysically in terms of Nietzsche's Will to Will, with his own view of Nature as the Presocratic *phusis* or the *aufgehend-verweilend Walten* (the emergent-enduring force).[63] Heidegger believes that he emancipates power from its subjectivist metaphysical interpretation, regarding it as something that overwhelms (*überwältigt*) man and the will. In turn, he likens the dangerous power game of Being, in which the latter stakes out beings, with the child's game played by the *aion*, the "world's age" (*die Weltzeit*), which is Heraclitus's metaphor for Being—fragment 52, we recall, is also one of Nietzsche's favored references.

63. Heidegger, *Einführung in die Metaphysik* (Tübingen, 1958), p. 23; hereafter *EM*.

And yet, even though Being flings beings loose into unconcealedness, it does not lose them; rather, it keeps them in balance or protected. In order to describe this paradox, Heidegger develops one of his famous series of playful etymologies and word associations, this time around *das Wagnis*, venture, *das Wagen*, daring, and *die Wage*, the old spelling of *die Waage*, balance, which in the Middle Ages, according to Heidegger, meant also something like hazard or risk: "The word *Wage*, in the sense of risk and as the name of the apparatus balance, scales, comes from *wagen*, *wegen*, to make a way, that is, to go, to be in motion. . . . What rocks is said to do so because it is able to bring the balance, *Wage*, into the play of movement, this way or that. . . . To weigh or throw in the balance [*Wagen*] as in the sense of wager means to bring into the movement of the game [*in den Gang des Spieles bringen*; to bring into play], to throw into the scales, to release into risk. What is so ventured is of course unprotected; but because it hangs in the balance, it is retained in the venture [*Wagnis*]. It is upheld" (pp. 103–104).

One is reminded here of the scales on which Zeus weighs the mortals' portions (within whose confines they can also be said to be shielded or safe), and the concept of Being as the play of venture bears a strong family resemblance to that of the Hellenic cosmos as the play of chance-necessity.

Rilke calls the force of Being, which both flings beings into the open and keeps them in balance, the "force of gravity" (*Schwerkraft*). This force of gravity, which appears in Rilke's poem "Schwerkraft," must be understood not as physical gravitation but rather as the center of beings as a whole; in another poem, Rilke names it the "unheard-of center" (*unerhörte Mitte*) in order to distinguish it from gravitational force. It is the center which, not unlike Socrates' divine lodestone in the *Ion*, draws and holds everything in relation to each other, gathering all beings in the play of venture (*das Spiel des Wagnisses*). This center is the "eternal playmate" (*ewige Mitspielerin*) in the world-play of Being (*Weltspiel des Seins*).

Needless to say, the world-play of Being in Rilke is the one interpreted metaphysically, as in Nietzsche, and Heidegger implicitly opposes to it his own view of *Weltspiel*, for example when he discusses Rilke's notion of the Open and the "widest Orbit." He insists that when Rilke speaks of the Open, he does not have in mind the "unconcealedness of beings that lets beings as such be present"; rather, Rilke intends to "designate the whole draft [*Zug*] or the force of gravity to which all beings, as ventured beings, are given over" (p. 106). Consequently, what Rilke experiences as the Open is "precisely what is closed up, unlightened"; it is a "confinement within the boundless," established by representational thinking. This kind of thinking "excludes man from the world and places him before the world," interpreted metaphysically as *das Seiende im Ganzen*. But the term *Open*, just like the term *venture*, is ambiguous insofar as it is part of the history of *Seinsvergessenheit*: it may signify "the whole of the unbounded drawings of the pure draft [*das Ganze der entschränkten Bezüge des reinen Bezüges*], as well as openness in the sense of a universally prevailing release from all bounds [*die überall waltende Entschränkung*]" (p. 107); the first meaning is presumably Rilke's, while the second belongs to Heidegger and is already present in "The Origin of the Art Work." Because Rilke's poetry "remains in the shadow of a tempered Nietzschean metaphysics" it cannot think the Open in this second sense, as the "essentially more primal lightening of Being [*Lichtung des Seins*; lighting-clearing of Being]" (p. 108).

A similar ambivalence, Heidegger claims, transpires in Rilke's use of the term "the widest Orbit" (*der weiteste Umkreis*; also the widest circle or circumference), which for the poet is another way of describing the Open, and therefore remains interpreted metaphysically, in terms of the beings as a whole. From a postmetaphysical (which for Heidegger is also a premetaphysical) point of view, the widest Orbit must be thought of as the Being of beings, and not only as *das Seiende im Ganzen*. Heidegger again resorts to Parmenides' fragment 8 in order to make his point. According to him, Parmenides has not yet entirely forgotten the ontological difference and calls Being *eon* to distinguish it from *eonta*, the beings as a whole. Furthermore, the Eleatic calls *eon* the *hen*, the unifying One, and describes it as a "well-rounded sphere" (*eukuklos sphaire*). Hence, this sphere should be conceived of as the "Being of beings, in the sense of the unconcealing-lightening unifying One [*das entbergend-lichtende Einen*]" (p. 123).

It is less important here to decide whether Heidegger interprets Parmenides correctly than to point out the way in which Heidegger distances himself, through Rilke, from Nietzsche's notion of Being as the *Weltspiel* of the Will to Power. Although in "What Are Poets For?" he does not yet make explicit his own view of the *Weltspiel* as the mirror-play of earth, sky, divinities, and mortals (we get only a veiled reference to it in his criticism of Rilke's express denial that "one may think of the Open in the sense of the openness of sky and space," p. 108), Heidegger nevertheless clears the way for this view by embarking upon a critique of the Nietzschean *Weltspiel* and its power-oriented, *representational* mentality. This mentality culminates, dangerously, in modern man's (self-)destructive technological quest, and the broad outlines of Heidegger's critique of technology are already evident in the passages quoted from his Nietzsche book.

In "The Thing" ("Das Ding," 1950, published 1951), Heidegger seemingly leaves behind Nietzsche's agonistic view of play; he now borrows the nonrepresentational language of such mystics as Laotze, the Zen Buddhists, and Meister Eckhart, to think Being in terms of the mirror-play (*Spiegel-Spiel*) of the fourfold (*das Gevirt*).[64]

Starting from a critique of the concept of object or thing in Western metaphysics, including the Kantian notion of the *Ding an sich*, Heidegger attempts to disengage this concept from the representational thinking which he criticizes in "What Are Poets For?" opening it toward the foundational thinking of Being. In terms of the latter, he sees the essence of the thing as "gathering" (*Versammlung*). The thing "things," that is, it emerges into being as thing, by bringing near, in their remoteness, the united four of earth, sky, divinities, and mortals. By thinging, the thing gathers "the united four, earth and sky, divinities and mortals, in the simple onefold of their self-united fourfold" (p. 178). The four facets of Being are to be thought of neither as engaged in an agon (in the manner of earth and world, in "The Origin of the Art Work,") nor as isolated entities. Rather, they are an all-embracing totality, the fourfold (*das Gevirt*), to be conceived of as a play of mutual mirroring or as mirror-playing: "Earth and sky, divinities and mortals—being at one with one another of their own accord—belong together by way of the simpleness of the united fourfold. Each of the four mirrors [*widerspiegelt*] in its own way the presence of the others. Each therewith reflects itself in its own way into its own within the simpleness of the four" (p. 179).[65]

In the present case, Heidegger insists, the mirroring must not be

64. For detailed discussions of the mystical elements in Heidegger's thought see Richardson, *Heidegger*, pp. 566–576; and Caputo, *The Mystical Element*, especially chap. 4, "Heidegger and Meister Eckhart," and chap. 5, "Mysticism and Thought." English quotations from "The Thing" will again refer to Hofstadter's translation in *Poetry, Language, Thought*, which I have used in parallel with the German text, "Das Ding," in *Vorträge und Aufsätze*, vol. 2; hereafter *VA*.

65. The "united four" or the "fourfold" belongs to a long tradition of number symbolism in Western and Eastern thought, in this particular case, the symbolism of the "quadrate." For this tradition, see Richardson, *Heidegger*, pp. 570–572, and Jean-François Mattéi, *L'étranger et le simulacre* (Paris, 1983), especially "Le Quadriparti," pp. 504–547.

understood in representational terms, as the "Darstellen eines Ab-bildes" (presentation of an image). Rather, it is to be conceived of as a shining forth, a play of mirror flashes, as it were. These flashes melt into each other at the same time that they remain distinguishable. In contra-distinction to the Platonic discussion of art as mirroring in the *Republic*, here one should look neither for mirrors nor for mirror-carriers. The four "mirrors" emerge into presence as light at the same time that they converge into a union that is binding in its freedom; whereas they cast light upon each other, they remain properly themselves (insofar as they remain partly concealed in darkness?): "None of the four insists on its own separate particularity. Rather, each is expropriated, within their mutual appropriation, into its own being. This expropriative appropri-ating [*enteignende Vereignung*] is the mirror-play of the fourfold [*das Spiegel-Spiel des Gevirts*]. Out of the fourfold, the simple onefold of the four is ventured [*getraut*, therefore also entrusted]" (p. 179).

The term *Spiegel-Spiel* is probably intended as an overcoming (*Über-windung*) of the Nietzschean and the Presocratic *Urstreit*. Pointedly avoiding any agonistic overtones, Heidegger's language now closely resembles the mystical language of Love, which, as a source of all-embracing harmony, binds souls into a free communion at the same time that it releases them from the binds of self(ish)ness—in much mystical thinking, for instance in the Cabbala, Love and Light are interchangeable.

The appropriating (*ereignende*) mirror-play of the fourfold also bears the name "world" (*Welt*). The world "worlds," that is, it comes into being as world, just as the thing things, or the united four fours, and Heidegger insists that his apparent tautologies are necessary tools in going beyond teleological thinking, with its will to represent, explain, and possess which ultimately goes back to the Will to Power. The world's worlding "cannot be explained by anything else nor can it be fathomed through anything else," because causes and grounds remain unsuitable for it. As soon as man attempts to master it, he "fails to transcend the world's nature and falls short of it" (p. 179).[66]

The definition of the world as the mirror-play of the simplefold of earth, sky, divinities, and mortals is a far cry from the one offered in "The Origin of the Art Work," where world could arise and manifest its essence only by engaging in an agon with earth. Accordingly, the play of

---

66. Cf. Heidegger, *Der Satz vom Grund* (Pfullingen, 1957), below, particularly his discussion of Angelus Silesius's poem "Ohne Warum."

the world is carefully pruned of its previous agonistic, Nietzschean implications; the prevailing image is no longer that of wrestling, but that of the (round) dance of the fourfold: "The mirror-play of world is the round dance [*Reigen*] of appropriating [*Ereignis*]. . . . The round dance is the ring that joins while it plays as mirroring. . . . The gathered presence of the mirror-play of the world, joining in this way, is the ringing [*das Gering*]. In the ringing of the mirror-playing ring, the four nestle into their unifying presence, in which each one retains its own nature" (p. 180).

The key word in understanding this passage, as well as all the others that I have so far quoted from "The Thing," is *Ereignis*. This word (which, we recall, replaces *Urstreit* in Heidegger's last revision of "Der Ursprung des Kunstwerkes") is now played upon throughout the last section of "Das Ding." The dictionary meaning of *Ereignis* is event, occurrence, happening, occasion, and Heidegger certainly intends us to keep this meaning in mind. But he also uses the word in the hyphenated form of *Er-eignis*, creating a playful etymology based on the adjective *eigen*, proper, own, individual, particular, spontaneous, strange, peculiar, and the like. Its verb form, *er-eignen* (cf. also *Vereignen, enteignen*) may mean to appropriate or make its own, but not in the possessive sense of, for instance, man's technological impulse. Rather, to appropriate for Heidegger is to gather together in essential belonging the world's (in)dependent facets that mutually preserve, in the very act of surrendering, their own freedom.

But Heidegger also brings into play the true etymology of *ereignen*, which comes from *eräugen*, to place before the eyes, to show, which in turn is connected with the noun *Augen*, eye. *Ereignis* is therefore tied in with the Heideggerian notion of truth as clearing, lighting (*Lichtung*) or as the self-(dis)closing of beings in the Open of Being.[67] In the last section of "The Thing," *e-reignen* is also associated, homophonically, with *Reigen*, the round dance of *Ereignis*, and then with *Ring*, the ring of the united four, which lightens them "in the radiance of their simple oneness." Both *Reigen* and *Ring* are other names for, or ways of describing, the mirror-play of the world as the "simple fourfold-onefold of earth, sky, divinities, and mortals" (p. 181).

*Ereignis*, then, seems to have the same function as the *Spiegel-Spiel*, that is, it plays counter to (*widerspielt*) Nietzsche's view of *Weltspiel* as an eternal contest of forces. One might argue that the round dance of the

67. See Hofstadter's introduction to *Poetry, Language, Thought*, p. xxi.

world seems akin to Zarathustra's ecstatic Dionysian dance, but Heidegger would of course counter that the latter still belongs to a *Weltspiel* interpreted metaphysically as the game of individuation and integration which the Will plays with itself; Heidegger's round dance, on the other hand, "leaps" beyond the Being of beings interpreted as the Will to Will to the Being of beings as the play of unconcealment and withdrawal of the totality of beings.

In "The Nature of Language" ("Das Wesen der Sprache," in *Unterwegs zur Sprache*, 1959) Heidegger further discusses the play of Being as the round dance of the world, this time in the context of language. The pre-text of his discussion is yet another poet, Stefan George, whose poem "Das Wort" ("The Word") occasions an analysis of "poetic language" (which is the same as "poetic thinking" whose function, in Heidegger, is to replace "metaphysical thinking") by explicit contrast with the traditional view of language as representation.[68]

For Heidegger, the relation of word to thing does not presuppose an ontological separation of the two; rather, "the word itself is the relation which in each instance retains the thing within itself in such a manner that it 'is' a thing."[69] Needless to say, here the word "thing" is to be understood in the sense in which Heidegger uses it in "Das Ding." George's poem, like any "essential" poetry, teaches us how to relate word to thing in this new manner, that is, it teaches us how to "undergo an experience with language" (*mit der Sprache eine Erfahrung zu machen*). By undergoing this experience, what we learn is not how to speak a language, but how to let language speak through us (p. 57).

Heidegger's premise is that man does not speak, but is spoken by language. As he says in an earlier work, *Der Satz vom Grund*, "It is language that speaks, not man" (*Die Sprache spricht, nicht der Mensch*). In *What Is Called Thinking?* (*Was heisst Denken?*, 1951–1952, published 1954), Heidegger further states that man risks himself in language, the way a swimmer plunges into the middle of a swift stream: "We thus venture ourselves in the play of language, on which our essence is staked [*Wir wagen uns dabei in das Spiel der Sprache, auf das unser Wesen gesetzt*

---

68. For extensive discussions of Heidegger's notion of "poetic thinking," see White, *Heidegger and the Language of Poetry*, and Halliburton, *Poetic Thinking*, especially chap. 6, "Poetic Thinking and the House of Being."

69. Heidegger, "The Nature of Language," in *On the Way to Language*, trans. P. D. Hertz (New York, 1971), p. 54. Further citations refer to this edition. I have used in parallel the German text in *Unterwegs zur Sprache* (Pfullingen, 1959); hereafter *US*.

*ist*]" (*WD*, p. 87). Relying on these previous formulations, Heidegger now indicates that Language and Being are interchangeable or, rather, that Being discloses itself as Language: his view of language as the "house of Being" (*US*, p. 63) is his counterplay to Nietzsche's view of language as man's "prison-house." Consequently, for Heidegger, the relation of language to man is another way of formulating the relation of Being to Dasein.

Being discloses itself as language in the saying (*die Sage*). In turn, what *die Sage* "says" is the play of the fourfold. The fourfold is no longer called simply *das Gevirt*, but *die vier Welt-Gegenden* (the four world regions) or *das Welt-Gevirt* (the world-fourfold). Its play is no longer called a mirror-play, presumably because this phrase has too many metaphysical and representational overtones, but an "encounter" (*das Gegen-einander-über*) in the play of stillness (*das Spiel der Stille*) of the time-space (*Zeit-Raum*; cf. the use of this term in contemporary physics, where it is usually translated as the "time-space continuum"). Likewise, whereas in "The Thing" Heidegger describes the mirror-play of the fourfold in spatial terms, now he introduces a temporal element into the play of stillness, which ultimately, however, must not be understood as sequence, but as simultaneity.

Just as the thing things, the time times, that is, it "makes ripe, makes rise up and grow." But time also times simultaneously, that is, it gathers together the past, the present, and the future; in the totality of its essence time "rests in stillness" (*ruht still*) (p. 106). If time times, the space spaces: it clears (*einräumt*)—both admitting and releasing—locality and place, and takes up simultaneity (*das Gleich-Zeitige*) as time-space. In the totality of its essence, space, just like time, does not move but remains still. Together, time and space form the play of stillness, also called "the Same" (*das Selbe*): "Time's removing and bringing to us, and space's clearing, admitting and releasing—they all belong together in the Same, the play of stillness. . . . The Same, which holds space and time gathered up in their nature, might be called Time-Play-Space [*Zeit-Spiel-Raum*]. Timing-clearing, the Same moves on its way [*bewägt*] the encounter [*das Gegen-einander-Über*] of the four world regions: earth and sky, god and man—the world-play" (p. 106).

It would seem, then, that in "The Nature of Language" Heidegger continues his attempt, initiated in "The Thing," to leap beyond Nietzsche's concept of *Weltspiel* as an agonistic play of forces. In his later descriptions of the *Spiel des Seins* he seems to have replaced the dynamic language of the will with the contemplative language of mystical unity. Thus, Heidegger's *Weltspiel*, whether as the mirror-play of the fourfold or as the play of stillness of the *Zeit-Raum*, now seems to bear almost no traces of the earlier *Urstreit*. And yet, ultimately, is Heidegger able to overcome Nietzsche's agonistic notion of play? Or, more generally, is he able to leap, through his own *Weltspiel*, beyond the power-oriented mentality of the West? Before we can answer these questions we need to turn to one last work, *Der Satz vom Grund*, where Heidegger further clarifies his notion of the play of Being. And he does so, again, in explicit opposition to that metaphysics of rationality which Nietzsche also sets himself against and claims to have overcome through his own view of *Weltspiel* as *Spiel der Kräfte*.

*The Principle of Ground* (*Der Satz vom Grund*, 1957) is a course of lectures which Heidegger delivered at Freiburg University during the academic year 1955–1956, in which he "retrieves" Leibniz's *principium rationis*, translated into German by Schopenhauer as *der Satz vom Grund* and better known in English as "the principle of sufficient reason."[70] According to this principle, all beings must have a cause or a reason for their existence, that is, they must be accounted for in rational terms: *Nihil est sine ratione*, nothing is without reason or ground. Truth itself is only that for which one can offer a ground or a rationale; falsehood is that which is groundless or *sine ratione*, without reason, a *nihil*, a "nothing." Furthermore, every being must have a ground in another— and eventually in the highest—being (God). Hence, in Leibniz, the Being of beings itself is interpreted as Reason or Ground. Although it is in Leibniz that it first reaches its self-awareness, the *principium rationis* has been operative, according to Heidegger (and to Schopenhauer), throughout the history of Western thought. This principle does not belong to Leibniz, but rather speaks through him, and in this sense, Heidegger argues, it belongs to the very dispensation of Being (*Seinsge-schick*) in the West, remaining in force to the present day. It is, as Leibniz says, "of great power" (*grossmächtig*), extending its dominion (*Macht-bereich*) throughout the field of Western metaphysics and, insofar as modern man looks for reasons or rational explanations everywhere, throughout the field of human and natural sciences as well.

But, if we listen attentively to what Being or Language says to us

70. In *Der Satz vom Grund* Heidegger shows a thorough knowledge of Schopenhauer's work, drawing upon *On the Fourfold Root of the Principle of Sufficient Reason*. Generally, Heidegger shares with Schopenhauer both an aesthetic view of the world and certain Buddhist, mystical leanings. In this regard, he also "returns" to Schopenhauer's "denial of the Will" both in his attack on Nietzsche's Will to Power, interpreted as Will to Will (see, e.g., "Who is Nietzsche's Zarathustra?" in *VA*, p. 117) and in his notion of *Gelassenheit* (releasement, letting-be).

through Leibniz's principle, we will be able to effect a leap (*Sprung*) and hear this principle in a different key. So far we have heard *Nihil est sine ratione* as "*Nothing* is *without* ground." If, however, we place the emphasis on "is" and "ground" we will hear, "Nothing *is* without *ground*." Read in the latter way, Leibniz's principle reveals that Being, present in "is," has always acted as the Ground of beings. Then, through a number of intricate leaps and detours that I cannot retrace here, Heidegger shows that the interpretation of Being as Ground (*Grund*, in the sense of firm land, solid surface, and reason or rationale) always also implies an interpretation of Being as Groundlessness or Abyss (*Ab-grund*). Thus, Being becomes the "nothing" or the "no-thing" (no being in particular) of *Nihil est sine ratione*, which now can be read as an affirmative, rather than as a negative, statement: (the) "Nothing is groundless." Being as the no-thing is an abyss (*Abgrund*) and as such it does not need a ground; at the same time, however, Being grounds the totality of beings that emerge into presence. Whereas metaphysics and its representational thinking can only understand the Being of beings as Ground, nonrepresentational poetic and mystical thinking (e.g., Christian negative theology) can understand it both as Ground and as Groundlessness, and Heidegger offers a pertinent example from the mystical poetry of Angelus Silesius, a Christian poet influenced by Meister Eckhart and held in high esteem by both Leibniz and Hegel. Through Silesius, Being as *Ab-grund* speaks to us in the following lines:

*Ohne Warum*
Die Ros' ist ohn' warum, sie blühet weil sie blühet,
Sie ach't nicht ihrer selbst, fragt nicht, ob man sie siehet.

*Without Why*
The rose is without why; she blooms while she blooms;
She pays herself no heed, asks not if one can see her.[71]

Angelus Silesius compares the rose (*die Rose*) with the soul (*die Seele*), suggesting that the latter should also leap beyond the search for "reasons," beyond the "why" of beings. Certainly, the rose could also be seen as falling within the dominion of the *principium rationis*—any

71. *Der Satz vom Grund*, p. 73. Apart from an excerpt in *Man and World* 7 (1974): 207–222, trans. K. Hoeller, there is no English translation of *Der Satz vom Grund* to date. All the translations are mine, and references are to the German edition. Normally *weil* means, and is translated as, *because*, but here Heidegger plays on its archaic, temporal sense.

botanist would argue that much. The point is, however, that it may also fall outside this dominion, in a region where representational thinking has no access to and cannot acccount for it. This does not mean that the rose remains groundless. It simply means that the rose comes into presence on its own ground, as a "thing" (in the sense defined in "Das Ding"), outside the representing subject who assigns it a reason, "classifies" it, and thereby always misses its true essence. The rose "roses," that is, it shines forth in its own Being, out of its own truth, rather than out of the truth of the will to measure, calculate, and classify. The soul, in turn, should no longer act as the being that searches for the meaning or the "why" of all other beings, including itself, but should let beings "be," let them emerge into presence of their own accord and on their own ground. Heidegger borrows the term *Gelassenheit* (releasement) from Meister Eckhart in order to name this letting be of beings, a term that also defines the role of Dasein in the game of Being: man is no longer the measure of all things, as in Protagoras, but rather, as in Plato, he is the toy of Being, and the most he can do is play along (*mitspielen*) with it.[72]

Heidegger specifically reflects on the essence of play in the thirteenth and last lecture of *The Principle of Ground*. According to him, play has always been interpreted metaphysically as a mere being and, as such, it has always been assigned some kind of "reason." Hence play as being has always been seen from the perspective of Ground (*Grund*) or *ratio*, as a dialectic of necessity and freedom, as a rule-determined, calculative activity (p. 186). In this sense, Leibniz's statement, *Cum Deus calculat fit mundus*, normally translated as "when God reckons/calculates, the world comes into being," would more appropriately be rendered as "while God plays, the world comes into being" (*während Gott spielt, wird Welt*). The question for Heidegger, however, is no longer to define the being of play, but the play of Being, and he performs another leap into a new key when he asks: "Does the essence of play allow itself to be properly defined in terms of Being as Ground, or must we think Being and Ground out of the essence of play? [*Lässt sich das Wesen des Spiels sachgemäss vom Sein als Grund her bestimmen, oder müssen wir Sein und Grund aus dem Wesen des Spiels denken?*]" Choosing the second path, Heidegger defines Being itself as play, or as an interplay of Ground and Groundlessness, of sending forth and withdrawal, which cannot be

72. For Heidegger's notion of releasement, see *Gelassenheit* (Pfullingen, 1959); historical background on this mystical notion can be found in Caputo, *The Mystical Element*, especially pp. 173–183.

"rationalized" or thought of in terms of any particular being. The play of Being, like the rose, has no "why." It remains purposeless, an inscrutable mystery.

Whereas in "Das Ding" and "Das Wesen der Sprache" Heidegger focuses mainly on the cosmic aspect of the play of Being as the mirror-play of the fourfold or the play of stillness of the Time-Space, in *The Principle of Ground* he brings up its other aspect, that is, the play of Being as dispensation (*Geschick*). This aspect seems to be of most concern to the mortals (and perhaps to the gods), for whom the play of Being comes into presence as an "epochal" sequence, that is, as history: Being plays (with Dasein) its game of advancing and retreating in different ways in different epochs. Epochal sequence (history), however, must not be understood as a rational chain of cause and effect; rather, it is a sudden, spontaneous, and arbitrary unfolding (p. 187). Thus, Heidegger sees the history of Being, in Hegelian fashion, not as the orderly progress of an "Absolute Spirit" but, on the contrary, as a series of unexpected and inscrutable turnings (*Kehren*). In order to make his point, he resorts again to Heraclitus's fragment 52, this time interpreting *aion* precisely as the *Seinsgeschick*, which is as wanton and unpredictable as a child at play: "The dispensation of Being is a child at play, moving pieces on a board; it is to the child that the kingship belongs—'kingship' meaning the *arche*, that is, what grounds, constitutes, rules: Being for the being. The dispensation of Being—a child at play" (p. 189).

It is as pointless to ask why Being plays its game of *Geschick* as it is to ask why the child plays: "Why does the great child, whom Heraclitus has seen in the *aion*, play? He plays because he plays. The 'because' disappears in the game. The game is without why. He plays while he plays [*er spielet weil er spielet*]. What remains is play—the highest and the deepest" (p. 189).

Perhaps we are now finally in a position to see to what extent Heidegger has been able to overcome Nietzsche's metaphysics of the Will to Power and, therefore, Nietzsche's agonistic concept of play as well. First, however, I should point out that the term *overcoming* (*Überwindung*) is itself part of an agonistic vocabulary; indeed, Heidegger drops it at the end of his thinking career, realizing that one cannot overcome metaphysics, but only walk away from it. Yet, despite his straying into the no-man's-land of the mystics, the question remains whether Heidegger's path ultimately steers clear of the power-oriented mentality of Western metaphysics and, specifically, of Nietzsche's agonistic *Weltspiel*.

By interpreting Nietzsche's Will to Power as the Will to Will, Heidegger certainly does away with the *Wille* of the *Wille zur Macht*, but without bypassing *Macht* itself. On the contrary, the Will to Will now allows him to reject a metaphysics of the subject (which he believes still to be present in both Schopenhauer and Nietzsche) while retaining its controlling presupposition, the notion of power: he simply transfers power from the Will to the Being of beings. Although he no longer thinks of Being as Will, Heidegger nevertheless thinks of it as a non-representable, inscrutable, and unpredictable force that overpowers man, playing with him a dangerous and "fearful" game (pp. 60–61), whose highest stake is death. As in Nietzsche's tragic, Dionysiac perspective, man has no choice but to play along in this game. In other words, like Nietzsche, Heidegger thinks of power in prerational terms, as arbitrary, spontaneous, and violent play. No less than Nietzsche's eternal play of forces, Heidegger's play of Being remains groundless while it grounds everything that comes into being. Heidegger also adopts a Nietzschean and a Presocratic perspective when he calls Being as ground *phusis* and defines it as the *aufgehend-verweilend Walten*, the emergent-enduring force. Thus, he adopts Nietzsche's prerational perspective not only in his critique of modern rational values, but also in his return to the Presocratics.

Although in his later thought, especially in "The Thing" and in "The Nature of Language," Heidegger seems to have left behind Nietzsche's agonistic concept of play, a look at *The Principle of Ground* shows that this is hardly the case. In the first two essays Heidegger simply considers the play of Being from the perspective of the fourfold or the four world-regions, and his language, which he borrows from the mystics, proves somewhat misleading. As soon as we look at the play of Being from the perspective of Dasein or the "mortals," as the dispensation of Being, we realize that this play has all along remained as agonistic as in Nietzsche and the Presocratics.

The competitive nature of Heidegger's concept of play is obvious not only in *The Principle of Ground*, where the play of Being discloses itself as the dangerous game of Death, "the still unthought measure of the measureless, i.e., of the highest game into which man is drawn on earth, upon which he is staked" (p. 187), but also in all of Heidegger's statements about the "essence of language," including those in "The Nature of Language" itself. In these statements Language, which is seen as the house of Being (in contrast to Nietzsche's prison-house), also plays a game of venture with Dasein, a dangerous and fearful game insofar as it is played literally to the death of the latter. Death is the essential way in which Language as Being toys with us, ventures us out into the draft of the Open and keeps us in balance there, for a while. When speaking about the essense of Language, Heidegger in effect retrieves from "What Are Poets For?" Rilke's (read: Nietzsche's) notion of play as risk taking and as *amor fati* or the joyful submission to the fateful power game of the world. For example, drawing a questionable, anthropocentric distinction between mortals (*die Sterblichen*) and animals (*das Tier* or *das Getier*), Heidegger remarks: "Mortals are they who can experience death as death. Animals cannot do so. But animals cannot speak either. The essential relation between death and language flashes up before us, but remains still unthought. It can, however, beckon us toward the way in which the nature of language draws us into its concern" (*US*, pp. 107–108).[73]

Language "draws us into its concern [*uns zu sich be-längt*]" whether we desire it or not. Man does not define Language or Being, but Language or Being defines man. When Heidegger says that man "risks himself" in Language, he actually means that Language itself risks man, stakes him out in the play of the world. From this point of view, even Western metaphysics with its *principium rationis* and its Will to Will is not some kind of avoidable human misprision, but an arbitrary turning (*Kehre*) in the hide-and-seek game that Language-Being plays with Dasein. Man's fateful mission (*Geschick*) is simply to play along.

Heidegger's *Spiel des Seins* as the "overpowering" (*das Überwältigende, EM*, p. 115) remains highly agonistic: it overwhelms man, turning him from a player into a plaything. Furthermore, man himself is by nature violent, accepting the challenge of the play of Being and venturing himself in this play (cf. Nietzsche's concept of *amor fati*).[74] In this respect, it is not very clear how, in Heidegger, *Gelassenheit*, or "the will not to will, to let things be," can be anything more than a strategy of Dasein in negotiating the dangerous power play of Being. Dasein could not practice *Gelassenheit* in the mystical sense, even if it wanted to, given the fact that its own will is determined by the unpredictable turnings of the Being's cosmic game of chance. Heidegger's use of Meister Eck-

73. For a remarkable development of Heidegger's thought on the relationship between death and language, see Giorgio Agamben, *Il linguaggio e la morte: Un seminario sul luogo della negatività* (Turin, 1982).

74. Cf. Caputo: "Man is a 'mortal' swept up in the power play of Being. . . . [He is] the venturer (*Wagender*) who dares to grapple with the groundless ground, to peer into the abyss of Being, risking vertigo, to win the high stakes of the truth of Being. . . . The interplay of Being and man is a strife. The play of Being and man is 'ant-agonistic' not 'quietistic'" ("Being, Ground and Play in Heidegger," pp. 39–41).

hart's term again seems somewhat misleading: in the German mystic, *Gelassenheit*, releasement, is man's way of achieving unity with God, understood as love. The dimension of mystical love is absent from Heidegger's thought, although he may, as we have seen, borrow its language to describe the mirror-play of the fourfold. But separated from its mystical religious context (and throughout his career Heidegger insisted on this separation), this language remains problematic.[75]

One can further argue that Heidegger's appeal to poetry and "poetic thinking" in his attempt to leap beyond Western metaphysics is, in some respects, also misleading: such appeals are bound to repeat the Socratic moment of the scapegoating of poetry by metaphysics. If one accepts the premise of this book that what we call "poetry" is only an older, more immediate form of power, then any metaphysician who will enlist poetry against metaphysics will return, in one way or another, to this form. This is precisely the case of both Nietzsche and Heidegger, who return to archaic values at the very moment that they abandon the "high road" of metaphysics (Kant) and stray into the "woodpaths" of poetic discourse.

Heidegger's view of poets and poetry remains as ambiguous as Nietzsche's. Like Nietzsche (and Kant), he sets up hierarchies among the arts, with poetry at the top, and among artists (we have seen that Hölderlin is closer to the "truth of Being" than Rilke). Again following Nietzsche, Heidegger ultimately dispenses with poets and retains only poetic discourse. For instance, in "Der Ursprung des Kunstwerkes" he makes a distinction between great and ordinary art on the basis of the artist's ability to consume himself in the work: "It is precisely in great art—and only such art is under consideration here—that the artist remains inconsequential as compared with the work, almost like a passageway that destroys itself in the creative process for the work to emerge" (*HW*, p. 40).

Here, then, we have Heidegger's polite version of Nietzsche's view of the artist as the "manure" on which art is permitted to grow. In turn, the artwork is seen as the locus (*Spielraum*) of the establishment (*Einrichtung*) of the truth of Being (*HW*, p. 61) and therefore is charged with carrying a heavy philosophical burden. Even though Heidegger's philosophy calls itself poetic thinking rather than metaphysics, it addresses

75. This is not to say, however, that the "divine love" of the mystics transcends the power-oriented mentality of Western or, for that matter, Eastern man (as Caputo, for one, seems to imply). To my knowledge, there is no major religion that has conceived of divinity otherwise than as power, even if the nature of this power is often supposed to be benevolent.

all the fundamental philosophical questions, including the most fundamental one, the question of Being—the fact that, at the end of his career, Heidegger no longer calls Being "Being" but, for example, in "Zur Seinsfrage," ~~Being~~ or the "Region," (*die Gegend*), in no way changes the essentially philosophical nature of his thought. His philosophy in a new key is far from renouncing the traditional claim of supremacy of metaphysical discourse over all other discourse. For instance, in listing the "essential ways" in which truth establishes itself in beings, he places philosophy as the "thinking of Being" (*Denken des Seins*) above science which, he argues, is not an "original happening [*ursprüngliches Geschehen*] of truth," and therefore is an "unessential" way of disclosing what is. Conversely, when a science "passes beyond correctness and goes on to a truth, which means that it arrives at the essential disclosure of what is as such, it is philosophy" (*HW*, p. 62).

Although he does not say so explicitly, Heidegger clearly implies the superiority of philosophy as the thinking of Being not only over the unessential but also over all the essential ways in which truth can emerge into presence, including the artwork itself: it is only through this thinking that truth can establish itself in an "essential" way in the first place. It is also philosophy as the thinking of Being that decides *where* and *to what extent* truth has established, or may establish, itself in the various fields of human activity. One can then conclude that Heidegger indeed brings "Nietzsche's accomplishment to a full unfolding," without, however, turning away from the power-oriented mentality that controls Nietzsche's thought as well as Western metaphysics at large. By transferring power from beings to Being itself, Heidegger has taken a decisive step in "overcoming" the metaphysics of the subject which he believes still to be present in Nietzsche's concept of the Will to Power, thus consolidating the latter's return to the prerational, archaic notion of power as *Weltspiel*—a violent, arbitrary, and ecstatic play of forces in which man is both player and plaything.

## SECTION 3

# Play and the Artist-Metaphysicians

With Kant, Schiller, Nietzsche, and Heidegger, play has gradually moved into a key position in modern philosophy. It appears in Kant as the negative condition of the possibility of metaphysical discourse, is interpreted positively in Schiller as the orderly *als ob* activity of reason, and finally, in Nietzsche and Heidegger, returns to its archaic form of violent and innocent manifestation of power. We have witnessed in these four thinkers not only a return of the play concept(s) to a dominant position in Western thought, but also a recurrence of the split between the rational and the prerational branches of the family tree. Their agon carries over to the conceptual level the contest between rational and prerational values that has since Antiquity been at the core of what I have called the Western mentality. Although one play group may gain temporary dominance over the other, its victory is never conclusive: it only manages to push its opponent into the background until the next round. One can further trace this agon in the work of some of the most influential contemporary thinkers, who can be called "artist-metaphysicians" both because, like Nietzsche and Heidegger, they turn to art and play in order to grapple with the consequences of a "nihilistic," self-devouring mode of thought, and because, again like Nietzsche and Heidegger, they in effect use art, aesthetics, and play to safeguard for philosophy the cultural authority that it has stood in danger of losing for the past one hundred years. These thinkers— whom, let me emphasize again, I employ here only as test cases in a history of the modern concepts of play (thereby to a certain extent bracketing the other aspects of their philosophical activity)—are Eugen Fink and Hans-Georg Gadamer in Germany and Gilles Deleuze and Jacques Derrida in France.

In the wake of Heidegger (who may undoubtedly bear the same title), the artist-metaphysicians follow Nietzsche in seeing the world as a work of art that incessantly creates and re-creates itself. They have all written on either Nietzsche or Heidegger, or on both—some of them influential, book-length studies. All of them recognize the importance of play in Nietzsche's or Heidegger's thought, but they differ in the way in which they preserve or obscure the link between play and power in this thought, and consequently in the way in which they give preference to one form of play over another in their own work. Finally, the artist-metaphysicians not only employ various notions of art and play in order to ground their philosophical speculations, but also display considerable (in some cases perhaps even excessive) artistry, playfulness, and stylistic virtuosity in their writing. Oftentimes, and not unlike their masters, they gleefully and daringly leap and dance on the borderline between logic and poetic thought, between philosophy and literature.

## 3·1 Eugen Fink and the Play of the World

In Nietzsche and the later Heidegger play is a first principle which remains groundless while it grounds their thought; consequently, play itself does not receive sufficient critical attention in their work. The latter task is assumed by Heidegger's lifelong disciple and friend, Eugen Fink, who undertakes both a historical investigation of the play concept in metaphysics and the elaboration of an onto-phenomenological theory of play which claims to transcend this metaphysics. Whereas he starts from Heidegger's ontological difference, Fink concentrates particularly on the relation of Dasein to Being on the one hand, and the relation of Being to the totality of beings on the other. We have seen that in Heidegger Being needs Dasein for its hide-and-seek game, and therefore Dasein appears as a privileged sort of being vis-à-vis all other beings. In principle, Fink does not deny Dasein's special place in the history of Being; nevertheless he asks such questions as: What is Dasein's relation to the totality of beings? What is the relation of the World to all that emerges into presence within it, including Dasein? Does the World "world" without man's participation or does emergence into presence occur only in the nearness of human consciousness? By way of answering these questions, Fink proposes a "cosmological" interpretation of the world which undoubtedly is already implicit in Heidegger's thought, but which clearly spells out Dasein's dual role of player (*Mitspieler*) and toy (*Spielzeug*) in the play of the world. He further develops Heidegger's notion of *Weltspiel*, by describing the "world-totality" (*Weltall*)—Fink's own, nonmystical, version of Heidegger's "Region" (*die Gegend*)—in terms of a "play without player(s)" (*ein Spiel ohne Spieler*).

Not surprisingly, Fink returns to Nietzsche and Heraclitus in order to support his cosmological view of play.[76] In his remarkable book on

76. For Fink (and Heidegger) the problematic of Western metaphysics concerns the question of Being interpreted as being, and is fourfold: the question of being as such (*das Seiende als solches*); the question of the total structure of being (*Gesamtgefüges des Seienden*); the question of the supreme being (*das höchste Seiende*); and the question of the unconcealment of being (*Unverborgenheit des Seienden*). Before Nietzsche this fourfold problematic found expression in the "four transcendentals" of Antiquity (*on, hen, agathon, alethes*) and of the Middle Ages (*ens, unum, bonum, verum*). In turn, according to Fink (and Heidegger), Nietzsche regards the being as such as the will to power; the totality of being as the eternal return of the same, appearing both in a negative form, as the death of God, and in a positive form, as the Apolline-Dionysiac counterplay in the realm of appearance; and the unconcealment of being (truth) as the Overman. Here, however, Fink and Heidegger part ways because Fink believes that Nietzsche transcends this problematic through his notion of *Weltspiel*. Fink differs from Heidegger not only in his interpretation of Nietzsche but also in his interpretation of the Presocratics, particularly Heraclitus. See, for example, Heidegger and Fink's *Heraclitus Seminar 1966/67*, trans. C. H. Seibert

Nietzsche, he gives the latter a Heideggerian interpretation against Heidegger himself; or, to put it in slightly different terms, he interprets Nietzsche through Heidegger, and Heidegger through Nietzsche.

For example, in his concluding chapter, significantly entitled, "Nietzsches Verhältnis zur Metaphysik als Gefangenschaft und Befreiung" (Nietzsche's relation to metaphysics as imprisonment and liberation), Fink criticizes Heidegger's "one-sided" interpretation of Nietzsche's will to power as the essential ground of Being (*Grund-Formel des Seins*). This interpretation allows Heidegger to see Nietzsche as still caught up in the metaphysics of subjectivity, which thinks the Being of beings as an object of representation (*ein Gegenstand des Vorstellens*), in other words, as the plenipotentiary (*Gemächte*) of a representing power (*vorstellende Macht*). And here Fink raises the question that has remained implicit throughout his study and that is designed to separate, in a decisive manner, his own interpretation of Nietzsche from that of Heidegger: "*Ist Nietzsche . . . nur das Ende der Metaphysik—oder der Sturmvogel einer neuen Seinserfahrung*? [Is Nietzsche . . . only the end of metaphysics—or is he the harbinger of a new experience of Being?]"[77] The answer to this question, Fink insists, can be found only in an examination of Nietzsche's concept of play as *Weltspiel*: Nietzsche's cosmological view of play does go beyond Western metaphysics and opens up the possibility of a new *Seinserfahrung*.

From the outset, Nietzsche "places himself within the mysterious dimension of play through his artistic metaphysics, his Heraclitean view of the world child Zeus—the *pais paizon*" (p. 187). His play, however, must not be understood in a Hegelian or idealist sense in general. Although the idealist philosophy of Kant, Schelling, and Hegel pays close attention to the relationship of play to the imagination, time, and freedom, in the end it always proclaims the primacy of spirit or will over

---

(University, Ala., 1980) and *Heraclitean Fragments: A Companion Volume to the Heidegger/Fink Seminar on Heraclitus*, ed. J. Sallis and K. Maly (University, Ala., 1980).

77. Eugen Fink, *Nietzsches Philosophie* (Stuttgart, 1960), p. 173. Further citations refer to this edition; all translations are mine. For discussions of Fink's concept of play see H.-G. Gadamer, "*Spiel als Weltsymbol*" in *Philosophische Rundschau* 9 (1961): 1–8; Otto Pöggeler, "*Zur ontologischen Frühgeschichte*," in *Philosophischer Literaturanzeiger*, 14 (1961): 115–119; H.-W. Jäger, "*Spiel als Weltsymbol*," in *Philosophisches Jahrbuch* 69 (1961): 189–191; and D. F. Krell, "Towards an Ontology of Play: Eugen Fink's Notion of *Spiel*," in *Research in Phenomenology* 2 (1972): 62–93. For a philosophy of play related to, and largely inspired by, that of Fink (as well as that of Nietzsche and Heidegger), see also Kostas Axelos, *Héraclite et la philosophie* (Paris, 1962) and *Vers la pensée planétaire* (Paris, 1964).

play.[78] With Nietzsche, human play, especially the play of the child and the artist, becomes the "conceptual key to the universe" (*der Schlüssel-begriff für das Universum*) or a "cosmic metaphor." This does not mean, however, that he uncritically projects the play essence of man upon the totality of beings (*das Seiende im Ganzen*); on the contrary, it means that he thinks the essence of man out of the totality of beings, conceived as the play of the world:

> The essence of man can be grasped and defined as play only if man is thought of as ecstatic openness to the reigning world [*waltende Welt*], rather than as a mere intraworldly [*binnenweltlich*] thing among other things, distinguished by the power of the spirit, of reason, etc. . . . The world plays—it plays as the Dionysiac ground . . . bringing together and breaking apart, mingling love and death, beyond good and evil, beyond all evaluation, because all values can arise only *within* this play. Dionysus is the name of this unspeakable play of all-embracing power (*All-Macht*). . . . Where Nietzsche conceives Being and Becoming as play, he is no longer caught in the trap of metaphysics. (p. 188)

According to Fink, however, whereas the Nietzschean play of the world remains purely arbitrary and beyond all value systems, man's play is rule determined and necessity bound. For Nietzsche, man the player, who "ecstatically opens himself to the formless, form-giving, playing god Dionysus, does not live in the vascillating arbitrariness of unconditional freedom" (p. 189); rather, he is a "playmate" (*Mitspieler*) in the game of the world, deeply desiring "what is necessary" (*das Notwendige*, in Heidegger's sense), and Nietzsche's formula for man's longing for necessity is *amor fati*. At the root of Nietzsche's poetic thinking lies the essential life experience, defined as the "cosmic unison [*Einklang*, in a musical sense as well] of man and world in the play of necessity" (p. 189).

In *Spiel als Weltsymbol* (1960), Fink further develops his own blend of the Nietzschean and Heideggerian notions of *Weltspiel* as well as certain insights from his earlier study of play, *Oase des Glücks: Gedanken zu einer*

---

78. Fink could have added Schiller to this list (cf. sec. 1.2). My views on the relation between play and power in Nietzsche, and on the history of the play concept in Western thought in general, come closer to those of Fink than to those of any other artist-metaphysician. At the same time, however, I hope it is by now clear that I do not share Fink's or any other artist-metaphysician's prerational premises, or their belief that power is "all that is." On the other hand, this is not to say that I favor the rational mentality that prevails in our culture; this mentality seems to me no less power oriented than its prerational counterpart.

*Ontologie des Spiels* (Freiburg, 1957). He examines play from both a historical and an onto-phenomenological perspective, distinguishing three main aspects of the play concept in Western culture: metaphysical, mythical or religious, and symbolical.

Fink argues that an examination of play in its metaphysical aspect needs to go back to Plato and his concept of mimesis. Whereas before Plato, notably in Heraclitus, play is thought of as the arbitrary, exuberant, and spontaneous movement of the cosmos, in Plato it becomes subordinated to Reason and Being as eternal, immovable order; it is turned into a good or bad imitation of the divine Idea. Plato's low estimation of play closely parallels his low estimation of poetry and art in general as an inferior form of mimesis-imitation. Through what Fink calls a "world-historical decision" (*eine welthistorische Entscheidung*), Plato brings about an epistemological split, in our culture, between art as play and philosophy and science as seriousness and morality. Plato further separates play from Being and Truth not only on epistemological but also on ontological grounds: he defines it as "unreal" or as mere "appearance" (*Schein*). At the dawn of Western metaphysics, play assumes the "character of a likeness [*Abbild*], indeed, of a mere reflection and is to be defined as mimesis. 'Unreality' signifies a lesser degree of power of being [*Seinsmacht*] in relation to solid, ordinary [*schlicht-wirklichen*] things. Play is only a paraphrase and a copy of everyday reality and, consequently, of no essential cognitive value for philosophy."79

In a Nietzschean move, Fink reverses the Platonic dialectic of reality and unreality and shows that the latter is in fact more "real" than the former, because it is a mode of knowledge that comes much closer to Being (in a Heideggerian sense) than the so-called natural objects and phenomena. Unreality is indeed appearance, but in the sense of "shining forth" (*Erscheinung*). Human play is an intertwining of reality and appearance through which the world-totality shines forth on a limited stage. In the case of play, one can no longer speak of copies, because appearances do not imitate or reproduce anything; rather, they stand in a symbolical (from the Greek *sumballein*, to fit together), and not a representational, relation to Being, which flashes through fragmentarily, in the manner of broken mirror pieces. As with Heidegger, Fink's mirror is not a Platonic one, but should be thought of as a lighting/clearing (*Lichtung*) that allows beings to emerge into presence. By

79. Fink, *Spiel als Weltsymbol* (Stuttgart, 1960), p. 229. Further citations refer to this edition; all translations are mine.

his critique of Plato's ontology of *Sein* and *Schein*, then, Fink prepares his own ontology of play as *Weltspiel*, based on Heidegger's notion of Being as a play of (un)concealment.

In its second fundamental aspect, mythical and ritualistic, play has always been seen, particularly by archaic man, as a heightened reality or being, as a means of rising to the same level with, or miming, the divine powers. In other words, in its mythical aspect play has a much greater power of being than in its metaphysical aspect. In turn, ritual play has three interrelated aspects: the handling of demons and other evil powers through the mask, which is a particular way of expressing the amphibolous character of the world as an interplay of *Sein* and *Schein*; the magic techniques of the medicine man, which are based on the relation of equivalence between the world and what is contained within it as both *pars pro toto* and *totum in parte*; and the solemn cult play of a whole community, which takes the form of a spectacle or a festival—according to Fink (and others) drama itself has its origin in this cult play. In ritual play, man both plays with and is played by the divinities and, therefore, he reveals himself as both player and plaything.

Fink concludes the section on play and myth by arguing that ritual play has a double character. On the one hand, it reveals the relation between world and intraworldliness (*Binnenweltlichkeit*) by making world-totality appear or shine forth (*erscheinen*) on a limited, intraworldly stage. On the other hand, however, ritual play conceals this relation. That ritual play is not itself the original relation of Being to beings is evident in the fact that archaic man perceives it as a means of reproducing this relation. Archaic man sees the original relation of world-totality and intraworldliness as a lost golden age that can be retrieved only temporarily, within a limited play sphere. In other words, archaic man has already created a distinction between sacred and profane that no longer concerns the relation of Being to beings, but intraworldly relations among beings. Hence, ritual play conceals the play of the world both as the sacred play of man with the divinities and as the play of the divinities with man. The divinities themselves remain within the world, which therefore transcends the distinction between sacred and profane. In this sense, man's sacred play cannot be a model for the play of the world any more than his profane or secular play can. Only by going beyond such distinctions can human play open itself to the play of the world (pp. 205–206).

Finally, Fink proposes to discuss human play in its third, symbolic aspect, that is, in its cosmic relation to the world-totality. According to him, there are five fundamental human phenomena: death, love, strife, work, and play. All these phenomena are social and may involve—but also transcend—language and theoretical comprehension. Yet play gains priority over the other four precisely because it expresses Dasein's essential relationship to the world-totality, while the others express only intraworldly relations between Dasein and other beings. This is partly so because all other human phenomena imply a distinction between reality and unreality (appearance), whereas play implies an interlacing of the two. In human play an "unreal sphere of meaning breaks into the total reality [*Gesamtwirklichkeit*] of actual things and processes, a sphere which is here and yet not here, present and yet not present" (p. 229). The word "unreal" points to the fact that the play world transcends the causal chain of phenomena or ordinary reality, overspilling into the realm of appearance. In turn, appearance must not be understood in the Platonic sense of a lesser power of being, of something superficial that is the result of a false perception. On the contrary, "appearance" describes the way in which world-totality may manifest itself within the world, in the play of Dasein (pp. 230–231).

It is, therefore, through its "unreality" that play expresses its essential relationship to the world-totality: the world shines forth in the play's realm of appearance. Through the medium of unreality or the "imaginary" (*das Imaginäre*), the all-producing whole appears within that which it produces. Viewed from the perspective of Dasein, in play "an intra-worldly fragment is destined to represent the world-totality, [or to be] the 'deputy' of an all-effecting power [*der 'Stellvertreter' der alleswirkenden Macht*]" (p. 234). The player "imitates" (*gleichtut*), as it were, the world-totality: he acts *as if* he were all-powerful and "irresponsible," as if he both contained within himself and transcended all possibilities. It is only in this sense, Fink argues, that one can see human play in its cosmic relation to the world-totality, as a world symbol (*Weltsymbol*).

But to see human play as a cosmic metaphor or a world symbol by no means implies that one can understand the play of the world on the analogy of human play; it only implies that human play shares certain features with the play of the world. The world reflects itself only in the unreality component of human play and therefore can be perceived only in a broken and fragmentary fashion (p. 238). On the other hand, it is the reality component of play that, paradoxically, obscures the true character of the play of the world. This component gives human play a meaning, a direction, a "reason," that is, a *structure*. Whereas all that is within the world has a reason and a finality, the world itself is meaningless and groundless: "The world in itself is devoid of all finality and has no 'value': it is above all ethical evaluation, 'beyond good and evil.' Without reason or end, without sense or goal, without value or plan, the world contains within itself all the reasons of all the intra-worldly beings that have a ground, it embraces in its universal futility the paths along which one attempts to reach any ends or goals" (p. 238).

The play of the world further distinguishes itself from human play by the fact that it is a play without player. In fact, human play can function as a cosmic metaphor only if one gives up the notion of the subjectivity of the player and that of the ludic world as a realm of appearance (*Schein*). The play of the world cannot be the play of a personal power (*personale Macht*), not even the play of a god, because the all-embracing power of the cosmos subsumes the divine powers as well. The play of the world, as opposed to human play, is the play of no individual; rather, it itself is the play of individuation, containing within itself all individual things, beings, and phenomena, including men and gods. In turn, the play of the world is not appearance (*Schein*) but shining forth (*Erscheinung*). The world makes everything appear and disappear within the time-space continuum and, in this sense, the play of the world must be understood, with Heidegger, as a play of presence and absence, in which all beings emerge into presence, are for a while lit up, and then disappear again into the groundless abyss of absence (which equally belongs to the world). All beings are cosmic toys and all players are in turn playthings. The world's *Erscheinung* is a mask that hides no face behind it, hides nothing but the nothingness itself.

Once man understands that the play of the world is the groundless, meaningless, and impersonal movement of the cosmic power, he will no longer attempt to measure himself against the gods and the stars; he will, indeed, renounce all measuring criteria, opening himself to the world and releasing himself into the total freedom of boundlessness. And Fink fittingly concludes his speculations on human and cosmic play with a quotation from *Also sprach Zarathustra*: "If I ever spread still heavens over me and flew into my own sky with my own wings: if I swam *playfully* into the deep Light Distance and my freedom became bird-wisdom: for thus speaks bird-wisdom: 'Behold, there is no up, no down! Throw yourself about, ahead, behind, you light one! Sing! Speak no more!'" (Fink, p. 240).

This brief discussion of Fink's concept of *Weltspiel* has shown that Fink consistently remains a prerational thinker, who never fluctuates (as

Heidegger does) between the language of power and the language of mystical love. Hence his work clearly reveals power to be the essential problematic not only of Western metaphysics but also of Western thought in general, and points to the inseparable link between power and play in this thought.

## 3·2 Play and Ontological Hermeneutics: Hans-Georg Gadamer

If from the point of view of a history of the modern play concept(s) Fink returns, via Heidegger, to Nietzsche and his *Machtphilosophie*, Gadamer returns to Kant, Schiller, and Hegel. But since Gadamer's return, like Fink's, is mediated by Heidegger and therefore indirectly also by Nietzsche, his play concept will appear as a forced marriage between rational and prerational play elements. At first sight, play in general seems to be incidental to Gadamer's project of elaborating a "philosophical hermeneutics": it is given theoretical treatment only in a short subsection of *Wahrheit und Methode* (1960; Eng. trans. *Truth and Method*, 1975), and then again, much later, in another short section of a lengthy essay, *Die Aktualität des Schönen: Kunst als Spiel, Symbol, und Fest* (The actuality of the beautiful: Art as play, symbol, and festivity, 1977). Yet a second look at Gadamer's project will reveal that here, no less than in Heidegger and Fink, play has an essential function: it serves both as a metaphor for describing the way in which the truth of Being occurs through man's hermeneutical activity and as the groundless grounding (*Ab-gründung*) of Gadamer's own thought.

In *Truth and Method*, Gadamer, following Heidegger, employs play as an ontological clue (*Leitfaden*) to the understanding of the mode of being (*Seinsweise*) of the artwork. This understanding is part of the larger question of the ontological grounding of truth in science. Whereas Gadamer preserves the traditional distinction between natural and human sciences (*Natur-* and *Geisteswissenschaften*), he implicitly criticizes both for their method, understood in its Baconian or Cartesian sense. His critique of modern science as the will to domination parallels Heidegger's and implies the ontological difference: the truth that concerns science is the truth of beings, whereas the truth that concerns philosophical hermeneutics is the truth of Being. As in Heidegger, the truth of Being is not something that man arrives at through an objective and rigorous scientific procedure, but rather something that happens or advents (*ereignet*) to him in the course of his history. In order to understand the advent-event (*Ereignis*) of truth as historical dis-closure, Gadamer turns, like Heidegger, to the work of art, and part 1 of his study is significantly entitled "Freilegung der Wahrheitsfrage an der Erfahrung der Kunst" ("The Opening [or Freeing Up] of the Truth Question in the Experience of Art"). But before one can properly address the question of the truth of art, Gadamer believes that one needs to address the question of (Romantic) aesthetics, which has, according to him, relinquished the traditional truth claim of art by undergoing a process of subjectivization.

According to Gadamer, it is the brand-new science of aesthetics that at the end of the eighteenth century begins to give up the truth claim of art in the form in which it is formulated by Aristotle and the Neoclassical tradition. Kant is the first modern thinker who emancipates art from scientific truth requirements, by showing its autonomous, disinterested (*interesselose*) mode of being between the rational and the natural. But Kant's high price for establishing the autonomy of art is to initiate the abandonment of all of art's traditional claims to knowledge. In his wake, art becomes increasingly abstract and removed from the object, and the artist loses his traditional place in the community, withdrawing into an ivory tower whence he issues his futile, narcissistic pronouncements.

Gadamer sees this "subjectivization of aesthetics" as the necessary consequence of the split between subject and object which occurs for the first time in the thought of Bacon and Descartes. Hegel is a positive moment in the history of aesthetics because he reestablishes the truth claim of art, by seeing it as exceeding the realm of subjectivity and becoming part of the objective history of the Absolute Spirit. Nevertheless, Hegel subordinates the truth claim of art to that of the philosophical concept, and in this sense he is one step both ahead and behind Kant, who seeks precisely to emancipate art from the truth of the concept. One would need, then, to confront both Kant and Hegel with Heidegger and retain the autonomy of art while not surrendering its truth claim. From a Heideggerian perspective, restoring the truth claim of the artwork without losing its autonomy means no less than bringing about a reunion of the subject and object. In turn, the work of art becomes the privileged locus of this reunion. And it is at this point in his historical argument of part 1 of *Truth and Method* that Gadamer introduces play as a metaphor for the *Seinsweise* of the artwork.[80]

80. Obviously, my version of the modern history of aesthetics differs substantially from that of Gadamer. See my foreword and introduction, as well as the introductory and concluding remarks to Part I.

Before he discusses the playful nature of art, Gadamer attempts to redefine the concept of play in Heideggerian ontological terms. His argument is reminiscent of that of Heidegger in "Der Ursprung des Kunstwerkes," although it is carefully pruned of any agonistic implications. Pointing out that the concept of play has always had a crucial role in aesthetics, Gadamer nevertheless charges that this concept has invariably been interpreted in subjectivist terms. His intention is to emancipate play from the "subjective meaning which it has in Kant and Schiller and which dominates the whole of modern aesthetics and philosophy of man."[81] He warns that when he speaks of play in relation to art, he does not refer to the attitude of the artist or that of the audience, nor to the "freedom of subjectivity expressed in play"; rather, he refers to the "mode of being of art itself" (p. 91). Art and play are alike insofar as they both involve an experience that transforms the persons experiencing it. Art, like play, does not occur for the sake of the participants but rather merely manifests itself (*kommt zur Darstellung*) through them.

Reinterpreting certain Neo-Kantian elements in Buytendijk's and Huizinga's phenomenological definitions of play, Gadamer proceeds to show that the essence of play is independent of the players, consisting of a to-and-fro movement without any goal except in and for itself.[82] Play, then, is a *natural* process and in this sense the metaphorical and the literal meanings of the word are indistinguishable: water, light, animals, and men "play" because they are all part of nature. In turn, nature, "inasmuch as it is without purpose or intention, as it is, without exertion, a constantly self-renewing play, can appear as a model for art" (p. 94).

The attitude of the player does not determine the nature of play;

81. Hans-Georg Gadamer, *Truth and Method*, trans. Garrett Barden and John Cumming (New York, 1975), p. 91. Further citations refer to this edition. I have used in parallel the German text of *Wahrheit und Methode: Grundzüge einer philosophischen Hermeneutik* (Tübingen, 1960; 3d ed., 1972). Among the critical appraisals of Gadamer's work that I have found helpful the following stand out: K. O. Apel, et al., eds., *Hermeneutik und Ideologiekritik* (Frankfurt, 1971); H. R. Jauss, *Literaturgeschichte als Provokation* (Frankfurt, 1970) and *Ästhetische Erfahrung und literarische Hermeneutik*, vol. 1 (Munich, 1977); James Hans, "H.-G. Gadamer and Hermeneutic Phenomenology," *Philosophy Today* 22 (Spring 1978): 3–17; D. C. Hoy, *The Critical Circle* (Berkeley/Los Angeles, 1978); Joseph Bleicher, *Contemporary Hermeneutics: Hermeneutics as Method, Philosophy, and Critique* (London, 1980); Wolfgang W. Holdheim, *The Hermeneutic Mode* (Ithaca, N.Y., 1984); and, especially, Joel Weinsheimer, *Gadamer's Hermeneutics: A Reading of Truth and Method* (New Haven, Conn., 1985).

82. See Huizinga, *Homo Ludens*, chap. 2, "The Play Concept as Expressed in Language," and F. J. J. Buytendijk, *Wesen und Sinn des Spiels* (Berlin, 1933).

rather, the nature of play determines the attitude of the player. The excitement of a game consists in its tendency to take over or master the players, that is, in its element of risk. Even the rules of the game are determined not by the players but by the nature of the play itself. In various games, the to-and-fro movement which is the essence of play is variously structured, and to follow the rules of a game means to follow its particular movement. Thus, in its essence, for Gadamer, as for Heidegger and Fink, all playing is a being-played (*alles Spielen ist ein Gespieltwerden*, p. 95).

If play is natural, then its mode of being is self-representation (*Selbstdarstellung*), which means that, like all natural processes, in addition to being purposeless play represents something. (Here "representation" must be understood in the sense of bringing forth or presencing, and not in the sense of reproducing a model. In German the ambiguity of the term is absent: *Darstellung* comes from *stellen* and *da*, literally *to place there*, *to bring to presence*, and therefore its more accurate translation would be "presentation.") Gadamer next draws a distinction between games and art (exemplified by drama) as two different forms of play. Whereas in games representation comes into being for its own sake, in drama it always occurs for someone, as the German word for a theatrical performance, *Schauspiel*, indicates. In a *Schauspiel*, play is no longer "the mere self-representation of an ordered movement, nor mere representation in which the child is totally absorbed, but it is 'representing for someone' . . . [which] is constitutive of the being of art" (p. 97).

Gadamer's distinction between games and art, however, turns out to be a hierarchy when he goes on to say that in art "human play finds its true perfection" (p. 99), its entelechy, as it were. As Plato, Aristotle, Kant, and Schiller have done before him, Gadamer divides play into higher and lower forms, and for him the higher form distinguishes itself by possessing a "structure" (*Gebilde* [p. 99]). The concept of the "transformation into structure" (*Verwandlung ins Gebilde*) allows Gadamer to define art not only as a higher form of play but also as an "independent and superior mode of being," to be distinguished from ordinary reality. Again following Schiller and other idealist thinkers, he defines reality as "what is not transformed" and art as the "raising up of this reality into its truth" (p. 102).

After he "rehabilitates" art as play by arguing that it is a higher kind of work, Gadamer also attempts to rehabilitate the Neoclassical concept of art as mimesis-imitation. In order to carry out this task, he predictably turns to Plato and Aristotle. When speaking of art as *Nachahmung*, he argues, one must retain the element of knowledge contained in imitation. Gadamer identifies this element with Platonic recognition (*anamnesis*), which he reinterprets in terms of a Neo-Aristotelian view of cognition as a necessary process of abstraction and generalization. He appeals, for example, to Aristotle's remark that poetry is more philosophical than history, arguing that since Plato considers all knowledge of being to be recognition and since recognition is also operative in art, the latter must also have the character of "genuine knowledge of essence" (p. 103).

Revising both Plato and Aristotle from a Heideggerian position, Gadamer further argues that the true being of a work of art as play occurs only as performance or interpretation, in other words, that the work of art is an interplay of subject and object. Through the "transformation into structure" the play of art replaces the players with the audience, and the game occurs as an interplay of the objectivity of the structure and the subjectivity of the interpreter. This does not mean that the work exists only in the mind of the reader, viewer, or listener, nor that it is a predetermined set of rules and directions to be filled in by the interpretive subject, and even less that it is an arbitrary and discontinuous series of subjective experiences. On the contrary, the audience is part of the structure of the work, that is, the interpreter is in turn being interpreted or transformed by the work, just as the player is always being played by the game. Since the game of art is repeatable, the artwork always changes at the same time that it remains the same or, as Goethe would put it, the artwork is experienced as *Dauer im Wechsel*. The true being of the work of art is the play of interpretation, and experiencing this being, according to Gadamer, is the model for genuine understanding in *all* human sciences.

Significantly, Gadamer returns to play at the very end of part 3 of his study, "Ontologische Wendung der Hermeneutik am Leitfaden der Sprache" ("The Ontological Shift of Hermeneutics Guided by Language"). Arguing for the "universal aspect" of hermeneutics, he emphasizes the linguistic foundation of the essential unity between understanding and interpretation. For Gadamer, as opposed to Fink, man's relation to the world is "absolutely and fundamentally linguistic in nature, and hence intelligible" (p. 473). Following Heidegger, Gadamer conceives of language as the advent-event of Being. Beings emerge into presence as language, which is neither a differential system of signs nor a reflection of a prelinguistic reality, but the essential unity of word and thing.

The universal ontological significance of language comes from its speculative nature, and here "speculative" is to be understood in its etymological sense of "mirroring" (from the Latin *speculum*, mirror). Yet Gadamer's notion of mirroring is no more re-presentational than that of Heidegger and Fink, and should equally be thought of in terms of *Lichtung* (lighting-clearing), bridging the gulf between the Platonic essence and appearance, between Being and Becoming. Being interprets itself through man in language, which reflects not something that was previously there, but something that presents itself and thus can be understood. Being mirrors itself in and as language, creating a distinction between its way of being and its way of presenting itself. But, just as there is a unity between the thing and its reflection in a mirror, there is a unity between the mode of being and the self-presentation of beings. The mode of being of language, then, can be understood on the analogy of the mode of being of the artwork, which in turn can be understood on the analogy of the mode of being of play. Like the work of art and like play, language does not have a "being-in-itself which is different from its reproduction or the contingency of its appearance" (p. 432); rather, it is a unity of appearance and essence, interpretation and understanding, tradition and individual subjectivity, past and present.

Gadamer now takes up his play metaphor in order to clarify what he means by the event-advent of the truth of Being as language and its relation to understanding. Here again he emphasizes the two main aspects of his concept of play: emergence into presence or self-(re)presentation and the player as a "being-played." He reminds us that "it is the game itself that plays, insofar as it draws the players into itself and thus itself becomes the actual *subjectum* of the play movement [*Spielbewegung*]" (p. 446). We do not reach truth in language, but truth reaches us, just as we do not speak through language but the latter speaks through us (cf. Heidegger's *die Sprache spricht*). By "language games" (and the reference to Wittgenstein is deliberate),[83] we must not understand a subjectivity that plays with language; rather, the "play of language itself, which addresses us, proposes and withdraws, asks and fulfils itself in the answer" (p. 446). In turn, understanding is not playing in the sense that the "person understanding holds himself back playfully and withholds a committed attitude to the claim that is made upon him." On the contrary, someone who understands is "always

83. In this regard Gadamer remarks in a note to the foreword to the second edition of *Truth and Method*: "Wittgenstein's concept of 'language-games' seemed quite natural to me when I came across it" (p. 500).

already drawn into an event through which meaning asserts itself" (p. 446). We do not claim truth, but truth claims us, and we understand despite ourselves, as it were, in the same way that a player is drawn into the game and becomes one with its movement.

Gadamer returns to art and play in *Die Aktualität des Schönen*, whose published version is based on a course of lectures on "Kunst als Spiel, Symbol, und Fest," delivered in the summer of 1974 in Salzburg. He describes his essay as a contemporary "defense of art," a defense that becomes necessary whenever the Western tradition undergoes radical changes. Modernity, whose beginnings can be traced back to the end of the Age of Reason and the dawn of Romanticism, is such a period of radical change. As in *Truth and Method*, Gadamer contends that, ever since Romanticism, art has increasingly cut itself off from community and tradition, taking refuge in its own, self-created world, and therefore again stands in danger of losing its cultural prestige. Yet Gadamer rejects the notion that what we call "art" today threatens the very identity of this concept, and attempts to redefine the identity of art in anthropological terms. He suggests that man has always experienced and will continue to experience art as play, symbol, and festivity.

In his definition of play, Gadamer again invokes its *natural* aspect as self-representation (*Selbstdarstellung*) and self-movement (*Selbstbewegung*) without any goal or purpose. To this notion of play as natural, spontaneous movement he adds Schiller's concept of play as *Überschuss*, excess of energy, which as we have seen is borrowed from Plato and is also used by Nietzsche and Heidegger in order to underscore the prerational character of play. When Gadamer turns to defining art as play, however, he emphasizes its orderly character. As in *Wahrheit und Methode*, art is a higher form of play because it has a repeatable structure (*Gebilde*), which gives it "sameness" (*Selbigkeit*) or identity and, consequently, renders it communicable. Since art as play implies an audience, it always implies meaning or intentionality: in the game of art, "something *is meant* as something, even when this something is not conceptual, pregnant, or purposeful, but rather the pure self-imposed order of the movement [*die reine selbstgesetzte Bewegungsvorschrift*]."[84] For Gadamer all artworks, including contemporary forms, preserve their identity as "works," although this identity is no longer necessarily connected with the classicist ideal of harmony and perfection; rather, it is con-

---

84. Gadamer, *Die Aktualität des Schönen: Kunst als Spiel, Symbol, und Fest* (Stuttgart, 1977), p. 30. Further citations refer to this edition; all translations are mine.

nected with the play space (*Spielraum*) that any work of art opens for and shares with the audience. It is this "hermeneutical identity" of the work that invites the participation of the audience, which is not arbitrary, but "guided" (*angeleitet*) and "pressed into a certain pattern for all possible materializations [*Erfüllungen*]" (p. 35). Even in the case of contemporary art, then, the hermeneutical principle of the artwork as an ongoing interplay of tradition and interpreter remains in force.

If in his notion of art as play Gadamer stresses the rational aspect of play, in his notion of art as symbol he attempts to deal with its prerational aspect. Like Fink, Gadamer returns to the concrete, etymological meaning of the word *symbol*: the Greek *sumbolon* originally denoted the *tessera hospitalis* or the "remembrance shard" (*Erinnerungsscherbe*). This was the half of a broken clay piece which the host gave his guest at parting while keeping the other half for himself, so that their heirs, should their paths cross, would remember or *recognize* the vows of friendship between the two houses by fitting the two broken pieces together. Gadamer also recalls the myth of the androgynous ancestors of man in Plato's *Symposium*, where the severed halves of these mythical beings wander around the world in search of each other, yearning for reunion. Thus "symbol" denotes a metonymic rather than an analogical or metaphorical relationship, and is an appropriate way of expressing the relation of beings to Being.

The artwork has a symbolical function insofar as it is the place where the coming into being of the truth of Being occurs. The work of art can be said to "represent" this truth, but this does not mean that it stands in for something that is absent, nor that it is a multiplicity of forms expressing the same content, and even less that it is an imitation of a model. Rather, the artwork represents truth in the same way that, in Christian ritual, bread and wine represent Christ's body: they do not "signify," they *are* Christ's flesh and blood (p. 46). Art as symbol constitutes a bridge between Being and appearance, and the Greeks expressed this symbolical function in their notion of art as mimesis. Here again mimesis does not mean to imitate something already known but rather to bring something into presence or make it appear (*etwas zur Darstellung bringen* [p. 47]). Thus, art as symbol and art as play come together in Gadamer's notion of self-(re)presentation: in art, as in play, something comes to presence that has never been "there" (*da*) before, emerging spontaneously and out of its own accord.

But whatever emerges into presence appears necessarily fragmented or "broken," and Gadamer, like Fink, invokes Heidegger when he describes the symbolical character of the artwork as an "irreducible counterplay of reference and concealment [*unauflösliches Widerspiel von Verweisung und Verborgung*]" (p. 44). Indirectly, then, he invokes the prerational hide-and-seek that Being plays with Dasein and that comes to pass in the work of art. The symbolical character of art points to the ambivalence and indeterminacy (*Unbestimmtheit*) of Being as well as to its determinacy, to its irrationality as well as to its rationality.

In considering art as festivity (*Fest*), Gadamer returns to the notion of structure (*Gebilde*), to which he now adds the notions of community (*Gemeinsamkeit*) and organic unity (*organische Einheit*). For Gadamer, festivity is the experience of togetherness par excellence: "Festivity means community and is the representation of community itself in its perfect form" (p. 52). Celebrating means coming together over something, and festivity exhibits the same common purpose that play does. What is essential is not "simply the coming together [*Beisammensein*] as such, but the intention which unites all participants and prevents them from lapsing into individual conversations or splitting into individual experiences [*Einzelerlebnisse*]" (p. 54). Gadamer proceeds to describe the time structure of the festivity—which is also characteristic of that of artistic play—as a recurring unity. Many festivities are connected with the seasonal cycle and they return to men, just as seasons do. Their recurrence does not depend on a time order (*Zeitanordnung*), but the time order depends on their recurrence, as such religious holidays as Christmas and Easter demonstrate. Festivity, like the work of art, has its own time, which may be called "fulfilled time" (*erfüllte Zeit*) or "spontaneous time" (*Eigenzeit*; cf. the use of this word in contemporary physics, where it is usually translated as "proper time"), in contradistinction to the "empty time" (*leere Zeit*) of everyday experience. Spontaneous time covers such basic time phenomena as childhood, youth, maturity, old age, and death, eluding clock time: it comes into presence or disappears all at once and cannot be divided into or measured by time units.

*Eigenzeit* is also characteristic of what we call the "organic unity" of a work of art. This does not mean that the artwork is born, reaches maturity, and dies like any other organism, but rather that the experience of every instant of the work is related to the experience of the whole. As in the case of a living organism, the work's intentionality is directed toward itself, toward its own vital activities, and according to Gadamer, it is this kind of self-directed intentionality that Kant has in mind when he describes art as *Zweckmässigkeit ohne Zweck* (p. 57). The work of art has its own "internally structured unity" (*in sich strukturierte Einheit*), just as it has its own *Eigenzeit* (p. 57).

In his conclusion Gadamer again stresses the hermeneutical nature of *all* art. Even in contemporary, avant-garde art forms, whether consciously or not, tradition is at work or indeed at play, and Gadamer invokes for the last time his metaphor of the player as plaything in order to describe the "power of the tradition" (*Macht der Tradition*) over the interpreter (p. 64). Finally, for Gadamer, as for Schiller and Neo-platonic thought in general, the greatest accomplishment of art is the transformation into an enduring structure of that which is unformed, incoherent, and transitory.

My brief examination of *Truth and Method* and *Die Aktualität des Schönen* has revealed the fluctuating character of Gadamer's concept of play. As opposed to Fink, who, following Nietzsche, is openly committed to a view of play as a prerational manifestation of power, Gadamer stresses the rational aspects of play, especially in their artistic guise.[85] For Gadamer, art as play is primarily the orderly "transformation into structure" of a chaotic, arbitrary, and purposeless natural movement. Like Fink, Gadamer acknowledges the original link between art as mimesis and play, but unlike Fink he ignores the Platonic decision through which art as mimesis-play is severed from knowledge

85. It is highly revealing that in his review of Fink's *Spiel als Weltsymbol*, in *Philosophische Rundschau*, Gadamer objects to Fink's view of play as goal free: "Charakterisiert es wirklich das Spielverhältnis als solches, dass es von der Zweck-welt frei ist und dass es seine Freiheit nur aus solchem Gegensatz hat? Ich meine, indem es Spiel ist, ist es zugleich unter seine eigenen Regeln und Gesetze gestellt, die auch ihre Strenge haben" (p. 6). But, as we have seen, Fink (or Nietzsche) does not deny that play may be goal oriented and follow rules. He only denies that the "Zweckwelt" is primary and that play should ultimately be subordinated to it. In other words, play may include, but also go beyond, games. Throughout his review, Gadamer visibly ignores the third or "symbolic" aspect of Fink's notion of play, i.e., play in its cosmic relation to the world-totality, this being also the (prerational) aspect that Fink discerns in Nietzsche's *Spiel der Kräfte*. Although Gadamer, following Heidegger, wants to separate the concept of play from its allegedly "subjectiv-ist" interpretations, he mostly shies away from Fink's (and Nietzsche's) prerational view of play as a violent contest of physical forces, as well as from their *Macht-philosophie* in general (see, e.g., nn. 34 and 35 to part 1, sec. 2 of *Truth and Method*, pp. 512–513). Yet this does not mean that Gadamer actually manages to transcend this *Machtphilosophie*: see, for example, his essay "The Power of Reason," trans. H. W. Johnstone, Jr., in *Man and World* 3 (1970): 5–15, and, especially, *Dialogue and Dialectic: Eight Hermeneutical Studies on Plato*, trans. P. C. Smith (New Haven, Conn., 1980), chap. 3, "Plato and the Poets." I briefly examine this essay in *God of Many Names*, chap. 4.

and truth and is turned into mere imitation thereof. He attempts to restore the cognitive value of art by revising Plato's notion of "recognition" via Aristotle, not realizing that in his *Poetics* the latter takes the Platonic decision for granted and thereby perpetuates the separation between art and knowledge throughout the Classical and Neoclassical aesthetic tradition. Consequently, Gadamer's examination of the aesthetic phenomenon in Western thought does not go far enough: he largely limits himself to a critique of Romantic subjectivist aesthetics in terms of the Cartesian division between subject and object, without probing into the pre-Cartesian history of this division. For Gadamer, as for Heidegger and Postmodernism in general, Romantic aesthetic subjectivism and Cartesian scientistic objectivism are the chief villains in the drama of Western consciousness. In contrast to other artist-metaphysicians, however, Gadamer advocates a return to a holistic, prerational mode of thought without being prepared to accept the full consequences of such a return (that is, giving up the Platonic and Aristotelian rationalist tradition). On the one hand, he obscures the archaic link between play, art, and unmediated power, emphasizing the orderly, tradition-oriented character of human play. On the other hand, he operates with Heidegger's prerational notions of aesthetics and play, which view man as both player and plaything in the violent play of Being (a modern, Heideggerian version of the archaic play of Becoming). By relating Western tradition to this play of Being, Gadamer ends up giving universal validity to a man-made, power-oriented value system that has, under various guises, prevailed and perpetuated itself in the Western world for the past two thousand years.

## 3·3  Gilles Deleuze: The Play of Simulacra

Deleuze's return to Nietzsche can best be understood against the Hegelian and Marxian background of Parisian intellectual life in the 1950s, from which he attempts to distance himself. If Heidegger's and Fink's Nietzsche is primarily antimetaphysical and antiscientistic, Deleuze's Nietzsche is primarily anti-Hegelian and antidialectical: He is the genealogist of morals, introducing "meaning" and "value" into classical philosophy; he is the diagnostician of *ressentiment*, bad conscience, and nihilism versus the master-slave dialectic, unhappy consciousness, and alienation; finally, he is the transvaluator of all values through the affirmation of a will to power, understood as an interplay of active physical forces, rather than as a transcendental, voluntaristic, or subjectivist principle. Because, unlike Fink or Gadamer, Deleuze does not return to Nietzsche via Heidegger, his concept of play does not operate in terms of the ontological difference. Yet like Heidegger, Fink, and to a certain extent Gadamer, Deleuze does turn away from both a rationalist and a subjectivist interpretation of play, and thus remains close to Nietzsche's prerational view of play as *Spiel der Kräfte*. Even though Deleuze does not speak of the "play of the world" or the "play of being," his philosophical project cannot properly be understood outside a notion of play as a fundamental mode of existence. As in the case of the other artist-metaphysicians, this notion grounds his thought at the same time that it itself remains groundless. In Deleuze, the correlation of play and power is as firm as in Nietzsche but, as in Nietzsche and the other artist-metaphysicians, the concept of power itself—as the implicit or explicit foundation of Western metaphysics—remains unquestioned. I shall briefly look at Deleuze's Nietzschean notion of play as he presents it in *Nietzsche and Philosophy* (*Nietzsche et la philosophie*, 1962) and then as he uses it in his later work, specifically in *The Logic of Sense* (*Logique du sens*, 1969).[86]

In his extremely influential study of Nietzsche, Deleuze introduces play in chapter 1, "Le tragique," in relation to Nietzsche's view of tragedy. Here, Deleuze emphasizes two main variants of what I have called the prerational play concept: play as the innocent, exuberant, and excessive manifestation of power, and play as risk taking or as chance-necessity. For Nietzsche the tragic is the expression of the active or affirmative forces in culture, symbolized by the divine patron of tragedy, Dionysus: "It is Dionysus' task to make us graceful, to teach us to dance, to give us the instinct of play. Even a historian hostile or indifferent to Nietzschean themes recognizes joy, buoyant gracefulness, mobility and ubiquity as characteristic of Dionysus."[87]

86. For other views of Deleuze's thought see M. Foucault, "*Theatrum philosophicum*," *Critique*, no. 282 (1970): 885–908; *Gilles Deleuze*, special issue of *L'Arc* 49 (Aix-en-Provence, 1972); J. E. Leigh, "Deleuze, Nietzsche and the Eternal Return," *Philosophy Today* 22 (Fall 1978): 206–223; Vincent P. Pecora, "Deleuze's Nietzsche and Post-Structuralist Thought," *Substance* 14 (1986): 34–50; Vincent Descombes, *Le même et l'autre* (Paris, 1979), especially pp. 182–195; J. J. Lecercle, *Philosophy in the Looking Glass* (London, 1985); and Ronald Bogue, *Deleuze and Guattari* (London, 1989).

87. Gilles Deleuze, *Nietzsche and Philosophy*, trans. H. Tomlinson (New York, 1983), p. 18. Further citations refer to this edition. I have used in parallel the French text of *Nietzsche et la philosophie* (Paris, 1962).

The spirit of play characterizes the "innocence" of existence itself. Innocence is the "truth of multiplicity" and "derives immediately from the principles of the philosophy of force and will" (p. 22). All that is relates to a force that interprets it. In turn, every force relates to what it can do, from which it is inseparable. It is this way of relating, of affirming or being affirmed, that is "innocent" and "just." But modern man prefers to separate force from what it can do, and creates grotesque, slavelike representations of force and will. He splits the will in two, sets up a "neutral" subject with an ability to act or refrain from action, employs a distorted concept of justice, invents morality and religion, and thus becomes divided against himself, becomes a bad player: "*Alas, we are bad players.* Innocence is the game [*jeu*] of existence, of force and will. Existence affirmed and appreciated, force not separated, the will not divided in two [*dédoublée*]—this is the first approximation of innocence" (p. 23).

The tragic thinker par excellence is Heraclitus, because for him life is essentially innocent and just and because he "understands existence on the basis of an *instinct of play* . . . as an *aesthetic phenomenon* rather than a moral or a religious one" (p. 23). He is also the philosopher of the affirmation of becoming, and here Deleuze presents for the first time his Nietzschean concepts of being as becoming, unity as multiplicity, and repetition as difference, which will have a crucial role in his later work and can hardly be understood outside Nietzsche's notion of play as *Spiel der Kräfte*. According to Deleuze, when Heraclitus affirms becoming, he also affirms the being of becoming (*l'être du devenir*), and these two thoughts are inseparable: there is no being beyond becoming, there is nothing beyond multiplicity. The relationship between being and becoming, between one and many can be understood in terms of a game (*jeu*) played by an artist, a child, and a god—three embodiments of Dionysus (p. 25).

The two moments of the Dionysian game, the affirming of becoming and the affirming of the being of becoming, can also be seen as the two moments of a dice throw (*un coup de dés*): the rolling of the dice and their coming to rest. These two moments bear the names of chance and necessity, and their relationship is identical to that of the many and one, or becoming and being (p. 26).

It is true that Nietzsche identifies chance with multiplicity, fragmentariness, and chaos. But he turns all these notions into an affirmation. Thus, what he calls "necessity" is not the abolition of chance, but the combination of chance itself. There is only one combination of chance as such, one way of combining all the fragments of chance, one fatal number, and it is sufficient for the player to affirm chance only once in order to bring back the winning number, the number that allows him to repeat the dice throw. To affirm chance is to know how to play. But man is a bad player, because he counts on a great number of throws—on the use of causality and probability—to produce the winning combination. "To abolish chance by holding it in the grip of causality and finality, to count on the repetition of throws rather than affirming chance, to anticipate a result instead of affirming necessity—these are all the operations of a bad player" (p. 27). To be a good player is to recognize that the universe is purposeless, that it has no cause or goal, and hence to affirm chance in one throw (cf. Fink).

The two moments of the dice throw cannot be thought apart, and it is during the second moment that the eternal return is affirmed and the two moments become one. The eternal return is the outcome of the throw or the affirmation of necessity, the number that reunites all the fragments of chance. But the eternal return is also the return of the first moment, the repetition of the throw, that is, the repetition of chance itself. For Nietzsche, in contrast to the whole metaphysical tradition, chance and necessity, chaos and cycle, becoming and eternal return are not mutually exclusive but rather are two simultaneous moments of the same Dionysian game.[88]

At the very end of his study, after a detailed analysis of Nietzsche's concepts of *ressentiment*, bad conscience, guilt, the ascetic ideal, and nihilism as products of reactive or negative forces, Deleuze returns to play. In the last chapter, "Le surhomme: contre la dialectique," Deleuze contrasts what he calls the "play of difference" (*jeu de la différence*), characteristic of the will to power, to the labor (in the sense of both work and suffering) of dialectics. Although both affirmation and negation are qualities of the will to power, their relation is not univocal

88. Deleuze is now in a position to contrast Nietzsche's *coup de dés* to Mallarmé's. He argues that although there are obvious similarities between Nietzsche's and Mallarmé's concepts of chance and necessity, these similarities remain superficial; unlike Nietzsche, Mallarmé "always understood necessity as the abolition of chance." Moreover, Deleuze subscribes to the common view that Mallarmé's poem "Un coup de dés" belongs to the "old metaphysical thought of the duality of worlds; chance is like the existence which must be denied, necessity like the character of the pure idea or the eternal essence" (p. 33). For a different view of Mallarmé's *coup de dés*, see J. Derrida, "La double séance," in *La dissémination* (Paris, 1978), where Derrida engages in a covert polemic with Deleuze's traditional interpretation of Mallarmé's "Mimique."

(*univoque*). Negation opposes itself to affirmation, but affirmation differs (*diffère*) from negation. To think of affirmation as opposing negation would mean to bring the negative within it. Whereas opposition is the essence of negation, it has no place in affirmation, whose essence is difference. Affirmation is the "enjoyment [*jouissance*] and play of its own difference just as negation is the suffering [*douleur*] and work [*travail*] of the opposition proper to it" (pp. 188–189). Dialectics is precisely the work of the negative, which thrives on opposition and therefore is a reactive force, a particularly advanced form of *ressentiment* and nihilism.

For Deleuze, the Nietzschean eternal return does not include the return of the reactive or negative. There are, however, two kinds of negation: a reactive one, belonging to dialectics, *ressentiment*, and the ascetic ideal; and an active one, saying no to negation itself and becoming affirmative through a point of conversion or transmutation. Through transmutation, "opposition ceases its labor and difference begins its play. . . . Instead of the labor of opposition or the suffering of the negative we have the warlike play of difference, affirmation and the joy of destruction."

Finally, according to Deleuze, the play of difference in the will to power can also be seen as a function of both Zarathustra and Dionysus, the "two unequal genetic lines" (p. 193) that nevertheless converge in the end. In relation to Zarathustra, play, which Deleuze now divides into dance, laughter, and dice throwing, is an affirmative power of transmutation-transvaluation: "Dance transmutes heavy into light, laughter transmutes suffering into joy and the game of throwing [the dice] transmutes low into high." In relation to Dionysus, play is an affirmative power of reflection and development: dance "affirms becoming and the being of becoming; laughter, roars [*éclats*] of laughter, affirm the multiple and the one of the multiple; the dice game affirms chance and the necessity of chance" (p. 194).

In *Logique du sens*, Deleuze places his Nietzschean notion of play in the context of a philosophy of becoming which now, however, he attributes less to Nietzsche and the Presocratics than to the Stoics and the Epicureans. In a crucial chapter, strategically placed in the middle of the volume and entitled, "Dix-huitième série [de paradoxes], des trois images de philosophe" (Eighteenth series [of paradoxes]: On the three images of the philosopher), Deleuze distinguishes three kinds of philosophy that arose in ancient Greece and have since recurred throughout Western thought. First, there is a "philosophy of depths" (*philosophie de la profondeur*), invented by the Presocratics, then a "philosophy of heights" (*philosophie de la hauteur*), invented by Plato, and finally a "philosophy of surfaces" (*philosophie de la surface*), invented by the Stoics. The "great Stoic discovery" challenges both the Presocratics and the Platonists, being characterized by the "autonomy of the surface, emancipated of height and depth, against height and depth; the discovery of incorporeal events, sense [*sens*] or effects [*effets*] that are irreducible to deep bodies [*corps profonds*] or to high Ideas [*Idées hautes*]."[89] All that occurs or is said takes place at the surface. The "double sense of the surface, the continuity of the verso [*l'envers*] and the recto [*l'endroit*] replace height and depth. . . . The sense occurs and plays at the surface" (p. 158). This does not mean that the surface is devoid of mystery and requires no exploration; it is simply that the exploration takes place horizontally, rather than vertically, implying a geography, rather than a speleology or a meteorology (in the etymological sense of these terms). As Borges suggests in "The Garden of Forking Paths," the deepest and most tortuous labyrinth is the straight line.

According to Deleuze, Nietzsche's project of reversing Platonism entails passing by the surface or "pure becoming" (*devenir pur*), but Nietzsche does not remain there, resinking into the Presocratic depths. What Deleuze himself attempts to do, in *Logique du sens*, is to bring Nietzsche back to the surface with the aid of the Stoics and elaborate a philosophy of surfaces or a logic of becoming that would replace the logic of being that has long dominated Western thought, first in its Platonic and then in its Hegelian guise. For this purpose, Deleuze turns, like Heidegger and other artist-metaphysicians, to art and aesthetics, in this particular case primarily to the literary work of Lewis Carroll, claiming that this work already contains a model for a *logique du sens*, based on "pure becoming." What are the basic principles of a logic of pure becoming, in contradistinction to a logic of being or presence? First of all, the world of becoming is two rather than three dimensional, and therefore one needs both to ignore such (traditional) logical principles as the *tertium non datur* or the rule of noncontradiction and to redefine such notions as space, time, event, cause, effect, necessity, chance, structure, sense, and—what is of particular concern here—play.

Deleuze begins by defining the notion of pure or unlimited becoming as a paradox: Because it always eludes the present, becoming is an infinite, simultaneous double movement in opposite directions (*sens*), the past and the future. In *Through the Looking Glass*, for example, when

89. Deleuze, *Logique du sens* (Paris, 1969), p. 158. Further citations refer to this edition; all translations are mine.

Alice grows taller, at the same time she grows smaller; she becomes taller than she was and smaller than she becomes: "Such is the simultaneity of becoming whose proper nature is to evade the present. Insofar as it evades the present, becoming does not tolerate the separation or the distinction between before and after, or past and future. It is the essence of becoming to run or pull simultaneously in two directions [*sens*]: Alice does not grow without diminishing and vice versa. Good sense [*bon sens*] says that all things have a determinable sense-direction [*sens*], but the paradox affirms both senses at the same time" (p. 9).

Deleuze's play on the word *sens*, which he employs in this passage to denote both "direction," that is, a spatial-concrete notion, and "meaning," that is, a semantic-ideal notion, underscores the fact that a *logique du sens* blurs the distinction between concrete and abstract, real and ideal, implying an essential continuity between things (as spatial entities) and words (as abstract or ideal entities). In a two-dimensional universe, without height or depth, things and words, as well as space and time, situate themselves on the same infinite line, which runs simultaneously in both directions.

Deleuze traces his notion of *pur devenir* or *devenir illimité* to Plato and then to the Stoics. Plato acknowledges two ontological realms: the realm of being, where things can be measured, defined, or limited, as temporary fixed quantities; and the realm of becoming, without measure or limits, without a present, where past and future, lack and excess, small and large coincide in the simultaneity of an intractable matter. This Platonic duality is not that between the intelligible and the sensible, or between Ideas and Matter. Rather, it concerns that which receives the action of the Ideas and that which eludes this action. It is not the distinction between model and copy, but that between copy and simulacrum: "Pure becoming, the unlimited, pertains to the simulacrum insofar as it evades the action of the Ideas, insofar as it contests both model and copy" (p. 10). Whereas Plato banishes the realm of pure becoming to the bottomless depth of the cosmos, the Stoics bring it literally to the surface.

The Stoics redistribute the Platonic cosmic hierarchy by making a distinction between bodies and "incorporeals." The bodies have physical qualities, tensions, actions, and passions, and create "states of things" (*états de choses*) by combining with other bodies according to an active-passive principle—here it becomes obvious that Deleuze interprets the Stoics in terms of Nietzsche's typology of forces. Ultimately, there is a unity of all the bodies in the primordial Fire, whence they all come and to which they all return. The unity of bodies exists in a cosmic, eternal present: it is only the bodies that fill space and only the present that fills time. There are only causes and no effects among the bodies: they are all causes for one another, and the unity of these causes is called Destiny, stretching into a perpetual present.

Although the bodies produce *effects* (*effets*), these effects are not other bodies, but "incorporeals." The effects are not physical properties but logical attributes. They are not things or states of things, but *events*. One cannot say that they "exist, but rather that they subsist or insist, having a minimum of being which is proper to that which is not a thing, a non-existent entity" (p. 13). Their time is not the present but an infinite division of this present into past and future. The Stoics do not acknowledge three successive temporal dimensions, but offer two simultaneous readings of time: only the present has a real existence, but only the past and the future "insist" in time, dividing each present ad infinitum. Thus the Stoics distinguish between "two levels of being: on the one hand, the profound and real being, the force [*la force*]; on the other hand, the level of events [*faits*] that play at the surface of being, forming an infinite multiplicity of incorporeal beings."[90]

According to Deleuze, the Stoics effect a far-reaching reversal of Platonism. It is not only that they bring to the surface what Plato has relegated to the abyss, but also that they bring the Ideas down to earth, denying them any high spirituality. Ideality, causality, and temporality lose their height and depth and become a play of surfaces or a play of *simulacra* (pp. 17–18). The events, understood as "effects" in the sense of both results of a cause (the combination of bodies) and sound or visual effects, are coextensive with becoming, while becoming is in turn coextensive with language. The Stoics are fond of paradoxes, which always occur at the borderline between things and sentences. For example, Chrysippus teaches: "If you say something, this something comes out of your mouth; if you say *chariot*, a chariot comes out of your mouth."

Deleuze compares the employment of such paradoxes to the teaching of Zen Buddhism and to Anglo-American nonsense word games. "What is the most profound is the immediate; on the other hand the immediate resides in language" (p. 18). This is precisely the kind of paradox that Lewis Carroll employs. If at the beginning of *Alice in Wonderland* the mystery of events is still sought in the depth of the

90. Deleuze bases his view of the Stoic doctrine on Emile Bréhier, *La théorie des incorporels dans l'ancien stoïcisme* (Paris, 1928).

earth, where the bodies combine and coexist, toward the end of the book the movement of vertical submerging or diving is replaced by horizontal sliding, the depth becomes surface, creatures and objects become flat, like playing-card figures. It is by following the borderline, by walking along the surface, that one passes from the corporeal to the incorporeal, from one side to its reverse, as in a Moebius ring. Alice's many adventures turn into a single great one: the adventure of "coming to the surface, of disavowing the false depths, of discovering that all takes place on the borderline" (p. 19).

Deleuze constructs a whole series of paradoxes as he unfolds his "logic of sense" derived from the Stoic doctrine of the incorporeals. The paradox that is most relevant here is what Deleuze calls "ideal play" or "ideal game" (*jeu idéal*). In a chapter entitled "Dixième série [de para-doxes], du jeu idéal" (Tenth series [of paradoxes]: On ideal play), Deleuze develops a theory of "pure play" (*jeu pur*) that is a consequence of his logic of pure becoming. Alluding to such famous Carrollian playful inventions as the Caucus race and the croquet party, Deleuze draws a distinction between "normal" or "ordinary" and "ideal" or "pure" games. Normal games are those which we encounter in everyday life. Although they can be divided into games of skill and games of chance, all ordinary games are ultimately governed by rational rules, designed to restrain their arbitrary and aleatory tendencies. Such games refer us to "another kind of activity, work or morality, of whom they are a caricature or a counterpart, but whose elements they also integrate in a new order." In cases like Pascal's bet or Leibniz's chess-playing God, play functions as an explicit model only because it itself implicitly imitates a nonplayful one: "the moral model of the Good or the Better, the economic model of causes and effects, of means and ends" (p. 75). Finally, the radical difference between normal and pure games resides in their attitude toward chance. Ordinary games *"retain chance only at certain points*, and leave the rest to the mechanical unfolding of conse-quences, or to skill as the art of causality." Pure games, on the other hand, leave *everything* to chance. They adopt chance in its totality and make it into an object of affirmation (p. 75).

The characterization of ideal play as an affirmation of the totality of chance shows, then, that Deleuze places his interpretation of Nietz-sche's notion of chance and eternal return in the service of the Stoic doctrine of the incorporeals. In this regard, therefore, he does not depart as radically from Nietzsche as one might have thought. Deleuze also retains Nietzsche's view of the cosmos as a play of physical forces in his interpretation of the Stoic doctrine of bodies. Consequently we now have two simultaneous eternal returns: the return of the bodies and their combinatory states, measured by a cyclical present that ceaselessly reabsorbs or contracts past and future; and the return of events-effects, which infinitely divide the present into past and future, affirming chance all at once, as a recurring totality of throws. We now also have two kinds of play: the deep play of forces, combining bodies according to an active-passive principle, which is an avatar of Nietzsche's division of affirmative forces into active and passive or "acted upon"; and the pure or ideal play of effects-events, the play of simulacra, affirming chance as a *lancet unique*, which distributes each throw along an unlimited, aleatory line, whose points can in turn be divided into infinite, coresonant series. Whereas the deep play of forces (which remains unnamed but implicit throughout *Logique du sens* and reappears only later on, in *L'anti-Oedipe*, as the play of the "desiring-machines" or the "bodies without organs") concerns the bodies and their combinatory states, the ideal or pure play is the province of (philosophical) thought and art:

> For only thought can *affirm the totality* of chance, making it into an *object of affirmation*. And if one attempts to play this ideal game anywhere other than in the realm of thought, nothing takes place, and if one attempts to produce anything other than a work of art, nothing is produced. This is, then, the play reserved for thought and art, where there are only victories for those who know how to play, that is, how to affirm and ramify chance instead of dividing it *in order to* dominate it, *in order to* bet, *in order to* win. This play, which takes place only in thought and results only in a work of art, is also what makes thought and art real, disturbing the reality, the morality and the economy of the world. (p. 76)

The word *reality* in this passage has obvious polemical overtones: the so-called real world of economy, morality, and politics is as much a world of surfaces or of events-effects as the world of thought and art. For Deleuze, in keeping with the Stoic doctrine, the real world would be that of the bodies and their combinatory states, remaining in the realm of the physical and the unconscious but at the same time producing both consciousness and events-effects or the world of simulacra. Here, however, as in his book on Nietzsche, Deleuze directs his polemic both against the dichotomy of play and seriousness (work, dialectics) and against rational notions of play. Like Nietzsche and other artist-metaphysicians, he reverses the Platonic hierarchy of good and bad play, based on Reason's disciplinary rules. For Deleuze good play, which he calls, probably with deliberate irony, "ideal" or "pure," is precisely that which for Plato is bad play, that is, the play of chance, "without rules, without winners or losers, and without responsibility, a game of innocence and a Caucus race, where skill and chance are indistinguishable" (p. 76). Bad play, on the other hand, is the one played with the loaded dice of Reason, which attempts to control chance through (bad) repetition, causality, and morality. The moralizing bet of Pascal is foul play (*tricherie*), the economic combinations of Leibniz are a bad throw (*mauvais coup*). These rational or normal games are certainly not the "world as the work of art" (p. 76), and here the allusion to Nietzsche is as transparent as it can be.

Moreover, art is openly associated, if not identified, with *la pensée*, philosophical thought, a far cry from Kant's, or even Schiller's, view of art as mere appearance or simulacrum of knowledge. The reversal of Platonism is again obvious: good knowledge is the aesthetic one, bad knowledge is the rational one. Like Nietzsche and other artist-metaphysicians, Deleuze repeatedly claims that his writings are best understood as aesthetic play. In his foreword to *Logique du sens*, for instance, he describes his book as "un essai de roman logique et psychoanalytique" (p. 7).[91] His discourse no longer seeks philosophical justification through the traditional or Platonic claims to truth and (rational) knowledge, but through play. This means that it no longer has to justify itself at all, or that it is its own justification (cf. Heidegger's *es spielet weil es spielet*)—art, like the play of the world, is notoriously "irresponsible" and "innocent." At the same time, however, as in the case of other artist-metaphysicians, it would be an error to claim that Deleuze abandons philosophy as a discipline (in all the senses of this term); to do this, he would have to abandon his view of the world as a play of forces. Rather, Deleuze rediscovers and reaffirms the prerational beginnings of metaphysics in poetic thought as a playful manifestion of unmediated power.

## 3·4  Writing and Play: Jacques Derrida

If Deleuze, in his later work (written in collaboration with Félix Guattari), relinquishes the play of simulacra for the deep play of bodies

91. Cf. Deleuze's foreword to *Différence et répétition* (Paris, 1968): "Un livre de philosophie doit être pour une part une espèce très particulière de roman policier, pour une autre part une sorte de science-fiction" (p. 3). Cf. also his remarks on Borges, Pierre Menard, and the fictional devices of the contemporary history of philosophy (pp. 4–5).

and active forces, Jacques Derrida continues the exploration of the world of unlimited lines and flat surfaces, or the world of becoming as a nonexistent present, infinitely divided into past and future. Nietzsche, as the relentless critic of Western onto-theology and the advocate of the cosmic play of becoming, is as important a landmark for Derrida as he is for Deleuze, but Derrida's Nietzsche is again mediated by Heidegger and the ontological difference. This difference, however, has in turn passed through the Stoic and Deleuzian doctrine of the play of simulacra, losing its ontological "depth," and turning into a linguistic event-effect (*différance*). Like Heidegger, Derrida identifies the foundation of Western metaphysics with the concept of being, understood as presence (*ousia*). But unlike Heidegger, he concentrates on "writing" (*l'écriture*) as what has constantly been excluded in a metaphysics of presence, which therefore is also primarily a metaphysics of the spoken word or the *logos*. In place of a metaphysics of presence, Derrida proposes a "grammatology" or a philosophy of the *gramme* (in Greek, letter or writing), based on a concept of language as sign, which he inherits from both Saussure and structuralist linguistics. Although Derrida preserves the double structure of the sign (signified and signifier), he no longer conceives of reference in terms of a transcendental signified (which in traditional metaphysics is as a rule identified with God), but in terms of *différance*, a play (*jeu*) of differences and oppositions which generates and distributes meaning while it itself remains meaningless. At the same time, Derrida's grammatology is a philosophy of becoming, where the present as such has no place, being perpetually "deferred" as an absent, imaginary origin. Thus, *différance* as a pure play of simulacra has both a spatial and a temporal component. The spatial component concerns the play of differences which Derrida traces back to Nietzsche's play of forces as interpreted by Deleuze. The temporal component concerns the infinite division of the present into past and future, which transforms Heidegger's ontological difference into a play of events-effects where the present is always deferred in two directions at once. The spatial and the temporal components of *différance* are inseparable and have to be thought of as one and the same movement: Derrida coins this word in order to convey the meaning of both "differing" and "deferring," an ambivalence that escapes the common French word, *différence*. The play of *différance*, then, is Heidegger's play of Being, understood as Nietzsche's play of forces, in turn understood as Deleuze's play of simulacra.

Play permeates Derrida's entire discourse—indeed he is perhaps the most playful of the artist-metaphysicians under consideration in this section—but here I shall examine only one essay in some detail: "La structure, le signe, et le jeu dans le discours des sciences humaines" (Structure, sign, and play in the discourse of the human sciences), included in *L'écriture et la différence* (1967). I have chosen to discuss this early essay both because it has proven extremely influential, especially in the United States (where it has become a sort of Poststructuralist manifesto) and because it contains relatively extensive theoretical statements on play that are not so easy to find in Derrida's more recent work. As in the case of Heidegger and some of the other artist-metaphysicians, play has an ambivalent status in Derrida's discourse: it founds this discourse at the same time that it itself remains without theoretical foundation.[92]

In "La structure, le signe, et le jeu," which was first presented as a paper at the 1966 International Colloquium on Critical Languages and the Sciences of Man at Johns Hopkins University, Derrida introduces his notion of "free play" (*jeu libre*), the equivalent of Deleuze's "pure" or "ideal" play and Fink's "play without player(s)." Interrogating the traditional notions of structure and sign in their relationship to *episteme* (knowledge) and *ousia* (presence), Derrida contends that these notions presuppose the existence of a "center, a point of presence, a fixed origin," located both within and outside the structure. The function of

---

92. Because Derrida's concept of play (as much as his thought in general) has been given ample treatment in recent years, I have limited my discussion to its most relevant aspects. Among the numerous critical commentaries on Derrida's work are Edward Said, "The Problem of Textuality: Two Exemplary Positions," *Critical Inquiry* 4 (Summer 1978): 673–714; Rodolphe Gasché, "Deconstruction as Criticism," *Glyph* 6 (1980): 177–215 and, more recently, *The Tain of the Mirror* (Cambridge, Mass., 1986); Robert Magliola, *Derrida on the Mend* (W. Lafayette, Ind., 1984); and Irene E. Harvey, *Derrida and the Economy of Difference* (Bloomington, Ind., 1986). On Derrida and play see, among others, James Hans, "Derrida and Free Play," *MLN* 94 (1979): 809–823; Robert R. Wilson, "In Palamedes' Shadow: Game and Play Concepts Today," *Canadian Review of Comparative Literature* 12 (June 1985), esp. 190–196; and Christine Froula, "Quantum Physics/ Postmodern Metaphysics: The Nature of Jacques Derrida," *Western Humanities Review* 39 (Winter 1985): 287–311, esp. 305–311. For an attempt at a synthesis between German hermeneutics and French poststructuralism, based on a phenomenology of play, see James Hans, "Hermeneutics, Play, and Deconstruction," *Philosophy Today*, 24 (Winter 1980): 299–317, and, especially, *The Play of the World* (Amherst, Mass., 1981). See also the first section of my essay "Mimesis and Contemporary French Theory," pp. 66–79, where I examine the relationship between mimesis and play in "La pharmacie de Platon" and "La double séance."

this center is not only to "orient, balance, and organize the structure . . . but above all to make sure that the organizing principle of the structure would limit what we might call the *play* of the structure."[93]

The center opens, but at the same time closes off the play of the elements within a given structure. In this sense, the concept of centered structure betrays a concept of play, "constituted on the basis of a fundamental immobility and a reassuring certitude, which itself is beyond the reach of play." Through centered play, one can master an anxiety that is "invariably the result of a certain mode of being implicated in the game, of being caught by the game, of being as it were at stake in the game from the outset" (p. 279). To this concept of structure as a centered, limited, or grounded play, Derrida opposes the concept of structure as a decentered, limitless, and groundless play, associating the latter with a rupture or a new turn in Western thought:

> It was necessary to begin thinking that there was no center, that the center could not be thought in the form of a present-being, that the center had no natural site, that it was not a fixed locus but a function, a sort of nonlocus in which an infinite number of sign-substitutions came into play. This was the moment when language invaded the universal problematic, the moment when, in the absence of a center or origin, everything became discourse—provided we can agree on this word—that is to say, a system in which the central signified, the original or transcendental signified, is never absolutely present outside a system of differences. The absence of the transcendental signified extends the domain and the play of signification infinitely. (p. 280)

Derrida pointedly relates this new turn to Nietzsche, Heidegger, and Freud, and then proceeds to consider the case of contemporary structuralist ethnology as practiced by Lévi-Strauss. For Derrida this ethnology exhibits both an awareness of the decentered, groundless play of the structure and an experiencing of this awareness as a loss of and nostalgia for presence. Derrida identifies the structuralist theme of "broken immediacy," which still turns yearningly toward the absent, irretrievably lost origin, with the "*negative*, nostalgic, guilty, Rousseauistic side of the thinking on play." He then formulates the "other side" of the structuralist thinking on play in terms of Deleuze's interpretation of Nietzsche, which in turn he recasts in a grammatological vocabulary. To

---

93. Derrida, "Structure, Sign, and Play in the Discourse of the Human Sciences," trans. A. Bass and R. Macksey, in *Writing and Difference* (Chicago, 1978), p. 278. Further citations refer to this edition.

the reactive and nihilistic structuralist view of play, Derrida opposes the "Nietzschean *affirmation*, that is the joyous affirmation of the play of the world and of the innocence of becoming, the affirmation of a world of signs without fault, without truth, and without origin which is offered to an active as opposed to a *reactive* interpretation." The immediate effect of this Nietzschean affirmation is a transmutation, whereby the "noncenter" is determined "*otherwise than as a loss of center*," and the secure play of the centered structure becomes a "play without security," governed by absolute chance, in which affirmation "surrenders itself to *genetic* indetermination, to the seminal adventure of the trace" (p. 292).

Finally, for Derrida there are two interpretations of structure, sign, and play, as well as two interpretations of interpretation. The first "seeks to decipher, dreams of deciphering, a truth or an origin which escapes play and the order of the sign, and which lives the necessity of inter-pretation as an exile." The second turns away from the origin, "affir-ming" play and trying to go "beyond man and humanism, the name of man being that being who, throughout the history of metaphysics or of ontotheology—in other words throughout his history—has dreamed of full presence, the reassuring foundation, the origin and the end of play" (p. 292). In turn, there are two kinds of play, according to the kind of structure that one adopts: the play of a centered and limited structure, in which the signifiers are strictly regulated and controlled by a transcendental signified; and the play of a decentered and limitless structure in which the signifiers become emancipated and obey no rule, except for the one of absolute chance. These two Derridian kinds of play clearly belong one to the rational, and the other to the prerational, group of play concepts. Interestingly enough, Derrida affirms the im-possibility of choosing between them, preferring instead to trace their differential play or *différance*, in an attempt to discover their condition of possibility, both in historical and logical terms (p. 293). Yet this self-imposed task has so far remained unfinished, and in practice, like all the other artist-metaphysicians, Derrida has been *forced* to choose between the two play concepts. This choice is already evident in "Structure, Sign, and Play," where he echoes Heidegger's description of the Play of Being in *Der Satz vom Grund*: "Play is always play of absence and presence, but if it is to be thought radically, play must be conceived of before the alternative of presence and absence. Being must be conceived as pres-ence or absence on the basis of the possibility of play and not the other way around" (p. 292). Through this Heideggerian choice, Derrida becomes not only a player but also a plaything of his own deconstruc-tive project.

This cursory examination of the play concept(s) in four of the most influential contemporary artist-metaphysicians shows that these thinkers clearly favor prerational over rational play. Some of the main prerational forms of play that they employ are already to be found in Nietzsche and Heidegger, and include play as the ecstatic, innocent, and violent movement of cosmic becoming or cosmic power (Fink); play as a spontaneous and exuberant natural movement or activity (Gadamer); play as a relentless agon of active physical forces (Deleuze, Derrida); play as risk taking or (ad)venture (Fink, Gadamer, Deleuze, Derrida); play as absolute or pure chance (Fink, Deleuze, Derrida); and play as an infinite, aleatory permutation of interchangeable elements, within a decentered structure or limitless series of events, linguistic and non-linguistic signs, or a combination thereof—the play of signs-events can also be called the "play of repetition and difference" or the "play of simulacra" (Deleuze, Derrida). At the same time, the artist-metaphysicians are far from ignoring rational play: they not only engage in a polemic with the advocates of such play (Plato, Leibniz, Kant, Schiller, Fichte, Schelling, Hegel, and German idealism in general), but also attempt to subordinate the rational play concepts to the prerational ones. One of the most common strategies in bringing about this subordination is to show that play is only secondarily the orderly, rational activity of a subjective will and that, in fact, the will itself is less of a player than a plaything in the overwhelmingly powerful play of the world. This critique of (Romantic) subjectivist and voluntaristic notions of play leads to such formulas as *Spiel ohne Spieler* (Fink), *alles Spielen ist ein Gespieltwerden* (Gadamer), *jeu de la différence* (Deleuze), and *jeu de la différance* (Derrida). Man as an individual or as a free agent gives way to either man as Dasein, who is both player and plaything in an impersonal, inscrutable, and unpredictable play of Being (Fink, Gadamer), or man as a genetic product or a differential function of the arbitrary, unconscious play of physical forces (Deleuze, Derrida).

Although all of the thinkers presented here give priority to the prerational play group, they concentrate on different ramifications of their common family branch, or treat the same ramifications in the specific context of their own philosophical tradition, thus allowing for a certain *Spielraum* or play of differences within the group. An expedient way in which one could formulate the difference between the German and the French notions of prerational play is by contrasting the concept of *Erscheinung* to that of *simulacre*. From a purely ontological point of view this difference is one of emphasis, concerning the Platonic distinction between model and copy on the one hand and that between good and bad copies on the other.

Fink and Gadamer attempt to erase the Platonic dichotomy between Idea and appearance, or that between model and copy, arguing that in reality the two polarities become a unity through the notion of *Erscheinung*. Deleuze and Derrida, on the other hand, argue that the crucial distinction in Plato is not that between model and copy or Idea and appearance but rather that among appearances themselves (simulacra), which for Plato can be either good or bad. Reversing Platonism, therefore, means not to reverse the hierarchy of model and copy, or Idea and image, but to proclaim the power (*puissance*) of the simulacrum. For both Deleuze and Derrida, the simulacrum is what Nietzsche understands by the will to power: the eternal play of the active or affirmative forces.[94]

The difference between *Erscheinung* and *simulacre* may also lead to different concepts of language, although here the French and the German thinkers are not necessarily divided along national lines. For example, in contrast to Heidegger and Gadamer, but somewhat like Fink, Deleuze does not posit language as all that is; rather, he posits it as all that is *on the surface*. It is true that for him words are coextensive with things and whatever takes place is a linguistic occurrence as well. But, in keeping with the Stoic doctrine, Deleuze also posits a "deeper" prelinguistic world, the world of physical bodies. In this respect, his notion of language as event-effect ultimately remains subordinated to his notion of the deep play of unconscious, active forces. By contrast, Derrida, at least in his early work, shares Heidegger's and Gadamer's concept of language as all that is, but passes this concept through the Deleuzian

94. For example, in his essay "Renverser le Platonisme" (1967), included as an appendix to *Logique du sens*, Deleuze suggests that it is precisely by proclaiming the power of the simulacrum that Nietzsche stands Platonism on its head: "Simulation is the phantasm itself, i.e., the effect of the functioning of the simulacrum as a mechanism, a Dyonisian machine. It is a question of the false as power, *Pseudos* in Nietzsche's sense: the highest power of the false [*la plus haute puissance du faux*]. Rising to the surface, the simulacrum causes both the Same and its Semblance [*le Semblable*], both Model and Copy, to collapse under the power of the false. It renders impossible within two co-resonant series the order of participations, the fixity of distribution, and the establishment of hierarchies. It installs the world of nomadic distributions and crowned anarchies [*anarchies couronnées*]. Far from being a new foundation, the simulacrum engulfs all foundation, ensures a universal foundering [*effondrement*] but as a positive and joyous event, as *found(er)ing* [*effondement*]" (p. 303).

play of simulacra. As a result, Derrida concentrates on the relation of the spoken word (*logos*) and writing (*gramme*), placing the first at the core of the Platonic philosophy of Being and the second at the core of a philosophy of (unlimited) Becoming.

Furthermore, because Derrida gives priority to writing, his philosophy of Becoming depends on a semiotic notion of language. Whereas for Heidegger and Gadamer language is a unity of words and things, for Derrida language is a free, unrestrained play of signs. The two German thinkers start from the notion of Being as appearance, arguing that what is can present itself only as language (both spoken and written). Derrida, on the other hand, starts from a notion of *writing* as appearance, and therefore not only subordinates the oral to the written but also operates with a structuralist concept of language as a differential sign system. He adopts the Saussurian distinction between signifier and signified and then unleashes the play of simulacra by turning the transcendental signified into merely another differential element within the infinite linguistic series or structure.

Yet, one may ask, is there anything more than a difference of emphasis between *Erscheinung* and *simulacre*? Although they go back to different Platonic distinctions, both the German play of appearance as self-presentation (*Selbstdarstellung*) and the French play of appearance as simulacrum affirm becoming and difference as force, ultimately stemming from the Platonic question of *Seinsmacht*. For all the thinkers concerned, the Platonic distinctions are a matter of authority or degree of power, and consequently they all remain faithful to Nietzsche's *Machtphilosophie*. Since all of them share Nietzsche's view of the world as *Spiel der Kräfte*, the differences among the artist-metaphysicians finally boil down to the degree of freedom each of them is prepared to allow for this *Spiel*. From this point of view, Fink, Deleuze, and Derrida seem to allow more freedom of play to power than Gadamer does. One can also see that the frequent criticism leveled at Derrida, especially in the United States, that he is less concerned with the so-called real world (read: power) than Deleuze, Foucault, Said, and others are lacks any serious foundation. Although Derrida does not particularly insist on the power struggle between *logos* and *gramme*—probably because for him this struggle is part of the larger agon between Being and Becoming, already given extensive treatment by Nietzsche, Deleuze, and others, and therefore is *sous entendu*—he asserts the power of the simulacrum (as writing) no less than Deleuze does. Derrida conceives of deconstruction as a violent, subversive movement within what he calls

"Western metaphysics" (meaning, of course, only the metaphysics of Being or presence). The play of *différance* is a power play, the play of simulacra raised to their highest power. That deconstruction itself is a contest for authority at the same time that it claims to subvert all authority has become only too obvious, especially in its less sophisticated versions, currently circulating in the Anglo-American academic world.

One last word on the distinction without a difference between *Erscheinung* and *simulacre* concerns the political implications of these concepts. Whereas Fink and Gadamer refrain from giving a definite ideological bent to their concept of *Erscheinung* (having perhaps learned their lesson from Heidegger's brief but highly dubious political involvement in the 1930s), Deleuze and Derrida place the *simulacre* squarely in the service of the French leftist movement. This ideological commitment is surely not a philosophical exigency, but rather a question of personal preference (of taste, one might say): the play of simulacra as a play of affirmative forces is blind to any political right, left, or center, and can be invoked effectively by liberals and conservatives alike, as the case of the *nouveaux philosophes* has most recently demonstrated.[95]

Finally, perhaps we are now in a better position than we were at the beginning of this discussion on play and modern philosophy to understand the various implications of the so-called aesthetic turn in Western thought, which is as a rule associated with the rise of both European Romanticism and German idealism at the end of the eighteenth century. How can one explain philosophy's reawakening of interest in its old, subdued enemy, literature (or fine art in general)? The answer is by no means simple and one must look for it in the (violent) beginnings of philosophy as the latter emerges out of its quarrel with poetry. This quarrel is part of the larger agon between rational and prerational values in Western culture. Plato challenges Homer and the tragic poets because he sees them as influential spokesmen for a prerational mentality. This mentality is based on a notion of unmediated power and presupposes a view of the world as ceaseless, arbitrary play of forces (unlimited Becoming). Poetry and the fine arts in general have always been associated with this world of restless forces, with the chaotic and violent

95. For a critique of the Deleuzian and Derridian (political) concept of simulacrum from the standpoint of *la nouvelle philosophie* see especially Mattéi, *L'étranger et le simulacre*, pp. 414–448. For a semiotic approach to the simulacra of contemporary pop culture, see Jean Baudrillard, *Simulations*, trans. P. Foss, P. Patton, and P. Beitchman (New York, 1983).

world of the senses, of opaque, slippery, and ambiguous matter, of an unrestrained and reckless play of the will to power (in the Schopenhauerian and Nietzschean sense). Philosophy sets itself the task of subduing poetry, of imposing upon it a spiritual world of order, clarity, and permanence, a world of rationality and morality—the world of Being in the Platonic sense. Thus philosophy inaugurates "literary criticism," whose beginnings also must be sought, appropriately enough, in Plato and Aristotle: those who defeat and tame poetry also become her masters, protectors, and judges, in short, become literary critics.

Although Plato and Aristotle convert heroic and tragic poetry into "fiction" or "literature," subordinating it to the serious and moral truth of metaphysics, the ancient agon between the poets and the philosophers comes back again and again to haunt Western thought. Whenever prerational values attempt to regain cultural supremacy, what has been repressed under the name of "literature" or "art" as mere play and illusion also reasserts its claim to knowledge and truth, that is, its claim to power. Faced with this challenge or threat, the modern philosophers may react in two ways: they either reenact the Platonic suppression of prerational values, relegating them again to the realm of "mere" art and play (the case of Kant); or they wholeheartedly embrace these values, turning literature or art into an effective weapon against their own philosophical opponents (the case of the artist-metaphysicians). In both cases, literature or art is again "scapegoated," being used by philosophy to reinforce its own cultural authority as a master discipline in Western thought.

The case studies presented in Part I have shown that, since the end of the Age of Reason, prerational values have made a gradual comeback in Western philosophy. This process implies a reversal of Platonic and Aristotelian rational modes of thought, and a return to archaic or Presocratic nonrational modes. Consequently, the modern history of the play concept(s) exhibits a similar pattern of return and reversal. As we have seen, Kant reintroduces, in a negative fashion, the notion of play in modern philosophy, subordinating its prerational (for him, "irrational") forms to its Platonic or rational forms. Schiller openly calls the heuristic fictions of philosophy "play," and it is no accident that it is a poet-philosopher who first dares to take this step. He nevertheless remains within the Platonic fold, seeing art and aesthetics as a rational, nonviolent, and orderly manifestation of play. It is Nietzsche who first ventures beyond Plato, going back to the archaic sources of art and aesthetics in the violent, arbitrary, and innocent play of physical forces, thus reintroducing the prerational play concepts in modern philosophy. His heirs, the artist-metaphysicians, complete the reversal of Platonism or of what has come to be called "Western metaphysics," fully working out the theoretical and practical consequences of this reversal. We should therefore speak of *two* aesthetic turns in modern Western thought, running in opposite directions in a sort of *devenir fou*, to adopt a Deleuzian phrase: one is consolidated by Kant and Schiller, in the wake of the eighteenth-century English and German aestheticians; the other is initiated by Nietzsche, in the wake of Schopenhauer, and pursued by the artist-metaphysicians throughout the twentieth century.

One cannot, however, stress enough the fact that the agon between the rational and the prerational values—and, consequently, between the rational and the prerational play groups—remains inconclusive and any victory on either side is only temporary. Part II will concentrate on philosophy's most powerful ally, modern science, and we shall see that on this particular battlefield the prerational values—and the prerational play concepts—have so far scored only limited and somewhat dubious local victories.

# Play and Modern Scientific Discourse

In science, play becomes a serious topic in the second half of the nineteenth century, primarily due to the success of evolutionary theories, especially as elaborated by Darwin and Spencer. Since the turn of the century, play has moved out of its predominantly evolutionary context, spreading to the majority of the natural sciences, such as physics, astronomy, biology, ecology, ethology, and primatology, as well as to the majority of the human sciences, such as psychology, sociology, anthropology, political science, economics, modern warfare, education, and statistics, and becoming a truly interdisciplinary subject with ramifications in all fields of scientific knowledge.

A discussion of play and contemporary science can proceed along two lines: there is play as a serious object of scientific investigation, and there is the playful, "aesthetic" attitude of science toward its object of study, methodology, and so forth. There is also a correlation: an increasingly playful attitude in science has gone hand in hand with an increasing interest in studying play. Both the scientific studies of play and the uses of play in science have greatly multiplied in the past few decades, and to examine them all thoroughly would be difficult. Moreover, the essentially interdisciplinary character of play studies makes it virtually impossible for the historian not to cut across the traditional boundaries of various scientific disciplines. In this respect, as I point out in the Preface, play indeed transcends not only all disciplines, but also all discipline. One needs therefore to resort to certain generalizations and simplications, or to a "simple paradigm," which of course is itself a playful scientific concept, first employed by the Presocratic *phusikoi* and later on refined by Plato and Aristotle. One such paradigm, my division of the family tree of play concepts into a rational and a prerational branch, applies here as well. Since modern science was, and still largely remains, the offshoot of the Age of Reason, one can reasonably expect that the rational play concepts will dominate the prerational ones. This domination does not go unchallenged, however, especially in such highly theoretical fields as contemporary biology, physics, and philosophy of science.

By pursuing the relationship between play and Darwinian evolutionary theory, one can conveniently cut across disciplinary boundaries (including the line between the natural and the human sciences). Evolutionary theory not only has vast ramifications in almost all scientific fields, but is in turn based on two age-old play concepts that can again be traced back to Hellenic thought: a "struggle for life" leading to a "natural selection" within and among the species, and an interplay of necessity and chance which governs this struggle and/or selection. On the other hand, the most expedient way of looking at the playful or aesthetic mentality of modern science would be to concentrate primarily on the philosophy of science, including the "philosophical" statements of some of the most influential contemporary scientists, such as Planck, Einstein, Heisenberg, and others. In Part II, as in Part I, I shall combine broad historical-theoretical considerations with specific case studies of influential figures who seem to have set the pattern for the contemporary scientific thinking on play as well as for the aesthetic turn in theoretical scientific discourse.

## SECTION 1

# Play and Human Evolution

For the past century, human play has been an object of research in psychology, education, anthropology, primatology, and ethology, being associated with evolution on the one hand and human affect on the other. The two problematics have several points of interference, especially through mimesis (in the sense of both mimesis-play and mimesis-imitation), and they can be traced back, at least in the Anglo-American scientific world, to Herbert Spencer. The play theories around which modern scientific research on play has been conducted have been categorized as "classical" and "modern," but the field seems to be too recent to warrant, or to benefit from, such a traditional taxonomy.[1] Neverthe-

1. See, for example, J. B. Gilmore, "Play: A Special Behavior," in R. N. Haber, ed., *Current Research in Motivation* (New York, 1966), pp. 343–355; and Michael

less, as we come closer to the present, these theories show a shift from a concept of play as separated from knowledge to one that postulates it as an indispensable cognitive instrument—a development in the history of the play concept in modern science that clearly parallels a similar development in the history of play in modern philosophy. What all of these scientific theories have in common is an emphasis on the *utility* of play, which either acts as second fiddle to work or serves some "higher" biological purpose. The most recent theories attempt to dissolve the opposition between play and work, but they retain play's biological usefulness; they actually come to favor play over work as a learning and arousal-seeking activity, or as a motor in the individual's physical and psychological development. The view of play as biological utility culminates in present-day communication theory, where play is considered a main factor in the process of "hominidization," particularly in the development of such metacommunicative systems as language and other sociocultural conventions.

Insofar as they deal with human affect, some of the contemporary scientific theories of play contain certain mimetic and cathartic elements that become predominant in the strictly psychological theories. These theories postulate play as compensation (it satisfies psychic needs that cannot be satisfied by work), as catharsis (it purges violent, destructive emotions while limiting them to socially acceptable events, such as popular games or sports), and as assimilation of unpleasant experiences.[2] Although these mimetic-cathartic theories still enjoy a great deal

---

J. Ellis, *Why People Play* (Englewood Cliffs, N.J., 1973). Ellis also divides scientific play theories into classical, recent, and contemporary or modern, identifying thirteen different kinds of such theories in the behavioral sciences. Joseph Levy, in *Play Behavior* (New York, 1978), adds a few more to the list. The most readable account of the major play theories in the human sciences, however, remains that of Susanna Millar in *The Psychology of Play*.

2. For a detailed presentation of the compensation theory of play see R. C. Atkinson and E. S. Hilgard, *Introduction to Psychology* (New York, 1967); for a discussion of play as catharsis, see S. Feshbach, "The Catharsis Hypothesis and Some Consequences of Interaction with Aggressive and Neutral Play Objects," *Journal of Personality* 24 (1956): 449–462, and more recently L. Berkowitz, "Aggressive Cues in Aggressive Behavior and Hostility Catharsis," *Psychological Review* 71 (1964): 104–122; for play as assimilation of unpleasant experiences, see my discussion of Freud below. I shall also refer in the next section to several other well-known scientific theories of play, including play as recreation (Schiller, as well as J. Schaller, in *Das Spiel und die Spiele* [Weimar, 1861], and M. Lazarus, in *Über die Reize des Spiels* [Berlin, 1883]); play as recapitulation (G. S. Hall, in *Adolescence* [New York, 1916]); play as surplus energy (Schiller, Spencer); and play as preexercise (Groos).

of prestige in certain quarters (witness the interminable debates about the positive or negative effects of violence in television programs), the tendency has been to move away from play as mimesis-imitation and emphasize its exploratory or *creative* character instead. In this context, imagination (and therefore also fine art) is again valued positively: During the ideological dominance of the Protestant work ethic, work was looked upon as being productive of cultural values and imagination as being merely playful self-indulgence (fit for children and poets but not for serious adults); in our postindustrial world the play of the imagination is given the productive function. In most contemporary scientific theory, however, play and the creative imagination remain separated from violent power and firmly bound to orderly, rule-determined process; they remain faithful servants of a rational mentality. The section below briefly examines the general cultural implications of several play theories in the human sciences, both older and more recent, particularly as they appear in the works of Spencer, Groos, Freud, Bateson, and a few other contemporary investigators.

## 1·1 Spencer, Groos, and the Play of Man

In *Principles of Psychology* (1872), Spencer writes: "Many years ago I met with a quotation from a German author to the effect that the aesthetic sentiments originate from the play-impulse. I do not remember the name of the author; and if any reasons were given for the statement or any inference drawn from it, I cannot recall them. But the statement has remained with me, as being one which if not literally true, is yet the adumbration of a truth."[3]

Spencer goes on to show, very much in the spirit (and sometimes the letter) of the German author whose name he "cannot remember," that play and art are intimately related activities because "neither subserves, in any direct ways, the processes conducive to life," and neither refers to "ulterior benefits—the proximate ends are their only ends" (§533). Here we have, translated into a Spencerian vocabulary, the notions of disinterestedness and purposiveness without purpose that "remained" with him after reading Schiller. But now these statements come from an empirical philosopher and scientist (in view of his position, would it not have been embarrassing for Spencer to admit that he was borrowing his

3. Herbert Spencer, *Principles of Psychology*, vol. 2, p. 693, in *The Works of Herbert Spencer* (Osnabruck, 1899; rpt. 1966). Further citations refer to this edition.

scientific theory of play from a poet? Be that as it may, his joyful forgetfulness serves him well), and therefore they mark an important moment in the history of play in modern science.

Following Kant and Schiller, Spencer distinguishes between the world of experience and the world of reality: while the latter cannot be known in itself, it seems to be made up of forces that stimulate the former. Nevertheless, he differs from both Kant and Schiller insofar as he believes that it is not man who imposes forms and categories on what he observes, but that, on the contrary, it is the external stimulant that imposes certain restrictions and limitations upon man. His modified epistemology understandably results in a modified view of the play-drive, although Spencer will ultimately arrive, by his own empirical path, at a view of play as civilizing function that is very similar to Schiller's own (transcendental) play-drive and aesthetic State.

Initially, Spencer seems to depart from Schiller when he takes the latter's material play-drive as energy surplus (*Überfluss*) and modifies it to suit his own evolutionary purposes: "Play is . . . an artificial exercise of powers which in default of their natural exercise, become so ready to discharge that they relieve themselves by simulated actions in place of real actions. For dogs and other predatory creatures show us unmistakably that their play consists of mimic chase and mimic fighting. . . . And so with the kitten running after a cotton-ball . . . we see that the whole sport is a dramatizing of the pursuit of prey" (§534).

Unlike Schiller's lion, Spencer's dog or kitten spends its energy not out of pure exuberance or sheer delight in its own power, but because nature compels it to do so for very precise utilitarian purposes: these animals "play" both in order to keep their organs in good condition and in order to expend the energy surplus produced by their bodies when these organs are not at work. Here we have what in later scientific literature will amount to three separate, although obviously interrelated, concepts of play: play as energy surplus, play as compensatory activity, and play as catharsis.

With one exception (the giraffe), Spencer's examples in §534 are all taken from the world of predatory animals. His Darwinism leads him to an explicitly agonistic view of play, which in Schiller remains largely implicit, or repressed. His examples of human play are equally agonistic, pointing to the "life-serving" purposes to which play is indirectly subordinated:

The sports of boys, chasing one another, wrestling, making prisoners, obviously gratify in a partial way the predatory instincts. And if we consider even their games of skill, as well as the games of skill practised by the adults, we find that, significantly enough, the essential element running through them has the same origin. For no matter what the game, the satisfaction is in achieving victory—in getting the better of an antagonist. This love of conquest, so dominant in all creatures because it is the correlative of success in the struggle for existence, gets gratification from a victory at chess in the absence of ruder victories. Nay, we may even see that playful conversation is characterized by the same element. . . . Through a wit-combat there runs the effort to obtain mental supremacy. (§534)

In the Spencerian version of evolution, power in its immediate form of "love of conquest" becomes the "correlative of success in the struggle for existence," and the play-drive becomes its direct manifestation, functioning both as disinterested or pleasurable simulation and as useful furtherance of its goals.

Spencer does, however, return to Schiller when he preserves the traditional distinction between the lower and the higher faculties, to which he assigns lower and higher forms of play: "The higher but less essential powers, as well as the lower but more essential powers, thus come to have activities that are carried on for the sake of the immediate gratifications derived, without reference to ulterior benefits; and to such higher powers, aesthetic products yield these substituted activities, as games yield them to various lower powers" (§354).

Whereas the agonistic play-impulse finds an outlet in the lower games (the Spencerian equivalent of the Kantian "anthropological" view of play and of Schiller's material play-drive), it becomes sublimated in the "higher" aesthetic emotions expressed through fine art. It is true that, in contrast to Kant and Schiller, Spencer regards the higher faculties as less "essential for life" (because they seem to be less agonistic) than the lower faculties, and this view reflects his commitment to evolution and to a materialist world view in general. As a result, his transition from the lower emotions to the higher ones is less strained than in Schiller's aesthetics. For Spencer, aesthetic feelings differ from ordinary feelings only insofar as they linger in consciousness and are dwelt upon for their own sake, "their nature being such that their continuous presence in consciousness is agreeable" (§535). Yet for Spencer evolution also implies the ancient "enlightened" concept of progress, according to which the reign of the senses is gradually replaced by the reign of the intellect (and this concept is operative in any rational mentality). For example, he ascribes to the secondary, higher faculties the same civilizing function that Schiller had ascribed to the transcendental play-drive. In superior organisms, whose existence is not wholly taken up with life-serving activities, aesthetic or higher play-activities become increasingly important: "The aesthetic activities in general may be expected to play an increasing part in human life as evolution advances. . . . A growing surplus of energy will bring a growing proportion of the aesthetic activities and gratification; and while the forms of art will be such as yield pleasurable exercise to the simpler faculties, they will in a greater degree than now appeal to the higher emotions" (§540).

Starting from the distinction between the lower and the higher faculties, Spencer also sets up an hierarchy of the arts, reminiscent of those of Aristotle and Kant: "Under the head of aesthetic feelings we include states of consciousness of all orders of complexity, some of which, originating in purely physical conditions, are merely perfected modes of sensation, while others, such as the delight in contemplating a noble action of a fictitious character, are re-representative in an extreme degree" (§536). The highest arts, then, are the ones that are least connected with raw sensation and have undergone the greatest amount of mediation or "re-representation." Accordingly, Spencer, like Kant, places music at the bottom of the ladder, and literature, especially fiction, at the top. His preference for fiction is of course symptomatic of the Victorian taste in general, which favors such "rational" forms of literature as the so-called novel of manners; for Spencer, as for the average cultivated Victorian, "good" fiction ought to achieve a perfect balance of emotion and intellect, in which aesthetic feelings "shall have in them as much as may be of the moderate, mingled with as little as may be of the violent" (§538). The remoteness from violence and from "life-serving functions" (i.e., from the struggle for survival) distinguishes a good work of art from a bad one, as well as a superior culture from an inferior one:

> When they are established, the higher orders of co-ordinating powers also come to have their superfluous activities and corresponding pleasures, in games and other exercises somewhat more remote from the destructive activities. But, as we see in the mimetic dances and accompanying chants of savages, which begin to put on a little of the character called aesthetic, there is still a great predominance of these substituted gratifications of feelings adapted to a predatory life. . . .
>
> When, however, a long discipline of social life, decreasingly predatory and increasingly peaceful, has allowed the sympathies and result-

ing altruistic sentiments to develop, these, too, begin to demand spheres of superfluous activity. Fine Art of all kinds takes forms more and more in harmony with these sentiments. Especially in the literature of the imagination we may now see how much less appeal there is to the egoistic and ego-altruistic sentiments, and how much more to the altruistic sentiments—a trait likely to go on growing. (§540)

No less than Schiller, Spencer ends up ascribing to play and the imagination a crucial role in man's intellectual and moral development. One of the first influential scientific minds in the Anglo-American tradition to give play positive scientific consideration, he takes his cue from Darwin and relates play to evolution, thus opening the way for the present-day view of play as a decisive factor in animal and human development. At the same time he brings together art and science, by implying (e.g., in the preceding quotation) that they are two sides of the same coin, or interrelated civilizing factors. This had of course been the contention of poets all along, at least since the days of the "apologies for poesie," but Spencer is among the first positivist thinkers to support this contention.

Although Spencer's view of play as civilizing function marks a turn in the history of play in modern science, it brings with it all the theoretical ambiguities already present in Kant's and Schiller's views. These ambiguities are compounded by the theoretical ambivalence inherent in evolutionism, and all of them seem to have a common source in the divided nature of power in any rational culture. As we have seen, most modern thinkers operate not only with polarized concepts of power but also with polarized concepts of play, and in Spencer this polarization is extended to evolution as well. For him there is evolution based on the "struggle for life," that is, on agonistic play, and evolution based on altruistic impulses, on nonviolent, cooperative play. One operates in both the animal and the primitive human worlds, the other only in the civilized human world. One determines the other, and their goals are mutually exclusive: peaceful evolution advances only insofar as agonistic evolution recedes or the "struggle for life" becomes less fierce; adverse environmental changes may presumably reverse the peaceful trend. Peaceful evolution, moreover, seems to apply only intraspecifically, and in this sense civilized behavior reminds us of that of the ideal citizen in the Platonic Republic: gentle and friendly toward fellow-citizens, vicious and merciless toward foreigners (another species). The tension between our two groups of play concepts is therefore also the tension between peaceful and agonistic evolution, between the animal and the human world, between savage and civilized man. As we shall see again and again, these tensions and polarizations do not disappear in the scientific treatments of play, but are carried over, in various degrees, both in the theoretical assumptions and in the research practices of modern scientists.

Another early scientist who sees play as a decisive factor in evolution is Karl Groos. Groos is currently known within the scientific community chiefly as the proponent of the "practice" or "pre-exercise" theory of play. He was a late-nineteenth-century Neo-Kantian aesthetician who turned ethologist and psychologist, thoroughly conversant not only with Darwin, Spencer, and Weismann but also with the German aesthetic tradition, including Kant, Schiller, and Nietzsche (whose near contemporary he was at the University of Basel). In turn, he left his imprint on such influential twentieth-century figures as Freud, Wittgenstein, Huizinga, and Piaget.

In two voluminous works, *The Play of Animals* (*Die Spiele der Tieren*, 1896) and *The Play of Man* (*Die Spiele des Menschen*, 1899), Groos links the notion of play (in which he initially became interested because, like Schiller, he was looking for a theoretical foundation for his aesthetics) to evolution and natural selection: through play, animals and men practice the skills necessary for survival in the struggle for life.

In *The Play of Animals*, Groos offers an extensive critique of Spencer's surplus-energy theory of play, which he traces back to Schiller (although one could of course trace it back all the way to Plato and Aristotle or even further, to Homer and the Presocratics). Groos argues that whereas this theory has obvious areas of application, it does not apply to *all* play. As he puts it, the overflow of energy is the "most favorable though not the necessary condition of play."[4] He accurately points out the relation of imitation to play in Spencer's theory, again showing that imitative play is not the only kind and consequently that imitation cannot constitute the basis for a universal explanation of play. For example, it does not take into account the play of the very young: "For such plays . . . are very often not *imitations* [*Nachahmungen*], but rather *premonitions* [*Vorahmungen*] of the serious occupations of the individual. The experimenting of little children and young animals, their movement, hunting, and fighting games, which are the most important elementary forms of play, are not imitative repetitions, but rather preparatory efforts" (p. 7).

4. Groos, *The Play of Animals*, trans. E. L. Baldwin (New York, 1898), p. 18. Further citations refer to this edition.

Once he establishes the practice of skills as the elementary, *biological* cause of play, however, Groos proceeds to describe a great variety of play forms such as experimentation, movement games, hunting games (with living real prey, with living mock prey, with lifeless mock prey), fighting games (teasing, tussling among young animals, playful fighting among grown animals), love games (among young animals, rhythmical movements, the display of beautiful and unusual colors and forms, the production of calls and notes, the coquetry of the female), constructive arts, nursing games, imitative games, and curiosity. To these he adds, in *The Play of Man*, the playful activities of the human motor-sensory apparatus (playful movements of the bodily organs, playful movement of foreign bodies, throwing, catching, etc.), playful use of the "higher mental powers" and the emotions, and various "socionomic" play forms (mental and physical contest or rivalry, teasing, enjoyment of the comic and the tragic, the destructive impulse, hunting, sexual games, and social play).

Groos integrates all the rival play theories that he discusses into his own theory of play as practice of skills. Although he criticizes Spencer's excess-energy theory of play, for example, or Schaller and Lazarus's theory of play as recreation, he shares with these scientists the linking of play with evolution. In the final chapter of *The Play of Animals*, "The Psychology of Animal Play," Groos returns to Spencer, arguing for a functional view of play. For him there is no such thing as disinterested play, or play for its own sake. In its psychological aspect, play is directly connected with the feeling of power. The joy of play is not only the sheer pleasure of the expenditure of superabundant energy, but also the joy in "being a cause," and the "joy of conquest":

> But what is this feeling of joy, in its last analysis? It is joy in success, in victory. Nietzsche has opposed the "struggle for power" to Darwin's "struggle for existence," and however contradictory it may seem to identify the survival of the fittest, which is usually no struggle at all, with a struggle for power, it is certain that striving for supremacy is instinctive with all intelligent animals. . . . In short, we see in this joy in conquest a "correlative to success in the struggle for existence," whether it concerns rivalry among comrades, victory over enemy, the proof of one's capabilities, or the subduing of an external object. (pp. 290–291)

Like many other advocates of the theory of evolution, and like Darwin himself, Groos acknowledges the metaphorical character of the "struggle for existence," but finds this metaphor expedient in describing what he considers a real state of affairs in both nature and society. He relates the "joy in being a cause" (or the joy of being in control) and the "joy in conquest" to the notion of "conscious illusion," which he extends in Nietzschean fashion to all human endeavors, and finally to the notion of freedom itself (freedom is the unfettered and innocent pleasure-illusion, produced by the feeling of power).[5] When he sees play as the free and exuberant movement of physical forces Groos comes close not only to Nietzsche, but also to the Presocratics.

Yet in *The Play of Man*, after he presents play from a physiological, biological, psychological, aesthetic, and sociological point of view, Groos ends his study with a pedagogical, ethical discussion of play, reminiscent of Plato, Kant, Schiller, and Spencer. For Groos, as for Plato, Schiller, and Spencer, play has an important civilizing and educational function (p. 400). Too much play, on the other hand, is dangerous, indulging the immature side of a child's character (cf. Kant's arguments in the *Anthropology*). Like his modern rationalist predecessors, Groos preserves the distinction between work and play; also like them, he ends up calling play a "higher kind of work." According to him, the "most serious work may include a certain playfulness, *especially when enjoyment in being a cause and of conquest are prominent*" (p. 400, my italics). Play may become like work when pleasure in being active as such (e.g., in gymnastics, athletic events, and so forth) becomes achievement oriented. Work in turn, may become like play, when "its real aim is superseded by the enjoyment of the activity itself." For Groos it "can hardly be doubted" that this kind of play is the "highest and noblest form of work" (p. 400).

The teacher should always direct and closely supervise children's play. He ought to encourage what is good and useful and discourage "injurious and improper forms of play" (p. 402). In this respect, Groos also operates with the distinction between savage and civilized play behavior, or good and bad play. Good play is the disciplined and orderly activity of reason; bad play is indulging one's elementary impulses, leading to unruliness, violence, trancelike or ecstatic states, and vertigo

5. Groos takes over and develops the notion of "conscious illusion" from Konrad Lange, the main theorist of art as conscious illusion at the end of the nineteenth century. See, especially, Lange, *Die bewusste Selbsttäuschung als Kern des künstlerischen Genusses* (Leipzig, 1895) and *Das Wesen der Kunst: Grundzüge einer illusionistische Kunstlehre* (Berlin, 1907). In the French tradition, see P. Souriau, *La suggestion dans l'art* (Paris, 1893).

(p. 405). Although educators should not directly introduce ethical elements in child play, they should do so indirectly, for greater effectiveness. One "legitimate means" for indirectly promoting development of ethical character through play is fine art, and Groos observes: "Those who with me regard aesthetic enjoyment of poetry as a play [*Spiel*] will recognize in it a wide field of positive influence" (p. 405). On the other hand, one should become aware of the dangers of excessive imagination, such as daydreaming (cf. Kant): "When a child becomes absorbed in solitary musing . . . he should be aroused by application to useful occupation or by social stimuli which bring him in every possible way in contact with the external world. Even the noble gift of the imagination may from overindulgence degenerate into a deadly poison" (p. 406). In short, play should always be practiced in moderation, and the "moral law of temperance" is its supreme law (cf. Plato's *Laws*, e.g., 1.647d, 3.685a, and 5.729). Thus, Groos puts play in the service of rationality, attempting to restrain its violent, prerational side.

## 1·2   Play and Psychoanalytic Theory

Sigmund Freud is a good case of a contemporary scientist who works with polarized concepts of play as well as with polarized views of evolution. Like Groos, he was deeply steeped in the German aesthetic tradition, and brought several of its methods of inquiry (such as Romantic hermeneutics and the Nietzschean genealogical method) to bear upon his own scientific research. Freud's view of play is intimately connected with his psychoanalytic theories and here I can only touch upon some of its complex ramifications, especially in his later work.[6]

6. Among the enormous amount of critical commentary on Freud's psychoanalytic theory, especially as it relates to play and to Western culture in general, are Millar, *Psychology of Play*, pp. 23–30; Anthony Wilden, *System and Structure: Essays in Communication and Exchange* (New York, 1972), which also contains discussions of Piaget and Bateson; Deleuze and Guattari, *L'anti-Oedipe* (Paris, 1972); Herbert Marcuse, *Eros and Civilization: A Philosophical Inquiry into Freud* (Boston, 1966); Mikkel Borch-Jakobsen, *Le sujet freudien* (Paris, 1982); J. Laplanche and J. B. Pontalis, *The Language of Psycho-Analysis*, trans. D. Nicholson-Smith (New York, 1973); Theodor Reik, *Freud als Kulturkritiker* (Vienna, 1930); Jean-Joseph Goux, *Economie et symbolique: Freud, Marx* (Paris, 1973); Ilham Dilman, *Freud and Human Nature* (Oxford, 1983) and *Freud and the Mind* (Oxford, 1984); Robert Steele, *Freud and Jung, Conflicts of Interpretation* (London/Boston, 1982); Vincent Brome, *Freud and His Disciples: The Struggle for Supremacy* (London, 1984); Yiannis Gabriel, *Freud and Society* (London/Boston, 1983); Edwin Wallace, *Freud and*

Up to the time of *Beyond the Pleasure Principle* (1920), Freud basically operates with such views of play as were available to him in nineteenth-century science, chiefly in the works of Spencer and Groos. During this initial stage, play for him is a function of the pleasure principle and consequently is generally opposed to the reality principle, or at least attempts to circumvent it. For example, in *Jokes and Their Relation to the Unconscious (Der Witz und seine Beziehung zum Unbewussten,* 1905) Freud sees jokes as arising precisely from an adult need to find an acceptable substitute for the pleasures of childhood play, or the need to satisfy the play impulse without incurring the criticism of reason. He starts from Groos's thesis that play obeys one of the instincts that compel children to practice their capacities in preparation for adult life, and then invokes another Groosian argument according to which play is linked to the "pleasure of recognition."[7]

Going one step further, Freud criticizes Groos for abandoning his Aristotelian and Kantian idea of play as recognition pleasurable for its own sake, and for tracing this pleasurable recognition instead to a "joy in power" (similar to that experienced by Schiller's lion or Spencer's dog), or a joy in overcoming a difficulty. Groos had originally argued, without any reference to power, that children intensify the pleasure of recognition by deliberately putting obstacles in its way or by creating a "psychical damming up" from which they would then obtain pleasurable relief or catharsis. Freud says he sees "no reason to depart from the simpler view [which does not link play to a "sense of power"] that recognition is pleasurable in itself—i.e., through relieving psychical expenditure—and that the games founded on this pleasure make use of the mechanism of damming up only in order to increase the amount of such pleasure" (p. 122). Freud temporarily separates children's play from power and sees this play merely as a pleasurable activity for its own sake because he wishes to support his hypothesis of the pleasure principle, according to which pleasure never gives up its goals, even though it may have to reach them through intricate detours.

Later on, however, when Freud argues that children take pleasure in

*Anthropology* (New York, 1983); J. N. Isbister, *Freud: An Introduction to His Life and Work* (Cambridge/New York, 1985); and Harold Bloom, ed., *Freud, Modern Critical Views* (New York, 1985).

7. See Groos, *Play of Man,* p. 153. Quoted in *Jokes and Their Relation to the Unconscious,* in *The Complete Psychological Works of Sigmund Freud,* 23 vols., trans. J. Strachey (London, 1960), vol. 8, pp. 121–122. Further citations from *Jokes* refer to this edition.

"nonsense" as a deliberate act of rebellion against the pressures of critical reason, he quietly returns, on a different level, to Groos's view of play as power: "Whatever the motive may have been which led the child to begin these games, I believe that in his later development he gives himself up to them with the consciousness that they are nonsensical, and that he finds enjoyment in the attraction of what is forbidden by reason. He now uses games in order to withdraw from the pressure of critical reason" (pp. 125–126).

Although children's play may come to an end in adolescence as a result of the strengthening of the critical faculty, man, that "tireless pleasure-seeker," returns to it in many direct and indirect ways, such as jokes and drunkenness: "Under the influence of alcohol the grown man once more becomes a child, who finds pleasure in having the course of his thoughts freely at his disposal without paying regard to the compulsion of logic" (pp. 126–127).

The pleasure-seeking play of the child also returns in the poet, who can equally be said to be "under the influence," or naturally inebriated, thus escaping the rigors of the reality principle. In this regard, in "Creative Writers and Day-Dreaming" ("Der Dichter und das Phantasieren," 1908), Freud extends his theory of play to fantasy and to the creative imagination. The poet and the child at play have several things in common. Both create a world of their own, in which they rearrange and order things in a new way that pleases them better. Both take their play very seriously, expending a great deal of energy on it: the opposite of play is not seriousness, but reality. The child and the poet draw a sharp line between play and reality, and in this respect they both differ from the daydreamer. But they are also symmetrical opposites of sorts. The child's play is determined by his wish to grow up. Through it, he imitates what he knows of adult life, and he has no reason to hide his wish. The adult, on the contrary, has suppressed *his* wish, which is, ironically, that of becoming a child again. The poet, like the intoxicated man or the neurotic, is one of the few adults who may behave like a child without shame: here the phrase *poetic license* assumes its full antithetical sense.

Imaginative creation, like daydreaming, is "a continuation of and substitute for what was once the play of childhood,"[8] and the writer is able to break down the emotional barrier or the inhibition which the

8. Sigmund Freud, "Creative Writers and Day-Dreaming," in *Complete Works*, vol. 9, trans. J. Strachey (London, 1959), p. 152. Further citations refer to this edition.

reality principle, in the guise of the critical or logical faculty, has placed between us and play. According to Freud, "our enjoyment of an imaginative work proceeds from a liberation of tensions in our minds," as a result of the writer's "enabling us . . . to enjoy our own day-dreams without self-reproach or shame" (p. 153). For the poet, as for the child, play is a compensatory activity, related to wish fulfillment, which attempts to circumvent the reality principle at the same time that it is subordinated to this principle. As in the case of Spencer, the artistic genre that is supposed to support this utilitarian view of play is fiction, that is, the artistic form which is the most accessible to logic and criticism (pp. 149–150).

During the first phase of his psychoanalytic theory, then, Freud sees play as a pleasure-seeking activity that "arises from an economy in psychical expenditure or relief from the compulsion of criticism" (*Jokes*, p. 127), that is, as a direct or indirect manifestation of the pleasure principle. This view is, to a certain extent, Freud's psychoanalytic version of Spencer's theory of play as energy surplus, catharsis, and compensation, although it does not yet do full justice to the evolutionary and the agonistic aspects of the latter. As in Kant and Schiller, play is opposed both to reality and to Reason, but the ethical polarization remains implicit, being for the most part couched in a neutral, scientific vocabulary.

In *Beyond the Pleasure Principle* (*Jenseits des Lustprinzips*, 1920), Freud's view of play, as well as his view of the psyche in general, changes radically. This change can be traced back to his attempt to account for those elements in the life of the psyche that resist being subsumed under the pleasure principle. These elements turn out to be connected with agonistic or (self-)destructive impulses, and now Freud postulates an interplay of a life instinct (served by the pleasure principle) and a death instinct. He also pays closer attention to agonistic play and returns to Spencer's dualistic view of evolution, presenting his own psychoanalytic version of the tension between the egoistic and the altruistic instincts in man.

Freud begins by reexamining the relationship between play and the pleasure principle. Invoking what has by now become a famous case history, he reiterates his view of play as a compensatory activity. But in this case the child at play also reenacts an unpleasant event, such as his mother's absence, in order to master and derive some pleasure from it. He achieves this either through repetition or through a scapegoating act. For example, if the child has a frightening experience at the doctor's, during his next game he hands on this experience to one of his playmates and "in this way revenges himself on a substitute."[9] Hence, Freud returns not only to Spencer's view of play as a manifestation of the aggressive instincts but also to Groos's theory of play as power, which earlier he had criticized. Play now appears as both "mastery" and the "pleasure of revenge," which can no longer be subsumed under the "life instinct."

Another new element in Freud's theory of play is "repetition," which is no longer connected only with the pleasure of recognition or with the pleasure of imitation, but with a disquieting compulsion to regress as well. To be sure, the "economic motive" or the "yield of pleasure" involved in play remains operative in this case, too. The child compensates for his mother's absence by staging a game in which he can control her appearance and disappearance at will, and he shows much more pleasure at the reappearance of the toy substituting for his mother than at its disappearance. Thus one can infer that his behavior still conforms to the demands of the pleasure principle. As Freud reminds us, this principle "does not abandon the intention of ultimately obtaining pleasure, but it nevertheless demands and carries into effect the postponement of satisfaction and the temporary toleration of unpleasure as a step on the long, indirect road to pleasure" (p. 10). The child makes his mother disappear only to postpone the pleasure of having her back, and the endless repetition of this game can also be ascribed to the pleasure of "recognition for its own sake." Likewise, Freud argues that it is not necessary to postulate a special imitative instinct to account for children's propensity to imitate, in play, the activities of the grown-up (and now he goes against Aristotle), since here again the pleasure principle provides ample motivation through the notion of play as compensation. But what bothers Freud is the compulsion to repeat, outside the demands of compensation or the economy of pleasure, regarded as the preservation of the life instinct, a compulsion that is clinically observed, for example, in some psychoanalytical sessions with neurotics: "If we take into account observations . . . based upon behavior in the transference and upon the life-histories of men and women, we shall find courage to assume that there really does exist in the mind a compulsion to repeat which overrides the pleasure principle. Now too we shall be inclined to relate to this compulsion the dreams which occur in traumatic neuroses and the impulse which leads children to play" (p. 23).

9. Freud, *Beyond the Pleasure Principle*, in *Complete Works*, vol. 18, trans. J. Strachey (London, 1955), p. 8. Further citations refer to this edition.

In order to account for this compulsive repetition Freud postulates a death instinct that functions in a way that is remarkably similar to the pleasure principle. Its conservative nature requires the return to an older, more "primitive" state, which is that of inorganic matter, and it is this death instinct that creates the compulsion to repeat until it effects, through intricate detours, a return to the inanimate. Freud links the death instinct to aggression and violence, opposing to it a life instinct, which he relates to sexuality or, more generally, to Eros. He distances himself from Jung, whose view of the *libido* as "instinctual force" he says is monistic, while his own is dualistic: "Our views have from the very first been *dualistic* and today they are even more definitely dualistic than before—now that we describe the opposition as being, not between ego-instincts and sexual instincts but between life instincts and death instincts. Jung's libido theory is on the contrary monistic; the fact that he has called his one instinctual force 'libido' is bound to cause confusion, but need not affect us otherwise. We suspect that instincts other than those of self-preservation operate in the ego, and it ought to be possible for us to point to them" (p. 53). In *Beyond the Pleasure Principle*, then, Freud goes back not only to Spencer and Groos but also to Empedocles, particularly to his dualistic view of the world as a contest between Love (*Philotes*) and Strife (*Neikos*).[10]

The archaic origin of Freud's "dualistic" outlook is even more obvious in *Civilization and Its Discontents* (*Das Unbehagen in der Kultur*, 1929–1930), where Empedocles' Philotes and Neikos become first Eros and Ananke, then Eros and Thanatos. Tracing the development of his own psychoanalytic thought, Freud confesses that he initially turned (not unlike Spencer) to Schiller for an explanation of life, adopting the poet-philosopher's observation that "hunger and love are what moves the world." For Freud, hunger becomes associated with the "ego-instincts" or the instincts of self-preservation, while love becomes associated with "libidinal instincts," being directed toward the identification with and preservation of objects. In Hellenic mythological terms, the ego-instincts assume the guise of Ananke, Necessity, while the libidinal instincts assume the guise of Eros, Love. Freud himself points out that in this first phase of psychoanalytic theory, Ananke is ultimately subordinated to Eros, through the notion of narcissism or self-love. This subordination would in fact make the libidinal instincts the only primary instincts, as Jung had advocated, giving psychoanalysis a "monis-

---

10. I discuss these Empedoclean concepts in *God of Many Names*, chap. 2.

tic" character. But then, Freud adds, in *Beyond the Pleasure Principle* he drew the conclusion that "besides the instinct to preserve living substance and to join it into ever larger units, there must be another, contrary instinct seeking to dissolve those units and to bring them back to their primeval, inorganic state." In other words, besides Eros there is also an instinct of death, and "the phenomena of life [can] be explained from the concurrent or mutually opposing action of these two instincts."[11]

Freud admits that it is not easy to demonstrate the activities of the death instinct, and suggests that part of this instinct is "diverted toward the external world and comes to light as an instinct of aggressiveness and destructiveness" (p. 119). In this guise, the death instinct can be listed in the service of Eros, in sadistic sexual behavior, for example. When this instinct cannot find any external outlet it will turn inward, accelerating the process of the individual's self-destruction, for example, in masochistic sexual behavior. Since the death instinct can manifest itself only as aggression or destructiveness, that is, as violence, we can readily see that it is the perfect equivalent of Empedoclean Neikos, Strife. As in the case of Philotes and Neikos, Eros and Thanatos never appear isolated, but are "alloyed with each other in varying and very different proportions," which also accounts for the difficulty one has in telling them apart (p. 119). They are locked in an eternal agon, whose arena encompasses both the animate and the inanimate worlds—indeed, the agon is carried on precisely between these two worlds. Civilization can be defined as "a process in the service of Eros, whose purpose is to combine single human individuals, and after that families, then races, peoples, and nations, into one great unity, the unity of mankind" (p. 122). Death, which shares the "world-dominion" with Eros, opposes the latter's action, and their struggle is "what all life essentially consists of." The evolution of civilization "may therefore simply be described as the struggle for life of the human species," at the same time being the true "battle of the giants" that myths tell us about (p. 122).

And yet, despite Freud's "dualistic" claims, in *Das Unbehagen* the death instinct turns out to be primary, and one can contend that his views remain consistently monistic: whereas at first his theory requires the primacy of Eros, later on it requires the primacy of Thanatos.[12]

11. Freud, *Civilization and Its Discontents*, in *Complete Works*, vol. 21, trans. J. Strachey (London, 1961), pp. 118–119. Further citations refer to this edition.
12. For the opposite view, see, e.g., Laplanche and Pontalis, *The Language of Psycho-Analysis*, pp. 97–103.

Aggression precedes Love on the evolutionary scale, and why and how the latter comes into being remains unclear. As in the case of Philotes versus Neikos, Eros is far from being incommensurable with Death. On the contrary, it engages in a contest with it, thereby revealing its equally agonistic character. In section 5, Freud reviews several notions of Love, including the Christian one, and then pointedly dismisses them in favor of a psychological-historical view of Eros as "identification" and "aim-inhibited relationship" with the object (p. 109); on this view, then, Eros is a *reactive* force, acting in response to, rather than independently of, Strife. Freud sees Strife as an unavoidable, built-in component of humanity, and appeals to "experience" to justify his belief:

> *Homo homini lupus.* Who in the face of all his experience of life and of history will have the courage to dispute this assertion? . . .
>
> Anyone who calls to mind the atrocities committed during the racial migrations or the invasions of the Huns, or by the people known as Mongols under Jenghiz Kan and Tamerlane, or at the capture of Jerusalem by the pious Crusaders, or even, indeed, the horrors of the recent World War [to which we can now add the even worse horrors of World War II]—anyone who calls these things to mind will have to bow humbly before the truth of this view. (pp. 111–112)

On the social level, primitive man is originally violent and aggressive; only later does he develop altruistic instincts. Moreover, these instincts have an ambiguous origin, if we are to believe Freud's hypothesis of the murder of the primal father by his banished sons. This hypothesis (first developed in *Totem and Taboo*, 1913, and then taken up again in *Das Unbehagen*) advances the profoundly pessimistic view that social cohesion is based on ambivalent feelings of love and hate and is gained at the expense of an increasingly unbearable sense of guilt (*Civilization and Its Discontents*, pp. 123–125; cf. Nietzsche's theses in the *Genealogy of Morals*).

The same ambiguity, inherent in any evolutionary view of life based on agon, appears in Freud's statements (again reminiscent of Nietzsche) regarding the adverse fate of the "individuals of the leader type" in egalitarian societies. On the one hand, Freud argues that civilization needs "mastery over the individual's dangerous desire for aggression by weakening and disarming it and by setting up an agency within him to watch over it, like a garrison in a conquered city" (p. 124)—note the Platonic overtones of this passage, which recalls Socrates' argument in the *Republic* regarding the need for the soul's superior part to achieve mastery over its inferior part. On the other hand, Freud deplores the increased, almost unbearable levels of guilt that are reached by certain members of the community, leading to what he calls the psychological poverty (*psychologisches Elend*) of groups. This poverty "is most threatening where the bonds of a society are chiefly constituted by the identification of its members with one another, while individuals of the leader type do not acquire the importance that should fall to them in the formation of a group" (pp. 115–116).[13]

It is clear, then, that Freud's "dualism" means in effect fluctuating between two monistic principles. In his later work Freud also continues to operate with the old concept of good and bad eris, perhaps because he still remains committed to a Spencerian version of evolution, in which the altruistic drives may eventually prevail over the egoistic ones. Consequently, he inherits all the ambiguities of Spencer's evolutionary theory, which presupposes an agonistic view of the world at the same time that it repudiates this presupposition. The same *Unbehagen* that Freud diagnoses so precisely in our culture manifests itself in his own work as well, and it is to his credit as a psychoanalyst that he is fully aware of this fact. In the closing paragraphs of *Civilization and Its Discontents*, for example, he confesses that he cannot offer any consolation to his fellow human beings, and then concludes with a question: "The fateful question for the human species seems to me to be whether and to what extent their cultural development will succeed in mastering the disturbance of their communal life by the human instinct of aggression and self-destruction. . . . And now it is to be expected that the other of the two 'Heavenly Powers,' eternal Eros, will make an effort to assert himself in the struggle with his equally immortal adversary. But who can foresee with what success and with what result?" (p. 145).

Freud's impact on the scientific views of play seems to me twofold. On the one hand, he revives scientific interest in the nineteenth-century theories of play, such as those of Schiller, Spencer, and Groos, consolidating their place in the main stream of Western scientific discourse; on the other hand, particularly through his disciples, he establishes play as essential in various forms of therapy, thereby enhancing its cultural prestige.[14] Freud's most important contribution is that he is among the

13. For a detailed discussion of the relationship between Freud and Nietzsche, see Paul L. Assoun, *Freud et Nietzsche* (Paris, 1980).

14. Among the best-known Freudians who have further developed the master's views on play, applying them to psychotherapy, are Anna Freud, e.g., in *The Ego and the Mechanism of Defense* (New York, 1946) and *The Psychoanalytical Treatment*

first influential contemporary thinkers who, in the wake of Nietzsche, point to the original link between play and violence, or between play and what I have called the "unmediated" forms of power, characteristic of a prerational mentality.

Within the psychoanalytic community itself, however, there are very few Freudians who are prepared to accept the full consequences of Freud's later views. They usually emphasize the libidinal and "therapeutic" aspects of play, to which they subordinate its darker side. Two of the most prominent psychoanalysts in the Anglo-American community, Erik Erikson and D. W. Winnicott, have not only used play therapy with children but have also developed their own theories of play. Starting from the Freudian premise that play reveals something about the unconscious life and motivation of the individual, Erikson has elaborated several diagnostic techniques on the basis of observing children's play. The one he has used most frequently is based on "play constructions" and is described in his lecture "Play and Actuality":

> In the last few years Peggy Penn, Joan Erikson, and I have begun to collect play constructions of four- and five-year-old children of different backgrounds and in different settings, in a metropolitan school and in rural districts, in this country and abroad. Peggy Penn acts as the play hostess, inviting the children, one at a time, to leave their play group and to come to a room where a low table and a set of blocks and toys await them. Sitting on the floor with them, she asks each child to "build something" and to "tell a story" about it. Joan Erikson occupies a corner and records what is going on, while I, on occasion, replace her or (where the available space permits) sit in the background watching.[15]

Both the "model situation" in which the children are placed and their play constructions exhibit "some repetitiveness." Recurrent themes include the working through of a traumatic experience, a playful renewal, a need to communicate, the joy of self-expression, the exercise of growing faculties, and the mastery of a complex situation (p. 131). To these

---

*of Children* (New York, 1964); Franz Alexander, e.g., in *The Psychoanalysis of the Total Personality* (New York, 1930) and, more recently, in "A Contribution to the Theory of Play," *Psychoanlytic Quarterly* 27 (1958): 175–193; and Melanie Klein, e.g., in "The Psychoanalytic Play-Technique," *American Journal of Orthopsychiatry* 25 (1955): 223–237.

15. Erik Erikson, "Play and Actuality," in M. W. Piers, ed., *Play and Development* (New York, 1972), pp. 127–128. Further citations refer to this edition.

themes, by now familiar (cf. Schiller, Spencer, Groos, and Freud), Erikson adds, following Huizinga, Heidegger, and Gadamer, the notion of *Spielraum*, which he translates as "leeway of mastery." The meaning of this word cannot be conveyed in a literal translation such as "playroom," he points out. Like Gadamer, Erikson observes that *Spielraum* "connotes something common also for the 'play' of mechanical things, namely *free movement* within *prescribed limits*. This at least establishes the boundaries of the phenomenon: where the freedom is gone, *or the limits, play ends*" (p.133). Here, then, we have one of the main topoi of modern play theory inserted into psychoanalysis, what Roger Caillois calls *ludus*, play governed by rules.

It is not that Erikson ignores the aggressive tendencies in man. On the contrary, much of his work is dedicated to an investigation of these tendencies, and in *Toys and Reasons* (1973), his most comprehensive discussion of play to date, he even considers them in the context of cultural play. For example, he analyzes the relationship between "ritualized interplay"—rule-governed play among the various members of the same community—and "pseudospeciation," which he defines in "Play and Actuality" as a "tendency of human groups to behave as if they were *the* chosen species" (pp. 151–152; although it is not given a scientific name, pseudospeciation is already operative in Plato's *Republic*, in the Socratic definition of the guardian as a watchdog, or in the Freudian corpus, in *Totem and Taboo* or "Why War?"). Under the effects of pseudospeciation, rule-governed play becomes "anarchic" play, leading back to aggression. Thus, Erikson still operates with the Platonic distinction between good (rule governed) and bad (uncontrollable) play. By the end of *Toys and Reasons*, violent play becomes "pseudoplay," whereas true play is linked to Eros. For Erikson, the main contribution of psychoanlysis to Western culture has been to demonstrate, "in history as well as in life histories, how the fixation on the past can hinder the anticipation of the future, undermining serious playfulness and emotional vitality."[16] Psychoanalysis "may well prove of help in studies of how a given world view fulfills its mission, namely to facilitate an optimal interplay of life cycles and institutions." But psychoanalysis could not successfully contribute to these studies if it "were not grounded in a deep belief in the power of Eros to imbue intimacy and communality, work, worship, and awareness with a mea-

16. Erikson, *Toys and Reasons* (New York, 1973), p. 175. Further citations refer to this edition.

sure of true play" (p. 175). Erikson's "true play" is Plato's serious play, stripped of its archaic violence and dressed up in a rational garb. While it may be an "exuberant leap," it nevertheless requires "firm landings" (p. 175). In Erikson, therefore, Freud's irresolvable conflict between the libidinal and the aggressive instincts is resolved in favor of Eros, and Freud's pessimistic ambivalence as to the outcome of this *gigantomachia* is replaced by an unbounded faith in the Power of Love.

In Erikson the tensions and ambiguities that beset modern theoreticians of the ludic phenomenon remain close to the surface and can still be traced back to the Freudian agon between Eros and Thanatos; in Winnicott they become transfigured, and therefore obscured, in the form of an onto-epistemological paradox.[17] For Winnicott, play is a "transitional" or a borderline phenomenon, having its own time and space between subjectivity and objectivity or between dream and reality. Winnicott's most explicit theoretical statements on play can be found in a collection of his papers entitled *Playing and Reality* (1971), in which he attempts to define play in the context of his theory of transitional objects and transitional phenomena. The transitional object is a material object, such as a corner of blanket or napkin, a bundle of wool, and the like, which has a special value for the infant between the ages of four and twelve months, particularly before falling asleep. In developmental terms, this object lies "between the thumb and the teddy bear." Although it is an "almost inseparable part of the infant," and thus distinct from the future toy, it is nevertheless the "first not-me possession."[18] The transitional object occupies the neutral space between the subjective and the objective. In this neutral space, the object is no longer part of the infant's body, yet it is not fully recognized as belonging to external reality either (p. 2). The transitional phenomena are various gestures and oral activities such as babbling, humming, mouthing objects, and so forth, with which Winnicott assumes "thinking or phantasizing gets linked up" (p. 4).

The transitional objects and phenomena are a preliminary step toward the creation of the self in the separation from the object or in the division between an inner and an outer world. Once this step is taken, however, they do not disappear, but have lasting effects on the subject's

17. As we have seen, in modern philosophical discourse play is often presented as a logical or onto-phenomenological paradox (cf. Fink and Gadamer, for example); see also Bateson's theory of play and fantasy, discussed below.

18. D. W. Winnicott, *Playing and Reality* (London/New York, 1971), p. 2. Further citations refer to this edition.

later development, being retained throughout life "in the intense experiencing that belongs to the arts and to religion and to creative scientific work" (p. 14).

Winnicott locates transitional phenomena and objects in a realm of "illusion." In this respect, his arguments are reminiscent of those of Konrad Lange and Karl Groos, the two most prominent theorists of "aesthetic illusion" at the end of the nineteenth century. Illusion is that "intermediary area of *experiencing* to which inner reality and external life both contribute." This area is not "challenged" or contested by anyone as long as "no claim is made on its behalf except that it shall exist as a resting place for the individual engaged in the perpetual human task of keeping inner and outer reality separate yet interrelated." When more powerful claims are made for it, the intermediary area of illusion, which is "allowed to the infant, and which in adult life is inherent in art and religion," loses its *neutrality* and becomes a "hallmark of madness." In this case, the adult "puts too powerful a claim in the credulity of others, forcing them to acknowledge a sharing of illusion that is not their own" (pp. 2–3). Here again one can detect the close link between illusion, play, and freedom (understood as an unconstrained play of forces), which is a recurrent theme in the history of the modern play concepts.

Play, like illusion (linked to the Latin *ludere* and *ludus*), is such an intermediary area of experiencing, and for Winnicott it specifically designates the space—or what Erikson calls the *Spielraum*—between mother and infant. In order to distance himself from other psychoanalysts who have been "too busy using play context to look at the playing child, and to write about playing as a thing in itself," Winnicott makes a distinction between the meaning of the noun "play" and that of the verbal noun "playing." Playing means "doing" and as such it has both a time and a place, being the "potential space between baby and mother" (p. 41). At the same time it is the potential space between the analyst and his patient (metaphorically speaking, the two spaces are probably one and the same): "*Psychotherapy takes place in the overlap of two areas of playing, that of the patient and that of the therapist. Psychotherapy has to do with two people playing together. The corollary of this is that where playing is not possible, then the work done by the therapist is directed towards bringing the patient from a state of not being able to play into a state of being able to play*" (p. 38). Finally, for Winnicott, psychoanalysis itself is a "highly specialized form of playing in the service of communication with oneself and others" (p. 41).

Some of the basic features of playing, in Winnicott's psychoanalytic sense, have much in common with those of Erikson's *Spielraum*. For Winnicott, as for Erikson, playing is first and foremost a creative rather than a destructive experience, "a basic form of creative living" (p. 50). Winnicott recognizes the "frightening" or "threatening" elements in play but, like Erikson, he believes that these elements are controllable. Playing presupposes a "positive social attitude," and even though it "must include recognition that play is liable to become frightening," this positive attitude implies that the frightening aspects of play can be mastered through rules and surveillance. In this regard, "games and their organization must be looked at as part of an attempt to forestall the frightening aspect of playing." Furthermore, "responsible persons" must be available to monitor the playing of children. Although these responsible persons (adults) must refrain from taking over the children's playing, which would mean taking away their creative freedom, they must nevertheless stay close by and intervene if the playing gets out of hand (becomes violent).

But what does Winnicott understand by the "frightening aspect of playing"? At first sight, he seems to relate it not so much to violence as to his notion of play as an onto-epistemological paradox: "The precariousness of play belongs to the fact that it is always on the theoretical line between the subjective and that which is objectively perceived" (p. 50). Play is a borderline phenomenon, hovering between reality and unreality, and because of this undecidability it is potentially disruptive to the self and its identity. This is an age-old argument, employed by Socrates in his attack on the Sophists and the poets in the *Ion* and *The Republic*. But, as in the case of Plato, what appears on the surface as a rational and objective ontological argument betrays a deep-seated fear of the unrestrainable world of the senses. In Winnicott the danger of playing comes primarily from the fact that it "involves the body": "Bodily excitement in erotogenic zones constantly threatens playing, and therefore threatens the child's sense of existing as a person. The instincts are the main threat to play as to the ego" (p. 52). Consequently, Winnicott is very careful in separating play from "excessive instinctual arousal" (p. 52). The Platonic distrust of the senses (which runs through most of the Western metaphysical tradition) leads Winnicott to shift the emphasis, in his theory of play, from the instincts to the relationship between subjective and objective reality—an ontological distinction that he ultimately leaves unquestioned: "Playing is inherently exciting and precarious. This characteristic derives *not* from instinctual arousal but from the precariousness that belongs to the interplay in the child's mind of that which is subjective (near-hallucination) and that which is objectively perceived (actual, or shared reality)" (p. 52).

Thus, allowing for obvious differences in psychoanalytic vocabulary, Winnicott's theory of play turns out to be as rational as that of Erikson, inscribing itself in a long Western tradition which runs from Plato to Schiller to the present-day humanists.

## 1·3  Piaget, Bateson, and Contemporary Play Theory

Far from being limited to psychoanalysis, the tendency to see (rational) play as a positive evolutionary factor is discernable throughout the human sciences, most prominently in child psychology and education. Play as a cognitive process and play as learning are two evolutionary concepts that have over the past two decades become well established in these fields. The beginning of this development is usually associated with the name of Jean Piaget, an extremely prolific and versatile writer who reportedly published his first scientific paper when he was ten years old. Piaget started out as a zoologist, but eventually became interested in the development of the human intellect, basing his theoretical conclusions on an empirical study of his own children's early years. His interest in play is closely related to his interest in the development of man's rational faculty, and his play theory needs to be placed in this larger context. Piaget presents his theory of play chiefly in *La formation du symbole* (*Play, Dreams, and Imitation in Childhood*, 1951), the third volume in a series dealing with the early years of the child's intellectual development. In the two preceding volumes, *La naissance de l'intelligence chez l'enfant* and *La construction du réel chez l'enfant*, Piaget concentrates on what he calls the "sensory-motor intelligence in the pre-verbal stage" of the infant, which to him constitutes a preparation for what much later will become reflective thought. In *La formation du symbole* he attempts to describe what he sees as a transition from the sensory-motor activity prior to representation to representational modes of thought. Piaget claims that it is during this transitional period that we encounter the phenomenon of play. For him play is the extreme end of a fluid and dynamic polarity between assimilation and accommodation, the other end being imitation.

For his definition of accommodation and assimilation Piaget goes to the infant's sensory-motor skills, which presuppose the existence of what he calls "schemas of action," that is, "coordinated systems of movement and perceptions, which constitute any elementary behavior capable of being repeated and applied to new situations, e.g., grasping, moving, shaking an object."[19] He defines *accommodation* (a term he borrows from biology, where, according to him, it means "individual variation under the influence of the environment") as the "modification of the movements and point of view of the subject under the influence of the movements and positions of external objects" (p. 275). Conversely, *assimilation* is the "objective modification of external movements and positions by the movements of the subject, as well as the subjective modification resulting from the fact that perception or comprehension of these movements and positions essentially depends on the subject's point of view" (p. 274). Piaget underlines the purely functional character of his distinction. The organs that perform the functions of accommodation and assimilation "can in principle be entirely arbitrary, since the two functional invariants are at work through the whole evolution from the reflex to sensory-motor intelligence" (p. 275). If the two functional invariants are in equilibrium, then one has what Piaget calls "adaptation," and the "higher forms" of adaptation result in intelligent activity. On the other hand, if these two invariants are unbalanced, then there is either the primacy of accommodation over assimilation, resulting in imitation, or the primacy of assimilation over accommodation, resulting in play. An important consequence of this functionalist approach is that Piaget's definition of play does not need to postulate a "play instinct" or a "play-drive" as other scientific definitions do; nor does it require a clear-cut opposition between ludic and nonludic activities: "The tonality of an activity is ludic in proportion as it has a certain orientation. This amounts to saying that play is distinguishable by a modification, varying in degree, of the conditions of equilibrium between reality and the ego. We can therefore say that if

19. Jean Piaget, *Play, Dreams, and Imitation in Childhood*, trans. C. Gattegno and F. M. Hodgson (New York, 1951; rpt. 1962), p. 274. Further citations refer to this edition. For critical material on Piaget and play, see Millar, *Psychology of Play*, pp. 50–58; Brian Sutton-Smith, "Piaget on Play: A Critique," *Psychological Review* 73 (1966): 111–112; "The Role of Play in Cognitive Development," *Young Children* 6 (1967): 361–370; and "Piaget, Play, and Cognition Revisited" in W. F. Overton, ed., *The Relationship between Social and Cognitive Development* (Hillsdale,, N.J., 1983), which I discuss in some detail later on in this section; and Greta Fein, "Piaget, Vygotsky and the Relationship between Language and Symbolic Play: Echoes from the Nursery," paper presented to the American Psychological Association, Toronto, 1978. For an intriguing view of Piaget as a "constructivist," see Ernst von Glasersfeld, "An Interpretation of Piaget's Constructivism," *Revue Internationale de Philosophie* 36 (1982): 612–635.

adapted activity and thought constitute an equilibrium between assimilation and accommodation, play begins as soon as there is predominance of assimilation" (p. 150).

At first sight this functionalist principle appears very flexible and can
be regarded as a breakthrough in the scientific understanding of play. A
second look, however, reveals that in practice Piaget is far from being
able to adhere to it. A major difficulty arises from the fact that he seems
to operate with not one but two definitions of play, one more restrictive
than the other. On the one hand he states that play "begins as soon as
there is predominance of assimilation," and on the other hand he defines
it as a "pole" or "extreme end" or even as a "continuation" of assimilation (p. 150). Throughout his argument, he oscillates between these
two definitions, employing them according to what suits him best in a
particular context.

According to Piaget, there are four major stages in the evolution of
intelligence, which can in turn be divided into a number of substages or
phases. The first major stage, that of sensory-motor development, lasts
from the infant's birth up to about eighteen months. During this stage,
the infant evolves from an initial phase, when he is still unable to
distinguish between the impressions he receives from his senses and his
own reflex response to them, to a second phase, when he begins to
develop the sensory-motor coordinations and adjustments that allow
him to perceive and manipulate objects as well as to see causal relations
between them. Play appears during this second, more advanced phase,
and in this respect Piaget explicitly distances himself from Groos by
denying that play arises during the initial phase of "purely reflex adaptations": "For an interpretation of play like that of K. Groos, for whom
play is pre-exercise of essential instincts, the origin of play must be
found in this initial stage since sucking gives rise to exercise in the void,
apart from meals. . . . But it seems very difficult to consider reflex
exercises as real games when they merely continue the pleasure of
feeding-time and consolidate the functioning of the hereditary set-up,
thus being evidence of real adaptation" (p. 89).

According to Piaget, one needs to distinguish between "real adaptation," which presupposes a balance between accommodation and assimilation leading to an acquisition of new skills, and pure assimilation,
which is a mere repetition of already acquired skills. Furthermore, one
needs to distinguish between what, following Kant, Baldwin and others
have called "autotelic" or "disinterested" activities and play proper.[20]

20. See J. Mark Baldwin, *Mental Development in the Child and the Race, Methods
and Processes* (New York/London, 1884; rpt. 1903) and *Social and Ethical Inter-*

Insofar as play is an exercise in the void of schemas temporarily out of use, one can certainly say that it is autotelic, and Piaget reinterprets Kant and Schiller through Spencer and Groos when he states, for example, that play "proceeds by relaxation of the effort at adaptation and by maintenance or exercise of activities for the mere pleasure of mastering them and acquiring thereby a feeling of virtuosity or power" (p. 89). But even though play has an autotelic component (which, as in Groos, turns out to be related to a feeling of power), not all autotelic activities are play. To make this point, Piaget could have argued that imitation itself can be said to be autotelic, insofar as it is "pure" accommodation or "a kind of hyperadaptation to models which are virtually though not actually usable" (p. 89). Yet, because he has a stake in downplaying the similarities between play and imitation (for him they are antithetical pairs), he chooses instead to draw a comparison between play and science, as exemplified by mathematics: "But all autotelic activities are certainly not games. Science has this characteristic and particularly pure mathematics, whose object is immanent in thought itself, but if it is compared to a 'superior' game, it is clear that it differs from a mere game by its forced adaptation to an internal or external reality" (p. 90).

Here Piaget implies that one may call science a "superior" game only as a figure of speech. Strictly speaking, even though it may have an autotelic component (which presumably accounts for the possibility of the metaphor), science goes far beyond mere play, being a prime example of "real adaptation."

One begins to understand why Piaget goes to such lengths in separating play from any useful or life-enhancing activities: the true opposition, in his theory, is not that between play and imitation, but that between play and work or seriousness, and in this sense he operates with an old dichotomy, favoring one term over the other. This is evident from the rest of his discussion of the first main stage of the child's intellectual development. Although he adopts all the play categories with which Groos and others operate, including play as pleasure in being a cause, play as exploration, play as make-believe or pretense, and play as a symbolic activity, Piaget's conclusion is invariably the same: whereas play consolidates by repetition the infant's newly acquired skills, it never has an active part in the acquisition of these skills, and therefore has a secondary role in the process of cognition itself. Both

---

*pretations in Mental Development: A Study in Social Psychology* (New York/London, 1902).

play and imitation have to be distinguished from intelligence. Intelligence is the result of the equilibrium between accommodation and assimilation, play and imitation are antithetical distortions of these two adaptive processes. Finally, Piaget even seems to favor imitation over play, by giving the former a more active role in the birth of representation: "In the deferred and interiorized behaviors which characterize the beginnings of representation, imitation, which then extends accommodation to absent as well as to present objects, thereby acquires a function which produces 'signifiers' related to the 'signified' [in a Saussurian sense], which are either adaptive or ludic according as they result from accommodated assimilation or from distorting assimilation, the former characteristic of intelligence, and the latter of play" (p. 104).

It is, then, imitation, not play, that produces signifiers, and Piaget distinguishes between "adaptive" and "ludic" signifiers: the former are the product of true representation or knowledge, the latter are merely the distorting reproduction of the others. Unexpectedly, imitation is no longer simply an extreme or pure form of accommodation, but is given an important cognitive role, which one would have expected Piaget to assign to a more "adapted" form of accommodation, and which he certainly denies to play. Imitation and play are no longer antithetical, but asymmetrical. Paradoxically, play becomes an imitation of an imitation, since its role is to repeat or reproduce the adapted signifiers, produced by imitation.

The second major stage of the child's intellectual development is characterized by "symbolic" or "make-believe" play, which continues its evolution from the end of the first stage. Here, again, symbolic play does not have the function of producing signifiers or generating representational thinking; rather, as pure, "ego-related" assimilation, it repeats and organizes representational thinking in terms of symbols that have already been acquired through adapted or accommodated assimilation. Symbolic play also receives the function of assimilating and consolidating the child's emotional experiences, and in this regard, Piaget draws on Freud's theory of play as compensation and catharsis.

During the third and fourth major stages (from the age of seven or eight onward), symbolic play comes closer to adapted assimilation, turning into "games with rules." These games evolve under the impact of the child's socialization, presupposing both cooperation with others and collective discipline. They steer the child away from merely ego-related motor-sensory and make-believe play toward more adapted or objective social behavior. But Piaget emphasizes that even in the case of these "advanced" games, one cannot speak of "intelligent adaptation." Again he goes back to Groos, suggesting that, far from having any substantial cognitive value, the game rules merely *rationalize* the child's functional pleasure in both his sensory-motor skills and his intellectual achievement or triumph over his peers; in other words, the game rules merely structure or rationalize the child's feeling of power or the "joy in conquest." Moreover, if during the first three major stages of the child's intellectual development play is needed to consolidate adapted or ac-commodated assimilation, during the fourth and last stage, which is that of reflective intelligence, it is "progressively less distorting and more nearly related to adapted work" (p. 140), until with the advent of maturity it becomes completely indistinguishable from the latter.

Finally Piaget distinguishes among three classes of games: "mere practice games" (a modified version of Groos's evolutionary concept of play as preexercise), which man shares with animals; "symbolic games"; and "games with rules." The latter two surpass the ability of animals and are characteristic of man only. These three classes of games correspond to the three major steps in the evolution of human intelligence: sensory-motor, representational, and reflective. They follow a hierarchical order, with the sensory-motor games having the lowest rank on the evolutionary scale and the rule-governed games the highest. There is a fourth class of games which Piaget calls "constructional" or "creative," such as building miniature boats, drawing, modeling, designing, and the like, but they have an ambiguous status: they do not "form a category of the same kind as the others, but are a boundary class between games and non-ludic behavior" (p. 110). They occupy "a position half-way between play and intelligent work, or between play and imitation" (p. 113). Constructional games appear during the sec-ond and third stages of the child's intellectual development, but during the fourth stage they merge into adapted social behavior or work, losing their ludic character altogether.

Needless to say, the ambiguous status of the constructional or cre-ative games reveals the limits of Piaget's theory of play as well as his own ambiguity toward the ludic phenomenon. Although in principle he seems to hold that play "begins as soon as there is predominance of assimilation," he seldom remains consistent with this position, in prac-tice ending up with a much more restrictive view of play. More often than not, he describes it in negative terms (which he never does in the case of imitation), as a "distortion of reality" or a "self-centered ac-tivity." And even though he gives play various functions in the process of cognition or learning, all these functions remain secondary in relation to those of imitation and work.

The reasons for Piaget's ambivalent attitude toward play are undoubtedly complex, but they are at least in part related to the demands of the work ethic, which remains strong in his country (Switzerland), as well as to his deep-seated distrust of play, which he shares with rationalist thinkers from Plato to Kant. He obviously operates with traditional rationalistic assumptions about mind and reality. For instance, his distinction between accommodation and assimilation—an offshoot of evolutionary theory, specifically of the concept of natural selection through adaptation—is based on the old rationalist dichotomy between subject and object. Although both imitation and play are a result of an imbalance between subject and object, Piaget ultimately favors imitation over play, precisely because for him the former is oriented toward the object and therefore seems free of the dangers of total subjectivity or arbitrariness. In turn, he undervalues play because he sees it as oriented toward the subject, and therefore as a self-indulgent, egocentric activity, feeding that feeling of power and appetite of conquest which no veneer of "civilized" behavior has been able to suppress completely. Hence, following Plato and Kant, Piaget attempts to discipline play, yoking it to rational rules and social order. Yet despite the ambiguities inherent in his rationalist position, Piaget performs the same service for play in developmental psychology and education that Schiller performs for it in modern philosophy: he turns the ludic phenomenon into a respectable scientific topic.

If Piaget is prepared to assign only a secondary cognitive role to play, many child psychologists and educators who come after him proclaim it to be a decisive factor in the development of intelligence and the creative imagination. They support this contention by allying themselves with the recent research on play, conducted in communication, cybernetics, ethology, primatology, and anthropology. A good deal of this research has been inspired by Gregory Bateson's frame or metacommunication theory of play. Possessor of a truly interdisciplinary mind, Bateson has done extensive work in anthropology, ethnology, psychiatry, biology, genetics, ecology, philosophy of language, communication, and systems theory. Some of his most significant writings are collected in *Steps to an Ecology of Mind* (1972), including his extremely influential paper "A Theory of Play and Fantasy" (1955), on which I concentrate here.

Bateson's interest in play comes primarily from his attempt to wed analytic philosophy to psychiatric theory, and in this regard he acknowledges his debt to Whitehead, Russell, Wittgenstein, Carnap, and Whorf. He distinguishes among three levels of abstraction in human verbal communication: the *denotative* level, where the subject of discourse is outside language ("the cat is on the mat"); the *metalinguistic* level, where the subject of discourse is language itself ("the word *cat* has no fur and cannot scratch"); and the *metacommunicative* level, where the subject of discourse is the relationship between speakers ("my telling you where to find the cat was friendly"). Play belongs to this last level. The metacommunicative level is highly abstract and is not necessarily verbal, always remaining implicit. According to Bateson it marks an advanced stage in the evolutionary process. At this stage, the organism no longer responds automatically to the mood-signs of other organisms (by a "mood-sign" Bateson understands a spontaneous action, such as a bite, which produces a spontaneous response, such as a retaliatory bite), but is able to recognize these signs *as* signs; in other words, it is able to "recognize that the other individual's and its own signals are only signals, which can be trusted, distrusted, falsified, denied, amplified, corrected, and so forth."[21] The metacommunicative level is precisely the one that makes communication at the other levels, including the verbal, possible. It is characteristic not only of man but also of other higher animals, as Bateson found out through observations at the zoo:

> I saw two monkeys *playing*, i.e., engaged in an interactive sequence of which the unit actions or signals were similar to but not the same as those of combat. It was evident, even to the human observer, that the sequence as a whole was not combat, and evident to the human observer that to the participant monkeys this was "not combat.". . .
> Now, this phenomenon, play, could only occur if the particular organisms were capable of some degree of metacommunication, i.e., of exchanging signals which would carry the message "this is play." (p. 179)

The message "this is play" is a complex communicative act. Logically, play denotes something that is "not play." Hence the signals exchanged in play are false and that which they denote is nonexistent. Bateson mentions other actions which, like play, differ from what they denote, such as bluffing, threatening, histrionics, fantasizing, ritual, drama, and the like. He suggests that they form a single complex of phenomena setting up a paradoxical frame of the Epimenidean type. Logical para-

21. Bateson, *Ecology of Mind*, p. 178. Further citations are in the text.

doxes of this type are self-contradictory propositions about themselves, such as "All statements within this frame are false." If this proposition were true, then it would be false; if it were false, then it would be true. Bertrand Russell describes this type of logical paradox as belonging to a class of classes that are not members of themselves.

After attempting to establish a connection among play, metacommunication, logical paradoxes, and psychological frames, Bateson draws a parallel between therapy and the ludic phenomenon. Although his approach is largely non-Freudian, he anticipates some of Winnicott's observations about psychoanalysis as a game between analyst and patient. According to Bateson, both play and therapy occur within a "delimited psychological frame, a spatial and temporal bounding of a set of interactive messages." In both processes, the messages have a paradoxical relationship to a "more concrete or basic reality": "Just as the pseudocombat of play is not real combat, so also the pseudolove and pseudohate of therapy are not real love and hate. The 'transfer' is discriminated from real love and hate by signals invoking the psychological frame; and indeed it is this frame which permits the transfer to reach its full intensity and to be discussed between patient and therapist" (p. 191).

Bateson further uses his game analogy to describe the interaction of therapist and patient. He imagines two players who engage in a game of canasta, abiding by the rules. As long as these rules remain unquestioned, the game remains unchanged, that is, no therapeutic change will occur. But if the players stop the game and start discussing the rules, their discourse will be of a different logical type from that of their play. Should they resume their game, they would probably proceed with changed rules. Therapy, like play, involves a combination of divergent logical types of discourse. Yet, whereas the canasta players can avoid paradox by separating their discussion of the rules from the game itself, the therapist and the patient cannot do so. As a result, they play a more fluid game, changing the rules as they go along: "As we see it the process of psychotherapy is a framed interaction between two persons, in which the rules are implicit but subject to change. Such change can only be proposed by experimental action, but every such experimental action, in which a proposal to change the rules is implicit, is itself part of an on-going game. It is this combination of logical types within the single meaningful act that gives to therapy the character not of a rigid game like canasta but, instead, that of an evolving system of interaction. The play of kittens or otters has this character" (p. 192). Bateson, then, makes an implicit distinction (which unfortunately he does not pursue) between the relatively "free play" of the patient and therapist, resembling the loosely structured play of animals, and the rigid and inflexible parlor—or even social—games in which the rules are established in advance.

According to Bateson, the psychotic—notably the schizophrenic—cannot play, that is, he cannot handle psychological frames: he treats all actions as mood-signs, unaware of their metaphorical or abstract level. He needs to discover, in the course of the therapeutic process, what these signs stand for, so that he will finally realize that they are only signs. Bateson concludes that the paradoxes of abstraction inherent in play are not mere philosophical inventions belonging to Russell's theory of logical types. Rather, they represent an advanced stage in all communication, going beyond mood-signs, and without them the evolution of communication could proceed no further. Life would then be an "endless interchange of stylized messages, a game with rigid rules, unrelieved by change or humor" (p. 193).

Despite its somewhat loose and unclear formulation, Bateson's metacommunication theory of play has proven seminal not only in psychology but also in biology, anthropology, and linguistics. It firmly links play to evolution, assigning it a crucial role in the development of mental or symbolic processes, which is precisely what Piaget was not prepared to do. Further, it associates play with the capacity for abstraction and simulation of the higher organisms and therefore with these organisms' ability to free themselves from strict biological constraints (an idea adopted by several other contemporary biologists). At the same time, Bateson's theory of play represents a decisive victory for the rational play concept in the human sciences. Because he links it mostly to the logical faculty, seeing it as an exclusively symbolic activity, Bateson "rationalizes" play to an even greater extent than Erikson and Winnicott, separating it completely from its prerational, violent origins. Note, for instance, that his monkeys, not unlike his patient and therapist, engage in "pseudocombat," exhibiting pseudolove and hate and thus limiting conflict to an abstract or symbolic level. Granted that Bateson's metacommunication theory may apply in the case of play among equals (for example, among members of the same species), what about the play of a cat with mice or that of a god with men? Are we to consider mice and men schizophrenic if, in this case, they fail to understand the "logical paradoxes of abstraction" or the symbolical content of the message "This is play" sent to them by the cat or the god? What I mean, of course, is that play is not always intersubjective nor is it always metaphorical and abstract; in short, it is far from being exclusively nonviolent and rational, as Bateson's theory presupposes.

Another influential figure in the current interdisciplinary studies of play who combines Bateson's symbolic approach with behavioral theory, remaining nonetheless highly skeptical of a purely rationalist interpretation of the ludic phenomenon, is Brian Sutton-Smith. Although his training is originally in developmental psychology and education, Sutton-Smith's work cuts across a variety of disciplines, including anthropology, folklore, narratology, linguistics, communication theory, and aesthetics. Of particular interest is his critique of Piaget's theory of play, presented in several papers over the past twenty years and recently summed up in "Piaget, Play and Cognition Revisited" (1983). Despite certain divergences in the interpretation of Piaget's theory of play, Sutton-Smith's critique of this theory parallels my own, revolving around three main objections: "1) that despite their apparent equipotentiality in his theory of intelligence, Piaget had contrived an asymmetry or imbalance between the contributions to be made to cognition by imitation and play—imitation was the star performer and play was its aborted partner; 2) that this inequality was brought about by Piaget's focus on directed or rational or convergent, rather than undirected or imaginative or divergent cognitive operations; 3) that it was also a result of presupposing play to be a predominantly infantile state of development, a not uncommon assumption in the work ethic ideology of Western culture."[22]

Reviewing the currently available empirical evidence for Piaget's theory of play in relation to what he considers its three main assumptions, Sutton-Smith points out that this evidence either remains partial and inconclusive or has been arrived at through objectionable methodological procedures. In turn, he employs Bateson's metacommunication or frame theory of play as well as Berlyne's "stimulus-response" or "arousal" theory in order to describe the structural characteristics of "undirected" thought, which is usually associated with imagination and play and is relegated to a secondary cognitive role by "directed," rational thinking.[23] These structural characteristics involve four classes of psy-

22. Sutton-Smith, "Piaget, Play, and Cognition Revisited," in Overton, *The Relationship between Social and Cognitive Development*, p. 230. Further citations are in the text.
23. See D. E. Berlyne, *Conflict, Arousal, and Curiosity* (New York, 1960). Berlyne's stimulus-response theory of play continues to have a great deal of authority in the behavioral sciences.

chological events: communicative (framing or reframing in Bateson's sense), conative (reversibility in Freud's sense), cognitive (abstraction of prototypes, themes and variations, boundaried space and time, which in turn includes miniaturization, hyperbolation, and circular repetition), and affective (modulation of excitement, in Berlyne's sense). Sutton-Smith demonstrates that what appears in Piaget as undirected thought or pure, distorting assimilation involves several levels of operations, some of them, such as reversibility, being also required in convergent or rational thinking. Others, such as abstracted prototypes, themes and variations, and modulation of excitement, are at the very "heart of divergent and imaginative thinking and therefore of playful and artistic productions" (p. 243). In the so-called hard sciences, one might add, theorists have begun to speak of divergent and imaginative thinking itself as playing a major role in scientific theory: witness, for example, the philosophical statements of such renowned physicists as Einstein and Schrödinger or the recent studies in the philosophy and history of science which emphasize the "scientific imagination and intuition."[24]

Sutton-Smith concludes that Piaget's concept of play as "pure assimilation" in fact describes only one kind of play, called "reverie" or "daydreaming," which seems to predominate during the child's early years. Piaget largely directs his attention to the study of the solitary play activities of his (middle-class) children, ignoring the social context in which these activities took place, including the interaction of his children with their mother or with himself, their supposedly objective observer. Therefore, Piaget still operates with traditional observational methods that fail to take into account the observer as part of the process.

Finally, Sutton-Smith argues for a larger cultural and cross-cultural context for the study of adult and child play. His main premise is that play is always the play of a certain social group; it cannot stand outside culture and it is functionally related to this culture. Furthermore, the cultural relationships of play are variable and flexible. In some cases play may be a mirror of sociocultural life: "More collaborative cultures have more collaborative kinds of games, more competitive cultures have more competitive kinds of games." In other cases, cultural play may be an "inversion of the larger cultural system, a message as to the dangerous affective life that underlies it and that should not be tampered

24. See, e.g., Gerald Holton, *The Scientific Imagination* (Cambridge, Mass., 1978) and Judith Wechsler, ed., *On Aesthetics in Science* (Cambridge, Mass., 1978). I refer again to these authors in sec. 3.3, below.

with if stability is to be maintained." In still other cases, the domain of play may be one of "instability and conflict" or, conversely, one of "communitas and unity, as compared with the disequilibrium of war and economics" (p. 245). According to Sutton-Smith, what all these cultural interpretations of play have in common is that play "enters always into some systematic pattern of social relationships and mythic beliefs." Far from being perceived as standing aside as a "nonentity and unimportant part of the cultural whole," play becomes a reading of "the total cultural structure that provides an underlying sense of its overall reality" (p. 245). In other words, culture does not only generate play and players but is itself "played," and in this respect Sutton-Smith comes close to the philosophical position of Heidegger, Fink, Gadamer, and others.[25]

The cases I have so far discussed in the scientific literature on play show that since the end of the nineteenth century there has been an increasing emphasis on the ludic phenomenon as a cognitive instrument and as an active evolutionary force. This scientific interest in play seems to have been initiated, in the Anglo-American scientific community, by Spencer, and although his surplus-energy theory is no longer regarded as scientifically valid, his prediction of the centrality of play in a postindustrial culture has proven correct. While discarding the physiological descriptions with which Spencer sought to support his view, evolutionists have adopted most of his insights, and nowadays psychologists, psychoanalysts, anthropologists, ethnologists, primatologists, and others proclaim play a decisive factor in evolution, not only in the transition from the higher primates to man, but also in the development of humanity itself.[26]

25. Sutton-Smith's research on play is extensive: one cannot even begin, in a study like mine, to do it justice by tracing its development from Sutton-Smith's first studies of children's play in the 1950s to such later books as *The Folkgames of Children* (Austin, Tex., 1972) and *A History of Children's Play: The New Zealand Playground, 1840–1950* (Philadelphia, 1981). Although some critics have charged him with a certain theoretical eclecticism or even inconsistency, for Sutton-Smith this eclecticism seems to be a conscious strategy in dealing with a complex and slippery phenomenon that cannot lend itself to any single methodology. One can also discern in his recent work an increasing awareness of the relationship between play and power, and in this he stands apart from a great number of his colleagues in child psychology, who have a tendency to "idealize" play (see Sutton-Smith, "The Idealization of Play," paper presented to the Second Annual Conference of the North American Society of the Sociology of Sport, Fort Worth, Tex., Nov. 12, 1981).

26. The psychological and anthropological literature on children's play is extensive, and one can consult two useful guides to it: Helen B. Schwartzman, *Transfor-*

Whereas the older scientists favor work over play, the recent ones attempt to dissolve this dichotomy, retaining nonetheless play's biological utility. As a result, in these later theorists, play effectively becomes privileged over work both as a learning or arousal-seeking activity and as a major factor in the individual's mental and emotional development. Michael Ellis, for instance, argues that play and work are the same activity: "If play is stimulus-seeking activity and if work is life-supporting activity, many, many activities are both at the same time. Frequently the life-support activities are sufficiently interesting to allow the worker

---

*mations: The Anthropology of Children's Play* (New York, 1980) and Bernard Mergen, *Play and Playthings: A Reference Guide* (Westport, Conn., 1982). Two related works are J. M. Hawes and N. R. Hiner, eds., *American Childhood: A Research Guide and Historical Handbook* (Westport, Conn., 1985) and Barbara Finkelstein, ed., *Regulated Children/Liberated Children* (New York, 1979). In anthropology, the most influential work (apart from Victor Turner's "liminality" theory of play, which I shall examine in detail elsewhere) has been a collective volume significantly entitled, *Play: Its Role in Development and Evolution*, ed. Jerome S. Bruner, Alison Jolly, and Kathy Sylva (New York, 1976), containing papers on play from an anthropological, primatological, ethological, psychological, psychoanalytical, sociological, linguistic, and literary point of view. According to the editors, "the contributors were interested in exploring the trends in the primate order as these reflect themselves in the play of human beings," all of them subscribing to the "hypothesis that the evolution of play might be a major precursor to the emergence of language and symbolic behavior in higher primates and man."

More recently, several collective and interdisciplinary studies have appeared under the auspices of The Association for the Anthropological Study of Play (TAASP), founded in 1974, including D. F. Lancy and B. A. Tindall, eds., *The Study of Play: Problems and Prospects* (West Point, N.Y., 1977); M. A. Salter, ed., *Play: Anthropological Perspectives* (West Point, N.Y., 1979); H. B. Schwartzman, ed., *Play and Culture* (West Point, N.Y., 1980); A. Cheska, ed., *Play as Context* (West Point, N.Y., 1981); J. Loy, ed., *The Paradoxes of Play* (West Point, N.Y., 1982); F. E. Manning, ed., *The World at Play* (West Point, N.Y., 1983); and B. Sutton-Smith and D. Kelly-Byrne, eds., *The Masks of Play* (West Point, N.Y., 1984). Sutton-Smith's edited volume, *Play and Learning* (New York, 1979), deals specifically with play as a cognitive process and includes contributions by such noted anthropologists, developmental psychologists, and educators as Mihaly Csikszentmihalyi, Catherine Garvey, Corinne Hutt, Helen Schwartzman, Jerome Singer and Dorothy Singer, and others. A dissenting view as to the importance of play for evolution and cognition can be found in Catherine Garvey, *Play* (Cambridge, Mass., 1977). For play, anthropology, and semiotics, see Thomas A. Sebeok, *The Play of Musement* (Bloomington, Ind., 1981). For play and sociology, see Georg Simmel, *Grundfragen der Soziologie (Individuum und Gesellschaft)* (Berlin, 1917) and, in his wake, Erving Goffman, *Frame Analysis* (New York, 1974), Robert Nisbet, *Sociology as an Art Form* (Oxford, 1976), and Richard Brown, *A Poetics for Sociology* (Cambridge, Eng., 1977).

to maintain arousal while earning the monetary rewards for existence. . . . Play and work lie on a continuum."[27]

Another behaviorist, Joseph Levy, replaces the distinction between work and play with that between work and effort: "Effort is autonomous, intrinsically motivated, and stressful, whereas work is allonomous, extrinsically motivating, and boring or over-arousing."[28] Needless to say, what Levy calls effort is just a cryptic "scientific" name for what others openly call play. Indeed, later on in his study, Levy himself remarks that "play, not work, has become the major source of personal dignity and identity in post-industrialist society" (p. 38).

The behaviorist view of play as work or work as play is shared even by such sophisticated behavioral theorists as Mihaly Csikszentmihalyi. Starting from Berlyne's concept of stimulus-response (like Ellis and Levy), Csikszentmihalyi develops a "flow" theory of play, locating the ludic phenomenon on a continuum between "boredom" and "anxiety." In this regard, he also attempts to eliminate the opposition between work and play. Nevertheless, for him, as for many other contemporary behavioral scientists, it is play, not work, that represents an awareness of existential choices and a restructuring of, rather than an adaptation to, reality.[29] These examples, to which one can add many others, reveal what Sutton-Smith has called an "idealizing tendency," which goes hand in hand with what I would call a "rationalizing tendency," in the contemporary scientific studies of play. These tendencies seem again to be most prominent in, although certainly not limited to, behaviorist science, where play has become a universal remedy for all our physical and spiritual problems (see, for instance, the last chapter of Levy's book, significantly entitled "Play and the Future: A Time for Renaissance," *Play-Behavior*, pp. 183–190). Voices like that of Sutton-Smith belong to a small minority and the rational play concepts remain predominant in the current discussions of play in the human sciences.

## SECTION 2

# Play and Natural Selection

As we have seen, a good number of the most influential concepts of human evolution remain tied up with a vague or ambivalent notion of

27. Ellis, *Why People Play*, p. 110.
28. Levy, *Play Behavior*, p. 185.
29. Mihaly Csikszentmihalyi, *Beyond Boredom and Anxiety* (San Francisco, 1975).

progress, for which play functions as a catalyst, if not a sine qua non. Even a cursory examination of the current scientific concepts of biological evolution shows that they often present a more complicated evolutionary picture, in which play has, with a few exceptions, a relatively minor role. If proponents of human evolution have occasional scuffles, those of natural evolution engage in heated wars—the young discipline of biology, for example, has been a battlefield of fiercely antagonistic theories. Darwinism and Neo-Darwinism have started losing ground on this battlefield lately, being again vigorously challenged even by some of their older, once-defeated, enemies such as Lamarckism and Cuvierism. This goes to show, perhaps not without irony, that the "struggle for life" of ideas, unlike that of the species, does not lead to natural selection, but only to temporary victory or defeat.

Though biologists rarely take the ludic phenomenon itself as their object of study, many of them have increasingly used play concepts as tools in understanding evolution by natural selection—the "central dogma" of Darwinism and Neo-Darwinism.[30] They usually conceive of natural selection either as a contest leading to the survival of the fittest (with the word *fittest* meaning different things for different biologists) or as an interplay of chance and necessity. They often combine these two positions, usually postulating an interplay of randomness and design that governs the competition leading to natural selection. The advocates of natural selection by an interplay of chance and necessity are, in turn, split in two camps, according to whether they give priority to necessity or to chance in the evolutionary process. The first camp sees natural selection as an immense game with infinitely complicated but in principle discoverable or specifiable rules, while the second one sees it as an immense lottery, arbitrary and unpredictable, governed by pure chance. Recently, a third camp has emerged, mediating between the other two and giving equal status to both chance and necessity. While not denying chance a significant role, this camp attempts to meet it halfway by postulating a spontaneous, self-assembling, and self-regulating "inner" necessity—the kind that seems to be inherent in biological entities, such as a living organism. On this view, necessity arises out of

---

30. A notable exception is Robert Fagen's extensive study *Animal Play Behavior* (New York, 1981). Unlike other biologists, Fagen attempts an interdisciplinary approach to his topic, even including a discussion of play and art from a biological point of view. One can further consult the brief sections on play in William H. Thorpe, *Learning and Instinct in Animals* (London, 1963). Thorpe also provides short discussions of researchers who have given specific treatment to play as a biological phenomenon.

chance, order out of chaos, although the details of this process often remain unclear. The first camp, then, obviously operates with rational play concepts. The second and the third camps would seem, prima facie, to operate with prerational play concepts, but this first impression may prove misleading. This may equally be the case in regard to the concept of natural selection as the outcome of a competition for natural resources, and it is this concept that I shall examine first.

## 2·1 Play, Struggle for Life, and Survival of the Fittest

Some contemporary Darwinists, especially those who regard natural selection as an interplay of chance and necessity, agree that *struggle for life* and *survival of the fittest* are ambiguous terms, susceptible to various readings and misreadings, and prefer to separate them from the concept of natural selection. Originally, Darwin meant them as mere metaphors, which came to him while perusing Malthus's theories on the growth of human population and its adverse effects on society at large. In *Origin of Species*—whose full title, one must not forget, is *On the Origin of Species by Means of Natural Selection, or the Preservation of Favoured Races in the Struggle for Life*—Darwin establishes the connection between natural selection (a term he coins on the analogy of the farmer's method of breeding cattle by selection), struggle for life, and survival of the fittest:

> All these results . . . follow from the struggle for life. Owing to this struggle, variations, however slight and from whatever cause proceeding, if they be in any degree profitable to the individuals of a species . . . will tend to the preservation of such individuals, and will generally be inherited by the offspring. . . . I have called this principle, by which each slight variation, if useful, is preserved, by the term Natural Selection, in order to mark its relation to man's power of selection. But the expression often used by Mr. Herbert Spencer of the Survival of the Fittest is more accurate, and is sometimes equally convenient.[31]

For Darwin, then, *natural selection* and *survival of the fittest* are equivalent terms, a view that contains no small historical irony since later Darwinists, forgetting the Malthusian origin of Darwin's and Spencer's

31. Charles Darwin, *Origin of Species* (New York, 1952), p. 52. Further citations are in the text.

metaphors, emphatically deny the relevance of natural selection to the social realm and dismiss Spencer's "social Darwinism."[32] In turn, struggle for life has a metaphorical function for Darwin, covering a variety of disparate phenomena:

> *The Term Struggle for Existence, used in a large sense.* I should premise that I use this term in a large and metaphorical sense including dependence of one being on another, and including . . . not only the life of the individual, but success in leaving progeny. Two canine animals, in a time of dearth, may be truly said to struggle with each other which shall get food and live. But a plant on the edge of a desert is said to struggle for life against the drought, though more properly it should be said to be dependent on the moisture. A plant which annually produces a thousand seeds, of which only one of an average comes to maturity, may be more truly said to struggle with the plants of the same and other kinds which already clothe the ground. . . . In these several senses, which pass into each other, I use for convenience's sake the general term of Struggle for Existence. (pp. 52–53)

What for Darwin may be "truly said" to be a struggle for life turns out primarily to be a competition for natural resources among various species or among the members of the same one. In this regard, as Nietzsche (who was a relentless anti-Darwinist) accurately sensed, Darwinian agon is not the gratuitous, "aristocratic" contest of free and arbitrary forces, and therefore cannot be seen as a prerational play concept. Rather, it is the utilitarian, early capitalist competition for natural resources and market rights which, despite certain abuses, remains on the whole based on rational principles of "fair play." Even so, struggle for life and survival of the fittest must evoke the occasionally raw and inhuman aspects of early capitalism (as portrayed, for example, in Victorian fiction, notably in Dickens's and Gaskell's novels) to our contemporary sensibilities, formed in an age of subtler competition and postindustrial leisure. This may partly explain why more recent Darwinists wish Darwin had stuck to his farming analogy, and not mixed his metaphors. They feel, not without justification, that these metaphors are too vague and imprecise, assembling too many heterogeneous elements within their operational field, to be of much scientific use. And

32. Lately, however, sociobiology or the "new synthesis" has reversed the trend. See especially the work of E. O. Wilson, the "father" of contemporary sociobiology. For a cogent critique of this allegedly interdisciplinary approach, see Marshall Sahlins, *The Use and Abuses of Biology* (Ann Arbor, Mich., 1976).

yet many other biologists, including certain Neo-Darwinists, seem unwilling to give them up and continue to reinterpret them in terms of their own theories of evolution.

One of the most articulate recent advocates of natural selection as survival of the fittest is Richard Dawkins, an Oxford-trained ethologist with a close interest in genetics and game theory. In his influential study *The Selfish Gene* (1976), Dawkins provides a highly readable account of the Neo-Darwinist position, established by Sir Robert Fisher in *The Genetical Theory of Natural Selection* (1930), and extended by such contemporary Anglo-American geneticists as J. B. S. Haldane, W. D. Hamilton, G. C. Williams, J. Maynard Smith, R. L. Trivers, and E. O. Wilson, according to which natural selection as survival of the fittest does not occur at the individual or even the group but rather the *gene* level. Dawkins's thesis is that the "predominant quality to be expected in a successful gene is ruthless selfishness" and that, in turn, this gene selfishness "will usually give rise to selfishness in individual behavior."[33] According to him, if one were to sum up the modern understanding of natural selection one could not use a more apt phrase than Tennyson's "nature red in tooth and claw" (p. 2). Dawkins is willing to push the Darwinian and Spencerian metaphors of struggle for life and survival of the fittest all the way to Hobbes's *bellum omnium contra omnes*, although unlike Hobbes or Spencer, and like many contemporary ethologists, he stops short of applying them to human societies.

The natural enemy of Dawkins's biology of selfishness is the biology of altruism, advanced in such ethological studies as Wynne-Edwards's *Animal Dispersion in Relation to Social Behavior* (1961), Lorenz's *On Aggression* (1966), Ardrey's *The Social Contract* (1970), and Eibl-Eibesfeldt's *Love and Hate* (1971). According to Dawkins, this biology makes the "erroneous assumption that the important thing in evolution is the good of the *species* (or the group) rather than the good of the individual (or the gene)" (p. 2). Dawkins defines as altruistic any behavior on the part of a biological entity (such as a mammal or an insect), which "increases another such entity's welfare at the expense of its own," with "welfare" in this case meaning chances of survival (p. 4). Usually the proponents of altruistic behavior are also advocates of "group selection," with "group" meaning anything from a herd to a population or an entire species. Dawkins sums up their point of view as follows: "A group such as a species or a population within a species, whose individ-

---

33. Richard Dawkins, *The Selfish Gene* (Oxford, 1976), p. 2. Further citations refer to this edition. Dawkins extends and refines some of the theses of *The Selfish Gene* in *The Blind Watchmaker* (Harlow, Essex, 1986).

ual members are prepared to sacrifice themselves for the welfare of the group, may be less likely to go extinct than a rival group whose individual members place their own selfish interest first" (p. 8).

To altruistic behavior Dawkins opposes selfish behavior that benefits only the individual, and to group selection he opposes individual selection, which in his case means gene selection. Although he does not deny that in certain cases an individual may behave in an apparently altruistic fashion, he argues that one needs to evaluate this behavior at the gene level; indeed, there are "special circumstances in which a gene can achieve its own selfish goals best by fostering a limited form of altruism at the level of individual animals" (p. 2). For him, however, most cases of so-called altruistic behavior are only a matter of false reading on the part of the observer, and he devotes a significant portion of his study to showing how these cases serve equally well as examples of selfish behavior.

Dawkins interprets survival of the fittest to mean "survival of the stable," and extends the Darwinian theory of evolution by natural selection beyond the species to the beginnings of life on earth. A stable thing, according to him, is a "collection of atoms which is permanent enough or common enough to deserve a name" (p. 12). The first stable organic matter may have been the amino-acid molecule that developed in the so-called primeval soup (the seas of thousands of millions of years ago) by a combination of water, carbon dioxide, methane, and ammonia in the presence of a powerful source of energy such as lightning. (This process has been simulated successfully in the laboratory.) A primeval natural selection operated among these and other organic molecules, preserving the stable ones and rejecting the unstable. At some point there came into existence, by pure chance, a special kind of molecule that was able to create copies of itself, which Dawkins calls a *replicator*. These replicators were the ancestors, or at least the primeval equivalents, of the modern DNA molecule. They were favored by natural selection because they were able to replicate either rapidly or accurately, thus tending toward more and more stability. Competition played as important a role in this process as it does in "modern" evolution. The primeval soup could support only a finite number of replicator molecules. The replicators that prevailed in the struggle for existence were the ones that built for themselves what Dawkins calls "survival machines." Similarly, their descendants or their modern equivalents, the genes, have built their own survival machines, in the form of humans, animals, plants, bacteria, and viruses.

Since any survival machine is made up of millions of genes, it would make sense to speak of "gene complexes" rather than of individual genes. The point Dawkins wants to drive home, however, is that while the combinations of genes that make up an individual organism live only as long as *it* lives, the genes themselves are potentially immortal. Sexual reproduction mixes and reshuffles genes in various combinations, and individual bodies are temporary vehicles for such combinations. But the genes survive beyond a particular combination, moving on, by sexual reproduction, into other bodies. A DNA molecule may "live in the form of *copies* of itself for a hundred million years" (p. 37). The individual gene, then, can be regarded as a "unit which survives through a large number of successive individual bodies" (p. 26).

But how do genes manipulate their bodies or "control" their survival machines? The genes work by controlling protein synthesis, but this is a very slow process, hardly geared to directing behavior on a day-to-day basis; therefore the genes need to program their survival machines *in advance*, to instruct them "not in specifics, but in general strategies and tricks of the living trade" (p. 59). The genes must be able to anticipate the future life conditions of their survival machines and "build in" the behavioral strategies most suitable to those conditions. For instance, if their survival machine will be a polar bear, they will program him to have a thick, white pelt that will both protect him from the Arctic cold and camouflage him in the snow.

The genes must not only predict the future of their survival machines and program them accordingly, they must also gamble on the accuracy of their predictions; they must take risks. To stay with the example of the polar bear, if the Arctic conditions were suddenly to change for tropical ones, the genes would have committed a grave error for which they would have to pay with their own lives. It is at this point that Dawkins introduces game theory into his argument. He spares the nonmathematical reader the abstract and complicated language with which this theory usually operates.[34] Instead, he presents its basic assumptions and objectives in the form of a "gambling" metaphor:

34. According to Martin Shubik, "Game theory is a method for the study of decision-making in situations of conflict. It deals with human processes in which the individual decision-unit is not in complete control of other decision-units entering the environment" (*Game Theory and Related Approaches to Social Behavior* [New York, 1964], p. 8). See also Martin Shubik, *Game Theory in the Social Sciences: Concepts and Solutions* (Cambridge, Mass., 1982) and Hervé Moulin, *Game Theory for the Social Sciences* (New York, 1982). Game theory can be applied to any state of affairs or natural phenomena that are based not only on conflict but also on an

Prediction in a complex world is a chancy business. Every decision that a survival machine takes is a gamble, and it is the business of genes to program brains in advance so that on average they take decisions which pay off. The currency used in the casino of evolution is survival. . . .

We can carry the metaphor of gambling a little further. A gambler must think of three main quantities, stakes, odds, and prize. If the prize is very large, a gambler is prepared to risk a big stake. A gambler who risks his all on a single throw stands to gain a great deal. He also stands to lose a great deal, but on average high-stake gamblers are no better and no worse off than other players who play for low winnings with low stakes. . . . Are there animal gamblers who play for high stakes, and others with a more conservative game? . . . Naturalists who read this book may be able to think of species which can be described as high-stake high-risk players, and other species which play a more conservative game. (pp. 59–60)

In gambling, game theory weighs the stakes against the odds, or calculates the risks involved, at the same time predicting which play strategies are more likely, or unlikely, to pay off. Outside gambling, game theory has attempted to predict the outcome of real and hypothetical ecological, social, economic, political, and military developments, usually involving a "conflict of interest" between two or more parties, and it bases its predictions on "cost-benefit" calculations, that is, on rational and utilitarian premises. Following John Maynard Smith, G. A. Parker, G. R. Price, and others, Dawkins applies game theory to natural selection and describes a considerable number of gene "strategies," his assumption all along being, of course, that these strategies are unconscious: genes, or even individual animals, do not think, they act "blindly." He reexamines, in this light, such controversial topics as animal aggression, kin relationships, childbearing and child-caring, the "battle of generations," the "battle of the sexes," animal symbiotic relationships, and so forth. In all these cases Dawkins concludes that individuals act primarily out of self-interest, being preprogrammed by their selfish genes to do so. Nevertheless, because *all* individuals are survival machines, working in the best interest of their own genes, in

---

interplay of chance and necessity. There is a huge number of studies based on game theory in economics, cybernetics, statistics, political and social science, and modern warfare, as well as in physics, chemistry, and biology. The best mathematical treatment remains that of John von Neumann and Oscar Morgenstern, *Theory of Games and Economic Behavior* (New York, 1944).

practice they arrive at what J. Maynard Smith and others have called "evolutionarily stable strategies," or ESS. Since all of them try to "maximize" their own success, the only "strategy that persists will be one, which, once evolved, cannot be bettered by any deviant individual." Selection itself will "penalize" any deviation from such a strategy (p. 74).

Dawkins uses ESS, for example, in his discussion of animal aggression. He rejects both the "naive" versions of the selfish gene theory, which would supposedly predict that animals will indiscriminately kill and then eat their enemies, and the group selection theory (in this case represented by Lorenz, in *On Aggression*), which "stresses the restrained and gentlemanly nature of animal fighting" (p. 72). According to Dawkins, animals will fight only when it is in the best interest of their selfish genes to do so, which is much less often than one might think: there are costs as well as benefits involved in "outright pugnacity," including such important considerations as time, energy, and a complex system of rivalry, in which killing an enemy might benefit another more than it would oneself. Consequently, ESS is "applicable wherever we find conflict of interest and that means almost everywhere," demonstrating how a group of selfish entities may come to look very much like a single organized and harmonious whole (p. 90). Apart from its scientific name, ESS is by no means a new discovery. It has been employed over the centuries by several social thinkers, such as Hobbes and Vico, in order to explain how a certain society can be fiercely agonistic and yet remain relatively stable. In all such agonistic societal models, the individual acting in his own selfish interest ends up acting in the best interest of the whole, with "best interest" meaning stability and "whole" meaning a balance of forces rather than an altruistic or neighborly community.[35]

Another interesting question Dawkins raises in relation to game and model theory is that of the techniques devised by the genes in order to predict the future of their survival machines. For this purpose, the genes have provided the machines with such sophisticated features as learning abilities and adaptive behaviors and, most important, a capacity for "simulation." Here again Dawkins borrows his metaphor from computer language and model theory, defining simulation as "vicarious trial and error" (p. 62): faced, for example, with a difficult decision involving

35. The Hellenic concepts of *isonomia* and *isomoiria* also bear a certain family resemblance to ESS, and I examine them in *God of Many Names*, chap. 2. See also my comments on Feyerabend's notion of a "free society" in sec. 3.3 below.

unknown future quantities, one may try out, hypothetically, all the courses of action available in that particular situation, and then decide which one seems best to follow in real life. Dawkins suggests that the evolution of the ability to simulate has culminated in man's subjective consciousness, which "arises when the brain's simulation of the world becomes so complete that it must include a model of itself" (p. 32). He sees human consciousness as a sign of the emancipation of the survival machines from their masters the genes by taking full control of the decision making. (The analogy with the self-programming computer or the "artificial intelligence" is obvious.) Dawkins then uses this hypothesis to support his theory of "memes," which are a qualitatively new kind of replicator that he believes will eventually replace the genes.

Dawkins proposes his theory of memes at the end of his book. Thus far he has mostly stayed away from human evolution (with the exception of the anthropomorphic metaphors with which he describes the behavior of genes and animals; but, then, the sole expressed purpose of these metaphors is to make his scientific topic more entertaining—a clear evidence of his playful or aesthetic attitude toward his discipline). Now we understand why: in matters of human evolution he turns out to be a self-avowed altruist after all. He operates with a fairly traditional notion of cultural evolution, which, predictably, he links to the idea of science and progress: "There is a sense in which modern science is actually better than ancient science. Not only does our understanding of the universe change as the centuries go by: it improves. Admittedly the current burst of improvement dates back only to the Renaissance, which was preceded by a dismal period of stagnation, in which European scientific culture was frozen at the level achieved by the Greeks. But . . . genetic evolution too may proceed as a series of brief spurts between stable plateaux" (p. 204).

Dawkins coins the word *meme* as an abbreviated form of *mimeme*, and makes no secret of the fact that what he offers is yet another version of the ancient theory of mimesis, interpreted as imitation. He intends "meme" to convey the "idea of a unit of cultural transmission, or a unit of *imitation*." Examples of memes may include "tunes, ideas, catchphrases, clothes fashions, ways of making pots or of building arches," and the like (p. 206). They also include scientific, philosophical, religious, and artistic ideas that have come down to us through the centuries. Dawkins's theory of memes has two basic aspects. The memes replace the genes as replicators by a process that he has already outlined in his discussion of subjective consciousness as simulation. Although they do not seem on the whole to be as "ruthless" as the genes, the memes still evolve by natural selection, that is, by competition, and their chances of survival depend, as in the case of their predecessors, on longevity, fecundity, and copying fidelity. On the other hand, they are both agents and enforcers of cultural authority, much the same way as, for instance, Neoclassical literary tradition perpetuated itself by requiring the imitation of the ancients. Consequently Dawkins has ambivalent feelings toward them. In one respect, he sees the memes as cultural liberators from the "blind" natural forces of the genes; in another, he sees them as a new form of authority that in some ways is no less blind than that of their predecessors. He ends his study, however, on a note of "qualified hope," in the best rationalist tradition: "It is possible that yet another unique quality of man is a capacity for genuine, disinterested, true altrusim. . . . Even if we look on the dark side and assume that individual man is fundamentally selfish, our conscious foresight—our capacity to simulate the future in imagination—could save us from the worst selfish excesses of the blind replicators. . . . We are built as gene machines and cultured as meme machines, but we have the power to turn against our creators. We, alone on earth, can rebel against the tyranny of the selfish replicators" (p. 215).

The question may be asked why, in view of their basic rational mentality, Neo-Darwinists like Dawkins persist in employing Darwinian and Spencerian metaphors that have caused so much methodological vexation among rationalist scientists and philosophers of science. In the light of the assumptions of this book the answer seems rather obvious. There is considerable rhetorical advantage in presenting a scientific theory (especially if, like Darwinism, it may appear as a revolutionary or a potentially upsetting one) in terms of well-worn metaphors that have from time immemorial appealed to the Western "collective unconscious": struggle for life and survival of the fittest are precisely such metaphors. I certainly do not mean to imply that Darwin, Spencer, and Dawkins use these metaphors in a dishonest or devious fashion, as a conscious stratagem of getting their theories accepted. Rather, they seem to share in the prevailing collective mentality that will "naturally" favor one set of values over another. Competition has consistently been a highly positive value in Western culture, and its scientific sanction is bound to be met with general, if not "universal," approval. On the other hand, our rational mentality favors only certain kinds of competition— rule-governed, nonviolent over unregulated, destructive ones. Undoubtedly this is one of the reasons that other Neo-Darwinists, such as

Lorenz and Wynne-Edwards, downplay struggle for life and survival of the fittest, stressing altruism, cooperation, and fair play in the natural world. Dawkins himself has devised a convenient solution to the tantalizing dilemma of having your cake and eating it too: he applies his agonistic metaphors mostly to the natural world, but downplays them as much as possible in the case of the cultural world. One can finally argue that the selfish and the altruistic positions in ethology are two sides of the same coin. As Dawkins himself points out, the altruists usually replace individual selection by *group* selection. Therefore, the altruistic position does not abandon natural selection (competition) any more than the selfish position does, but simply moves it from the intraspecific to the interspecific level. One is again reminded of the Socratic watchdog in Plato's *Republic*. If the altruistic position can be seen as a sort of socialism of the natural world, in which the individual works for the common good of the species, the selfish position can be seen as an ethological, scientific version of the "look-out-for-number-one" mentality, most recently associated, for example, with the so-called New Right in American politics.

## 2·2  Chance and Necessity

Although ethologists and sociobiologists still speak of natural selection in terms of struggle for life and survival of the fittest, other biologists, particularly in molecular genetics and biochemistry, prefer to separate natural selection from its agonistic implications, seeing it simply as a differential rate in reproduction. Consequently, they will also be inclined to see it more as a product of chance and necessity than one of competition: chance at the level of variation or small mutations, necessity at the level of reproduction or identical duplications. Of course, the concept of natural selection as an interplay of randomness and design is not limited to molecular genetics and biochemistry, having implications that go far beyond science. Particularly in our century, this concept has assumed general ideological overtones, being enlisted in the fierce struggle for authority in which modern science has, ever since its birth in the Renaissance, been engaged with religion or the onto-theological tradition. Gordon Rattray Taylor makes this point in unequivocal terms:

> If Darwinism fails, this is a critical point in human rationality, of much more than merely scientific consequence. The reason Darwin's

ideas caused such a furore when they were first announced was that they presented the living world as a world of chance, determined by material forces, in place of a world determined by a divine plan. . . .

The issue underlying any debate about Chance vs Purpose is, or can be seen as, a political one: Left vs Right. At the same time, there is something repellent about the idea that we live in a meaningless, fortuitous world. Darwinism, therefore, has always aroused fierce feelings and has been attacked and defended with great ferocity.[36]

If the concept of natural selection as survival of the fittest has its methodological and ideological problems, so does its next of kin, natural selection as a pure product of unguided chance. While natural scientists are more than willing to summon chance to their aid in order to do battle with the world as divine order, they soon discover that chance is a double-faced ally. Order, predictability, and certainty are the raisons d'être of science, and chance means uncertainty, unpredictability, and chaos. By inviting chance into the stronghold of Reason, these scientists bring in the "irrational" and thereby sow the seeds of Reason's downfall. Consequently, they remain forever wary of this potent *pharmakon* and invariably throw in a good measure of necessity to counteract its poisonous effects. This holds true even for those scientists who, like Jacques Monod, seem to give priority to chance over necessity in the evolutionary process.

In *Le hazard et la nécessité: Essai sur la philosophie naturelle de la biologie moderne* (Chance and necessity: An essay on the natural philosophy of modern biology, 1970), Jacques Monod, a Nobel Prize winner for physiology and medicine (1965) and professor of biochemistry at the prestigious Collège de France, presents the recently developed molecular theory of the genetic code (launched in 1952 by Francis Crick and James Watson with their discovery of the so-called central dogma of modern biology) in the larger framework of contemporary science and modern culture in general. According to Monod, this theory is the first general theory of living organisms, giving our concept of life a rigorous chemical and physical basis, and being an irrefutable genetic confirmation of Darwin's theory of evolution by natural selection. But, although the molecular theory of the genetic code can explain and even predict the existence, the properties, and the interaction of certain *classes* of objects and events in the biosphere, it can never account for the exis-

36. Gordon R. Taylor, *The Great Evolution Mystery* (New York, 1983). Further citations refer to this edition.

tence and properties of any *individual* object and event. Monod's central thesis, then, is that the biosphere is a *unique occurrence*, compatible with, but not deducible from, first principles, and therefore essentially unpredictable. In other words, life on earth is entirely the product of chance rather than necessity or design, and consequently its "mystery" can never be fully unraveled by science or the human mind in general.

Although life itself is a product of chance or what Monod calls, in a different context, the "gratuitous play of physical forces" (*jeu gratuit des forces physique*)[37]—a phrase reminiscent of Nietzsche and Deleuze— living organisms possess three main characteristics that distinguish them from all inorganic objects (except for crystals, which have the same structure as living beings, only much less complex): teleonomy, autonomous morphogenesis, and reproductive invariance. Organisms are "objects endowed with a purpose or a project which they both exhibit in their structure and carry out in their performances" (p. 5). Monod calls this property of exhibiting and carrying out a goal *teleonomy* (from the Greek *telos*, purpose, end). Living organisms also differ from other physical objects insofar as their shape or form owes almost nothing to the action of outside forces, but only to the microscopic internal forces that put them together in macroscopic structures. Organisms are machines that are able to put themselves together. Monod calls this self-generating ability *autonomous morphogenesis*. Finally, living beings are able to build exact copies or replicas of themselves, a property that Monod calls *invariant reproduction* or simply *invariance*.

Teleonomy, autonomous morphogenesis, and reproductive invariance are closely interrelated. For example, invariance manifests itself only through the autonomous morphogenesis of the structure constituting the teleonomic equipment. Moreover, all teleonomic activities are subordinated to a "unique, primary project, which is the preservation and multiplication of the species" (p. 14). One may speak of the "teleonomic level" of a species, which corresponds to the quantity and complexity of the information that must be transmitted from generation to generation in order to preserve the specific content of reproductive invariance. Here are included not only activities connected with reproduction itself, but all the other activities contributing, however indirectly, to the survival and multiplication of a certain species, and for Monod play is precisely such an activity: "For example, in higher

37. Jacques Monod, *Chance and Necessity: An Essay on the Natural Philosophy of Modern Biology*, trans. A. Wainhouse (New York, 1971), p. 4. Further citations refer to this edition.

mammals the play of the young is an important element of psychic development and social integration. Therefore this activity has teleonomic value, inasmuch as it furthers the cohesion of the group, a condition for its survival and for the expansion of the species" (p. 15).

In the middle of his book, Monod concentrates on the evolutionary process as an interplay of invariance and teleonomy at the molecular level. After he discusses a number of teleonomic molecular structures and performances, he arrives at what he sees as their *ultima ratio*: the sequences of residues that make up the polypeptide fibers of the globular proteins. If one were to understand these sequences, one would finally possess the "secret of life." And yet, when the "logic" of these sequences was finally discovered (by Sanger in 1952), this discovery was both a "revelation and a disappointment": they are completely "random" in the sense that even if one knew the exact order of 199 residues in a protein containing 200, one would not be able to predict the nature of that final residue. At the same time, however, the random sequence of each protein is reproduced again and again, in cell after cell of each organism, for generations on end, with an accuracy that guarantees the invariance of the structure. Thus, the "secret of life" revealed by the globular protein is randomness "caught on the wing, preserved, reproduced by the machinery of invariance and thus converted into order, rule, necessity" (p. 98). The globular protein, Monod concludes, behaves like a machine in its functional operations, but not in its deep structure, where one can find nothing but a "play of blind combinations" (p. 98).

Monod finds the same interplay of accident and design in the case of the DNA molecule, which he calls the "biological fundamental invariant." After he describes in some detail its teleonomic structure (the double helix) and its twin performance of replication and translation, Monod points out that only chance can be responsible for the mutations that will occur in a DNA sequence: "We call these events [mutations] accidental; we say that they are random occurrences. And since they constitute the *only* possible source of modifications in the genetic text, itself the *sole* respository of the organism's hereditary structures, it necessarily follows that chance *alone* is at the source of every innovation, of all creation in the biosphere. Pure chance, absolutely free but blind, at the very root of the stupendous edifice of evolution" (pp. 112–113).

In order to clarify his concept of randomness, Monod makes a distinction between "operational" and "essential" chance. Examples of operational chance can be found in such games as dice and roulette. Chance is brought into these games only because of the "practical impossibility of governing the throw of dice or the spinning of the little ball with sufficient precision" (p. 113). The same lack of precision or statistical ability in dealing with exceedingly small or large quantities leads, for purely methodological reasons, to the use of chance and the theory of probability in certain fields, and here Monod clearly alludes to game theory and its various areas of application (mathematics, economics, biology, sociology, etc.). Essential chance, on the other hand, governs what one might call "absolute coincidences," resulting from the intersection of two completely independent chains of events (p. 114). The principle of uncertainty in quantum physics and in molecular theory is based precisely on such a concept of essential chance (see sec. 3.2, below).

Judging solely on the basis of his "essential chance," Monod appears to come rather close to the prerational notion of play employed by the Presocratics (one of the epigraphs to Monod's book comes from Democritus) and, in modern times, by Nietzsche and other artist-metaphysicians. Like these thinkers, Monod seems to espouse an antiteleological, materialist philosophy of becoming. Where he seems to differ from them, however, is in his separation of the concept of chance and necessity from a prerational notion of power. He does employ phrases like the "gratuitous play of physical forces" or the "play of blind combinations," but he never quite explains what he means by them. This may be deliberate: if Monod were to be wholly consistent with his philosophy of becoming, he would have to give up science and rationality, which he is certainly not prepared to do. He is fully aware of this dilemma, which is reflected even in the way he presents his topic. Throughout his argument he shifts back and forth between chance and necessity. For Monod, Western thought has always been divided between two opposed attitudes: the Platonic one, according to which the ultimate truth of the world resides in the immutable, invariable, and eternal forms; and the Heraclitean one, according to which this truth resides in flux, change, and evolution (in the sense of becoming, not progress). He acknowledges that whereas science studies the flux and evolution of matter, it nevertheless shares the Platonic attitude insofar as it always looks for "invariants," for that which is stable, identical, and symmetrical, formulating all its basic truths as universal "conservation principles." Monod even entertains the possibility that all the invariants, conservations, and symmetries of science might be "fictions substituted for reality in order to obtain a workable image of it" (p. 100).[38] He concludes, however, that even if this were the case, human reason seems incapable of doing without such fictions (a Neo-Kantian position shared by many modern scientists). In science "there is and will remain a Platonic element which could not be taken away without ruining it. Amidst the infinite diversity of singular phenomena, science can only look for invariants" (p. 101).

Monod visibly wavers between the two basic attitudes in Western thought which he himself identifies, and we have seen that he is far from being the only scientist (or philosopher) caught in this dilemma. This wavering produces interesting, occasionally even surprising, interpretations of some of the biological and sociological issues related to the Darwinian theory of evolution. For instance, for Monod natural selection is not a matter of struggle for life, as it is for some of his Anglo-American colleagues, including Dawkins. In fact he denies altogether that the concept of natural selection as a struggle for life has anything to do with Darwin, attributing it (inaccurately) to Spencer: "Some post-Darwinian evolutionists have tended, when they discussed natural selection, to propagate a stark, naively ferocious idea of it: that of the no-holds-barred [*pure et simple*] 'struggle for life'—an expression which comes not from Darwin but from Herbert Spencer" (p. 119). According to Monod, the Neo-Darwinists of the first quarter of this century were closer to the mark when they saw natural selection as a differential rate of reproduction. This position is more or less to be expected from an advocate of natural selection as an interplay of chance and necessity. But what is surprising is that Monod does *not* see natural selection as a product of chance, either. Because it operates at the level of organisms, for him it occurs not in the microscopic realm of chance, but in the macroscopic realm of necessity. Natural selection "operates *upon* the products of chance and can feed nowhere else; but it operates in a domain of very demanding conditions, and from this domain chance is

38. According to Monod, however, modern physics, in contrast to its classical counterpart, is no longer satisfied with such logical fictions as the principle of identity, requiring that this principle have a "substantial reality" or material basis (*Chance and Necessity*, p. 101). In fact, many contemporary quantum theorists still treat atoms and subatomic particles as convenient fictions or conventional descriptions of interacting energy fields. For the question of the fictionality of our scientific concepts, as well as for the issues of causality, chance and necessity, and determinism vs. indeterminism in contemporary theoretical physics, see secs. 3.1 and 3.2.

barred" (p. 118). This view, according to which natural selection is guided by teleonomy rather than by chance, allows Monod to make a smooth transition from natural to human evolution. He introduces the notion of "higher selective pressures," which in the "higher organisms" include behavior and consequently, in man, individual and social responsibility (p. 126). Thus, by the time he comes to man Monod effectively manages to eliminate any significant effects that chance might have on evolution, and gives full priority to teleonomic performance.

For Monod, as for Dawkins, one of the most important factors in human evolution is the simulative capacity in the higher mammals. Unlike Dawkins, however, Monod squarely relates this capacity to play, discerning its beginnings in the animal world:

> Simulation is not an exclusively human function, however. The puppy that manifests its joy at seeing its master getting ready for the daily walk obviously imagines—that is, simulates through anticipation—the discoveries it is about to make. . . .
>
> In animals, as in young children too, subjective simulation appears to be only partially dissociated from neuro-motor activity. Play is its outward expression. But in man subjective simulation becomes the superior function par excellence, the creative function. This is what is reflected by the symbolism of language which, transposing and summarizing its operations, recasts it in the form of speech. (p. 155)

Nevertheless, in the wake of Piaget, Monod seems to place play at the lower end of an ascending evolutionary line, the culmination of which is the creative faculty and language. Again, as for most rationalist thinkers, for him play seems to be evolutionarily inferior because it remains tied up with the neuro-motor activity, with the body. Although Monod does not offer a systematic discussion of play in his book, his occasional remarks enable us to conclude that he operates with polarized concepts of play. On the one hand, there is the "gratuitous play of physical forces" which, as in Kant, resists rational analysis; on the other hand, there is play as a teleonomic activity or the play of natural selection, contributing either to the psychic development and social integration of the young or to the birth of language and the "higher" creative function in man.

One would expect Monod to dispense with the notion of the survival of the fittest, just as he did with that of struggle for life, yet he surprises the reader again: he now applies *both* metaphors to human evolution, and attempts to explain man's violence in terms of "selective pressures." In a first evolutionary stage, man "extended his dominion over the subhuman sphere," and consequently channeled his violence outside his own species. But once he managed to dominate his environment, he had no dangerous competitor to face except his own kind: "Specialists all agree in thinking that direct strife, Spencer's [*sic*] 'struggle for life,' has played only a minor role in the evolution of the species. This is not so as regards mankind. Somewhere in the human species' development and expansion the point was reached where tribal or racial warfare came to be an important evolutionary factor" (p. 161).

Monod, then, takes exactly the opposite view from that of Dawkins: he discerns altruism in the world of animals and selfishness in the world of man. For him violence and strife (read: competition) are productive of culture, and he deplores the fact that there is no longer anything "natural" about selection in modern societies. It is in this context that he employs the phrase "survival of the fittest," which he interprets genetically. In modern societies, "intelligence, ambition, courage and imagination are still factors of success . . . but of *personal*, not genetic success, the only kind that matters in evolution" (p. 163). Those who possess these qualities are also those who have the fewest children and therefore are in danger of becoming a "shrinking elite in relative numbers." (Of course, Dawkins would argue that genetically controlled characteristics are distributed *throughout* the gene pool, and therefore one "genius" would not necessarily give birth to another.) Until recently the "weeding out of the physically and . . . mentally least fit was automatic and ruthless," while today, because of the advances in science, "many of these genetic cripples live long enough to reproduce" (p. 163). Monod employs sociobiological arguments that have a certain currency in the United States as well and incidentally were also invoked, albeit in a more ruthless fashion, by the Nazis (in whose case I suppose one might also say that evolutionary "selective pressures" ran very high).

In fairness to Monod, however, one must quickly add that he certainly does not advocate National Socialism, but only a middle-of-the-road kind of socialism (throughout his book he also does ideological battle with Marxism), a position that he again attempts to justify in evolutionary terms. Some may find this approach objectionable, but it is in fact perfectly consistent with Monod's biological views. Like Dawkins, he believes in the selection of ideas and therefore in the evolutionary value of ideological strife or competition. The only kind of socialism that Monod believes to be favored by evolution is the one based on "scientific objectivity" and the "ethics of knowledge," which he opposes to the "animist" and "vitalist" beliefs in Western culture. For him, both vitalism and animism are teleonomic (teleologic) systems of thought, the difference between them being that the first restricts the idea of a universal or grand design to the biosphere, while the second extends it to the inanimate world as well.

According to Monod, the principle of scientific objectivity requires a distinction between values and knowledge which the animist and the vitalist views are both unwilling and unable to make. This does not mean, however, that science is devoid of values. On the contrary, the quest for objective truth or knowledge is by definition an ethical one: it is "from the ethical choice of a primary value that knowledge starts" (p. 171). Thus, in fact, science *practices* an ethics of objectivity or knowledge. Finally, the ethics of knowledge which "created the modern world is the only ethic compatible with it, the only one capable, once understood and accepted, of guiding its evolution" (p. 176).

To Monod the scientist, scientific thought naturally appears as a culmination of the evolutionary process and as the superior product of a rigorous selection of ideas. His argument reveals the sort of circularity that often plagues evolutionary discourse, particularly when it attempts to justify its own status in relation to ideological strife or to the so-called selection of ideas: Monod explains evolution through science and science through evolution. In one way or another, evolutionary success always seems to be its own justification, to prove that nothing succeeds like success. But even though Monod's arguments are tautological, they are certainly not gratuitous. If one recalls that he defines scientific objectivity in terms of a view of the world as governed by chance rather than by design and science as the teleonomic endeavor par excellence, then one can readily discern the telos behind his ideological polemic. Monod attempts to gain for science the cultural authority that, according to him, has belonged for centuries to the animist ideologies (including religion, science's chief rival), by attacking these ideologies for their teleonomic orientation while safeguarding science's own prerogative to a teleonomic way of thinking.

In view of the fact that Monod primarily employs his concept of chance to defend science against competing modes of knowledge rather than to undermine its teleonomic nature, it is rather ironical that he should have come under violent attack in certain scientific quarters. Perhaps one reason for these attacks is that, as Monod himself points out, many scientists still remain uncomfortable with having chance or uncertainty as a fundamental principle of hard science. They must feel that this principle seriously endangers the solid teleonomic premises of their enterprise, appearing more like an admission of ignorance than a sound scientific foundation on which to build vast and secure teleonomic structures. Another reason is clearly ideological in nature: Monod uses his scientific concepts of chance and objective knowledge to espouse a form of existentialist philosophy—the epigraph of his study contains not only a quotation from Democritus but also one from Camus—coupled with a (non-Marxist) form of scientific socialism which must sound distasteful to those scientists who do not share his philosophical and political views. These reasons become particularly evident in Manfred Eigen and Ruthild Winkler's study significantly entitled *Das Spiel: Naturgesetze steuern den Zufall* (Play: Natural laws steer chance, 1975).

Eigen, a Nobel Prize winner for chemistry (1967) and director of the biochemistry section of the Max Planck Institute in Göttingen, and Winkler, his coworker at the institute, base their study, as does Monod, on the molecular theory of evolution by natural selection. Although they largely agree with Monod's concept of molecular biology, they claim to "differ from him greatly in the conclusions he draws from it for mankind and society." According to them, Monod's ideological beliefs derive from an "animistic inflation of the role of chance" and a neglect of the "complementary role played by natural law."[39] They claim to start, unlike Monod, from the premise that chance and necessity or "law" play an equal role in evolution. For all practical evolutionary purposes, however, their position on chance and necessity hardly differs from that of Monod, despite their ideological quarrel with him.

Eigen and Winkler also base their study on the premise that evolution, as well as the world at large, can best be described as an immense game of which chance and necessity are the fundamental components:

> Everything that happens in our world resembles a vast game in which nothing is determined in advance but the rules, and only the rules are open to objective understanding. . . .
> We see this game as a natural phenomenon that, in its dichotomy of chance and necessity, underlies all events. (pp. xi–xii)

39. Manfred Eigen and Ruthild Winkler, *Laws of the Game: How the Principles of Nature Govern Chance*, trans. Robert and Rita Kimber (New York, 1983). Since this translation is not always reliable (as one can see even from the English title), I have used in parallel the German edition (Munich/Zurich, 1975). Further citations, however, refer to the English translation.

One can see from the outset that the game of the world envisaged by Eigen and Winkler is certainly not Nietzsche's or Heidegger's *Welt-spiel*—the latter thinkers would want to know in advance *who* or *what* determines the rules. Rather, it is a game metaphor that attempts to provide a rational or scientific account of the inanimate world and the biosphere while taming the effects of both chance and the chaotic play of physical forces (in fact, part 1 of *Das Spiel* is appropriately entitled "Die Zähmung des Zufalls," The taming of chance).

That Eigen and Winkler's concept of play is as ambivalent as those of other rationalist thinkers becomes evident in the first few chapters, which set up the theoretical framework for the rest of the book. The authors create a myth of the origin of play which is based on the "big bang" theory in physics:

> The history of play goes back to the beginnings of time. The energy released in the "big bang" set everything in motion, set matter whirl-ing in a maelstrom of activity that would never cease. Ordering forces sought to bring this chaotic striving [*Auseinanderstrebende*] under control, to tame chance. What they forged, though, is not the rigid order of the crystal, but the order of the living. From the outset, chance has been the essential counterpart of the regulating forces.
>
> Chance and rules are the elements of play. Once begun by the elementary particles, atoms, and molecules, play is carried on by our brain cells. Man did not invent play. But it is "play and only play that makes man complete." (p. 3)

Like all myths, this one is rather vague and confusing, but what Eigen and Winkler seem to mean is that after the "big bang" (itself an obvious power-oriented concept), the play of physical forces takes the form of an interplay of chance and necessity; chance is presumably the manifesta-tion of chaotic forces, whereas necessity is the manifestation of ordering forces. The question might be asked (if indeed it is fair play to question a myth—the point is, however, that Eigen and Winkler certainly do not see their story as a myth but as a scientific hypothesis) where the ordering forces came from in the first place, or how the chaos produced by the "big bang" came to be guided or regulated. A prerational thinker like Nietzsche would reply that there are no such things as ordering and chaotic forces, but only relatively stronger and weaker ones. Order is the temporary subordination of the weaker by the stronger forces; it is always a *hierarchy*, and consequently both order and chaos are only a matter of perspective. From the perspective of the ceaseless play of physical forces, there is no such thing as an interplay of chance and necessity, but only chance *as* necessity or necessity *as* chance. In this passage, however, Eigen and Winkler are clearly thinking not of Nietzsche but of Schiller, whom they quote not only here (their reference is to letter xv of the *Aesthetic Education*) but throughout their book. When they come to man, they interpret the "ordering" or the "regulating" forces as rational forces, and the play of these forces as the play of Reason. This play (*Spiel*) attempts to tame the effects of chance by turning them into games (*Spiele*), and the symbol Eigen and Winkler want the reader to remember is certainly not Nietzsche's "dancing floor for divine chances" or "table of the Gods for divine dice and dice-players," but Hesse's Glass Bead Game: "There is something mysterious about glass beads. The refraction of light makes them glow, and as we explore the idea of play in this book, Hesse's glass beads will take on a new life. . . . The course the bead game takes is determined by the roll of the dice, yet at the same time it is also influenced by the rules of the game, just as chance in nature is subject to the laws of physics. The dice and the rules of the game—these are our symbols for chance and natural law" (p. 5).

Although they start out speaking of play, the authors quickly move on to games, and for a good reason: it is not play, but only games, or rather only *certain* games, that will bear out their scientific hypothesis of the interplay of chance and necessity in nature. They will, predictably, approach most of their theoretical questions in terms of game theory, which operates, as we have seen, on utilitarian and rational premises, attempting to minimize uncertainty and chance and optimize predictability and necessity.

Eigen and Winkler distinguish among several categories of games, including games of chance, games of strategy, and mixed games (chance combined with strategies attempting to reduce or control its effects). Because these games are based on a large number of possible choices, they will be played differently each time, according to the particular decisions of the players and the individual dice throws. One can visualize the sequence of moves in a game following the imaginary branches of a "decision tree," with each roll of the dice and each player's decision opening new directions for the game. Each player attempts to anticipate the decisions of the other(s) and constructs his game strategy not only in relation to the roll of the dice, but also in relation to what he thinks the other player(s) might do. He weighs the unpredictable against the predictable, formulating an "optimal" strategy that will enable him to win. This is basically the authors' model for the interplay of necessity and chance, in a competitive situation, which they will later employ to describe evolution by natural selection. The rolls of the dice represent the possible and unpredictable variants or mutants, whereas the players' decisions stand for those variants or mutants that are actually selected as being the most advantageous in the game of life, which for Eigen and Winkler is also a game of winning or losing, that is, a competitive game.

Eigen and Winkler attempt, however, to correct the impression that the "motivating force behind all games is competition or even outright battle" (p. 17). They offer examples of games that are played by one person, such as solitaire, and games that are based on cooperation rather than contest. But the one example of cooperative games they mention, *kemari*—the traditional ball game of the Japanese royal house, in which the players move around in a circle trying to kick the ball to each other in such a way that it never touches the ground—seems ill chosen: since there is considerable pressure on each player *not* to be the one to drop the ball, the game remains competitive in nature. What this game seems to be designed to teach the royal family is group solidarity, uniting them against outside enemies; in evolutionary terms, it reflects group, rather than individual selection.

The authors further refer to the autotelic, gratuitous character of play and its capacity for generating pure excitement. They even cite Huizinga's statement that "we play and know that we play, so we must be more than merely rational beings, for play is irrational." But they quickly qualify this statement: "Perhaps we would do better to say that play is beyond reason [*jenseits von Vernunft*]. It makes sense only in and of itself" (p. 18). In other words, they gloss over the "irrational" character of play, falling back on the Kantian and Neo-Kantian concept of play as an autotelic activity. Finally, after they briefly acknowledge the existence of noncompetitive games and skirt the issue of "irrational" play, they proceed to employ competitive game models in their biological theories.

Eigen and Winkler's version of natural selection comes very close to that of Monod. They first point out the tautological character of the phrase *survival of the fittest*, which in certain modern biological versions of natural selection simply means *survival of the survivor*; they argue that a precise characterization of selection would be possible only "under conditions of extreme competition," which do not obtain in nature. In terms of the macromolecular theory of natural selection, however, survival of the fittest is still an accurate phrase to employ and, moreover, without running the risk of tautology. At the macromolecular level *fittest* indicates optimal selective value, which depends not only on direct competition but also on a large number of other local factors, such as available space and available amounts of matter and energy. The mechanisms of selection exist at the basic level of the macromolecules—the nucleic acids and the proteins—and are required by the great number of possible variations occurring at that level. Only by means of these mechanisms "can those rare viable variants be selected and preserved from extinction" (p. 59). The evolutionary process is the result of reproduction, mutation, and selective evaluation according to the laws of molecular dynamics, combining chance and necessity (p. 59).

Eigen and Winkler criticize Monod, arguing that "examination of the dynamic underlying processes of selection and evolution shows that the completely unregulated chance situation that Monod celebrates does not occur in evolution" (p. 162). They further contend that Monod's "absolute, blind chance" applies exclusively to the "historically conditioned uniqueness of events." There is no causal link between the triggering of a mutation and its selective evaluation, which takes place at a different level. Nevertheless, the fate of a mutant is determined by natural law: "The number of 'permitted' routes, large as it may be, is relatively small in comparison to the total number of possible routes. The preferred direction imposed by selective evaluation cuts down tremendously the number of possible binary decisions. Natural law here means a channeling, if not a taming of chance" (p. 168).

But as we have seen, this is precisely what Monod argues as well: selection occurs at the macroscopic level and is itself not a product of chance; rather, it *operates upon* the products of chance, choosing only those mutants that are most viable for survival. Again, when they address the question of the self-organization of living matter or what Monod calls autonomous morphogenesis, Eigen and Winkler give the same priority to necessity over chance that Monod does. For the German authors, the elements of order such as structure, shape, regular pattern, and symmetry prevail because they are selected as being functionally superior. When considering symmetrical structures, for instance, they remark: "We find so many symmetrical structures in biology today because they were more efficient in exploiting their advantage and consequently won—a posteriori—the selection competition" (p. 130). This remark is in perfect consonance with Monod's idea of the increasingly efficient teleonomic organization of living matter as one goes up the evolutionary scale.

As far as human evolution is concerned the differences between Eigen/Winkler and Monod seem to be more of an ideological than a biological nature. For the German authors, just as for their French colleague, man is the product not of chance but of selective pressures, that is, competition—especially intraspecific competition. The ideological differences between them surface, however, in regard to defining a "just social order." For instance, Eigen and Winkler disapprovingly cite an official statement by a German student-socialist according to which "the [capitalist] system encourages waste, exploitation, and lust of profit, all of which work against the optimal utilization of the unlimited possibilities of the high productivity of our times" (p. 133). In defense of the "system," the authors quote figures from the annual report of a leading West German chemical firm which show that, compared with the amount spent on wages and salaries, the percentage allotted to dividends is "minimal." Their point is that in industrial societies a higher standard of living can be achieved only by the increased productivity of all and not by a redistribution of capital (an alleged socialist goal). To Monod's socialist ideal, they oppose the capitalist philosophy of profit earned by hard work, a philosophy deeply routed in competition, the "legacy of our evolution": "A high standard of living has to be earned by hard work. We cannot do without the incentives [profit] that produce that kind of work. Motivation presupposes rewards. We cannot simply discard this legacy of our evolution. If we want to establish norms of behavior, we cannot ignore human nature in doing so" (p. 135).

For Eigen and Winkler (and again, in this regard there is little difference between them and the socialist Monod), the idea of a just social order is "normative, not natural." The biological order has developed first and foremost from the "natural process of competitive behavior." If human beings want to establish norms for a just social order they first have to emancipate themselves from this biological legacy. But in doing so, they "have to retain their individuality as it is expressed in personally motivated actions" (p. 131). In other words, the authors advocate a mild competitive form of capitalism, in which the state intervenes to redistribute "excessive" profits in the form of social services; they advocate the system that is already in place in West Germany.

However, Eigen and Winkler show more ideological flexibility than Monod does when they argue that natural selection cannot account for or justify any specific historical route of human evolution, socialism being no more evolutionarily "inevitable" than any other social order. Thereby, they prudently avoid the controversial issue of the selection of ideas. They also argue, against Monod, that one cannot claim absolute validity for an ethic of objective knowledge: "Whether we choose to emphasize the 'laws of material existence' or the 'absoluteness of human existence,' a just human order needs for its realization not only objective—and always incomplete—knowledge but also a humanism based on hope, charity, and love" (p. 172).

In keeping with their humanistic ideals, Eigen and Winkler do not exclude art and aesthetics from their scientific considerations (thereby also remaining faithful to the aesthetic turn that has occurred in the theoretical sciences in the past few decades). At the end of their book, the authors discuss art in terms of their concept of evolution as an interplay of chance and necessity. They contend that, in the case of art, one cannot strictly apply the concept of optimal functionality which is operative in the case of natural selection, or even in that of language and thought in general. As a result, chance—individual uniqueness or difference—plays a larger role in art than in other fields of knowledge. Yet they agree with Adorno, against Huizinga, that art cannot be *all* play, that it has to conform to certain rules, canons, or forms of expression; in other words, that it involves not only chance but also necessity. They sum up their views on art by presenting an imaginary round table whose participants include Huizinga, Adorno, Mann, and Beckett. Huizinga and the two artists present, with slight variations, the view of art as pure play, while Adorno presents the view of art as a mirror of the creative play of nature, combining necessity and chance. Needless to say, this view is also shared by Eigen and Winkler, who favor a Romantic concept of art as creation or production, rather than imitation or reproduction (p. 330). Imitation obviously remains operative in this Romantic model as well, however, with the difference that the artist now imitates nature's creative processes rather than her finished products.

Despite their ideological disagreements with Monod, Eigen and Winkler support the same view of biological evolution by natural selection as the French scientist.[40] As far as human evolution is concerned,

40. As for the ideological disagreement between the German scientists and their French counterpart—a question of secondary interest for the present argument—one would have to take into consideration not only the individual temperaments of these scientists but also the historical context of their work. Monod was writing in Paris in 1969, during the student movements and the rise of leftist radicalism. But leftist ideas have long been fashionable in Parisian intellectual circles, and in this sense Monod is far from expressing extravagant political views in relation to his immediate ideological environment. Eigen and Winkler, on the other hand, were writing in Göttingen in the mid-seventies, after the radical wave that swept across West European universities had subsided. Again, in relation to their own intellectual environment, their political views are the norm, rather than the exception. In

they circumvent the specific issue of the selection of ideas, concentrating on the larger issue of the competitive behavior inherent in human "nature." Unlike Monod, they employ game theory to support their view, but they thereby gloss over some of the theoretical difficulties (which Monod attempts to meet head on) encountered by scientific thought when dealing with the concept of chance. As Monod himself points out, game theory uses operational rather than essential chance, that is, it uses a "tamed" or rational version of this notion. Operational chance is a mathematical fiction or artifice, based on a process of abstraction which treats individual or unique natural events as a large group of similar phenomena. This fiction, in turn, engenders the statistical fiction of the "average behavior" of natural phenomena, which has no more historical reality than the "average man" of opinion polls. In this respect, the artist-metaphysicians, for example, would argue that what appears to the scientist as shape, pattern, or symmetry is determined not by natural necessity but by his own will to order, which he projects as "natural law."

For all these scientists, Darwin's theory of evolution by natural selection is not just another scientific hypothesis but an incontrovertible natural law. Undoubtedly, Monod would fully subscribe to Eigen and Winkler's formulation of this dogmatic belief: "But Darwin*ism* as such is obsolete. This is not so because his opponents, the vitalists, proved him wrong, for they did not and have not. It is so because a natural law which can be traced back to fundamental principles of physics should not be designated an 'ism.' It is instead, where its preconditions are met, a law, and it permits of no alternatives" (p. 164).

For all these scientists, science remains a highly teleonomic activity, revealing the objective laws of nature, placing them in the service of man, and thereby decisively contributing to the latter's ever-higher development. Finally, whereas Monod seems to waver somewhat between prerational and rational play concepts in dealing with natural evolution, he joins his German colleagues in favoring rational over prerational play concepts when dealing with human evolution. He would again fully agree with Eigen and Winkler's assessment of man's role in the game of the world, where he has a choice between controlling his fate or becoming a plaything of chance (p. xiv; cf. the artist-metaphysicians, for whom man has no such choice, being always both player and plaything in the violent play of Becoming).

---

both cases, then, the scientific community out of which and for which these scientists were writing was likely to receive their ideas favorably.

## 2·3 René Thom and Biological Play

The work of René Thom offers a somewhat different approach to evolutionary theory: although he shares the biochemical assumption that physical phenomena are atomic in nature, he attempts to describe these phenomena through qualitative rather than quantitative methods. In this he follows the lead of such English biologists as D'Arcy Thompson and C. H. Waddington, who approach biological phenomena through morphological rather than atomistic models and therefore go against the mainstream of Neo-Darwinism. A mathematician by training, Thom is particularly interested in differential topology, the principles and methods of which he has applied to biology, model theory, and linguistics (especially semantics). Differential topology is also the basis of his "catastrophe theory," which attempts to describe the mechanism of the succession of forms in nature or "morphogenesis." He presents this theory in his influential study *Stabilité structurelle et morphogénèse: Essai d'une théorie générale des models* (*Structural Stability and Morphogenesis: An Outline of a General Theory of Models*, 1972).

Like Monod, Thom is fully aware of the fact that science faces a fundamental dilemma. On the one hand, it seems "indisputable that our universe is not chaos." We see objects and beings around us to which we give names and which have a relatively stable structure or form; they occupy a certain space and last for a certain time (cf., in a different context, Dawkins's similar definition of stability). On the other hand, the world we see is a "ceaseless creation, evolution, and destruction of forms." Now the purpose of science is to "foresee this change of forms, and, if possible, explain it."[41] The problem is, however, that the change of forms does not seem to obey any determinate rules, so that the "same local situation can give birth to apparently different outcomes under the influences of unknown or unobservable factors." Thus science is placed in the ironic position of having to predict unpredictable changes, and modern biology shares this dilemma.

Although Thom does not deny the importance of the physicochemical substratum of evolution, he believes that this substratum will always remain indeterminate, unpredictable and subject to chance. Therefore, he is far from subscribing to any "foundation of certainty" (Francis

41. René Thom, *Structural Stability and Morphogenesis: An Outline of a General Theory of Models*, trans. D. H. Fowler (Reading, Mass., 1975), p. 1. Further citations refer to this edition.

Crick) that the molecular evolutionary theory claims to provide, and in this he follows the basic postulates of quantum mechanics (cf. sec. 3.2, below). Despite his indeterminism, however, Thom is no more prepared to give up law and order in science than Monod is. Instead, he proposes qualitative rather than quantitative models in dealing with the reality of morphogenesis.

Thom points out that morphogenetic phenomena are not readily amenable to quantitative analysis, because the "characteristic of all form . . . is to display itself through discontinuities of the environment, and nothing disturbs a mathematician more than discontinuity, since all applicable quantitative models depend on the use of analytic and therefore continuous functions" (p. 9). His qualitative model is therefore designed to deal precisely with these discontinuities, by proceeding in the opposite direction from the quantitative models; it attempts to reconstruct the dynamic underlying a process by a macroscopic examination of its morphogenesis and a local and global study of its singularities. This means that it treats morphogenesis independently of its atomic substratum, without reference to its "more-or-less chaotic underlying structures." Thom's solution to the problem of indeterminism is to employ limited models, formalizing local or accidental biological phenomena without claiming any definite knowledge about the "ultimate nature of reality" (p. 7).

At first sight, Thom's biological views seem closely related to those of Monod, who after asserting the uncertain nature of the atomic substratum of phenomena proceeds with his teleonomic enterprise at the macroscopic level. Yet Thom goes farther than Monod in specifying the nature of the "play of physical forces," a concept that he traces, like Nietzsche, back to the Presocratics. Thom imagines every object or physical form as being a structurally and temporarily stable "attractor." He defines morphogenesis as the "disappearance of the attractors representing the initial forms, and their replacement by capture by the attractors representing the final forms," and it is precisely this process that he calls "catastrophe" (p. 20).

Thom himself points out that his model attributes all morphogenesis to conflict, or to a struggle between two or more attractors, and that this is the "2,500 year-old idea of the Presocratic philosophers, Anaximander and Heraclitus" (p. 323). For him, evolution by natural selection is no longer struggle for life or survival of the fittest, but an incessant agon of physical forces that create and destroy an infinite number of natural forms—a position that comes much closer to that of the artist-metaphysicians than to that of Darwin and the Neo-Darwinists. Moreover, Thom follows Nietzsche in defending the Presocratics against the charges of anthropomorphism leveled at them by modern science:

> [Anaximander and Heraclitus] have been accused of primitive confusionism, because they used a vocabulary with human and social origins (conflict, injustice, etc.) to explain the appearance of the physical world, but I think that they were far from wrong because they had the following fundamentally valid intuition: *the dynamical situations governing the evolution of natural phenomena are basically the same as those governing the evolution of man and societies*, profoundly justifying the use of anthropomorphic words in physics. Inasmuch as we use the word "conflict" to express a well-defined geometrical situation in a dynamical system, there is no objection to using the word to describe quickly and qualitatively a given dynamical situation. (p. 323)

In arguing for the essential identity of natural and social dynamic processes, Thom, following Nietzsche and Heidegger, proclaims the unity of interpreter and object interpreted, or more broadly, the unity of culture and nature. In this regard, he undermines science's claim to "objective knowledge," going beyond the dichotomy of subject and object and coming close to Nietzsche's concept of interpretation as the differential function of the play of physical forces or as Will to Power.

Thom's concept of play as a biological phenomenon is also related to the struggle among attractors. In the animal and human world, these attractors are called "predator" and "prey": "The essential regulation constraint on an animal is feeding, which alone allows it to replace its loss of chemical energy and to restock its reserves. Now feeding implies predation, the presence of another living being (animal or plant), the prey, which is to be captured or ingested" (p. 297). According to Thom, the predator identifies with its prey up to the point of a "perception catastrophe," when it recognizes the prey and becomes itself again. This identification or mimesis is observable in archaic man as well, taking the form of ritual participation (*methexis*), during which man assumes the guise of his prey or predator. In this sense, the nervous system of higher animals is an "organ of alienation," allowing them to be something other than themselves (p. 299). The ability to identify with the prey is precisely what Dawkins and Monod understand by the simulative capacity of the higher animals, and Thom, like Monod, relates its development to play. For him, play has an important function in stabilizing the animal's fragmented identity or "ego," which is an "aggregate of local charts, each associated with a well-defined motor or psychological activity (areas for hunting, congregating, sleeping, etc.)" (p. 303). Play is an *as if* behavior by which the predator simulates the capture of its prey, thereby creating a fictitious ego which enables it to separate itself from the prey: "Observe, for example, a young cat in the process of playing; it will behave as if attacking genuine prey in front of an object like a ball of wool or string, having only a distant morphological analogy with its prey. The animal is certainly not deceived; it has created a playful ego that is not at all disturbed by the lack of final reward when the pseudoprey is found to be inedible" (p. 304).

Play is often a highly structured combination of rules, but for Thom its essential freedom consists in the fact that it releases the animal from its biological constraints. The absence of effective reward makes play into a free activity that the animal may abandon or resume at will (p. 304). At the same time, however, play remains a useful activity: predatory play "gives valuable experience in distinguishing between edible and inedible objects" (p. 305). In fact, in both animal and man, the state of wakefulness is a state of "continuous virtual predation." Although only edible objects trigger the capture process, the animal treats every object as a virtual prey, weighing it by perception, in the etymological sense of this word: *percipere* means to "seize the object continually in its entirety" (p. 305). This sort of playful exploration by seizing and handling is most obvious in human babies between eight and eleven months of age, who practice it almost incessantly. Thus, according to Thom, play originates in the predatory activity of the animal, and despite its relative freedom, ultimately remains determined by this predatory activity. In this regard, his view of play as virtual predation bears a certain family resemblance to that of Spencer and Groos.

The kinship between Thom's view and the traditional evolutionary views of biological play becomes even more evident when he turns to adult human play. For him, this play is a combinative *mental* activity through which man constructs semantic models closely simulating the "structures and forces of the outside world" (p. 317). Like animal play, human play may be determined by rules. But the rules are often "not powerful enough to determine the system completely," in which case play will appear as a "kind of artistic activity in which the player, motivated by some esthetic sense, tries to form the most attractive and effective moves" (p. 317). Nevertheless, games are "fundamentally different" from artistic activity precisely because their set of rules "must be consciously kept in mind" at all times. Formalized thought, such as logic and mathematics, can be considered as a "game whose rules, forming the organizing center, are codified as a system of axioms" (p. 317). Thus, Thom's distinction between artistic and formal thought is in fact the traditional, rationalist distinction between unorganized play (*jeu*) and rule-oriented games (*jeux*). Furthermore, he operates with another traditional distinction between gratuitous or trivial and useful or reality-oriented play: "Playful activity, left to itself, is not slow in creating gratuitous, worthless examples of semantic models with no other semantic realization than their own combination, nor is it slow to decline into trivia. Although some of modern mathematics is perhaps guilty of this charge, it is no less true that mathematical activity among mankind has essentially been inspired by reality and finds there its constantly renewed fecundity" (p. 317).

The reality-oriented play of mathematics has an important evolutionary role. It is "significant play *par excellence* by which man can deliver himself from the biological bondage that weighs down his thought and language, and can assure the best chance for the survival of mankind" (p. 318).

Even this brief overview of Thom's scientific uses of the play concept reveals that he operates with two conflicting views of play: a prerational and a rational one. On the one hand, like Nietzsche, Heidegger, and other artist-metaphysicians, Thom employs prerational play as a groundless ground of his scientific speculations, tracing all phenomena back to the incessant "play of physical forces." On the other hand, he sees biological play as an important factor in evolution, being itself subject to an evolutionary process. Although it originates in the predatory activity of the animal, being ultimately determined by this activity, at the human level play becomes more and more abstract, losing its violent aspect in the combinative, rule-determined activity of logic and mathematics.

The four cases examined in this section have shown the intimate relation of agonistic play to the Darwinian concept of evolution by natural selection. Irrespective of the level at which it is supposed to operate (gene, organism, group, population, or species), natural selection always retains its agonistic features. This also holds true of the concept of natural selection as an interplay of chance and necessity and of the various mathematical, statistical, probabilistic, and stochastic models that it has generated. Chance and necessity are two age-old philosophical concepts that are closely related to the (Hellenic) notion of play as agon; they are not "neutral" or "objective" natural phenomena, but are very much tied up with other power-oriented values in our culture. They are often combined, as we have seen, with such metaphors as survival of the fittest and struggle for life, a combination that again bespeaks their agonistic origin.

However, the Darwinian concept of evolution by natural selection finally presupposes a rational, rather than a prerational, notion of agon. Survival of the fittest and struggle for life are certainly a far cry from the heroic and tragic contest. Survival per se is hardly a highly regarded value within a prerational, agonistic mentality: witness Achilles' choice, in the *Iliad*, of a short and heroic life on the battlefield over a long and peaceful one at home. Nietzsche ranks survival rather low in his hierarchy of aristocratic values. He sees "survival of the fittest" as an expression of herd mentality, and Darwinian evolution by natural selection as the product of socialist ideology (indeed, ironically, many twentieth-century evolutionists advocate a form of socialism or populism when it comes to human societal evolution). For Nietzsche the "fittest" are the mediocre, and we have seen that ESS always favors the golden mean, the shrewd and calculating individual that grazes safely in the middle of the herd and never "lives dangerously," venturing on its margins.

Some artist-metaphysicians would also challenge the utilitarian view of play that most Neo-Darwinists, including Thom, are reluctant to abandon. They would further accuse the Neo-Darwinists of being "bad players" as far as the interplay of randomness and design in natural selection is concerned, of loading the dice in favor of necessity, of failing to affirm chance all at once, by one decisive dice throw, retaining it instead only at certain points and leaving the rest to the mechanical unfolding of cause and effect. But more important, it is also on its own turf, in biology, that natural selection—the cornerstone of Darwinism—is increasingly attacked on the same nonutilitarian, aesthetic grounds. Taylor is only one of a growing number of biologists who have recently rebelled against the utilitarian aspects of the Darwinian concept of evolution by natural selection. To the seriousness and the teleonomic functionality of the struggle for survival Taylor opposes the purely aesthetic motivation, the *gratuity* of the evolutionary process. For instance, when speaking of the echinoderms (starfish and sea-urchins) as possible ancestors of the vertebrates, he remarks:

> Incidentally the echinoderms were perhaps the most variable of all these early groups. They assembled their armour plate in scores of fancy, imbricated patterns, like a fashion model trying on dress after

dress. I mention this because it seems such a long way from the dour Darwinian picture of organisms precisely fitted in their niche in the struggle to survive. Many of these early creatures experimented with their entire body form, moving their mouth up to the end or down to the side, extending their feet or their neck, shifting their eyes (some had eyes in their tails, useful to tell you if you are truly out of sight in your burrow) and . . . twisting and contorting themselves. Far from being a struggle to survive, it looks more like one glorious romp. (*Great Evolution Mystery*, p. 195)

Biologists are increasingly concentrating on the problems with which the Neo-Darwinists are least comfortable, such as the gaps in the fossil record and the mechanisms of nongenetic inheritance. They question the Neo-Darwinist thesis that all evolution can be explained solely by the natural selection of random mutations and they are no longer certain about the fundamental relevance of the atomic substratum to the evolution of organic life. Ironically, the revival of the organicist view (which was prevalent in the Romantic biological models of the nine-teenth century) is largely due to the *physicists*, especially those who adhere to the Copenhagen interpretation of quantum theory. Niels Bohr applies his notion of complementarity not only to physical but also to biological phenomena, attempting to correct what he sees as the purely mechanic, reductionist nature of genetic evolutionary theory. For Bohr this theory is as extreme as its old vitalistic enemies. What contemporary biology needs instead is a complementary view, in which the physicochemical processes discovered in living organisms comple-ment, rather than substitute for, the basically unexplainable phenome-non of life. In "Biology and Atomic Physics" Bohr says: "First of all we must realize that every experimental arrangement with which we could study the behavior of the atom . . . in the fundamental experiments of atomic physics will [when applied to biological units] exclude the possibility of maintaining the organism alive. . . . In this sense, the existence of life itself should be considered, as regards both its definition and observation, as a basic postulate of biology, not susceptible of further analysis, in the same way as the existence of the quantum of action, together with the ultimate atomicity of matter, forms the ele-mentary basis of atomic physics."[42]

Adopting the same complementary view of organic life, some con-

42. Niels Bohr, *Atomic Physics and Human Knowledge* (London, 1958), pp. 20–21. See also my discussion of Heisenberg and his relation to Bohr in sec. 3.2.

temporary biologists again stress necessity and determinism (in a relative rather than an absolute form—see sec. 3.2), instead of natural selection, with regard to living organisms. They form the third camp mentioned at the beginning of this section. While not denying chance an important role, they concentrate on the "self-organization" of living organisms and the "hierarchical levels of order" in the universe (or, indeed, the pluriverse), conceiving order as spontaneously arising out of chaos.[43] In this respect, the biologists who form this third camp no longer see the "central dogma" of Darwinism as an absolute law that "permits of no alternatives," but rather as one element in a very complex and essentially mysterious holistic process.

Other contemporary biologists concentrate on the question of the multiplicity and change of biological forms, which far exceed the exigencies of natural selection and therefore are another embarrassment for the Neo-Darwinist evolutionary theory. We have seen, for instance, that René Thom, in the wake of D'Arcy Thompson and C. H. Waddington, attempts a taxonomy of biological forms that is independent of both the physicochemical substratum and natural selection, going against the Neo-Darwinist notion that the constraints of form are functional, depending on the natural selection in the struggle for survival. Thom assumes that these constraints are *structural*, arising from natural necessity. But the emerging pattern in the current evolutionary

43. See, for example, Ilya Prigogine and Isabelle Stengers, *La nouvelle alliance* (Paris, 1979), translated into English as *Order out of Chaos* (New York, 1984). Cf. also David Bohm's view of chance and necessity in terms of hierarchical levels of order in sec. 3.2. Along the same lines, the "anthropic cosmological principle" is, philosophically speaking, a contemporary sophisticated version of Leibnizian (teleological and melioristic) cosmological thought. Although this principle does not exclude chance, it ultimately subordinates it to necessity, at least on a local level such as inside our universe. For example, two contemporary proponents of the anthropic principle in cosmology, John D. Barrow and Frank J. Tipler, state: "The sizes of the stars and planets, and even people, are neither random nor the result of any Darwinian selection processes from a myriad of possibilities. These and other gross features of the Universe are the consequences of necessity; they are manifestations of the possible equilibrium states between competing forces of attraction and repulsion. The intrinsic strengths of these controlling forces of Nature are determined by a mysterious collection of pure numbers that we call the *constants of Nature*" (*The Anthropic Cosmological Principle* [Oxford, 1986], p. 5). Note that the anthropic cosmological model bears a strong family resemblance to the isonomic cosmological models of the Presocratics; it is also agonistic and power oriented, because it assumes, like its Presocratic predecessors, that our universe is a result of the conflict between various controlling forces.

studies seems above all to be pluralistic, and certainly does not exclude Darwinist theory. Again Taylor sums up the situation well: "Punctuationism is significant in that once it is conceded that some other mechanism than natural selection operates in evolution, even if only from time to time, natural selection is ousted from its unique position and Darwin's idea becomes merely a part of a larger theory. Of course, once one admission of this calibre is made, the situation becomes much more fluid and scientists will feel free to look around for new interpretations in a much less inhibited manner, free of any fear of having their careers damaged by the awful charge of unorthodoxy" (*Great Evolution Mystery*" (p. 245).[44]

There are no signs, however, that future evolutionary studies will favor prerational over rational play, any more than their current rivals do. Whereas many contemporary biologists no longer hesitate to use an aesthetic or playful approach in presenting their arguments (as we have seen in Dawkins, Eigen, Winkler, Thom, and Taylor), acknowledging the creative imagination and the unfathomable mystery of the world, they are by no means ready to abandon the traditional scientific reliance on rational thought, and their play is, with very few exceptions, the play of Schiller rather than that of Nietzsche. In section 3, I shall examine in some detail the nature of the aesthetic turn in modern science and its consequences for the agon between the rational and the prerational play concepts in contemporary culture.

## SECTION 3

# Play and the Aesthetic Turn in Contemporary Science

If in philosophy the first aesthetic turn occurs at the end of the eighteenth century, in science this turn takes place a century later. The reasons for this historical *décalage* are complex, but here I would like to emphasize one that is not often discussed. Since its rise during the Renaissance, modern science has been as tightly organized and rule governed as its chief cultural rival, religion. The public image which it

---

44. Punctuationism is a form of evolutionary theory that revises Cuvierism, suggesting that evolution is not gradual but "punctuated" by abrupt discontinuities. For a full exposition, see Stephen J. Gould, *Ever Since Darwin: Reflections in Natural History* (New York, 1977).

has wrought for itself over the centuries, and which it owes in part to its contest with religion, is a highly liberal one. Science sees itself and is seen by others as a neutral and objective pursuer of knowledge and truth, as an enlightened champion of freedom and progress. This image, however, does not wholly reflect the state of affairs within science's enclave. The scientific communities are as closely knit as the religious ones, and unorthodoxy on the part of their members is punished as severely in the one as in the other.[45] Hence, although its claims as a

45. Cf. sec. 3.3. Here one can also point out the disciplinary nature of scientific language in general. Over the centuries, science has developed various highly specialized, technical vocabularies, with terms borrowed from foreign or dead languages, such as Greek and Latin (cf. the similar origins of Church vocabulary). As a rule, these terms are abstractions or metaphors that originally had a concrete meaning in everyday language; moreover, the most common of them, such as *dunamis*, *phusis*, and *energeia*, can be traced back directly to a prerational language of power. Through its technical vocabularies, science effectively sets itself apart from the rest of the community and assumes a mystical aura similar to that of many secret religious societies (such terms as *laymen*, *temple of science*, *the high priests of science*, used by Einstein, Planck, and many other influential contemporary scientists, certainly reinforce this analogy). For a cogent critique of scientific language as power see, among others, Feyerabend, *Science in a Free Society* (London, 1978) and Michel Foucault, e.g., in C. Gordon, ed., *Power/Knowledge: Selected Interviews and Other Writings, 1972–1977* (New York, 1980).

Another related issue is that of the interplay between science and technology. Traditional philosophers and historians of science have drawn a distinction between pure and applied science, implying that the first is disinterested (in a Kantian sense; cf. Schrödinger, below) and therefore separated from the so-called real world (i.e., the world of power). It is only applied science or technology that is seen as power oriented and is constantly subjected to cultural critiques. Both Heidegger and Gadamer point out the fallacy of this distinction and in their wake have appeared a host of critiques of science and technology from a philosophical-hermeneutical standpoint. The view of science for science's sake is as untenable as that of art for art's sake: both scientific and artistic discourse are engaged in a contest for cultural authority, and their claims of neutrality or impartiality often turn out to be competitive strategies, aimed at gaining special cultural privileges (cf. my discussion of Schiller, in sec. 1.2). On the other hand, Postmodern technology is increasingly seen as going beyond traditional power structures. Computers and artificial intelligence, so the argument goes, will decenter our power-oriented world, ushering in a New Age of global peace and cooperation. This argument is an obvious Postmodern avatar of the old rationalist myth of progress. Yet even though Postmodern technology may no longer be recognizable as androcentric and may render the traditional Western power configurations obsolete, it will nevertheless remain as power oriented as its earlier versions. No matter how sophisticated Postmodern machines become, they will still be a product or an extension of the Western (rational) mentality; they will merely expand—and perhaps further obscure—

privileged source of knowledge and truth have frequently been challenged from outside, science has been able to resist internal pressures for change much better than its main modern counterparts, philosophy and art. When the Classical mechanism of producing and transmitting cultural values, based on mimesis-imitation, began to disintegrate during the Romantic period, science was able to preserve largely unchanged what had, by the end of the seventeenth century, become its traditional values. We have seen, for instance, that in the third *Critique* Kant continued to proclaim the superiority of the scientist over the artist on the criterion of mimesis-imitation at the very moment that he repudiated this same principle in art, where he replaced it with *poiesis* (the imitation of the processes rather than the products of nature).[46]

Science was able to withstand the Romantic revolution partly because it had broken away from speculative philosophy in the seventeenth century, a moment that was marked, for example, by the controversies between the followers of Descartes and those of Newton, resulting in the victory of the quantitative over the qualitative approach to natural phenomena. When, during the last quarter of the nineteenth century, change became inevitable, it appropriately took the form of a "Romantic" emphasis on natural process, intuition, creativity, and the subjective and qualitative character of knowledge in general. As new, or newly revived, hypotheses were replacing old dogmas, the theoretically oriented scientists and the philosophers of science who promoted these hypotheses sought to support them not only with conventional scientific methods but with philosophical and aesthetic arguments as well.

Since the changes that occurred in science at the turn of our century can in part be seen as a belated Romantic revolution, it is not surprising that among the most vocal philosophical supporters of this revolution were the Neo-Kantians, including such figures as Friedrich Albert Lange and Hans Vaihinger. Apart from Kant, the most revered Romantic philosophical figure for the Neo-Kantians was Schiller, and we have seen that Spencer alludes to him as well, although in a veiled fashion. What the Neo-Kantians borrow from Schiller is precisely his

---

rather than change, the nature of this mentality. In other words, technology is only as "good," or as "evil," as its creators (an insight that is already present in Mary Shelley's *Frankenstein*). For a recent examination of contemporary technology as power see Marike Finlay, *Powermatics: A Discursive Critique of New Communications Technology* (London/New York, 1987).

46. Cf. my discussion of Kant's third *Critique* in Part I, sec. 1.1 and my discussion of Kuhn's notion of scientific revolution in sec. 3.3.

theory of aesthetic play, with its peculiar blend of the rational and the imaginative faculties, and with its *as if* approach to knowledge. Vaihinger, for example, speaking of his *Lehrjahren*, remarks: "Many of Schiller's verses made an indelible impression on me, for instance the words 'In error only is there life, and knowledge must be death,' words which in certain respects have become the foundation of my theory of Fiction. Schiller's philosophical treatises were of course still too difficult for me to attempt, but I understood his theory of play as the primary element of artistic creation and enjoyment; and it had great influence on the development of my thought, for later on I recognized in play the 'as if,' as the driving force of aesthetic activity and intuition."[47]

Vaihinger correctly observes that F. A. Lange recognizes as his immediate precursor not Kant but Schiller, who, according to Lange, "with the insight of the diviner, grasps the innermost kernel of the Kantian doctrines" (quoted by Vaihinger, p. 332). Schiller's concept of play and aesthetics will be invoked by virtually every twentieth-century German scientist who takes upon himself the task of presenting the aesthetic turn in modern science to the public at large, and we have already examined, to this effect, the case of Eigen and Winkler. Finally, the Neo-Kantians were ideally suited for advocating the scientific revolution because, whereas they introduced aesthetic and intuitive elements into scientific discourse, they never abandoned the empiricist and positivist assumptions of modern science.

Neither is it surprising that the aesthetic turn in the hard sciences began with physics, where Newton had ruled practically unchallenged for almost two centuries. His famous dictum *hypotheses non fingo* (I do not feign hypotheses) implied that the purpose of science was to discover, not to create, natural laws. The physicists at the beginning of this century maintained just the opposite: they no longer claimed to disclose a certain objective reality, but rather to invent it as they went along. Referring to the Einsteinian revolution in physics, Herbert J. Muller remarks:

47. Hans Vaihinger, "Autobiographical: The Origin of the Philosophy of 'As If,'" *The Philosophy of "As If": A System of the Theoretical, Practical and Religious Fictions of Mankind*, trans. C. K. Ogden (London, 1924), p. xliv. Further citations refer to this edition. I have also used in parallel the first German edition, *Die Philosophie des Als Ob: System der theoretischen, praktischen und religiösen Fiktionen der Menschheit auf Grund eines idealistischen Positivismus* (Berlin, 1911). This first edition does not contain the autobiographical section included in Ogden's English edition.

This revolution might be summarized as the triumph of the postulate over the axiom. A postulate is something assumed, to be tested for its usefulness not a law laid down by God but a logical fiction consciously invented by man. "No one can say," declared Descartes of the properties of the triangles, "that I have invented them"; mathematicians and scientists now say just this. . . .

In *The Evolution of Physics* Einstein talks constantly of the "important invention" of the electromagnetic field and all the other realities "created by modern physics."[48]

Despite Newton's gallant cry (he was not unaware of the fictional character of his theory of gravitation),[49] it was psychologically easier for

---

48. See Herbert J. Muller, *Science and Criticism: The Humanistic Tradition in Contemporary Thought* (New Haven, Conn., 1943), pp. 78–79. Cf., however, my comments on Muller in secs. 3.2 and 3.3.

49. Newton expresses his awareness in terms of an ancient play metaphor: "I don't know what I may seem to the world. But as to myself I seem to have been only like a boy playing on the seashore and diverting myself in now and then finding a smoother pebble or prettier shell than ordinary, while the great ocean of truth lay all undiscovered before me" (quoted by Werner Heisenberg, in *Philosophic Problems of Nuclear Science* [New York, 1952], p. 79). Here Newton views play in a typically negative, Neoclassical fashion, as lacking any cognitive value in contrast to the "great ocean of truth." Recent reappraisals of Newton's thought emphasize Newtonian attacks on Cartesian and Leibnizian concepts of rational order. Richard Westfall, for example, notes: "The basic issue between Newton and the traditional mechanical philosophers lay in his willingness to employ an ideal of science which accepted the ultimate inscrutability of nature" (*The Construction of Modern Science: Mechanisms and Mechanics* [New York, 1971], p. 158). These reappraisals, however, do not sufficiently stress the fact that such attacks are merely "family quarrels," being largely aimed at replacing qualitative by quantitative models of physical reality, without endangering the fundamental assumptions of the Western ontotheological tradition. Cf. my views on the Copenhagen school and rationality, below. For recent reappraisals of Newton see, among many others, R. E. Butts and J. W. Davis, eds., *The Methodological Heritage of Newton* (Toronto, 1970), including N. R. Hanson's fine essay, "Hypotheses Fingo," pp. 14–33; J. E. McGuire and Martin Tamny, *Certain Philosophical Questions: Newton's Trinity Notebook* (Cambridge, Eng., 1983), especially pp. 127–174; and Gale E. Christianson, *In the Presence of the Creator: Isaac Newton and His Times* (New York, 1984). For the debates between Newton and Leibnitz, and Newton and the Cartesians in general, see Pierre Brunet, *L'introduction des théories de Newton en France au XVIIIe siècle* (Geneva, 1970) and A. Rupert Hall, *Philosophers at War: The Quarrel between Newton and Leibniz* (Cambridge, 1980). For discursive critiques of the seventeenth-century Scientific Revolution see, among others, Richard H. Popkin, *The History of Scepticism from Erasmus to Spinoza* (Berkeley/Los Angeles, 1979) and, in the English context, Steven Shapin and Simon Schaffer, *Leviathan and the Air-Pump: Hobbes,*

physicists than for other scientists to (re)acknowledge the fictive nature of their scientific tools, because physics, like mathematics, has always employed conscious fictions, such as the concept of force, the atom, and, more recently, subatomic particles.

In modern biology, by contrast, the aesthetic turn came later than in physics, not least because Darwinism had first to establish itself as a serious scientific enterprise, or had to prove that it was not operating merely with fictions. This it proved with the aid of atomic physics. As is well known, the success of biology as a modern discipline is mainly due to its combination of the Darwinian evolutionary theory with genetics, which is in turn based on an atomistic view of organic life. Only after their field became securely established could such scientists as Monod, Thom, Eigen, and Winkler invoke aesthetic criteria in support of their biological theories—criteria that again they borrowed from theoretical physics.

Although the aesthetic turn has made itself felt in most scientific disciplines, in this section I shall concentrate on its impact in the new physics (precisely because this physics had a leading role in the twentieth-century scientific revolution) as well as on its impact in the contemporary philosophy and history of science, the new physics' closest ally. I shall also cast a preliminary look at Hans Vaihinger, one of the early promoters of the aesthetic turn in the philosophy of science. Thereby I shall stray somewhat from the well-worn path of the contemporary history of science, where it is customary to trace the theoretical foundations of the revolution in physics back to Mach, Poincaré, and logical positivism in general. In this respect, few historians stress the equally important role played by the particular brand of Neo-Kantian positivism that revised Kant through Schiller. Several influential theoretical physicists, including Planck and Einstein, while starting out as Machian positivists, move on to a Schillerian kind of Neo-Kantianism, and it is precisely this Schillerian tradition that contemporary historians of science do not pay enough attention to.[50]

*Boyle and the Experimental Life* (Princeton, N.J., 1986), as well as Simon Schaffer, "Making Certain," *Social Studies of Science* 14 (1984): 137–152, and Peter Dear, "*Totius in verba*: Rhetoric and Authority in the Early Royal Society," *Isis* 76 (June 1985): 145–161.

50. In his *Thematic Origins of Scientific Thought: Kepler to Einstein* (Cambridge, Mass., 1973), for example, Gerald Holton correctly observes: "Phenomenalistic positivism in science has always been victorious, but only up to a very definite limit. It is the necessary sword for destroying old error, but it makes an inadequate plowshare for cultivating a new harvest. I find it extremely significant that Einstein

## 3·1   Hans Vaihinger's Philosophy of *As If*

Although he only published his *Philosophie des "Als Ob"* in 1911, Vaihinger had already worked out the basic outlines of his theory of scientific fictions by 1876, when he presented it as an inaugural dissertation at the University of Strasbourg.[51] His philosophy of *as if* attempts to reconcile German idealism with the various forms of scientific empiricism and positivism that had come to prominence by the end of the nineteenth century. Vaihinger proposes to effect this reconciliation by emphasizing that element in Kant and Schopenhauer which was also used by Nietzsche as well as by a host of utilitarians, pragmatists, and logical positivists from J. S. Mill to William James to Mach: a skeptical theory of sense perception which may be traced back to the empiricism of Locke and Hume. Vaihinger calls his philosophical position an "idealist positivism" or "positivist idealism," and this position, which is a brand of Neo-Kantianism, is still shared explicitly or implicitly by a great number of theoretical scientists and philosophers of science.

From Schopenhauer Vaihinger also borrows, like Nietzsche, his concept of the will, but, unlike Nietzsche, he interprets this concept in utilitarian terms. For Vaihinger, the origin of the will must be sought in the "strivings [*Streben*; cf. Eigen and Winkler] which probably exist in the most elementary physical processes" (p. xliv). In organic beings, these strivings become impulses which, in higher animals and especially man, have evolved into will and action. Thought itself is an instrument "in the service of the Will to live and dominate . . . a means in the struggle for existence and to this extent only a biological function" (p. xlvi). Apart from his Darwinian interpretation of the Schopenhauerian will as a struggle for existence, here Vaihinger does seem to come close to Nietzsche's view of thought as a biological function of power. Like Nietzsche (and Schopenhauer), he goes against the Hegelian notion of

---

saw this during the transition phase of partial disagreement from the Machist philosophy" (p. 240). Holton falls somewhat short of specifying to what kind of "plowshare" Einstein and others turn in order to cultivate their new harvest (cf. sec. 3.2).

51. One can certainly object that, since Vaihinger published his major work relatively late and since his Strasbourg dissertation could not have reached a wide audience, his influence on the scientific community at the turn of the century must have been rather small in comparison to that of Mach (whose views were well publicized). But the basic principles of Vaihinger's philosophy of *as if* were quietly absorbed not so much through his treatise as through the two extremely influential journals that he founded, *Kant-Studien* and *Annalen der Philosophie*.

the universal spirit and that of human consciousness as a representation of external reality, which also means that he goes against the traditional concept of Reason: "If intellectualism or rationalism be identified with the assumption of an original theoretical reason as an inherent human faculty with certain problems to be determined by it, then my exposition must be termed antirationalism or even irrationalism" (p. xlvi). For Vaihinger all thought processes and constructs are not rational, but biological phenomena. Many of them are "consciously false assumptions" which contradict reality or are even self-contradictory, but which have a practical value, being instrumental in attaining the goals of the will (to live and dominate).

Vaihinger defines reality as the observable unchangeability of phenomena, their relations, and their unalterable sequences and coexistences. Everything else is a "mere illusion with which the psyche plays about" (p. 124). Because our conceptual world is itself a *product* of reality, it cannot at the same time be a reflection of this reality. It can only serve as an instrument within reality, by means of which the higher organisms carry out their activities. It is a "symbol by means of which we orientate ourselves; and it is in the interest of science to make this symbol more and more adequate and utilizable, but a symbol will it always remain" (p. 65). Logical thought is no different. By regarding it simply as a means for a practical purpose, the "superstitious admiration of logical forms diminishes and the logical products no longer appear as revelations of reality but as purely mechanical instruments, whereby thought may move forward and attain its practical objects" (p. 172). Here, then, Vaihinger seems to go back, like Nietzsche, to a prerational view of thought as a practical instrument of the will to power, the *metis* of the archaic Greeks. We shall see, however, that he is ultimately unable to remain consistent with this position precisely because of his divided allegiances to idealism and logical positivism.

Although thought has a biological origin and a purely utilitarian purpose, it is subject to what Vaihinger calls the "law of the preponderance of the means over the end." According to this law the biological means serving a certain purpose ultimately become overdeveloped; they emancipate themselves from their original purpose and become ends in themselves. This is also the case of thought, which in the course of time has gradually forgotten its original function and has become theoretical and contemplative, practised for its own sake. As a result, thought poses itself unsolvable problems, such as the origin and meaning of the universe, the relation of body and spirit, subject and object, sensation and motion. Vaihinger's law of the preponderance of the means over the end (which he claims to have discovered before Wundt) remains the basis for the widely accepted contemporary view of symbolic thought, as we have seen in the case of Bateson, Dawkins, Monod, and others; for Vaihinger, however, this law has a negative side, whereas our contemporary theorists interpret it in an entirely optimistic fashion, as man's emancipation from his biological constraints, leading eventually to his complete biological self-transcendence.

From the foregoing exposition, it might appear that for Vaihinger, no less than for Nietzsche, all thought, including the logical faculty, is a fictive activity, producing ideational constructs that further the goals of the will to live and dominate. But it turns out that this is not the case. Fictions are a peculiar kind of logical product, a special manifestation of the logical function. Vaihinger attempts to illustrate his point by drawing a distinction between the *rules* and *artifices* of thought. The rules are the "totality of all those technical operations in virtue of which an activity is able to attain its object directly"; in logic these operations, particularly the inductive ones, are appropriately called the "rules of thinking" (p. 11). The artifices are those operations which allow logical thought to attain its object indirectly, and they have an "almost mysterious," magical character. As in the case of certain techniques pertaining to the arts and crafts, they are kept secret as long as possible (pp. 11–12). When the material encountered resists known rules, the logical faculty exhibits an "instinctive, almost cunning ingenuity," overcoming the material's resistance with the help of "accessory concepts." It is precisely these accessory concepts or logical artifices that Vaihinger calls *fictions*.

On the other hand, however, the fictive activity is also a manifestation of fundamental psychical forces, and for Vaihinger fictions are mental structures, forged in the struggle for survival: "The psyche weaves this aid to thought out of itself; for the mind is inventive; under the compulsion of necessity, stimulated by the outer world, it discovers the store of contrivances that lie hidden within itself. . . . In necessity and pain mental evolution is begun, in contradiction and opposition consciousness awakes, and man owes his mental development more to his enemies than to his friends" (p. 12).

The fictive activity, therefore, has the same biological origin as the logical function in general and, ontologically speaking, the distinction between fictions and other ideational constructs is one without a difference. Yet Vaihinger continues to insist on drawing epistemological and logical distinctions, particularly when he embarks upon his main topic, scientific fictions.

Before proposing his classification of scientific fictions, Vaihinger observes that the object of science is to develop ideas that correspond to some kind of reality, eliminating all "admixture of the subjective." Our natural tendency is to "adjust our representations, to test them by comparison with reality, and to render them free of contradictions" (p. 15). The scientific ideal would be to have an ideational world made up exclusively of congruous, well-ordered, and noncontradictory constructs. If one remembers, however, that our customary modes of thought already contain a great number of subjective and fictional elements and that, furthermore, the aim of the world of ideas as a whole is not to represent reality but to provide us with an *"instrument for finding our way about more easily in this world"* (p. 15), then one realizes that the scientific ideal would be very hard to reach. In scientific practice, therefore, one finds ideational constructs that correspond to reality (which does not mean that they are copies of it, but merely that they are accurate gauges for measuring the changes in it), others that contradict reality, and still others that contradict both reality and themselves. Most scientific constructs belong to the second and third categories. Thus Vaihinger draws a distinction between real scientific fictions, which are "not only in contradiction with reality but self-contradictory in themselves," such as the concept of the atom or that of the *Ding an sich*, and scientific semifictions that "only contradict reality as given" (p. 16), such as artificial classifications. All scientific fictions are "provisional methods" to be discarded as soon as they attain their objective or as soon as more accurate methods are found. (Vaihinger uses the image of the scaffolding to be removed once the edifice is built, a metaphor that crops up as a commonplace in contemporary scientific treatises.) It is this provisional status that gives fictions their *as if* character: the scientist who employs them proceeds as if they were true or corresponded to reality.

Vaihinger reviews a large number of scientific and philosophical real and half fictions, dividing them into taxonomical, abstractive, schematic, paradigmatic, utopian, analogical, personificatory, heuristic, summational, and mathematical ones; he also devotes special chapters to such crucial fictions as infinity, matter, atom, *Ding an sich*, and the main conceptual tools of mechanics (gravity, motion, forces, etc.). From the point of view of this book, his most important logical distinctions are those between good and bad fictions, between fictions, hypotheses, and dogmas, and between scientific and aesthetic fictions. For Vaihinger, good fictions are those which further the objectives of the will in general and of thought in particular, in other words, those which have a utilitarian value; bad fictions, on the other hand, are those which do not have such value, being a "mere play of ideas" (cf. Kant). Among the good or useful fictions Vaihinger includes what he calls "practical" or "ethical" fictions, comprising most religious notions as well as the major philosophical constructs of German idealism. Thus he argues for the practical value of such religious and ethical fictions as God, immortality, duty, the moral world order, infinite perfection, and infinite progress, as well as for the utility of what we call "ideals" in ordinary life: "From a logical point of view [ideals] are really fictions, but in practice they possess tremendous value in history. The ideal is an ideational construct contradictory in itself and in contradiction with reality, but it has an irresistible power. *The ideal is a practical fiction.* . . . We include as fictions not merely indifferent theoretical operations but ideational constructs emanating from the noblest minds, to which the noblest part of mankind cling and of which they will not allow themselves to be deprived. Nor is it our object so to deprive them, for as *practical fictions* we leave them all intact; they perish only as *theoretical truths*" (pp. 48–49).

In this passage Vaihinger puts to work not only his distinction between good and bad fictions but also his distinction between fictions and hypotheses. For him, this latter distinction is both logical and epistemological. A hypothesis is an ideational construct that is oriented toward reality: it wants to correspond to a certain state of affairs and it demands verification. Whereas a hypothesis looks forward to being established as truth, a fiction is a "mere auxiliary construct, a circuitous approach, a scaffolding afterwards to be demolished" (p. 88). The fiction is "artificial," the hypothesis is "natural." Hypotheses attempt to produce knowledge, establishing what is "ultimately and primarily unalterable." Fictions have only a practical purpose, and do not lead to real knowledge. Hypotheses aim at eliminating all logical contradictions while fictions thrive on these contradictions. The former seek to *discover*, the latter to *invent*.

The fiction and the hypothesis differ also in their methodology. The hypothesis operates on the principle that its assumptions are possible not only for thought but also in actuality, that the facts of experience agree with it. One fact that is at variance with a hypothesis may demolish it, while a fiction remains undisturbed by its contradiction of experience. But if a hypothesis must be verified, a fiction must be justified: the former must be confirmed by experience, the latter must prove its usefulness to science. In sum, the governing principle of "hypothetical method is the *probability of the conceptual constructs*, that of fictional method is their *expediency*" (p. 89). Vaihinger concludes his comparison between fictions and hypotheses by sounding a warning in regard to fictions: "If a fiction has finally been accepted, the principal requirement is that of being careful not to transform it either into an hypothesis or into a dogma, and not to substitute for reality what has been deduced from the fiction, without first having made the necessary corrections. . . . We must not become attached to these fictions as if they were the essential thing, but we must recognize them as fictions and be content with this knowledge, and refuse to allow ourselves to be enticed and confused by the illusory questions and the illusory problems arising out of them" (p. 90).

After having set up these careful logical distinctions in the best tradition of Neo-Kantian critical positivism, Vaihinger all but erases them again in what he calls the "law of ideational shifts" (*Gesetz der Ideenverschiebung*). According to this law, certain ideas "pass through various stages of development, namely those of fiction, hypothesis, and dogma; and conversely dogma, hypothesis, and fiction" (p. 124). Now Vaihinger partly shifts his distinctions from a logical and epistemological to a psychological level, formulating his law in terms of an empiricist theory of belief and psychic conservation. He divides the psychic elements into well-established and fluctuating groups of ideas. Dogmas belong to the first group, whereas hypotheses belong to the second, their objective validity being always in doubt. Because the mind accepts it only provisionally, the hypothesis interferes with the psyche's tendency toward stability and equilibrium; it creates a state of psychic tension that the mind naturally attempts to relieve. Consequently the mind starts working at stabilizing the hypothesis through "repeated confirmation" and this is the "legitimate way" of transforming a hypothesis into a dogma. There are cases, however, when repeated confirmation is impossible or involves centuries of labor, so the psyche circumvents it by transforming the hypothesis into dogma through some "illegitimate" method, that is, without "gradual verification." In this case, the idea is "shifted one place in value either gradually or suddenly, and this may therefore be called the law of ideational shifts" (p. 126). The transformation of a fiction into dogma, either directly or through the intermediary stage of a hypothesis, is due to the same psychic process of conservation, except that now there is no legitimate method available since, logically speaking, a fiction will be a fiction under any circumstances.

We see, then, that even in his law of ideational shifts Vaihinger does not completely move the ground of his argument to the psychological level, and therefore does not completely erase his logical distinctions among dogmas, hypotheses, and fictions. Unlike Nietzsche, he shies away from the more radical consequences of his own theory of fictions, attempting to keep it within the confines of logical positivism. His distinction between legitimate and illegitimate methods of transforming a hypothesis into dogma is merely another logical fiction, if we accept his own argument that the psyche operates on the principle of expediency rather than on that of verification and that, from the will's point of view, it simply does not matter whether the mind's ideational constructs correspond to or deviate from reality as long as they carry out the will's goals quickly and effectively. After all, it is Vaihinger himself who, in a different context, insists that the "boundary between truth and error is not a rigid one" and that "what we generally call truth, namely a conceptual world coinciding with the external world, is merely *the most expedient error*." (p. 108) There is really no good reason for science, or for Vaihinger, to insist on verification, unless this were invariably the most direct and expedient way of achieving the will's goals, which, according to Vaihinger himself, it is not. In this respect, it is scientific method and not the purely fictive activity that seems to be "circuitous" and "auxiliary." The inescapable conclusion is either that science's concern with verification is a luxury or that it is itself a useful *artifice* or fiction which ultimately allows its dogmas to prevail over and endure longer than those of any other cultural endeavor.

If one accepts the second alternative, it becomes obvious that through his law of ideational shifts Vaihinger serves the goals of science rather than, say, those of philosophy or religion. In order to carry out these goals, he employs not only a double perspective (logical and psychological) but also a double standard: one for science and one for other fields. The first presupposes a scientific process of regression through which nonscientific dogmas are exposed as fictions and (false) hypotheses, and the second presupposes an unscientific process of transformation through which scientific dogmas are indirectly legitimized. There are legitimate and illegitimate dogmas and fictions, and it is only in and through science that the legitimate ones can be arrived at and be securely established. One might finally wonder why, after going to the trouble of disclosing the fictional character of innumerable scientific dogmas, Vaihinger still clings to this double standard, thereby running the risk of seriously damaging the plausibility of his arguments from a purely logical standpoint. As it turns out, he runs all this risk for the sake of only one scientific hypothesis, which he treats as a de facto dogma: the Darwinian theory of evolution by natural selection (pp. 85–86).

Vaihinger employs the same double perspective (logical and psychological) and the same double standard in his distinction between scientific and aesthetic fictions. In part 1, chapter 20, "The Separation of Scientific from Other Fictions, Particularly from the Aesthetic," Vaihinger begins by acknowledging the common psychological ground of *all* fictional constructs. The psychological genesis of fictions is the same in all fields of inquiry, going back to the imaginative faculty. According to him, the very etymology of the word *fiction* points to the close link of the fictive activity to the imagination. The Latin *fictio* is both an activity and a product of *fingere*. As an activity it means "constructing, forming, giving shape, elaborating, presenting [*Darstellen*], artistically fashioning [*künstlerisch Formieren*]," as well as "conceiving, thinking, imagining, planning, devising, inventing." As a product of *fingere* it designates a "fictional assumption, fabrication, creation, or imagined case" (p. 81). For Vaihinger mythology, the "common mother of religion, poetry, art, and science," is the first historical manifestation of the "free constructive activity of the inventive faculty, of imagination and of fantasy." The most salient feature of the fictive activity is its "unhampered and free expression," that is, its playfulness. Thus, not only the mythical but also other fictions are the result of the "free creative play of psychical activity, expressing itself in arbitrary combinations and alternations of the elements existing in the world of fact" (p. 82).

But after pointing out the common psychological origin of all fictions, Vaihinger immediately introduces a logical and epistemological distinction between mythical or religious and scientific fictions. Whereas the mythical or religious fiction is merely an error, its scientific counterpart is a consciously false construct which proceeds as if it were true. When the latter fails to recognize its *as if* character, it turns from a correct fiction into an incorrect judgment (p. 82). Nevertheless, Vaihinger reminds us that we should not discard the religious fictions altogether: even though they are incorrect judgments, they remain useful, especially in their theological guise (e.g., in German idealist philosophy). The aesthetic fictions, on the other hand, seem to have an intermediary logical status between the religious or mythical and the scientific ones, being closely related to both. They are in part poetic adaptations of the mythical fictions and in part newly created. The fact that they are closely related to scientific fictions seems "quite natural when we remember that the same elementary processes contribute to the construction of both" (p. 82). But Vaihinger never specifies what the logical distinction between the aesthetic and the scientific fictions is, proceeding as if this distinction were self-evident. We are left to infer that it might be somewhat similar to the distinction between scientific and mythical-religious fictions: the aesthetic constructs are presumably less close to the world of fact than their scientific counterparts, although closer than the mythical fictions. In any case, Vaihinger suggests, in a note, that "in the future we should call scientific fictions *fictions*, and the others, the mythological, aesthetic, etc. *figments* [*Figmente*]," because this would "certainly facilitate distinctions" (p. 81). In the main text, though, he prefers to emphasize the similarities rather than the differences between the aesthetic and the scientific fictions (note that in the case of his comparison between the scientific and mythical fictions he does exactly the opposite), basing these similarities on utilitarian criteria.

Aesthetic fictions serve the purpose of "awakening within us certain uplifting or otherwise important feelings." Like the scientific ones, they are "not an end in themselves but a means for the attainment of higher ends" (p. 82). Moreover, both the aesthetic and the scientific fictions have come under attack for similar reasons: they have been overused. According to Vaihinger, these attacks are part of an old dispute concerning the uses and abuses of fantasy (and play). The criterion in resolving this dispute, he argues, is the practical value of these fictions, being decided upon by good taste and logical tact: "As in science so in poetry . . . fictions have been greatly abused, and this has frequently led to reactions, based on exactly the same grounds as those resulting from the misuse of scientific fictions. The real criterion as to how far such fictions are to be admitted into either field, and which has always been adopted by good taste and logical tact alike, is simply the practical value of such fictions" (pp. 82–83).

Here one can see that, like so many of his predecessors, Vaihinger attempts to settle the quarrel between philosophy-science and poetry on the *former's* terms. His defense of the aesthetic fictions in effect promotes the interests of science rather than those of poetry. Vaihinger argues for the "poetic" quality of the scientific fictions without giving up their higher claims to cultural authority, which he justifies on util-

itarian grounds (later on, he will employ the same strategy in attempting to settle the quarrel between science and religion; see particularly his
discussion of F. A. Lange's "standpoint of the ideal," pp. 328–330). By
applying the same utilitarian criteria to the aesthetic fictions, Vaihinger
simply reaffirms the authority of science and philosophy to judge art by
their own standards, rather than by art's.

In turn, Vaihinger's view of play is inseparable from his concept of
fictions as products of the imaginative faculty. All fictions are created
through the free play of this faculty, and *Spielbegriffe* (play-ideas) is one
of the terms that Vaihinger lists as expressing the same meaning as the
word "fictions" (p. 97). Since he inherits his concept of play, together
with that of the imaginative faculty, from Kant and Schiller, one will
find in Vaihinger the same ambiguities that one finds in his predecessors
regarding these concepts. On the one hand, Vaihinger traces human
play back to the prerational (for him, irrational) play of cosmic forces.
For example, when he argues that the ideational world is not a copy of
the cosmic process, but a part of it, he remarks: "The world as we
conceive it is only a secondary or tertiary construction, arising in our
heads through the play of cosmic process and solely for the furtherance
of this process. This conceptual world is not a *picture* of the actual world
but an *instrument* for grasping and subjectively understanding that
world" (p. 63).

Likewise, he invokes play in support of another antirational argument (related to the previous one), namely that intuition and experience
are superior to reason. Unlike reason, they confine themselves to their
legitimate function, viz., serving the practical purpose of the will to live
and dominate, and do not seek the autonomy of the means over the end,
creating needless speculative riddles: "Experience and intuition are
higher than all human reason. When I see a deer feeding in the forest,
when I see a child at play, when I see a man at work or sport, but above
all when I myself am working or playing, where are the problems with
which my mind has been torturing itself unnecessarily? We do not
understand the world when we are pondering over its problems, but
when we are doing the world's work" (p. xlv).

In this passage, Vaihinger invokes the intuitive and existential, or the
spontaneous, character of play, an idea inherited from a prerational
mentality. At the same time, however, Vaihinger couples play with
work, implying its utilitarian side. In the case of play, too, the "practical
reigns supreme" (p. xlv). Finally, as we have seen, he links play to the
freely creative activity of the imagination. Fictions are the result of this

"free creative play of psychical activity," and Vaihinger, again following an ancient tradition, emphasizes the close relation of the concept of play to that of freedom.

On the other hand, for Vaihinger, as for his rationalist predecessors, too much free play is just as harmful as too much imagination or fantasy and needs to be disciplined by the logical function. Like Schiller and Lange, Vaihinger starts by emphasizing the positive aspects of Kant's concept of the imaginative faculty and the aesthetic judgment. For him, the "realization that imagination also plays a great part in science is one of the main advances of modern epistemology" (p. 55). Scientific fictions as the playful product of the imaginative faculty have an "immense practical importance," playing an "indispensable intermediary role." Without them, the "satisfaction of understanding, the ordering of our chaotic material . . . all advances in science, and finally all higher morality would be impossible" (p. 50). But they play *only* an intermediary role and, according to Vaihinger, Kant was "quite correct and circumspect when he spoke of a 'transcendental imaginative faculty.'" The free creative play of the psyche ultimately remains tied down by the actual sequence and coexistence of the sense-data (p. 56). If the criterion of fictions "is to be of value, we must always be able to find our way back to reality again." Despite the great importance of the imaginative function, its products "must only be regarded as fictions, without any corresponding reality, arising by immanent necessity from the mechanistic play of ideas, as aids and tools created by the purposive logical activity with the object of lightening and perfecting its labor, whether in relation to science or life" (p. 50). In other words, the creative play of the imagination is a mere tool of the logical faculty, and as such it must obey its directives. Thus Vaihinger, despite his irrationalist posturing, remains safely within the rationalist fold.

The aesthetic turn that Vaihinger and other Neo-Kantian thinkers both advocated and helped to bring about in modern science at the beginning of the twentieth century has several points in common with the aesthetic turn that their Romantic predecessors engineered in philosophy at the end of the eighteenth century. Like their forerunners, Vaihinger and his fellow Neo-Kantians argue for the important function of the creative play of the imagination in philosophy and science, and, in their wake, the aesthetic and intuitive side of the scientific activity will be emphasized again and again by a host of twentieth-century scientists and philosophers of science. But like their Romantic forerunners, the Neo-Kantians distrust what they see as the fundamentally chaotic and arbitrary, and therefore unscientific, character of imaginative play, strictly subordinating it to the logical faculty. The aesthetic revolution that they advocate in modern science is certainly not Nietzsche's aesthetic project of transvaluating all values but, like many revolutions, has a conservative rather than a subversive tenor, and Vaihinger's attitude toward Nietzsche is exemplary in this regard as well.

Although he is Nietzsche's contemporary and is fully aware of his thought—*Philosophie des "Als Ob"* concludes with a chapter called "Nietzsche's Doctrine of Conscious Illusion"—Vaihinger ignores the more daring implications of this thought. He interprets Nietzsche's theory of "truth and lie in an extra-moral sense" in terms of his own utilitarian view of fictions, disregarding Nietzsche's profoundly non-utilitarian, aristocratic system of values. He mistakenly charges Nietzsche with attacking both Schopenhauer and Darwin while quietly adopting their insights (cf. Groos's similar attempt to draw a parallel between Nietzsche and Darwin), and he equates his own "will to live and dominate" with Nietzsche's "will to power." What Vaihinger does not seem to realize is that the Nietzschean will is a purely prerational notion, requiring a sweeping critique of all rational values, including those of science. Hence he also fails to see that his own theory of fictions, if applied consistently, would inevitably lead to a Nietzschean transvaluation of all values.

Vaihinger constantly wavers between the rational values that make up the scientific mentality and the prerational values that are inherent in Schopenhauer's concept of the Will and are openly affirmed by Nietzsche. If he had chosen a consistently prerational perspective, for example, Vaihinger might have avoided some of the more glaring logical contradictions and double standards that plague his arguments. He might have realized that his distinction among fictions, hypotheses, and dogmas is a purely axiological one, in the sense that a certain group of values determines logic and epistemology, rather than the other way around. Then Vaihinger's "fictions" would not have remained amphibolous, paradoxical logical categories, assuming the guise now of hypotheses, now of dogmas. Instead, his law of ideational shifts would have stipulated that in the course of their history *all* ideational constructs may at one time or another be treated as if they were fictions, dogmas, or hypotheses, that is, they may be upgraded or downgraded in value, according to how successful they are in their contest for cultural authority. In turn, this radicalized theory of the shift of ideational constructs could have given rise to a functionalist history of the interplay, in Western culture, of such major stretches of discourse as philosophy, science, religion, and art. But these are questions that go

258 · Play and Modern Scientific Discourse

beyond the confines of the present section. For the time being, therefore, let us return to scientific theoretical discourse and examine the uses
of aesthetics and play in what has come to be known as the "new
physics," uses that are, moreover, remarkably similar to those we find in
Vaihinger's philosophy of *as if*.

## 3·2 Play and the New Physicists

The principal landmarks that led to the foundation of the new physics
are well known: a few of them are the Michelson-Morley experiment
(1887) and the theoretical debates around it; Max Planck's quantum
hypothesis (1900); Albert Einstein's photon theory and special theory
of relativity (1905); Niels Bohr's planetary model of the atom (1913);
Einstein's general theory of relativity (1915); Louis de Broglie's hypothesis of matter waves (1924); Erwin Schrödinger's wave equation
(1926); Bohr's theory of complementarity or of the wave-particle duality of light (1927); Werner Heisenberg's uncertainty principle
(1927); and the Copenhagen interpretation of quantum mechanics
(1927). What is of interest here is certainly not a more or less technical
discussion of the new developments in physics, but an examination of
the general philosophical and cultural-theoretical assumptions—or the
scientific mentality—behind these developments. I shall briefly consider the cases of Planck, Einstein, Schrödinger, and Heisenberg, then
cast a quick look at the more recent theoretical developments in the field
and their relevance to what I have called the aesthetic turn in modern
scientific discourse.

The cultural-theoretical assumptions of the new physics reveal some
of the same thematic polarities that appear in other fields of knowledge.
These thematic polarities can to some extent also be traced back to the
age-old conflict between a rational and a prerational mentality, of
which, as we have seen, the conflict between the chaotic, violent, and
indeterminate play of physical forces and the orderly, necessary, and
rule-governed play of reason is a special case. Monod's distinction
between a Heraclitean and a Platonic scientific attitude, for example,
and Thom's dichotomy between uncertainty and determinacy or between a qualitative and a quantitative approach, are equally operative in
theoretical physics—in fact, as I have already pointed out, Monod and
Thom borrow their distinctions from this field.[52]

52. Gerald Holton lists other polarities that, although not necessarily connected
with the rational/prerational dichotomy, are nevertheless illustrative of the agonis-

One might also be tempted to see, in contemporary physics, a replay of the two aesthetic turns that the sequence Kant-Schiller-Nietzsche-Heidegger mark in modern philosophy. More specifically, one might be tempted to treat the philosophical controversies surrounding the general relativity and quantum theories as another chapter in the ceaseless contest between rational and prerational values, with the relativists generally leaning toward a rational world view and the quantum theorists toward a prerational world view. Even though such an approach would not be totally unjustified, the complexity of this particular scientific conjuncture defies any neat generalizations. Indeed, whereas certain developments in the quantum field are susceptible to prerational interpretations, the majority of the theoretical physicists from both camps reaffirm their allegiance to rational values, adopting Neo-Kantian positions similar to that of Vaihinger.

In his numerous essays on the contemporary philosophy of science, Max Planck anticipates most of the onto-epistemological questions which continue to concern theoretical scientists today, and which he answers from a Neo-Kantian rationalist standpoint. In "Causality in Nature," not unlike his direct heirs Eigen and Winkler, Planck resolves the issue of chance and necessity in science in favor of necessity, relating it to what he calls the "law of causality" and "determinism."

Planck begins by acknowledging that there are no satisfactory scientific definitions of causality, suggesting that a good practical approach to this concept would be to attach it to the capacity of predicting future events: a physical event is "causally conditioned if it can be foretold with certainty."[53] Even in this case, however, the available facts "compel us

tic mentality of Western science: "Not far below the surface, there have coexisted in science, in almost every period since Thales and Pythagoras, sets of two or more antithetical systems or attitudes, for example, one reductionist and the other holistic, or one mechanistic and the other vitalistic, or one positivistic and the other teleological. In addition, there has always existed another set of antitheses or polarities, even though, to be sure, one or the other was at a given time more prominent—namely between the Galilean (or, more properly, Archimedean) attempt at precision and measurement that purged public, 'objective' science of those qualitative elements that interfere with reaching reasonable 'objective' agreement among fellow investigators, and, on the other hand, the intuitions, glimpses, daydreams, and a priori commitments that make up half the world of science in the form of a personal, private, 'subjective' activity. . . . Science has always been propelled and buffeted by such contrary or antithetical forces" (*Thematic Origins*, p. 69).

53. Max Planck, "Causality in Nature," in *The Philosophy of Physics*, trans. W. H. Johnston (New York, 1936), pp. 47–48. Further citations refer to this edition.

to admit . . . that in no single instance is it possible accurately to predict a physical event" (p. 49). Planck then points out that there have been two prevailing views regarding causality in physics. The first view, which is common in quantum physics, assumes that there is no genuine causality or law in nature; the only valid laws are the statistical ones or the laws of probability. Planck calls the advocates of this view "indeterminists." The second view, which is common in classical physics, assumes that there is natural causality; Planck calls its advocates "determinists."

The determinists safeguard the law of causality by introducing a theoretical fiction that Planck terms the "physical world-image" (*das physikalische Weltbild*). This world-image is admittedly arbitrary, being "merely an intellectual structure," a kind of "model or idealization" which replaces the real world of the senses (Planck does not take into account the possibility that the empiricist notion of the "real world of the senses" may be equally fictitious). Within the physical world-image every event can be determined with precision and the law of causality remains perfectly valid. The indeterminacy arises only in regard to the connection between the world-image and the world of the senses. Planck proceeds to show that the indeterminists also operate with a physical world-image, within which they are as rigidly deterministic as the classical physicists; they differ from the determinists only insofar as they employ different symbols and operating rules (this argument is fully borne out, as we have seen, by the examination of the theoretical assumptions of such indeterminists as Monod and Thom).

That Planck's "physical world-image" is a scientific fiction in Vaihinger's sense becomes evident when Planck states that the only criterion of judging the validity of the two positions regarding causality in physics is their practical value or usefulness. Each position implies generalizations and extrapolations that can "neither be proved nor disproved by logical processes" and consequently it can be judged "not in accordance with its truth but only in accordance with its value" (p. 76).[54] After he presents

---

Planck also addresses the question of causality and determinism in *Where Is Science Going?* trans. J. Murphy and W. H. Johnston (New York, 1959), chap. 3, "The Scientist's Picture of the Physical Universe," chap. 4, "Causation and Free Will: The Statement of the Problem," and chap. 5, "Causation and Free Will: The Answer of Science."

54. Cf. Planck, "Scientific Ideas, Their Origin and Effects," in *The Philosophy of Physics*: "We find that the importance of a scientific idea depends, frequently enough, upon its value rather than on its truth. This applies, e.g., to the concept of the reality of an external world or to the idea of causality. With both the question is not whether they are true or false, but whether they are valuable or valueless" (pp. 112–113).

both the advantages and disadvantages of each position, Planck ultimately pronounces himself in favor of determinism. Although the law of causality cannot be demonstrated any more than it can be logically refuted, being a heuristic principle, in Planck's eyes it is nevertheless the "most important pointer that we possess in order to find a path through the confusion of events, and in order to know in what direction scientific investigation must proceed so that it shall reach useful results" (p. 83). Furthermore, the indeterminists are compelled to "set a limit to their impulse for knowledge at a much earlier stage than the determinists since they renounce the attempt to set up laws valid for individual cases—a degree of resignation so surprising that one asks how it comes about that so many physicists have declared their allegiance to the doctrine of indeterminism" (p. 81).

Planck points out that the deterministic position also depends on setting a limit to the scientific impulse for knowledge, and this limit is the "ideal intellect," which is another Vaihingerian fiction: "The most perfect harmony and consequently the strictest causality in any case culminates in the assumption that there is an ideal spirit having a full knowledge of the action of natural forces as well of events in the intellectual life of men; a knowledge extending to every detail and embracing present, past, and future" (p. 78).[55]

Whereas the ideal intellect has total cosmic knowledge, it is itself only partially accessible to the human intellect, because of the latter's necessarily subjective and limited character. The ideal intellect, however, presents a constant challenge to its human counterpart, which ceaselessly strives for a better grasp of it, without ever attaining its goal—this is the theoretical foundation of Planck's concept of science as perpetual

55. Here Planck simply restates the often quoted Laplacian formula of absolute determinism: "An intellect which at a given instant knew all the forces acting in nature, and the position of all things of which the world consists—supposing the said intellect were vast enough to subject these data to analysis—would embrace in the same formula the motions of the greatest bodies in the universe and those of the slightest atoms; nothing would be uncertain for it, and the future, like the past, would be present to its eyes" (Laplace, *Introduction à la théorie analytique des probabilités*, *Oeuvres complètes* [Paris, 1886], p. vi).

For a detailed discussion of the Laplacian "static" determinism of Newtonian physics in opposition to the dynamic model of indeterminism of quantum theory, see Milič Čapek, *The Philosophical Impact of Contemporary Physics* (New York, 1961), especially pt. I, chap. 8, "The Implicit Elimination of Time in Classical Physics," pt. II, chap. 16, "The End of the Laplacian Illusion," and chap. 17, "The Reinstatement of Becoming in the Physical World." For further references to Čapek's book, see below.

progress, based on self-criticism, a concept that has been fully developed by Karl Popper and remains highly authoritative in contemporary scientific discourse.

The logical status of the ideal intellect remains ambiguous in Planck's argument. On the one hand, he places it above the physical world-image; the ideal intellect is his answer to the question whether it "might be possible to endow the concept of causality with a more deep and direct significance than that offered by the world-image by making it independent of the introduction of an artificial human product" (p. 74). On the other hand, Planck acknowledges the unscientific and illogical character of the ideal intellect (a Neo-Kantian version of Hegel's universal spirit or of a rationalist God). Yet he insists that this notion cannot be dismissed as scientifically useless merely because it lacks logical foundation. Such "narrow formalism obstructs the source from which men like Galileo, Kepler, Newton, and many other great physicists drew their scientific inspiration. Consciously or unconsciously a devotion to science was a matter of faith for these men; they had an unshakable faith in the rational order of the world" (p. 78). For Planck faith is at the root of science as much as it is at the root of religion; science ultimately means "unresting endeavor and continually progressing development towards an aim which the poetic intuition may apprehend, but which the intellect can never fully grasp" (p. 83). Thus, following Vaihinger, Lange, and other Neo-Kantians, Planck employs the concept of poetic intuition to ground his scientific fictions ontologically.

In other essays Planck also argues that when it comes to first principles it is "impossible to make a clear cut distinction between science, religion, and art."[56] He explicitly links scientific progress to the imagination and the "irrational": "Ultimately any new idea is the work of its author's imagination, and to this extent progress is tied to the irrational element at some point even in mathematics, the most exact of the sciences; for irrationality is a necessary component in the make-up of any intellect."[57] Finally, Planck refers both science and art to ethics or,

56. Planck, "Physics and World Philosophy," in *The Philosophy of Physics*, pp. 34–35.

57. Planck, "Scientific Ideas," p. 105. Cf. also "Physics and World Philosophy": "It should never be forgotten that the most vital ideas in physics have [a] twofold origin. In the first instance the form which these ideas take is due to the peculiar imagination of the individual scientist; in the course of time, however, they assume a more definite and independent form" (p. 29). This Planckian distinction lies at the origin of such recent dualistic notions of science as that of Gerald Holton, who draws a distinction between the private and the public aspects of the scientific

more precisely, to Kant's moral imperative, which for him, as for Lange and Vaihinger, is the supreme arbiter of value.

Despite his emphasis on the role of the intuition and the imagination in scientific knowledge, Planck does not surrender the truth claim of science to art and aesthetics any more than his Neo-Kantian predecessors do. For example, in "Is the External World Real?" he rejects positivism in science because, among other things, he believes it to lead (ironically) to aestheticism and relativism.[58] The reference to art and artistic creation occurs when Planck selects a well-known cosmological controversy (the Copernican versus the Ptolemaic theory) to illustrate positivism's relativist assumptions in epistemology:

> On the positivist principle the one theory is as good as the other, when considered from the scientific viewpoint. They are merely two different ways of making a mental construction out of sensory reactions to some outer phenomena; but they have no more right to be looked upon as scientifically significant than the mental construction which the mystic or poet may make out of his sensory impressions when face to face with nature. . . . Therefore Copernicus is not to be judged as a pioneer discoverer in the realms of science any more than a poet is to be judged as a pioneer discoverer when he gives fanciful and attractive expression to sentiments that are known to every human breast.[59]

Since Planck's method of argumentation here is that of the reductio ad absurdum, he obviously expects his readers to reject the alleged

enterprise; it can also be seen as the model for the recent distinction between a context of discovery and a context of justification in science. For a critique of these distinctions, however, see Feyerabend, sec. 3.3.

58. Planck defines positivism in the narrow sense of what one might call Mach's phenomenalist positivism (Einstein), without distinguishing between philosophical positivism and positivist scientific practice. Although Planck's remarks are entirely justified in the case of positivist scientific practice (much of which, indeed, is content to "describe the order observed in studying various natural phenomena"), no serious positivist thinker—including Mach, against whom Planck's polemic is largely directed—would deny the role of theory in the progress of science. If, however, one interprets Mach's philosophy as having done away with the Kantian *Ding an sich*, then one could say that Planck comes much closer to the Neo-Kantians and their *as if* approach than to Mach's strict adherence to logical empiricist principles. In this case, one would also have to distinguish between Machian logical empiricism, which is strictly phenomena-oriented, and the logical empiricism of a more recent vintage, such as that of Carnap, where logical processes have a more complex relation to and therefore are farther removed from physical phenomena.

59. Planck, "Is the External World Real?" in *Where Is Science Going?* p. 72. Further citations are in the text.

positivist equation of science and art from an epistemological point of view. For his part, Planck is ready to acknowledge the validity of the aesthetic and ethical standpoints as long as they are kept out of the realm of science. He vaguely excludes them from this realm because "they belong to another way of looking at nature" (p. 73). His obvious implication is that this way, unlike the way of science, leads merely to a description of sensory experiences or subjective feelings, rather than to objective knowledge. On Planck's view, the poet merely invents, whereas the scientist (such as Copernicus) both invents and discovers.

Finally, Planck's position regarding the use of imaginative play in science is identical with that of any Neo-Kantian rationalist: the scientist can allow free rein to his creative imagination, but *within reason*. In one sense, in constructing his picture of the physical universe the researcher has "an entirely free hand." He may freely indulge "his own spirit of initiative and allow the constructive powers of the imagination to come into play without hindrance." This means that the scientist has a "significant measure of freedom in making his mental constructions." In another sense, however, Planck insists that "this freedom is only for the sake of a specific purpose and is a constructive application of the imaginative powers." In this respect it is not a "mere arbitrary flight into the realms of fancy" (as art presumably is).[60] Like any modern scientist, then, Planck naturally favors the rulebound and orderly play of reason over the "unruly" free play of the imagination.

Einstein's philosophical views have been discussed extensively, and Gerald Holton, not without justification, labels them "rational realism" (a close relative of Vaihinger's "idealist positivism").[61] One can further remark, with Max Born, that for Einstein the "real world" is the creation of a rational God and that he "believed in the power of reason to guess the laws according to which God has built the world."[62] Here, however, I shall examine the close affinity between the Neo-Kantian (specifically Vaihingerian) aestheticism in science and Einstein's own aesthetic attitude toward scientific knowledge and its relation to the play of the

60. All of the quotations in this paragraph are from "The Scientist's Picture of the Physical Universe," in *Where Is Science Going?* p. 86.

61. See especially Gerald Holton, "Mach, Einstein, and the Search for Reality," in *Thematic Origins*, pp. 219–259. Holton's essay is an excellent account of Einstein's philosophical progress from Machian phenomenalist positivism to Planck's positivist idealism. For other commentaries on Einstein's natural philosophy, see P. A. Schilpp, ed., *Albert Einstein: Philosopher-Scientist* (Evanston, Ill., 1949).

62. Max Born, *Physics in My Generation* (London, 1956), p. 205.

imagination—an aesthetic attitude that he shares with Planck and with other influential contemporary theoretical scientists.

Like Planck, Einstein starts from the age-old dichotomy between the world of the senses (*mundus sensibilis*) and the world of the intellect (*mundus intelligibilis*), which are the sources of our empirical and our rational knowledge respectively. For Einstein there is an unbridgeable logical gulf between these two worlds and these two kinds of knowledge, a gulf that usually goes unperceived because of our "habit of combining certain concepts and conceptual relations (propositions) . . . with certain sense experiences."[63] Changes in science, indeed in epistemological paradigms, come only when these habitual combinations are no longer taken for granted and new combinations are formed (cf. Vaihinger's theory of psychic conservation as a basis for his law of ideational shifts). It is a logical error to believe that the world of the intellect can be derived inductively from the world of the senses. Rather, our concepts and conceptual relations are "free inventions of the human intellect, which cannot be justified by the nature of that intellect or in any other fashion *a priori*."[64]

In the manner of Vaihinger, Einstein points out the "purely fictitious character of the fundamentals of scientific theory." The recognition of this fictitious character is what separates the new physics from the old one:

> Newton, the first creator of a comprehensive workable system of theoretical physics, still believed that the basic concepts and laws of his system could be derived from experience. . . .
> 
> The natural philosophers of those days were . . . most of them possessed with the idea that the fundamental concepts and postulates of physics were not in the logical sense free inventions of the human mind but could be deduced from experience by "abstraction"—that is to say, by logical means. (p. 273)

Along the same lines, Einstein criticizes Mach for believing that "theories arise through *discoveries*, not through inventions."[65] He questions a whole positivist mode of theorizing in science, which has, under

63. Albert Einstein, "Remarks on Bertrand Russell's Theory of Knowledge," in *Ideas and Opinions*, trans. S. Bargmann (London, 1954), p. 22. Further citations refer to this edition.

64. Einstein, "On the Method of Theoretical Physics," *Ideas and Opinions*, p. 272. Further citations refer to this edition.

65. Einstein, "Letter to Besso," quoted in Holton, *Thematic Origins*, p. 231.

Mach's impact, given rise to what Einstein calls a "phenomenal" as opposed to a "metaphysical" physics. This mode of theorizing assumes that "all the concepts and propositions which cannot be deduced from the sensory material are, on account of their 'metaphysical' character, to be removed from thinking" ("Remarks on Russell," p. 23). In turn, "metaphysical" physics is simply the kind that recognizes the need for a free constructive theoretical element and goes beyond a mere ordering of empirical material. In this regard, Einstein deplores the "fear of metaphysics" of such philosophers of science as Bertrand Russell, a fear "which has come to be a malady of contemporary empiricistic philosophizing" (p. 24).

If physical concepts are free mental constructions, then the imagination, rather than the logical faculty, has a decisive role in their production. This is one of the reasons Einstein favors the imagination over rational knowledge: "Imagination is more important than knowledge. For knowledge is limited, whereas imagination embraces the entire world, stimulating progress, giving birth to evolution. It is, strictly speaking, a real factor in scientific research."[66] (Cf. Vaihinger's statement according to which "the realization that imagination also plays a great part in science is one of the main advances of modern epistemology.")

For Einstein, as for Kant and Schiller, imagination and intuition also have the important function of mediating between the world of the senses and the world of the intellect. As we have seen, Einstein assumes in a Kantian and Neo-Kantian manner that there is an unbridgeable logical gap between these two worlds. Consequently, the empirical world will always defy reason, and the "eternal mystery of the world is its comprehensibility" ("Physics and Reality," p. 292). According to Einstein, comprehensibility implies the production of some kind of order among sense impressions, and this order is created with the aid of general concepts, their interconnections, and certain lasting associations between concepts and sensory experience. Yet the concepts remain logically independent of the sense experiences and their relation is "not analogous to that of soup to beef but rather of check number to overcoat" (p. 294). It is only in this sense that the empirical world can be said to be comprehensible. That it should be comprehensible at all is a "miracle" (p. 292). But where logic fails, imagination and intuition succeed: "The connection of the elementary concepts of everyday think-

66. Einstein, "On Science," in *Cosmic Religion with Other Opinions and Aphorisms* (New York, 1931), p. 97. Further citations refer to this edition.

ing with complexes of sense experiences can only be comprehended intuitively and is unadaptable to scientifically logical fixation" (pp. 292–293).

For Einstein, therefore, the role of the imagination and intuition is twofold. On the one hand, they freely provide concepts for the rational faculty to play with, and on the other, they furnish the stable associations between concepts and sensory experience. Einstein consistently describes the imaginative and logical processes of building conceptual systems in terms of play. In "Remarks on Russell's Theory of Knowledge," he insists that a conceptual system is a "free play with symbols according to (logically) arbitrarily given rules of the game"; this applies as much to the "thinking in daily life as to the more consciously and systematically constructed thinking in the sciences" (p. 23; cf. Vaihinger's view of scientific fictions as *Spielbegriffe*). Or again, in "Autobiographical Notes": "All unser Denken ist von dieser Art eines freien Spiels mit Begriffen" (all our thinking is of this nature of a free play with concepts).[67] Finally, Einstein uses a game analogy to describe the fictitious nature of a conceptual system: "One may compare [the] rules [of a conceptual system] with the rules of a game in which, while the rules themselves are arbitrary, it is their rigidity alone which makes the game possible. However, the fixation will never be final. It will have validity only for a special field of application (i.e., there are no final categories in the sense of Kant)" ("Physics and Reality," p. 292).

In true Neo-Kantian fashion, Einstein no longer sees such basic scientific concepts as time, space, or causality as "final categories," but as useful constructs with limited and relative validity. In other words, these constructs are real in the sense in which a game can be said to be real: its rules remain operative only within the playing space and for the duration of the game. The economy of a conceptual system, no less than that of a game, demands the greatest possible sparsity and simplicity of rules (basic concepts and axioms) which shall nevertheless account for the greatest number of situations: "The aim of science is, on the one hand, a comprehension, as *complete* as possible, of the connection between the sense experiences in their totality, and, on the other hand, the accomplishment of this aim *by the use of a minimum of primary concepts and relations*. (Seeking, as far as possible, logical unity in the world picture, i.e., paucity in logical elements)" (p. 293). This demand for logical unity is an aesthetic one and has been imposed on artistic works

67. Einstein, "Autobiographical Note," in Schilpp, *Albert Einstein*, p. 7.

from Aristotle onward; it is also what most contemporary philosophers of science mean when they refer to the aesthetic attitude of modern science.

But how free is Einstein's play of the conceptual system? Since this play involves definite rules, it certainly cannot be granted absolute freedom. Despite his polemic with Machist positivism, Einstein does not depart from its basic tenet any more than Planck does: empirical reality is both the ultimate justification and the final test of any conceptual system. As Einstein points out again and again, in a theoretical physical system the concepts and their interconnections are in the long run answerable to experience, even though they may not be logically deduced from it: "The structure of the system is the work of reason; the empirical contents and their mutual relations must find their representation in the conclusions of the theory. In the possibility of such a representation lie the sole value and justification of the whole system, and especially of the concepts and fundamental principles which underlie it" ("On the Method of Theoretical Physics," p. 272).

Thus, in Einstein, no less than in Vaihinger and Planck, the so-called free play of the logical faculty remains tied down by the actual sequences and coexistences of the sense-data (Vaihinger). In practice, Einstein operates with a Kantian distinction between the unrestrained play of the imagination, which "embraces the entire empirical world," and the rule-determined play of the rational faculty, which imposes a certain (arbitrary) order on this chaotic world. The criterion of the distinction is again, as in the case of Vaihinger and Planck, a utilitarian one: the scientific conceptual system can justify itself only through its practical value. In the creation of a specific order of sense experiences, "success is the determining factor" ("Physics and Reality," p. 292). Likewise, in "Autobiographical Notes," after saying that our thinking is a "free play with concepts," Einstein hastens to add: "The justification for this play lies in the measure of survey over the experience of the senses which we are able to achieve with its aid" (p. 7). Although scientific concepts are "free creations of the human intelligence," they have a definite role. They are, as in Vaihinger's philosophy of *as if*, "tools of thought, which are to serve the purpose of bringing experiences into relation with each other, so that in this way they can be better *surveyed*" ("Relativity and the Problem of Space," p. 364, italics mine).

Indeed, for Einstein, as for the whole Platonic rationalist tradition, the world of the senses remains suspect, and it is the task of the logical faculty to survey and control it. The play of the logical faculty in science is therefore far from being a mere "empty" play with concepts and must be clearly distinguished from the play of the imagination. For instance, answering an inquiry from Jacques Hadamard on the psychology of invention in mathematics, Einstein observes that the "combinatory play" of the imagination is at the root of his thought mechanism. But for him this combinatory play, which consists of certain preverbal signs and vague images, is only the first stage in the creative process, to be superseded by the logical stage. Furthermore, it is already during this first stage that the play of the imagination is *directed* by the "desire to arrive finally at logically connected concepts," a desire that is the "emotional basis of this rather vague play with [preverbal signs and more or less clear images]" ("A Mathematician's Mind," p. 25). The play with these prelogical entities is, therefore, already "aimed to be analogous to certain logical connections one is searching for" and will be incorporated in the play of the logical faculty as soon as the "associative play of the imagination is sufficiently established and can be reproduced at will" (p. 26).

The play of the logical faculty is also distinguished from that of the imagination in terms of freedom: the first enjoys a different kind of licence from the second. To illustrate his point, Einstein compares scientific and artistic invention, a comparison with which we are by now all too familiar (cf. Planck): "The liberty of choice of scientific axioms . . . is of a special kind; it is not in any way similar to the liberty of the writer of fiction. Rather, it is similar to that of a man engaged in solving a well-designed word-puzzle. He may, it is true, propose any word as the solution; but, there is only *one* word which really solves the puzzle in all its parts" ("Physics and Reality," p. 295).

Einstein's "word-puzzle" is an obvious game metaphor which, moreover, turns out to belong to a *theologia ludens*. That the cosmos is a huge puzzle designed by God is something that we have to accept: "It is a matter of faith that nature—as she is perceptible to our five senses—takes the character of such a well-formulated puzzle" (p. 295). Although Einstein does not state it openly, the implication is that the scientist takes upon himself the task of solving the cosmic puzzle, and insofar as he accepts God's challenge to solve it he engages in a divine game.

Like Planck, Einstein attempts to defend his determinism on aesthetic and ethical grounds. For him, as for Planck, determinism is not a logical requirement of the scientific enterprise, although it motivates this enterprise, deriving from what Einstein calls the "cosmic religious sense." This sense is hard to explain to "those who do not experience it, since it does not involve an anthropomorphic idea of God." Rather, the believer feels the "nobility and marvelous order which are revealed in nature and in the world of thought," and he seeks to "experience the totality of existence as a unity full of significance" (*Cosmic Religion*, p. 48). According to Einstein, it is the role of art, as well as that of science, to nurture this cosmic religious feeling in man: "It seems to me that the most important function of art and of science is to arouse and keep alive this feeling in those who are receptive." (p. 50; cf. Vaihinger's argument that aesthetic fictions serve the purpose of "awakening within us certain uplifting or otherwise important feelings"). Finally, far from "undermining morals," the cosmic religious experience is the "strongest and the noblest driving force behind scientific research" (p. 52). To prove his point Einstein invokes the same examples from the history of science that Planck does: "What a deep faith in the rationality of the structure of the world and what a longing to understand even a small glimpse of the reason revealed in the world there must have been in Kepler and Newton to enable them to unravel the mechanism of heavens, in long years of lonely work!" (pp. 52–53).

It is also his deterministic world view that impels Einstein to go against some of the theoretical principles of quantum physics (indeterminacy, statistical rather than causal laws, and so on) at the risk of becoming a lonely voice in the scientific community. As in the case of Planck, this choice is not so much of a scientific as of an ethical and aesthetic nature. In a letter to his old friend and fellow physicist Max Born—an early advocate of the principle of indeterminacy in quantum physics— Einstein writes: "Quantum mechanics is certainly imposing. But an inner voice tells me that it is not yet the real thing. The theory says a lot, but does not really bring us any closer to the secret of the 'old one.' I, at any rate, am convinced that *He* is not playing dice."[68] And

68. Einstein, "Letter to Born," December 1926, in *The Born-Einstein Letters*, trans. I. Born (London, 1971), p. 91. For Born's own indeterminist or statistical concept of chance and necessity, see Max Born, *Natural Philosophy of Cause and Chance* (Oxford, 1949), esp. chap. 10, "Metaphysical Conclusions," where Born voices his disagreement with Einstein. Finally, note that Einstein's *theologia ludens* is an ideal point of intersection between the aesthetic and the religious turns in recent scientific theory. For some of the issues involved in the latter turn see, among many others, P. C. Davies, *God and the New Physics* (New York, 1983); Barrow and Tipler, *The Anthropic Cosmological Principle*, especially chap. 2, "Design Arguments" and chap. 3, "Modern Teleology and the Anthropic Principles"; and Anthony Zee, *Fearful Symmetry: The Search for Beauty in Modern Physics* (New York, 1986). It can

eighteen years later, after each of the two friends has tried in vain for years to get the other to adopt his point of view: "We have become Antipodean in our scientific expectations. You believe in the God who plays dice, and I in complete law and order in a world which exists, and which I, in a wildly speculative way, am trying to capture. I firmly *believe*, but I hope that someone will discover a more realistic way, or rather a more tangible basis than it has been my lot to find. Even the great inital success of the quantum theory does not make me believe in the fundamental dice-game, although I am well aware that our younger colleagues interpret this as a consequence of senility" (letter to Born, September 1944, p. 149). And finally after a lapse of another five years: "But our respective hobby-horses have irretrievably run off in different directions—yours, however, enjoys far greater popularity as a result of its remarkable practical successes, while mine, on the other hand, smacks of quixotism, and even I myself cannot adhere to it with absolute confidence. But at least mine does not represent a blind man's buff with the idea of reality. My whole instinct rebels against it irresistibly" (letter to Born, 1949?, pp. 180–181).

In these passages Einstein's reasons for rejecting the principles of

---

be argued, as one reader points out in regard to the religious turn in contemporary science, that "physics always poses a metaphysics, a means of situating one's limited discoveries of physical phenomena within a holistic vision." This may, to some extent, be the case. Yet the aforementioned studies, no less than the Einstein-Born controversy, seem also to reveal that religion in science remains, as it has always been, a matter of taste or personal choice (that is, it remains part of the *aesthetic* dimension of scientific discourse) and does not affect scientific practice, or the scientific *mentality*, in any essential way. The religious and the nonreligious scientist work side by side in the laboratory, they are part of the same community, sharing the same (power-oriented) institutional goals and research methods. Once religion is no longer a serious competitor for cultural hegemony in modern Western society (as it was up to the second half of the nineteenth century), science may soften its attacks against it, or even enlist it as an ideological ally. (On the other hand, religion may also find it expedient temporarily to befriend Satan, or to seek accommodation with its former foe; in this way, it may hope to regain "relevance" to modern life, i.e., some of its former cultural authority.) Perhaps it is this vague realization that has led, in recent times, to a reconciliation between science and religion, which is also advocated, as we have seen, by Lange, Vaihinger, and other Neo-Kantians.

The unessential nature (from the standpoint of a power-oriented mentality) of the dispute between religion and science is caustically dramatized by Gustave Flaubert's *Madame Bovary*, where the eternal ideological enemies, Homais the pharmacist and Bournisien the priest, become at last "reconciled" (by falling asleep) over the heroine's dead body.

quantum mechanics are certainly not logical and have little to do with scientific proof (in fact they go against it), revolving around such imponderable aesthetic categories as intuition, instinct, inner voices, illusion, and hobbyhorses. Note also the game metaphors that now Einstein employs in a negative sense, referring to the uncertainty principle in quantum physics: God "does not play dice," there is no "fundamental dice-game," the true believers in the theory of general relativity do not play "blind man's buff with reality." Here Einstein obviously criticizes the prerational view of play as chance-necessity from the standpoint of a rational concept of the interplay of chance and necessity, according to which "natural laws steer chance" (Eigen and Winkler). For Einstein, the cosmos is not the result of an irrational dice game (cf. Nietzsche) but the orderly, harmonious creation of a rational God: a masterfully conceived enigma, puzzle, or labyrinth, with a secret but nevertheless crackable code.

Finally, Einstein's *determinism*, *cosmic religion*, and *divine puzzle-maker* are aesthetic and ethical concepts that have the same ambiguous logical status as Planck's *ideal intellect*. They can best be described as practical fictions, to use Vaihinger's terminology. From a strictly logical point of view, these concepts are "really fictions, but in practice they possess a tremendous value in history." As we recall, Vaihinger further points out that ideals are ideational constructs, contradictory in themselves and in contradiction to reality, which nevertheless have an "irresistible power." They are fictions emanating from the "noblest minds, to which the noblest part of mankind cling and of which they will not allow themselves to be deprived" (*Philosophy of "As If"*, pp. 48–49). Since Einstein is fully aware of the fictitious character of his theoretical concepts (e.g., when he remarks that his hobbyhorse, the general theory of relativity, "smacks of quixotism and even I myself cannot adhere to it with absolute confidence"), one may equally describe these concepts as *bewusste Selbsttäuschung*, a phrase that is usually applied, as we have seen, to aesthetic play. In this regard, Einstein, no less than Planck, clearly belongs to a Neo-Kantian aesthetic tradition that begins with Schiller and has, in our century, become particularly strong not only in German philosophy and literary studies, but also in German science.

Another contemporary representative of the Neo-Kantian aesthetic tradition in science is Erwin Schrödinger, who of all the exemplary figures presented here is perhaps the most open advocate of the purely playful character of scientific theory. For instance, in "Science, Art and Play" Schrödinger argues that science, along with all other forms of intellectual activity, belongs to the sphere of play. Following Schiller, Spencer, and Groos, Schrödinger defines play as the manifestation of a "surplus force" left over in the higher animals after they satisfy their basic needs in the struggle for existence. In man, "the same surplus of force produces an intellectual play by the side of physical play or sport. Instances of such intellectual play are games in the ordinary sense, like card games, board games, dominoes, or riddles, and I should also count among them every kind of intellectual activity as well as Science;—and if not the whole of Science at any rate the advance guard of Science, by which I mean research work proper."[69]

Although Schrödinger does not discount the practical results of scientific research, he in effect argues that these are the by-product of "learned leisure." For him, research is primarily motivated not by the "bare struggle for existence" but by "pure and lofty pleasure." Like art and play in general, science is a "noble luxury" which intensifies the joy of living (p. 29). The pleasure derived from pure scientific knowledge contains a "strong esthetic element and is closely related to that derived from the contemplation of a work of art" (p. 30). Schrödinger attributes to science the same disinterestedness and purposivenesss without purpose that Kant, Schiller, and their present-day followers attribute to art or play: "Play, art and science are the spheres of human activity where action and aim are not as a rule determined by the aims imposed by the necessities of life; and even in the exceptional instances where this is the case, the creative artist or the investigating scientist soon forget this fact—as indeed they must forget it if their work is to prosper. Generally, however, the aims are chosen freely by the artist or student himself, and are superfluous" (p. 28).

The duty of a science teacher is not only to transmit to his audiences knowledge that they can use in their daily activities but also to perform this task in "such a way as to cause them pleasure" (p. 29; cf. the traditional view of art as being both *dulce et utile*). Finally, for Schrödinger science is not "such a desperately serious affair," contributing less to material well-being and more to "purely ideal pleasures" than is generally assumed (p. 33).

In keeping with his view of science as intellectual play, Schrödinger is not worried in the least about the so-called epistemological crisis in modern science, regarding this crisis as a positive rather than a negative

69. Erwin Schrödinger, *Science, Theory and Man* (London, 1957), p. 28. Further citations refer to this edition.

development. (His position in this regard differs radically from that of the other theoretical physicists discussed here; see, e.g., Planck, "Is the External World Real?" pp. 65–68.) Far from deploring the state of intellectual turmoil in contemporary physics, Schrödinger welcomes it as a necessary condition for future progress not only in this field but in all other fields of knowledge. He believes that "its results can only be advantageous: no scientific structure falls entirely into ruin; what is worth preserving preserves itself and requires no protection" (p. 38).

Schrödinger's aesthetic attitude toward scientific theory is also apparent in the peculiar manner in which he deals with the issue of determinism versus indeterminism in science. In "The Law of Chance: The Problem of Causation in Modern Science" he points out that ultimately the choice between a determinist and an indeterminist position in natural science is a matter of personal taste, because the validity of either position cannot be decided by rational proof or by experiment (cf. Planck). His own preferences, however, are not immediately apparent.

Since Schrödinger very often employs philosophical arguments against determinism and in support of indeterminism, one might be tempted to label him as an indeterminist. But this would be seriously misconstruing his aestheticist philosophical position: Schrödinger largely remains consistent with his playful approach to scientific theory and, in principle, neither rejects nor completely embraces either determinism or indeterminism. He examines no less critically such indeterminist assumptions as Heisenberg's uncertainty principle in quantum mechanics, claiming not only that this principle is already implicit in classical mechanics (despite Heisenberg's arguments to the contrary), but also that statistical laws are no less deterministic than those of absolute causality (cf. Planck). After pointing out that one theoretical consequence of Heisenberg's uncertainty principle is to prohibit the construction of any models extending through space and time because the world that can be observed appears as no continuum at all, Schrödinger adds: "Of course, when faced with the question of how to represent it *otherwise* [than as a continuum], we are still confronted by an insoluble conundrum. I do believe that we cannot be satisfied in the long run with the answer which I once received in conversation with a young physicist of outstanding genius [Paul Dirac]: Beware of forming models or pictures at all!" ("Conceptual Models in Physics," p. 160).

Schrödinger's own wave mechanics was at first hailed by such determinists as Planck or Einstein as a philosophical victory over the principle of discontinuity advocated by quantum mechanics. And yet, in a typical relativist fashion, Schrödinger makes it clear in his Nobel address, "The Fundamental Idea of Wave Mechanics" (1933), that wave mechanics cannot replace particle or quantum mechanics, and that both are simply different ways of dealing with individual, finite observations rather than with the "real structure of the Universe." Nevertheless, this does not necessarily mean that scientists need give up their efforts of connecting these observations with some hypothesis postulating the existence of such a structure (pp. 190–192); in other words, the idea of the "real structure of the Universe" remains a useful scientific fiction.

Schrödinger's aestheticist and relativist approach to scientific theories goes hand in hand with his awareness of the historical character of scientific truth and of science in general. In "Is Science a Fashion of the Times?" he argues that science is not an objective and perennial body of truths, independent of its cultural milieu; on the contrary, not unlike painting, literature, or music, it is a product of its age, undergoing as many historical changes as art does. For Schrödinger scientific knowledge depends as much on the personality of the researcher and on his cultural environment as it does on objective and impartial observation. In this regard, the general consensus within a scientific community is no proof of scientific objectivity as such; this consensus simply indicates that a large or small group of scientists share the same goals and priorities during a given historical period. These goals and priorities are in turn determined by the scientist's cultural milieu or the spirit of the age: "In all branches of our civilization there is one general world outlook dominant and there are numerous lines of activity which are attractive because they are the fashion of the age, whether in politics or in art or in science. These also make themselves felt in the 'exact' science of physics" (p. 100).

Among the fashionable ideas that have prevailed in our age Schrödinger mentions evolution both in its general and in its special, Darwinian form, an idea that, largely owing to Hegel's philosophy, has prolonged its life "far beyond its natural span" (p. 103). If such an idea had been put forward in a former age, it would certainly have been rejected as preposterous (p. 104).

In "Physical Science and the Temper of the Age," Schrödinger examines the modern age in terms of his notion of the historical and relative character of scientific knowledge, trying to determine to what extent the "picture of the physical universe as presented to us by modern science has been outlined under the influence of certain contemporary trends which are not peculiar to science at all" (p. 106). For example, contemporary physics adopts the concept of simplicity and functionality which prevails in the contemporary arts and crafts: "Just as we are no longer afraid of bare surfaces in our furniture and our dwelling rooms, so in our scientific picture of the external world we do not try to fill up the empty spaces. We try to exclude everything that in principle cannot be the object of experimental observation. And we think it better to leave our feeling of incompleteness unsatisfied rather than to introduce mental constructions which cannot by their nature be experimentally controlled or tested for their correspondence to external reality" (p. 109).

The desire for change and freedom from authority that makes itself felt throughout contemporary culture has also reached physics, in the form of the theory of relativity and quantum theory. The latter even questions the principle of causality. Because we can never determine experimentally whether causality obtains or does not obtain in nature, we ought to be free to maintain or alter this principle at our convenience, in whatever way makes for a simpler description of natural phenomena. This means that we are free not only to "drop a long-accepted principle when we think we have found something more convenient from the viewpoint of physical research," but also to "re-adopt the rejected principle when we find we have made a mistake in laying it aside" (pp. 116–117). An ever-developing empirical science such as physics "need not and must not be afraid of being taunted with a lack of consistency between its announcements at subsequent epochs" (p. 117).

The theory of relativity itself is neither new nor limited to physics, Schrödinger points out: He traces it back to the Sophists, the "first historically known relativists of the Occident" (p. 117). The Sophists' claim that they could establish the truth of either one of two contradictory assertions must not be interpreted solely in a self-serving political or legal sense; what they meant to emphasize is that a "statement is very seldom simply either right or wrong, but that nearly always a point of view is to be found from which it is right and another point of view from which it is wrong" (p. 117). In physics, this relativist principle takes the form of the reference system. In the Einsteinian special theory of relativity, the movement of a body can be directly observed only in relation to another body that acts as a frame of reference. In turn, the concept of the reference system is complemented by that of invariance. The latter presupposes that certain things can be independent of the reference frame and do not change when it does. Schrödinger offers as an example his own discussion of science as a relative or an absolute form of knowledge. For him this question can also be posed in terms of invariance: Are the statements of physical science "invariants" in reference to their cultural environment, or must they be related to this environment as a reference frame? If the latter is the case, as Schrödinger believes, it follows that when the cultural ambience "undergoes a radical change, the conclusions of science, even though they may not become false in detail, would yet acquire an essentially different meaning and interest" (p. 122).

By adopting a relativist epistemology and an aestheticist philosophical standpoint, as well as by viewing science as the product of a specific cultural historical context, Schrödinger lays the foundations for a thematic and paradigmatic approach to the history of scientific thought which will later be taken up and developed by such influential historians and philosophers of science as N. R. Hanson, Thomas Kuhn, Gerald Holton, and Paul Feyerabend. In this regard, Schrödinger is also a precursor of an "anarchist epistemology" in science (a question to which I shall return shortly). Finally, he is one of the rare scientists who refrain from giving cognitive priority to science over other modes of discourse, such as literature. For Schrödinger the truth-claim of science is no more or less valid than that of art or any other form of human endeavor. Despite his reference to the Greek Sophists and their relativist approach to truth, however, Schrödinger's own playful approach to scientific theory remains well within the rationalist camp. As we have seen, his play is not that of the artist-metaphysicians but that of Schiller, Spencer, and Groos, finding its ultimate justification in the Darwinian theory of evolution.

As the inventor of the *uncertainty relations* or of the *principle of indeterminacy* in quantum mechanics, Werner Heisenberg is considered, along with Niels Bohr, one of the chief advocates of the indeterminist position in scientific theory. Heisenberg's indeterminism, however, does not involve giving up the rational mentality of modern science, any more than Schrödinger's relativism does. Although he is fully aware of the prerational origins of the modern atomic theory, for example, Heisenberg ultimately justifies his scientific enterprise from a Neo-Kantian rationalist standpoint that is very similar to that of Schrödinger. Despite his polemic with the determinist opponents of the Copenhagen interpretation of quantum mechanics (which substitutes statistical laws for deterministic natural laws), and with Schrödinger in particular, Heisenberg shares most of the latter's epistemological assumptions.[70] In this sense his own aestheticist and relativist approach to knowledge is, like Schrödinger's, much more in line with the epistemology of Vaihinger than with that of the artist-metaphysicians.

Like Monod and Thom (who were undoubtedly familiar with his interpretation of quantum theory at the time that they were formulating their own biological theories), Heisenberg inherits his concept of nature as a ceaseless play of physical forces from the Presocratics, particularly from Heraclitus and Anaximander. In *Physics and Philosophy: The Revolution in Modern Science*, Heisenberg says that if one interprets Heraclitus's basic element fire as energy, that is, as "both matter and a moving force," then the views of modern physics are very close to those of the Ephesian: "Energy is in fact that which moves; it may be called the primary cause of all change, and energy can be transformed into matter or heat or light. The strife between the opposites in the philosophy of Heraclitus can be found in the strife between two forms of energy."[71]

Heisenberg also points out that Anaximander's notion of a fundamental substance that makes up all known substances but is essentially different from them reappears in the most modern part of quantum mechanics, the theory of elementary particles. In this respect, Heisenberg rejects the idea (also of Greek provenance) that the physical world can be reduced to a "few fundamental elementary particles," an idea that inspired physical research during most of the first half of the twentieth century. Rather, he believes that "all different elementary particles could be reduced to some universal substance which one may call energy or matter, but none of the different particles could be preferred to the others as being more fundamental" (pp. 61–62). Thus, Heisenberg returns to a Presocratic, monistic view of the physical world. For him, as for Heraclitus and Anaximander, the cosmos is made up of the same substance, which is moved by the same forces, although these forces divide and connect it in ever new ways (cf. Nietzsche's view of the world as an eternal play of physical forces). Consequently, this cosmos appears

70. For the controversy between Heisenberg and Schrödinger, which, again, involves mostly aesthetic criteria or differences in taste, see, e.g., Holton, *Thematic Origins*, introduction, pp. 26–27.

71. Werner Heisenberg, *Physics and Philosophy: The Revolution in Modern Science* (New York, 1958), pp. 71, 61. Unless otherwise specified, further citations refer to this volume.

as a "complicated tissue of events, in which connections of different kinds alternate or overlap or combine and thereby determine the texture of the whole" (p. 107).

Although Heisenberg's ontology can be described as essentially pre-rational, his epistemology is clearly of Neo-Kantian origin, relying on a rational *as if* approach to knowledge that is very similar to that of Vaihinger. For Heisenberg the world is basically unknowable, if by knowledge one understands the reflective act of consciousness. As in Vaihinger and Schrödinger, reason is not a mirror but a part of nature; it is a human instrument that arises in man's struggle for existence, helping him to find his way about the world. "Pure Reason" can never arrive at absolute truth, a meaningless concept in Heisenberg's episte-mology. Rather, rational concepts can adequately be defined with re-gard to their connections, that is, when they are integrated into a closed system of definitions and postulates that can be expressed coherently through a mathematical scheme. In this form, they can apply to a wider or a narrower field of experience and will aid us in finding our way through that field. Hence, for Heisenberg the function of physical science is no longer to divide the world into different groups of objects, as classical science does, but into groups of correlations. In turn, these correlations are formed by the scientist himself, who is no longer a purely objective or disinterested observer but an active participant in the processes of nature. It is from this Neo-Kantian standpoint that Heisenberg criticizes Cartesian epistemology and advocates a return to a subjective or explicitly interpretive element in scientific theory.

According to Heisenberg, modern scientific thought experiences a decisive turning point in the seventeenth century, with the Cartesian division between subject and object (*res cogitans* and *res extensa*). This division has led to the great success of classical physics and conse-quently, appears as "almost a necessary condition for natural science in general" (p. 81). Quantum theory, however, reveals the arbitrary char-acter of the Cartesian division at the same time that it seeks to restore the unity of self and world which had been the foundation of Hellenic scientific thought before Plato and Aristotle. The Copenhagen inter-pretation of quantum mechanics starts from the premise that natural science "does not simply describe and explain nature; it is a part of the interplay between nature and ourselves; it describes nature as exposed to our method of questioning" (p. 80). Like Schrödinger, then, Heisen-berg points out that the relative or "subjective" character of scientific truth is inevitable, deriving from the fact that science is a human product and thus is inextricably bound with human subjectivity and human interests.

Heisenberg further suggests that Einstein and other determinist scientists have such great difficulties in accepting the Copenhagen interpretation of quantum theory because they still operate under the premises of the Cartesian division which, during its three centuries of almost unchallenged reign, has "penetrated deeply into the human mind," giving rise not only to "metaphysical realism" (according to which *res extensa* "really exist") in philosophy, but also to "dogmatic realism" in science. On the latter view, the scientist's statements concerning the physical world are independent of the conditions under which they can be verified, and therefore are objectively true for all time. This dogmatic realism (defended, e.g., by Einstein) should be replaced by "practical realism," which assumes, more modestly, that the scientist's statements concerning nature are subject to the conditions under which they can be verified, in other words, that they depend on what Schrödinger calls a "reference frame."

Practical realism, according to Heisenberg, may also suggest an acceptable compromise among the various views of causality in contemporary scientific theory. Although the law of causality as formulated by Kant (whenever we observe an event we assume that there is a foregoing event from which the second must follow according to some rule) no longer applies to atomic events, it nevertheless remains a necessary condition for the observation of these events. What Kant has failed to realize is that an a priori concept like causality can be a necessary condition of science and at the same time have only a limited range of applicability, being a "relative truth" (p. 91).

There is no way of knowing how far these conceptual systems can aid us or where their range of applicability comes to an end and other systems become operative. As long as they are in force, however, the scientist may for all practical purposes treat them *as if* they were a priori (p. 92). Thus, Heisenberg does not discard the determinist assumptions of classical physics as invalid or antiquated. On the contrary, he preserves them intact, at the same time granting them the logical status of relative truths. The new system of definitions and axioms of quantum mechanics does not exclude its Newtonian counterpart, but shares certain boundaries with it. The two conceptual systems act as "limiting cases" for each other and are in a relation of complementarity.[72] This

72. The term *complementarity* appears for the first time in Niels Bohr's 1928 lecture "The Quantum Postulate and the Recent Development of Atomic Theory,"

relativist approach to scientific knowledge and truth, which Heisenberg shares with Schrödinger, is in perfect consonance with Heisenberg's functional view of science: the latter must create ever-new systematic connections in order to help man in his struggle for existence.

Heisenberg presents as complementary not only the relationship between the new and the old physics but also the relationship between quantum mechanics and other parts of natural science. Of special interest here are his observations with regard to the impact of atomic physics on biology in general and on the Darwinian theory of evolution in particular. Although the present tendency in biology to explain biological phenomena solely in terms of physicochemical processes has met with considerable experimental success, especially when related to evolutionary theory, Heisenberg (following Bohr) warns against the widespread belief among geneticists that the physicochemical elements suffice in accounting for *all* biological phenomena. There are two major views in contemporary biology, he points out. According to the predominant reductionist view, the combination of Darwin's theory with physics and chemistry gives an adequate explanation of organic life. According to the organic view, suggested by Bohr and shared by Heisenberg himself, our knowledge of an organism being alive may well be complementary to the knowledge of its complete molecular structure. Because a full knowledge of this structure can be attained only by destroying the life of the organism, it is "logically possible that life precludes the complete determination of its underlying physicochemical structure" (p. 105). Biological science, no less than quantum theory, should take into consideration the fact that its questions are asked by the "species man which itself belongs to the genus of living organism," or that we "already know what life is even before we have defined it scientifically" (p. 107). In other words, biological science, like any other

included in *Atomic Theory and the Description of Nature* (Cambridge, Eng., 1934). Bohr uses it to express the relation between spatiotemporal and causal descriptions in quantum theory: while they are mutually exclusive, both of these descriptions are necessary in understanding quantum phenomena. In a restricted sense, one could also say that Heisenberg's uncertainty principle (1927) expresses a complementary relation, during the process of measurement, between the position and the momentum of a particle. For useful historical background on Bohr's principle of complementarity, see Holton, *Thematic Origins*, pp. 135–161. Cf. also my discussion of Bohr's biological views at the end of sec. 2.3. For an excellent introduction to quantum theory in general, see Max Jammer, *The Conceptual Development of Quantum Mechanics* (New York, 1966).

science, should not forget that in the great "drama of existence, we are both players and spectators."[73]

Heisenberg's relativist concept of reality also allows him to regard art and science as complementary, rather than antagonistic, modes of knowledge. Like Schrödinger, he grants art the same status of relative truth that he grants science. In this sense, Heisenberg deplores the traditional division between art and science (and that between science and religion), which he attributes largely to classical science's own imperialist claims, based on the Cartesian ideal of an all-powerful rationality. Since all human knowledge is based on subjective idealizations that are "part of the human language that has been formed from the interplay between the world and ourselves, a human response to the challenge of nature," science and art share the same fictional nature.[74] In this respect, scientific conceptual systems can be compared to various artistic styles. In turn, an artistic style, like a closed scientific conceptual system, can be defined by a set of formal rules. Although these rules cannot be exactly expressed by a set of mathematical formulas and equations, their fundamental elements are akin to those of mathematics. In both art and mathematics, "equality and inequality, repetition and symmetry, certain group structures play the fundamental role" (p. 108).

As in the case of a scientific conceptual system, it takes the effort of several generations to develop the formal system of rules that later becomes the mark of a certain artistic style. Once this system of rules is fully worked out and becomes "closed" (*abgeschlossen*), the artists lose interest in it and move on to another formal system which, when completed, will in turn create a new "style." Again, as in the case of

73. The phrase again belongs to Bohr. See, for example, "Unity of Knowledge": "On the scene of existence we are ourselves actors as well as spectators" (*Atomic Physics*, p. 81). Of course, this play metaphor is a very old one that can be traced back not only to Hindu thought but also, in the West, to Pythagoras and, more recently, to the *theatrum mundi* of medieval and Renaissance literature. Lately, one can also see a reverse movement: scientific concepts are now again employed in literary theory. For example, in *The Cosmic Web: Scientific Field Models and Literary Strategies in the Twentieth Century* (Ithaca, N.Y., 1984) N. Katherine Hayles convincingly argues for the relevance of the "field concept" in modernist and Postmodernist fiction. Her first chapter, "Spinning the Web: Representative Field Theories and Their Implications," is also a useful introduction to the more general cultural theoretical implications of certain new physical concepts. For some of the recent questions that concern the interdisciplinary study of literature and science, see the special issue of *The Annals of Scholarship* (1986) devoted to literature and science.

74. See Heisenberg, *Philosophic Problems of Nuclear Science* (New York, 1952), p. 22.

science, one cannot determine to what extent the formal rules of art represent reality. Art, like science, will always remain an idealization that is nevertheless necessary for understanding (p. 108).

Finally, Heisenberg addresses the traditional argument that science, as opposed to art, represents objective reality, and therefore its conceptual systems are not arbitrary, but a "necessary consequence of our gradually increasing experimental knowledge of nature" (p. 109). Turning this argument around, he asks whether the artistic formal system of rules is really any more subjective than its scientific counterpart. Here again one must not be misled by the Cartesian division. A certain artistic style does not arise in an arbitrary manner any more than scientific systems do; rather, it is a direct product of the interplay between the world and the artist in a specific historical context. In this sense, art no less than science is, in Schrödinger's words, "a fashion of the times." For Heisenberg, as for Schrödinger, the *Zeitgeist* is "probably a fact as objective as any fact in natural science." He adds, however, that this *Zeitgeist* reveals features of the world that are independent of time, if not eternal. (On this point, Heisenberg differs from Schrödinger and returns to Goethe and Schiller's concept of art as *Dauer im Wechsel* or as a dialectic of temporality and permanence, a concept shared by most nineteenth- and twentieth-century German intellectuals; cf. Gadamer, Eigen and Winkler.) Heisenberg thus concludes that the processes of art and science are very similar. Both create over the centuries a "human language by which we can speak about the more remote parts of reality, and the coherent sets of scientific concepts as well as the different styles of art are different words or groups of words in this language" (p. 109).

It is obvious, however, that Heisenberg's notion of art is a thoroughly rational one. In this respect, he consciously or unconsciously adopts a modified version of the traditional scientific view of art. For him, as for Schrödinger, art is primarily a set of formal rules, a formal structure that the artists gradually "fill up" with the sensual material of the world. Although this formal structure may change with the *Zeitgeist*, the rational idea of art as rule-determined structure or form remains valid for all time. Heisenberg's notion of aesthetics is again a rational (Neo-Kantian) one. He remains unaware of the prerational origins of art and embraces the Platonic philosophical decision that emphasizes art's fictionality over its unmediated link to power. This Platonic emphasis allows Heisenberg to see art as a different aspect of the same rational enterprise that science is involved in (the subordination of nature to man's goals). His parallel between science and art is based on rational criteria of symmetry, order, and structure. For Heisenberg, as for Schiller and Gadamer, art no less than science must deal with an essentially irrational and unpredictable sensuous world on which it imposes its own ideals of order and stability.

Heisenberg's philosophical reflections on quantum theory are not designed to undermine the rational foundations of science, but rather to reaffirm them through a Neo-Kantian *als ob* approach to scientific knowledge. He replaces the universal validity of the scientific conceptual systems (presupposed by classical science) with a limited validity which, however, neither precludes nor limits the application to reality of rational thinking in general. On the contrary, for Heisenberg it is rational thinking itself that requires a limited applicability of scientific concepts. He notes, for example, that although the nineteenth-century concept of the universe can be called "rational" because its center, classical physics, is constructed from a handful of axioms subject to rational analysis and rests on a belief in the rational understanding of all reality, "the hope of gaining an understanding of the whole world from a small part of it can never be supported rationally."[75] But this fallacy of classical physics does not affect rational thinking per se: "The misunderstanding that the transformations in exact science have brought to light certain limits to the application of rational thinking must immediately be countered. A narrower field of application is given to certain ways of thought only, and not to rational thought in general" (p. 24).

Whereas modern physics has "purged classical physics of its arbitrary belief in its unlimited application," it has also revealed that various scientific fields such as mechanics, electricity, and quantum theory create scientific systems that are "complete in themselves [*abgeschlossen*], rational, and capable of complete investigation." Within their limited areas of application, these fields "state their respective laws, probably correctly, for all time" (p. 24). Finally, the notion of the limited validity of the scientific conceptual systems must not stand in the way of the scientists' dream of creating an "all-embracing yet unified and logical concept of science." In this regard, Heisenberg adds, it is "perhaps not too rash to hope that new spiritual forces will again bring us nearer to the unity of the scientific concept of the universe which has been threatened during the last decades" (p. 26). Heisenberg's philosophical statements, then, are meant less to emancipate quantum theory from

75. Heisenberg, *Philosophic Problems of Nuclear Science*, p. 23. Further citations are in the text.

the dominant rational scientific tradition than to carve a place for it within that tradition.

The most recent developments in theoretical physics still follow the two directions described by Heisenberg.[76] Physicists, especially in the field of elementary particles, continue the atomistic quest of finding the smallest bits of matter, the so-called building blocks of the physical universe. The scientists who are engaged in this quest are usually concerned only with the experimental, practical aspects of quantum theory and largely ignore its broad philosophical implications; consequently, they often continue to operate on the old Cartesian assumption of the split nature of reality (*res extensa* and *res cogitans*). Those theoretical physicists who are on the frontiers of their field, on the other hand, attempt to work out the consequences of the monistic view of physical reality presupposed by quantum theory, especially in its Bohrian and Heisenbergian version. They also attempt to come closer to an "all-embracing yet unified and logical concept of science," by bringing together relativity and quantum theory in a comprehensive theory of the unified fields. Much like Bohr and Heisenberg, however, all these physicists oscillate between an essentially prerational ontology, which gives primacy to the ceaseless play of physical Becoming, and a rational epistemology, which stresses the determinate and orderly nature of reality and is based on a Neo-Kantian *as if* approach to scientific knowledge. A good example of this amphibolous philosophical position is offered by David Bohm's theoretical work.

In his book significantly entitled *Wholeness and the Implicate Order*

76. For popular discussions of recent developments in theoretical physics, see Fritjof Capra, *The Tao of Physics* (rev. ed., New York, 1984); Gary Zukav, *The Dancing Wu Li Masters* (New York, 1980); John Gribbin, *In Search of Schrödinger's Cat* (New York, 1984). For brief overviews, see David Finkelstein, "The Quantum Paradox," in *Encyclopedia Britannica, Yearbook of Science of the Future*, pp. 185–207, and Jack Sarfatti, "The Physical Roots of Consciousness," in J. Mishlove, *The Roots of Consciousness* (New York, 1975), pp. 279–293. See also the contributions in B. De Witt and N. Graham, eds., *The Many-Worlds Interpretation of Quantum Mechanics* (Princeton, 1973). Christine Froula, in "Quantum Physics/Postmodern Metaphysics: The Nature of Jacques Derrida," attempts to draw a parallel between the philosophical implications of quantum mechanics and what she calls the "Postmodern metaphysics" of Derrida. Contrary to her argument, however, we have seen that Bohr, Heisenberg, and the other advocates of the Copenhagen School (no less than Einstein or, for that matter, Derrida, as Froula herself is fully aware) remain within the Western metaphysical tradition precisely because they openly or tacitly embrace the power-oriented mentality of this tradition, be it in its rational or prerational guise. Cf. also below.

(1980), for instance, Bohm points out that most modern views of physical reality are dominated by a fragmentary, atomistic bias. These modern scientific views tend to reinforce the fragmentary way of thinking and being of our society in general because they give us a "picture of the whole world as constituted of nothing but an aggregate of separately existent 'atomic building blocks'" and because they provide experimental evidence that seems to impose the conclusion that this fragmentary way of thinking and being is necessary and inevitable.[77] For Bohm, the division of self and world is the main reason for the endless conflict and confusion that reign in modern society.

Bohm further points out that some of the more radical implications of quantum and relativity theory make it impossible to continue regarding reality as fragmentary. If one accepts the fundamental premises of these theories, then one can no longer maintain the division between subject and object, the observer and the observed, that is implicit in the atomistic view (for which the subjective and the objective realms are two separate aggregates of atoms). On the contrary, both quantum mechanics and the theory of relativity imply the need to look at the world as an "*undivided whole*, in which all parts of the universe, including the observer and his instruments, merge and unite in one totality" (p. 11). This new way of looking at the world can be termed "Undivided Wholeness in Flowing Movement," and it suggests that flow or flux is ontologically prior to the "things" that form and dissolve within it. On this view, "there is a universal flux that cannot be defined explicitly but which can be known only implicitly, as indicated by the explicitly definable forms or shapes, some stable and some unstable, that can be abstracted from the universal flux. In this flow, mind and matter are not separate substances. Rather, they are different aspects of one whole and unbroken movement" (p. 11).

All that is is the "process of becoming itself, while all objects, events, entities, conditions, structures, etc., are forms that can be abstracted from this process" (p. 49). Hence, the atomistic view equally has its place within this flowing totality of being, but only as another simplification or abstraction, valid in a limited context (cf. Heisenberg's view of the limited validity of classical physics).

Bohm traces his concept of the flowing totality of being (which bears a remarkable family resemblance to Heidegger's and Fink's *Weltspiel*) back to Heraclitus and to Eastern holistic modes of thought, as well as, in modern times, to Bergson and Whitehead. Like Heidegger and other

77. David Bohm, *Wholeness and the Implicate Order* (London, 1980), pp. 15–17. Further citations refer to this edition.

artist-metaphysicians, Bohm grounds his concept aesthetically, seeing it as a formative, *poetic* act of creation. For him the comprehension of totality is not a representational correspondence between thought and reality as a whole, but rather an "art form, like poetry, which may dispose us toward order and harmony in the overall dance of the mind" (pp. 55–56). The function of the concept of totality, like that of poetry, is "primarily to give rise to a new perception, rather than to communicate reflective knowledge of 'how everything is'." In this regard, there can "no more be an ultimate form of such thought [totality] than there could be an ultimate poem (that would make all further poems unnecessary)" (p. 63).

In the wake of Bohr and Heisenberg, then, Bohm no longer operates in terms of either the Cartesian division between observer and observed or the classical Laplacian notion of determinism (according to which the totality of world events is predetermined for all time). He also replaces the notion of absolute truth by that of relative truth with regard to scientific knowledge. As he puts it, scientific theories are no longer true or false, but only "clear in certain domains and unclear when extended beyond these domains" (p. 5). Bohm criticizes Popper's thesis of the falsifiability of scientific theories, arguing that these theories ought to be regarded essentially as "ways of looking at the world as a whole, rather than as 'absolutely true knowledge of how things are'" or as a steady series of approximations to absolute truth (p. 5). Where Bohm differs from the Copenhagen interpretation of quantum mechanics, however, is in his approach to the question of indeterminacy, probability, and statistical law.

According to Bohm, the Copenhagen version of quantum theory does not go beyond the classical principle of local causes or locality. On this principle, what happens in one area of the universe cannot affect or be affected by what happens in another area if the two areas are sufficiently distant from each other so that no light signal can connect them; in other words, the principle of local causes assumes that because nothing in the universe can travel faster than the speed of light, the causal interconnections of physical events are local in character. Bell's theorem, however, indirectly challenges this principle, by showing that information can be transmitted and received at superluminal speeds and therefore that nonlocal connections among physical events are possible.[78] Nonlocality can thus explain why local quantum events should appear as the product of chance and at the same time obey statistical or

78. For a detailed examination of the various implications of Bell's theorem, see Nick Herbert, *Quantum Reality: Beyond the New Physics* (New York, 1985).

probabilistic laws. If one accepts the principle of nonlocality, then the concepts of indeterminacy and probability lose their absolute character and assume only a limited validity, becoming subordinated to a higher level of determinism. Bohm sees the nonlocal connections between quantum events as a manifestation of the cosmic "undivided wholeness" and replaces the indeterminist concept of probability with the (non-Laplacian) determinist concept of hierarchical levels of order. This determinist concept operates in a nonlocal, "nonmanifest" manner, which creates the appearance of chance at the local, "manifest" level.[79]

In order to clarify his (nonclassical) concept of order, Bohm draws a distinction between an "implicate" and an "explicate" cosmic order, describing their interrelation on the analogy of a hologram. Cosmic totality is "implicate" or enfolded in each of its parts, just as each part of a hologram contains the whole. Bohm lends a dynamic quality to his cosmic metaphor by suggesting the term "holomovement" to describe not the pattern of objects or "things" but that of events or processes, enfolded in the cosmic order. Also, in keeping with the quantum notion of the unity between subject and object, Bohm postulates consciousness as an integral part of the holomovement. For him, mind and matter are not causally related in the classical sense (one does not "determine" the other). Rather, they are interdependent and correlated: both are implicate elements of a higher level of order which is neither mind nor matter.

Despite his sophisticated notion of the world as a totality in flowing movement (strongly reminiscent of Fink's notion of *Weltall*—see Part I, sec. 3.1) Bohm, unlike Fink, remains unaware of its prerational character, nor is he willing to give up the rational foundations of the scientific enterprise; rather, he attempts to create new ways of justifying this enterprise. In this regard, his epistemological position does not differ essentially from that of Bohr and Heisenberg. Although Reason is no longer asked to divide but to unify the world, nor is it seen as an eternal order established once and for all (as in Laplacian determinism), it remains the faculty that perceives and therefore creates order in the name of an ever-changing world totality. As Fritjof Capra aptly points

79. Cf. also Bohm's earlier book, *Causality and Chance in Modern Physics* (London, 1957); and, more recently, Prigogine and Stengers, *La nouvelle alliance* (1979), mentioned at the end of sec. 2.3. According to these authors, new physics attempts to replace a philosophy of Being with a philosophy of Becoming. This thesis is also cogently argued in Čapek's *The Philosophical Impact of Contemporary Physics* (1961)—see below.

out, "the ability to recognize order seems to be an essential aspect of the rational mind; every perception of a pattern is, in a sense, a perception of order."[80]

In Bohm's case, moreover, the world totality enfolds or implicates an infinite number of hierarchical levels of order and the function of science remains that of revealing (*creating?*) these levels. Thus, atomism, causality, necessity, chance, and all the other tools of classical physics preserve their validity intact. Bohm relativizes this validity, it is true, but he does it in the name of a higher determinism, imposed, as he puts it, by the "force of overall necessity" (p. 193). Although he replaces the static determinism of classical physics with a dynamic determinism, required by quantum and relativity theory, Bohm clearly safeguards reason as the main instrument of this new determinism.

The cases discussed here have, then, revealed that the new physicists return to a prerational ontological position, especially through the Copenhagen interpretation of quantum mechanics and through Bohm's attempt to construct a quantum-relativistic theory of physical reality. This position comes close to that of such artist-metaphysicians as Heidegger, Fink, and Deleuze. Yet, unlike the artist-metaphysicians, the new physicists remain reluctant to recognize the prerational character of their ontological position (and therefore implicitly conceal the power-oriented nature of their physical views). This recognition would bring with it epistemological consequences that are far too radical for the essentially rational goals and methods of modern science and would ultimately endanger the very existence of science as a major field of human endeavor. Instead, the new physicists adopt a Neo-Kantian *as if* or aesthetic approach to scientific knowledge, an approach that allows them to preserve the institutional structures of science unchanged. Even an enlightened theoretical physicist like Fritjof Capra—who, as a "boot-strap" theorist, is seen by some as working at the frontiers of physical science—continues to justify the old objectives of the scientific enterprise in a new language.[81] In his popular book *The Tao of Physics* he

80. See Capra, *The Tao of Physics*, p. 308. Further citations are in the text.

81. The "bootstrap" theory, elaborated by Geoffrey Chow of U. C. Berkeley, attempts to understand nature entirely through its self-consistency and is an essentially holistic and dynamic approach to physical reality. It sees particles not as individual or independent bits of matter, but as interrelated patterns of energy in constant movement or as interconnections among various parts of an inseparable cosmic web (cf. Bohm and Prigogine). As Capra points out, the bootstrap theory (which has so far remained largely qualitative but has recently gained some author-

uses Bohr's concept of complementarity precisely to that effect. After arguing for a holistic view of physical reality that would resemble certain Eastern religious and psychological beliefs, Capra remarks: "I see science and mysticism as two complementary manifestations of the human mind; of its rational and intuitive faculties. . . . Science does not need mysticism and mysticism does not need science, but men and women need both. Mystical experience is necessary to understand the deepest nature of things, and science is essential for modern life. What we need, therefore, is not a synthesis, but a dynamic interplay between mystical intuition and scientific analysis" (p. 297).

Capra's dynamic interplay between mystical intuition and scientific analysis is, as we have seen, the formula of all contemporary theoretical physicists from Planck to Einstein to Heisenberg to Bohm. Far from questioning the nature of our reality, this formula simply allows science to pursue its analytic, rational goals. In turn, complementarity becomes a convenient way of justifying the existence of what Capra calls the "modern world," which is largely the product of the scientific mentality and depends on this mentality for its perpetuation. Like all the other theoretical physicists who turn to Eastern mysticism for support of their holistic models of reality, Capra never considers the possibility that mystical intuition and scientific analysis can each belong to its own power-oriented mentality and that their "dynamic interplay" can lead only to the creation of yet another power-oriented world, perpetuating all the human dilemmas and predicaments that Capra deplores (pp. 297–298). Note also that the word *dynamic* itself comes from the Greek *dunamis*, physical force, and consequently, any dynamic model of reality, including those of Heisenberg, Bohm, and the Berkeley physicists, will necessarily remain a power-oriented one.

The split philosophical position of the new physicists is equally shared by some of the most sophisticated contemporary philosophers of science. For example, in his influential study on *The Philosophical Impact*

---

ity in the physical community at large, especially after being related to S-matrix theory and thereby yielding certain quantitative results) is the one that comes closest to the Hindu mystical view of reality. This view can also be presented in terms of a play metaphor, the "dance of Shiva," which is the eternal dance of cosmic creation and destruction. Cf. also Capra's discussion of *lila*, divine play, in chap. 13, "The Dynamic Universe." For the violent origins of Western physics, however, see Michel Serres, "Lucretius: Science and Religion," in *Hermes: Literature, Science, Philosophy*, ed. J. V. Harari and D. F. Bell (Baltimore, 1982), pp. 98–124, as well as my remarks below.

*of Contemporary Physics,* Milič Čapek shows convincingly that the new physics in effect replaces the classical philosophy of Being with a philosophy of Becoming. But he fails to recognize the prerational nature of this philosophy, attempting both to dispel the charges of "irrationality" directed against it and to safeguard determinism and causality, the main tools of scientific reason: "The alleged irrationality of indeterminism in physics disappears when we realize that the Laplacian model of physical reality is not the only rational model of the universe [cf. Heisenberg] and that the established inadequacy of classical determinism implies nothing more than a reinstatement of becoming in the physical world. . . . The applicability of probability laws to microphysical events clearly indicates that the concept of causality should be broadened rather than given up; what is to be eliminated is only its obsolete static necessitarian form."[82]

What Čapek does not seem to take into account is not only that a philosophy of Becoming always brings back into the foreground prerational values that are incompatible with science, but also that the nature of science no less than its origins will forever remain amphibolous. Even when it postulates Becoming as the fundamental nature of reality, science will always attempt to impose Being upon it; in other words, it will always attempt to find new ways of imposing law and order upon the ceaseless and arbitrary play of physical forces, subordinating this play to its own rational goals.

Finally, although a small minority of theoretical physicists, such as Schrödinger, Heisenberg, Bohm, Capra, Finkelstein, and others, no longer give primacy to the scientific mode of knowledge over other cognitive modes, the vast majority of physicists (especially those engaged in what Thomas Kuhn calls "normal science") still share the traditional scientific attitude toward art and religion. While recognizing the importance of the intuitive, aesthetic mode of knowledge favored by the latter two, traditional science subordinates this mode of knowledge to its own ideals of objective rationality. This traditional scientific attitude is well expressed by Herbert Muller, whom I have quoted at the beginning of this section in relation to the aesthetic turn in the hard sciences, and remains as much in force today as it was over forty years ago when Muller was active in his field:

In attempting to draw out the implications of the new concepts in physics, one has first to forgo a deal of pleasing phantasy. Literary men

82. See Čapek, *Philosophical Impact,* pp. 394–395.

have been inspired particularly by the Fourth Dimension. . . . More dangerous is the cocktail chatter about relativity and uncertainty, the giddy scepticism about the reliability of any human knowledge. In physics, the theory of relativity has not destroyed all constants but introduced more fundamental constants, made possible still more exact measurements of time-space relations. . . . And so with the romantic [read: prerational] misinterpretation of the scientific worlds of ceaseless process: all is flux, all is whirl. To the scientist, change emphasizes continuity; he does not deny constants and uniformities but simply looks for them in relations and processes instead of essences and lumps. Change itself is inconceivable without reference to something constant. (*Science and Criticism*, pp. 83–84)

Muller's clear-cut distinction between scientific fact and literary fiction, between the exact measurements of hard science and the playful indulgences of the imagination, shows again that despite its emphasis on Becoming and process, the aesthetic turn in the new physics remains largely of a rational nature. One can therefore conclude that, unlike its counterpart in contemporary philosophy, the aesthetic turn in contemporary physics has not yet reached, indeed perhaps never will reach, its second Nietzschean, prerational phase.

## 3·3   Play and Anarchistic Epistemology in the Contemporary Philosophy of Science

*Anarchistic epistemology* is largely a polemical term, introduced in the philosophy of science by Paul Feyerabend. In his provocative essay *Against Method: Outline of an Anarchistic Theory of Knowledge* (1975), Feyerabend attacks the current "law-and-order" methodologies in the philosophy of science such as Karl Popper's methodological falsificationism and Imre Lakatos's methodology of scientific research programs.[83] Feyerabend carries out his attack in the name of what he calls

83. For Karl Popper's critical rationalist philosophy of science, see especially *The Logic of Scientific Discovery* (New York, 1959) and *Objective Knowledge: An Evolutionary Approach* (Oxford, 1972). Apart from that of Feyerabend, critiques of Popperianism can be found in I. Lakatos and A. Musgrave, eds., *Criticism and the Growth of Knowledge* (Cambridge, Eng., 1970), esp. Thomas Kuhn, "Logic of Discovery or Psychology of Research?" and Imre Lakatos, "Falsification and the Methodology of Scientific Research Programmes." The latter is also the best exposition of Lakatos's own critical rationalist theory of research programs. For a helpful survey (largely from a Kuhnian perspective) of the general problems and concerns of the contem-

"theoretical anarchism." He argues that this anarchism (which he expressly limits to epistemology, distancing himself from the more unsavory political uses of the term) is "more humanitarian and more likely to encourage progress" than its rationalist competitors. But even though it takes up the bulk of his essay, Feyerabend's polemic against the rationalist theories of science is only a first step toward a more comprehensive goal. He ultimately directs his attack against modern science in general, which he perceives as an essentially totalitarian and imperialist enterprise that needs to be drastically reduced and restrained. Needless to say, here I can examine only those aspects of Feyerabend's central thesis which are directly relevant to aesthetics and play. Although this approach may at first sight appear somewhat marginal, I hope that it will in the long run cast a fresh light on Feyerabend's cultural critical project as a whole.

Feyerabend skillfully employs play and aesthetics both in support of his arguments and in their presentation. He adopts a playful, *as if* approach in his critique of the uses of rationality in the contemporary history and philosophy of science. He proceeds *as if* he shared the values of the rationalists (progress, objective criteria of scientific knowledge, logical consistency, etc.), but only to show that these values are far from motivating scientific practice itself. He warns the reader that the demonstrations and the rhetoric he uses do not express any "deep convictions" of his: they "merely show how easy it is to lead people by the nose in a rational way." In this respect he acts like an "undercover agent who plays the game of Reason in order to undercut the authority of Reason (Truth, Honesty, Justice, and so on)" (pp. 32–33). Feyerabend even undercuts the authority of "theoretical anarchism," replacing it by "Dadaism" and thereby emphasizing again the purely playful, aesthetic nature of his approach. For him the term "anarchism" is too ponderous, containing "precisely the kind of Puritanical dedication and seriousness which I detest." By contrast, Dadaism assumes that lighthearted attitude toward existence and human affairs which is also adopted by Nietzsche (e.g., in *Ecce Homo*): "A Dadaist is utterly unimpressed by any serious enterprise and he smells a rat whenever people stop smiling and assume that attitude and those facial expressions which indicate that something important is about to be said. A Dadaist is convinced that a worthwhile life will arise only when we start taking things *lightly* and when we remove from our speech the profound but already putrid

porary philosophy of science, see Mary Hesse, *Revolutions and Reconstructions in the Philosophy of Science* (Bloomington, Ind., 1980).

meanings it has accumulated over the centuries ('search for truth'; 'defense of justice'; 'passionate concern'; etc., etc.). . . . I hope that having read the pamphlet the reader will remember me as a flippant Dadaist and *not* as a serious anarchist" (p. 21).[84]

Feyerabend invents a Dadaist (anti-)methodology, which he playfully offers as a substitute for the rationalist methodologies he criticizes. This Dadaist research program is based on two interrelated principles: *anything goes* and *the more theories, the merrier* (my own term for Feyerabend's "proliferation of theories"). These principles are required by the very logic that seeks to repudiate them. Feyerabend reasons that no rationalist methodology can fully and adequately account for scientific practice which, like nature or life in general, is in continuous flux and therefore is unpredictable. If scientific practice itself resembles an anarchistic enterprise (following no rigid, predetermined set of rules), then it *stands to reason* that the best way of approaching it is through not one theory, but as many as possible. By the same token, the appropriateness or effectiveness of a methodology depends not on a universally applicable canon of rational rules and procedures, but on its ability to solve the concrete problems that arise in the course of scientific research. Hence the logical necessity of *anything goes* and of *the more theories, the merrier*.

Behind Feyerabend's playful Dadaist rhetoric one can discern Nietzsche's historical hermeneutics and genealogy of knowledge. For him, as for Nietzsche, facts do not create the theory; the theory creates the facts. Contrary to critical rationalist beliefs, scientific theories are not different interpretations of the same empirical data; they create their own data. In this sense one cannot say that new theories are in conflict with reality, but only that they are in conflict with older, more established theories that have already created their empirical support or reality. That theories create the facts, however, is only a polemical formulation—directed against positivism—of the Nietzschean concept of interpretation (see Part I, sec. 2.1), which Feyerabend at least partially shares. In reality, the relation between theory and experience is a dynamic interplay. Both belong to an inseparable process, and Feyerabend uses a game analogy to describe this process.

For Feyerabend scientific knowledge, indeed all knowledge, develops its tools the same way that infants develop their language skills: by playing games with new words or new concepts.[85] Children repeat

84. Feyerabend, *Against Method: Outline of an Anarchistic Theory of Knowledge* (London, 1975), p. 21, n. 12. Further citations refer to this edition.
85. Feyerabend's sympathy for Wittgenstein's concept of language games is apparent throughout his book. For his ambivalent relationship to Wittgenstein's

words ad nauseam, placing them in ever new combinations and contexts until they "grasp a meaning that has so far been beyond their reach." In this sense, the "initial playful activity is an essential prerequisite of the final act of understanding. . . . Creation of a *thing* and creation plus full understanding of a *correct idea* of the thing *are very often parts of one and the same indivisible process* and cannot be separated without bringing the process to a stop" (p. 26). As in the case of infant language acquisition, a new scientific theory-practice needs time to develop both its conceptual tools and its empirical data by *playing* with them, that is, by constantly repeating and combining them until they become common usage or reality. (Cf. Nietzsche's and Vaihinger's notions of truth and fiction as psychological rather than logical or onto-epistemological categories.) Here, then, Feyerabend employs not only the hermeneutical concept of language-games (cf. Wittgenstein and Gadamer) but also the Nietzschean idea of play as creativity, in the sense of both exploration and risk taking. He does not, however, trace his view of creativity back to Nietzsche but to Kierkegaard, calling the creative play of physical forces a "vague urge" or "passion" (it would nevertheless be easy to show that "passion" in Kierkegaard's sense bears a close family resemblance to the Schopenhauerian Will). This passion gives rise to a "specific behavior which in turn creates the circumstances and the ideas necessary for analyzing and exploring the process, for making it 'rational.'" (p. 26)

If science is essentially historical *practice* or a fashion of the times, then it may succeed even when it employs contradictory, irrational methods ("irrational" by the standards of the critical rationalists). Schrödinger makes a similiar point when he argues that physics must "not be afraid of being taunted with a lack of consistency between its announcements at subsequent epochs," and Feyerabend himself several times mentions Einstein's polemical remark that the practicing scientist will appear as the worst kind of opportunist to the philosopher of science. Scientific theories may prevail, for example, even when they proceed counterinductively (from speculation to facts), when they ignore the so-called consistency condition (new hypotheses must not contradict well-confirmed theories or well-established experimental results), and when they disregard the logical correlation of observation and theory (which assumes the relative autonomy of empirical data with respect to all theories).

Feyerabend examines the case of Galileo in great detail, showing how

---

work in general (which he helped edit and translate into English), see "Origins of the Ideas of This Essay," in *Science in a Free Society*, pp. 114–116.

the Italian scientist breaks every rule in the rationalist book in order to convince his contemporaries of the superiority of the Copernican theory of the motion of the earth over its Ptolemaic competitor. Galileo tampers with his observational data, uses ad hoc hypotheses to smooth over theoretical difficulties, misrepresents the properties of his newly invented telescope, and generally ignores all the (for Feyerabend "Puritan") standards of hard-nosed professionalism that the modern rationalists attempt to impose, at least in print, upon the scientific community. According to Feyerabend, Galileo is successful "because of his style and his clever techniques of persuasion, because he writes in Italian rather than in Latin, and because he appeals to people who are temperamentally opposed to the old ideas and the standards of learning connected with them" (p. 141). Feyerabend concludes that a theory may succeed neither because of its increased empirical content nor because it can provide a more satisfactory explanation for physical phenomena than its competitors, but because of favorable sociocultural circumstances or, at times, purely by chance.

After presenting his historical argument in a serious and impeccably scholarly manner, Feyerabend gives it a final twist by claiming that it would retain its full force (in relation to his strategic goals) even if it turned out to be a "fairy-tale." This "fairy-tale" would then still show that a "conflict between reason and the preconditions of progress is *possible*, it [would indicate] how it might arise, and it [would force] us to conclude that our chances of progress *may* be obstructed by our desire to be rational." Feyerabend finally points out that he defines progress as a "rationalist lover of science would define it, i.e., as entailing that Copernicus is better than Aristotle and Einstein better than Newton." This definition is quite narrow and there is no need to accept it. Feyerabend employs it only to prove that an "idea of reason accepted by the majority of rationalists (including all critical rationalists) may prevent progress as defined by the same majority" (p. 156).

In keeping with his Dadaistic antimethodology, Feyerabend argues not only for the abolition of the empiricist dichotomy between theory and observation, but also for the abolition of the dichotomy between the context of discovery and the context of justification, as well as that between historical description and methodological prescription. It is all these dichotomies that are in fact responsible for the false barriers between the history and the philosophy of science.

The domain of discovery, the rationalists argue, is concerned with retracing the "historical origins, the psychological genesis and development, the socio-political-economic conditions for the acceptance or rejection of scientific theories"; the domain of justification, on the other hand, provides a "logical reconstruction of the conceptual structure and of the testing of scientific theories."[86] Consequently, discovery is largely irrational and is not bound to any conscious method, while justification always proceeds rationally, beginning only *after* the process of discovery has been completed. Feyerabend's counterargument is that in scientific practice the two contexts are never found apart. Thus, science appears as a dynamic interplay of discovery and justification, and the two contribute equally to its advance. The same can be said of the distinction between methodological prescription and historical description. The two activities go hand in hand and scientific progress can be achieved "only if the distinction between the *ought* and the *is* is regarded as a temporary device rather than a fundamental boundary line" (p. 167).

If the distinctions between theory and observation, justification and discovery, philosophy and history of science turn out to be specious, so do the distinctions between science and art, and science and religion ("myth"). The logical necessity of abolishing these latter distinctions arises again from the Dadaist principle of *anything goes*. If what is regarded (by the critical rationalists) as scientific knowledge can have no special onto-epistemological claim to truth, then science should not be afraid of adopting any cognitive models that may aid its advance. Instead of rejecting them out of hand as "lies" and "fairy-tales," science should reexamine not only the older or dated scientific models of the Western and non-Western traditions but also the beautiful fictions of literature and myth in order to reassess their cognitive value or their scientific usefulness. Art proves particularly valuable during times of scientific upheaval: "Once it has been realized that close empirical fit is no virtue and that it must be relaxed in times of change, then style, elegance of expression, simplicity of presentation, tension of plot and narrative, and seductiveness of content become important features of our knowledge. . . . They *create* and maintain interest in a theory that has been partly removed from the observational plane and would be inferior to its rivals when judged by the customary standards" (p. 157).

Indeed, as Anaïs Nin points out in her *Diary*, "what restitutes to scientific phenomenon its life, is art" (quoted by Feyerabend, p. 157). Religion or myth is equally valuable to the scientific enterprise because

---

86. Herbert Feigle, "The Orthodox View of Theories," quoted by Feyerabend, *Against Method*, p. 166.

it offers alternative world views against which scientific theories can constantly measure themselves. A theoretical scientist who wants to increase the empirical content of his theories is compelled to adopt a pluralistic methodology. He must "compare ideas with other ideas rather than with 'experience' and he must try to improve rather than discard the views that have failed in the competition." For example, he may retain the cosmological views he finds in Genesis or the Pimander, expanding them and using them to "measure the success of evolution and other 'modern' views" (p. 30). Only by proceeding in this way can he satisfy the critical standards of scientific rationalism. And these very standards may conceivably lead him to the discovery that the theory of evolution is "not as good as it is generally assumed and that it must be supplemented, or entirely replaced, by an improved version of Genesis" (p. 30).

Even from this partial account of Feyerabend's Dadaist research program it is obvious that, like other contemporary artist-metaphysicans, he operates with an aestheticist and relativist world view. His rhetorical strategies are borrowed from the Sophists (as he himself points out) and are designed to turn reason against itself. The ultimate aim of this playful rhetorical exercise is twofold. On the one hand, Feyerabend hopes to demonstrate that reason is only an *instrument* (cf. Nietzsche and Vaihinger) that can be put to various uses and can therefore support any number of conflicting value systems or world views; and that rationalism, or the worship of reason for its own sake, is only one tradition among several others in Western thought—this fact is often forgotten or repressed because rationalism has for some time now managed to prevail over the other traditions. On the other hand, through his subversive play Feyerabend hopes to provide a corrective to the totalitarian ambitions of scientific rationalism. As he sees it, the present task of the philosopher of science, which converges with that of the historian of science and that of the scientist himself, is to restore the other traditions to their rightful place in modern science and in modern culture in general. In order to achieve this task the scientist-philosopher-historian has "'*to make the weaker case look the stronger,*' as the sophists said, *and thereby to sustain the motion of the whole*" (p. 30). In this respect, Feyerabend's philosophical position resembles not only that of the Sophists (Feyerabend himself praises, e.g., Protagoras for his cosmopolitan relativism) but also that of Nietzsche, and his critique of rationalism parallels Nietzsche's project of reversing all rational values as a first step toward a full return to a prerational mentality.

In turn, Feyerabend's play comes close to the rhetorical games of the Sophists, as well as to the exuberant stylistic play of Nietzsche's *Ecce Homo*. There are obvious similarities between Feyerabend and Nietzsche with regard to style, temperament, caustic sense of humor, and, above all, a never-tiring delight in polemics. For Feyerabend as for Nietzsche (or Schopenhauer or, in Antiquity, the Sophists, the Cynics, Socrates, and even Plato), the *agones logon* or fighting a worthy opponent is a vital source of both enjoyment and creativity, a particularly productive form of intellectual play.[87] All of this would certainly be enough justification for seeing Feyerabend's play (and his mentality in general) as essentially prerational. But is a full return to prerational values Feyerabend's ultimate goal? And can his play be unqualifiedly described as prerational? Family resemblances often conceal important differences, and a quick look at Feyerabend's critical project in relation to that of Nietzsche reveals features that help us understand not only Feyerabend's unique place in the modern history of the agon between rational and prerational values (and rational and prerational play) but also the ambiguous nature of the aesthetic turn in the contemporary philosophy of science in general.

To begin with, we have already seen that for Feyerabend, as for Nietzsche, scientific knowledge is not a series of self-consistent theories that move steadily toward an ideal and unreachable goal (Planck); nor is it a gradual, if never-ending, approach toward an eternal and immovable Truth (critical rationalism in general). Rather, knowledge is the product of a ceaseless contest of interpretations (again in Nietzsche's sense). Consequently, it appears as "an ever increasing *ocean of mutually incompatible (and perhaps even incommensurable) alternatives*, each single theory, each fairy tale, each myth that is part of the collection forcing the others into greater articulation and all of them contributing, via this process of competition, to the development of consciousness. Nothing is ever settled, no view can ever be omitted from a comprehensive account. . . . Experts and laymen, professionals and dilettanti, truth-

87. What Nietzsche says of Schopenhauer in the *Genealogy of Morals* applies equally well not only to Nietzsche himself but also to Feyerabend: "We must take into account the fact that Schopenhauer . . . absolutely required enemies to keep him in good spirits; that he loved atrabilious words, that he fulminated for the sake of fulminating, out of passion, that he would have sickened, become a *pessimist* (which he was not, much as he would have liked to be) had he been deprived of his enemies, of Hegel, of woman, of sensuality, of human will to survival. . . . Just as with the ancient Cynics, his rage was his balm, his recreation, his compensation, his specific against tedium, in short, his happiness" (p. 241).

freaks and liars—they all are invited to participate in the contest and to make their contribution to the enrichment of our culture" (p. 30).

Like Nietzsche in his early essays on archaic Greece, Feyerabend stresses the high cultural value of agon, which he regards as particularly productive in the field of scientific knowledge (thereby going against Kant and the Neo-Kantians, who, as we have seen, consider the *consensus omnium* a necessary condition of this knowledge). It is precisely from this Nietzschean agonistic standpoint that Feyerabend conducts his vigorous critique of modern science as an expression of a totalitarian mentality. He consistently shows how, in the guise of ideological neutrality (which presupposes a dispassionate pursuit of Truth, objective and universally valid standards of knowledge, fair play, and scrupulous professional honesty), the modern institutions of science impose a dogmatic ideology not only upon their own members but also upon society at large, in our schools, hospitals, free economy, government, and so forth. Despite its liberal image of ideological pluralism, of healthy skepticism toward rigid dogmas, and of openness to all ways of thinking and being, science has in fact ruthlessly suppressed its opponents; its dogmatic intolerance surpasses even that of religious institutions like the Inquisition. For Feyerabend, Western science is a form of myth that has defeated and replaced its older Western and non-Western competitors. Today science reigns supreme because "its practitioners are *unable to understand*, and *unwilling to condone*, different ideologies, because they have the *power* to enforce their wishes, and because they *use* their power just as their ancestors used *their* power to force Christianity on the peoples they encountered during their conquests" (p. 299).

Feyerabend's (at least temporary) antidote to the totalitarian tendencies of modern science is again of a prerational origin and bears a certain family resemblance to the Greek concept of *isomoiria*. *Isomoiria* means equal political shares for equally powerful contestants, with individuals having ceaselessly to contend for their shares. Feyerabend substitutes institutions and traditions for individuals, demanding that no tradition should be given an unfair edge over the ones it has temporarily defeated. For example, Feyerabend suggests an equalitarian model of general education in which science would certainly have its place—indeed, would be *put* in its place. According to him, science should be treated like any other subject in the curriculum rather than be given priority and be allowed to indoctrinate the pupils' minds with its own special standards. And Feyerabend characteristically uses a game analogy to describe his model: "The standards [of the various disciplines] will be *considered*, they will be *discussed*, children will be encouraged to get proficiency in the more important subjects, *but only as one gets proficiency in a game*, that is, without serious commitment and without robbing the mind of its ability to play other games as well. Having been prepared in this way a young person may decide to devote the rest of his life to a particular profession and he may start taking it seriously forthwith" (p. 218).

In *Science in a Free Society*, the spirited sequel to *Against Method*, Feyerabend extends his equalitarian model of education to modern society at large. He defines a "free society" in terms of *isomoiria*, again substituting traditions for individuals: "A free society is a society in which traditions are given equal rights, equal access to education and other positions of power."[88] Feyerabend points out that his definition differs radically from the customary definitions of (democratic) freedom: in the latter, "*individuals* have equal rights of access to positions *defined by a special tradition*—the tradition of Western Science and Rationalism" (p. 9). He criticizes the present-day American liberals who advocate social and racial equality for the individual, but not equality of traditions. For them, equality means in effect right of access to one particular tradition—the tradition of the white man. When in the aftermath of the civil rights movement liberal whites finally opened the Land of Opportunity to minorities, this was a "Promised Land built after their own specifications and furnished with their own favorite playthings" (p. 76).

Feyerabend insists, however, that what he advocates is not a general return to older, discarded traditions (in other words, he is not a political conservative or a "reactionary"), but the creation of a truly pluralistic and relativistic society in which every tradition including modern science can be practiced freely *if* an ethnic or a social group is interested in continuing this tradition (examples: astrology, folk medicine, Voodoo). A first step toward this goal would be to limit the ubiquitous authority of science by separating it from the modern state; this separation would simply follow the older historical model of the separation between state and church, which led to the creation of the modern state in the first place. But then, apart from this first step (which would already encounter enormous obstacles), what are the cultural conditions under which a free society in Feyerabend's sense may come about? It is in answering this question that Feyerabend parts ways with Nietzsche, *isomoiria*, and a purely prerational mentality.

88. Feyerabend, *Science in a Free Society*, p. 30. Further citations are in the text.

Whereas Nietzsche's ideal society would be created by a new breed of philosophical men of power or artist-tyrants, Feyerabend's free society would come about through a gradual development of the democratic structures that, to some extent, are already in place in the contemporary Western democracies. Nietzsche detests modern democracy, which to him is a direct expression of herd mentality, while Feyerabend has faith in the democratic instincts of the private citizen, who can be relied upon to pursue his own interests without seriously damaging anybody else's. In this respect Feyerabend comes much closer to J. S. Mill's pragmatic political philosophy (he frequently refers to Mill's essay *On Liberty*, for example) than to Nietzsche's aristocratic political views, and his model of the ideal state is not Sparta, but a combination of Switzerland and the United States. For Feyerabend, as for Mill, the role of the state is protective rather than intrusive and repressive. The state ought to be an ideologically neutral frame (with a strong police force at its disposal), an objective umpire who presides over the contest of various sociopolitical forces, intervening only when one force (such as modern science) does not play fair and is about to defeat and silence all the others. Hence Feyerabend's demand that the modern democratic state be separated from science. Yet this demand remains problematic for a number of reasons.

On the one hand, Feyerabend introduces a historical argument in support of his political model. He argues that at one time science was a progressive force in, and a natural ally of, the modern state, aiding it in its struggle against the totalitarian ambitions of religion. Today, however, the situation is reversed: science has replaced religion as a totalitarian force, threatening democracy (in the sense of a free play of social forces). Therefore it is science that now needs to be separated from the state and put in its place. What Feyerabend does not say (although as a good anarchist he is probably aware of it) is that this separation would in effect lead to the abolition of the modern state in its present form. The modern democratic state has from its inception been directly and inseparably correlated with the development of science-technology and rational mentality in general, and therefore will always *naturally* favor rational values, including those of modern science. Now unfortunately (or fortunately, depending on your point of view), there is no single cultural force in the present democratic state that is strong enough to seriously endanger scientific and rational values, and therefore any radical change, including Feyerabend's ideal state, would either have to depend on the goodwill of science and rationality or have to be imposed from outside.

Feyerabend does not find outside interference distasteful; on the contrary, he advocates it. His favorite example of a successful political intervention in the internal affairs of science is the action of the Chinese Communists in the 1950s, who reintroduced traditional folk medicine in their country's health-care system. However, even though this political intervention may, when regarded from outside (especially by a Western observer), create the illusion of pluralism within the Chinese medical establishment, it must surely be incompatible with Feyerabend's own standards of political pluralism: the Chinese Communist state is anything but an ideologically neutral entity, intervening only if the rules of fair play are infringed upon by freely contending social forces.

Far from illustrating the competitive mentality of a "free society," endorsed by Feyerabend, the example of the Chinese Communists only underscores the difference between Feyerabend's own politically restrictive model and a truly prerational, agonistic model. Political *isomoiria* depends on a delicate and tenuous inner balance of contending forces. This balance remains relatively stable only as long as there is a sufficient number of equally powerful forces to keep each other in check. In this regard, Feyerabend's idea of outside interference or protective frame (which he moreover wishes to back up with a large police force) would only lead to a super police state of the kind that we already have in place in several right- and left-wing dictatorships around the world. Besides, has Feyerabend considered the possibility that the majority of the citizens in the present democratic state *share* the rational values of science and wish to lead the kind of "easy" life that modern technology offers them, without pausing to think of—perhaps even joyfully *accepting*—all the risks involved in this technology? As Feyerabend himself is aware, a human community is only as good or bad as its members, and no protective frame is going to change its nature.

On the other hand, if Feyerabend's ideal free society has any chance of advancing beyond the stage of a beautiful fiction, it is because it is itself a *rational* model and as such it may conceivably become palatable to a rational mentality. This model depends on the agreement, if not the cooperation, of all citizens, including those who live in "subsocieties" that practice unrestrained violence (p. 132). Since a precondition of Feyerabend's free society is the pursuit of a "common aim" on the part of all its members, one wonders in what sense these violent subsocieties can be said to pursue a common aim with all the rest. If this aim be, say, "happiness," would not the meaning of the term vary so greatly from one subsociety to another that all sense of common purpose would be lost? And who will constitute the federal police force that would ensure that subsocietal boundaries are not crossed? Or would they be "robo-cops," programmed to enforce fair play?

Feyerabend himself is fully aware of the ideal nature of his free society. He points out, for example, that the separation of state and science, which for him is an essential step toward a general separation of state and traditions (subsocieties), cannot be introduced by a single political act. Rather, what is required is Mill's (rational) concept of political and ethical maturity: "Many people have not yet reached the maturity necessary for living in a free society (this applies especially to scientists and other rationalists). . . . The maturity I am speaking about is not an intellectual virtue, it is a sensitivity that can only be acquired by frequent contacts with different points of view. It can't be taught in schools and it is vain to expect that 'social studies' will create the wisdom we need. But it can be acquired by participation in citizens' initiatives" (p. 107).

Feyerabend's notion of pluralism, which he sees as a precondition of democratic maturity, is a thoroughly rational one as well, requiring the kind of sensitivity that belongs to fair play, a quality that simply cannot be postulated in a strictly agonistic model. In a society based on contest (as Feyerabend's ideal state is) pluralism does not mean urbane tolera-tion of the other's point of view; rather, as Hobbes and Nietzsche, among others, have observed, it means coming to terms with forces that are equal to yours because you have no other choice (short of leaving the power game). Thus, pluralism in isomoirian political models, and in an agonistic world at large, depends again on a balance of forces and not on a sense of fair play (as the behavior of today's so-called superpowers constantly reminds us).

On the other hand, it may well be that what Feyerabend's "free citizens" will gradually come to learn through their initiatives is to question the notion of competition and free society itself (which Feyer-abend does not yet seem prepared to do), in which case, instead of demanding "equal access to positions of power," they may quietly decide to drop out of the power contest altogether. As long as Feyera-bend's ideal scheme will be based on various forces alternately challeng-ing and gaining authority, it will perpetuate the same problems that he currently associates with the reign of scientific rationalism. It is in the nature of any agonistic world (Feyerabend's ideal state included) to keep moving back and forth between political totalitarianism and politi-cal fragmentation or "anarchism," and no ideologically neutral super-authority will be able to stop this movement. Not unlike the critical rationalists he attacks, then, Feyerabend remains caught up between rational and prerational values; he wants competition or *free play* but he also wants protective structures or *fair play*, and these two desiderata are incompatible if not incommensurable in Feyerabend's own sense.[89]

If, from the point of view of this book, one cannot but regard Feyerabend's "free society" with skepticism (because of its amalgam of rational and prerational values), one can nevertheless emphasize the usefulness of his critique of science as a (rational) form of power. To this critique one might add Thomas Kuhn's detailed description of the specific power-mechanisms developed by the institution of modern science, which has created a vast network of closed communities of experts or initiates who jealously guard their disciplinary turfs. In *The Structure of Scientific Revolutions* Kuhn argues that scientific communities function according to a dynamic model in which relatively long periods of stability, dominated by one theory, alternate with short periods of so-called scientific revolutions, dominated by free competition among theories or by what Feyerabend would call "epistemological anarchy."

Kuhn characterizes the stable periods (which may vary in length and content from one scientific community to another) as *normal science.* Normal science revolves around a dominant theoretical *paradigm,* a term that in his later work Kuhn partially replaces by *disciplinary matrix.* As he explains in "Second Thoughts on Paradigms," he calls it *disciplinary* because it is the "common possession of the practitioners of a

89. Feyerabend, *Against Method,* especially chap. 17. Feyerabend again employs a game analogy in order to explain his notion of incompatibility or incommensurability among scientific theories: "*One must learn to argue with unexplained terms and to use sentences for which no clear rules of usage are as yet available.* Just as a child who starts using words without yet understanding them, who adds more and more uncomprehended linguistic fragments to his playful activity, discovers the sense-giving principle only *after* he has been active in this way for a long time—the activity being a necessary presupposition of the final blossoming forth of sense—in the very same way the inventor of a new world view (and the philosopher of science who tries to understand his procedure) must be able to talk nonsense until the amount of nonsense created by him and his friends is big enough to give sense to all its parts" (p. 257).

Feyerabend's concept of incommensurability is essential for my own notion of the plurality of worlds. For me, however, the incommensurability obtains between power-oriented and other worlds. Within the power-oriented worlds themselves, various mentalities (such as rational and prerational ones) may be incompatible, but not incommensurable. See the introduction to this volume.

professional discipline," and a *matrix* because it is "composed of ordered elements of various sorts, each requiring further specification."[90] Nevertheless, Kuhn is still justified in calling the disciplinary matrix a *paradigm* because it is transmitted through scientific practice, in other words, because it is a model, to be "imitated" by successive generations of scientists. In this sense, the attribute *disciplinary* is doubly appropriate because the individual members of a scientific community are hardly expected to deviate from the matrix-paradigm, adopted by that community and are frequently punished if they do so (by losing credibility, by being denied research grants, even by being driven out of the profession). According to Kuhn, the main function of the researcher within normal science is "puzzle-solving" (note Kuhn's game metaphor, which, like that of Einstein, belongs to the rational branch of the play family); always remaining within the confines of his disciplinary matrix, the researcher concentrates on solving the main problems that this matrix still has to overcome in order to become perfectly consistent with the observational data (or, as Feyerabend would say, the researcher concentrates on *creating* the empirical data needed to support and consolidate the matrix).

The periods of scientific revolution, on the other hand, are the domain of what Kuhn calls *extraordinary science*. It is during these periods that a few daring and creative theoretical scientists depart from the disciplinary matrix accepted by their community and attempt to replace it with a new one. If this attempt is successful (for some of the reasons described by Feyerabend), then normal science can resume its puzzle-solving activity around the new disciplinary matrix, developing, consolidating, and perpetuating it for one or several generations.

Kuhn is fully aware that what he describes through his dynamic model of scientific practice is a power-mechanism, based on an "essential tension" between tradition and limited innovation. Unlike Feyerabend, however, he seems to have no *unglückliches Bewusstsein* about this power-mechanism; on the contrary, he seems to admire it a great deal, justifying it in terms of a Neo-Darwinist notion of progress. For example, toward the end of *Scientific Revolutions*, he first points out that the process of acquiring and transmitting a disciplinary matrix (through textbooks, closely monitored laboratory research, and so forth) involves "a narrow and rigid education, probably more so than any other except perhaps in orthodox theology."[91] He goes on to say that his descrip-

90. Thomas Kuhn, *The Essential Tension* (Chicago, 1970), p. 297.
91. Kuhn, *The Structure of Scientific Revolutions*, 2d rev. ed. (Chicago, 1970), p. 166. Further citations refer to this edition.

tions of normal scientific practices will inevitably suggest that the "member of a mature scientific community is, like the typical character of Orwell's *1984*, the victim of a history rewritten by the powers that be," a suggestion, moreover, which is not totally inappropriate because "there are losses as well as gains in scientific revolutions, and scientists tend to be peculiarly blind to the former" (p. 167). But Kuhn then hastens to qualify these statements which, he says, certainly do not mean to imply that "in the sciences might makes right." The choice of paradigms is the prerogative of the scientific communities themselves and is in no way determined by an outside authority, such as the state. In this respect, the "very existence of science depends upon vesting the power to choose between paradigms in the members of a special kind of community" (p. 162). In other words, science is *ultimately* a democratic process and can flourish only in a truly democratic society (cf. Feyerabend's arguments against this rationalist view, which to him is mere scientific propaganda).

For Kuhn, moreover, the choice of a scientific paradigm is *not* a random process. Despite the inevitable losses that accompany the switch to a new paradigm, the peculiar nature of the scientific community provides a "virtual guarantee that both the list of problems solved by science and the precision of individual problem-solutions will grow and grow" (p. 170). Here Kuhn invokes what Feyerabend would call the "fairy-tale" of scientific progress, even though he tailors it to fit contemporary evolutionary theory:

> The developmental process described in this essay has been a process of evolution *from* primitive beginnings—a process whose successive stages are characterized by an increasingly detailed and refined understanding of nature. But nothing that has been or will be said makes it a process of evolution *toward* anything. . . .
> But need there be such a goal? Can we not account for both science's existence and its success in terms of evolution from the community's state of knowledge at any given time? (pp. 170–171)

This relativist model of evolution, based on Schrödinger's and Heisenberg's relativist notions of determinism, still allows Kuhn to say that there is a sense in which Copernicus is "better" than Ptolemy or Einstein is "better" than Newton and, therefore, it does not amount to much more than a change in rationalist rhetoric. Like its older version, absolute progress (based on Laplacian determinism), relative progress hardly affects the normal goals and methods of scientific practice.

Feyerabend effectively challenges the idea of scientific progress (be it in its relative or its absolute form). Kuhn can still hold on to this idea because he does not sufficiently take into account the profoundly conservative nature of scientific revolutions (although he is not unaware of it). As he himself points out, the theories around which new disciplinary matrixes are developed are borrowed, as a rule, from older scientific or even religious and literary traditions. A scientific revolution almost always involves a "return" to older fictions which are then (re)vested with the authority of knowlege and truth. (Here Kuhn might profit from our modified version of Vaihinger's law of ideational shifts.) Finally, what returns in all revolutions (whether scientific or political) is not necessarily the same power structure but the same power-oriented *mentality*, which periodically regenerates itself by creating new communal and institutional frameworks. In Kuhn's notion of progress, then, we can discern the reluctance of some of the most liberal philosophers and historians of science to give up both the special claims to cultural authority of their own field and an essentially rational scientific mentality that will deny (not only to others but also to itself) that might makes right, even when it itself follows this principle *in practice*.

It is also easy to see (and Kuhn makes no secret of it) that his dynamic model of scientific practice is borrowed from the history of fine art, where the "essential tension" occurs between Classical and Romantic values. Whereas Classical artistic practices revolve around the imitation of a traditional model (for instance, Homer and Vergil), their Romantic counterparts allow themselves a certain free play, stressing originality, creativity, and innovation. It is in this sense that I have called the theoretical changes that led to the establishment of the new physics a belated Romantic revolution (see the introductory remarks to sec. 3). And if we are to adopt, for the moment, Kuhn's distinction between normal and extraordinary or revolutionary science (always keeping in mind, however, that this distinction has a systematic, heuristic rather than a historical character: in scientific practice, as Feyerabend points out in the case of other such distinctions, the two terms will ceaselessly engage in a dynamic interplay), then we can say that the aesthetic turns in science affect only its extraordinary domain and are certainly not part of the normal values of scientific practice. In other words, aestheticism in science appears mainly during scientific revolutions and is simply an instrument of supporting the new candidate for a disciplinary matrix in its contest with the already established theoretical paradigm. In turn the process of *normalization*, which occurs in the wake of any scientific revolution and is characteristic of political, religious, and artistic revolutions as well, will always involve a qualified rejection of aestheticism and play as well as a clear separation between science and other disciplines (including those which during revolutionary periods were science's allies); that is, it will always involve a return to a more traditional and authoritarian position. This fact is perfectly illustrated by the passage from *Science and Criticism* that I have quoted at the end of sec. 3.2. In this sense, it is important to remember that its author, Herbert Muller, was writing in the 1940s, that is, at a time when relativity and quantum theory (at least in its Copenhagen version) were already undergoing a process of normalization.

Finally, the kind of aestheticism and play that extraordinary science favors is that of Kant and Schiller rather than that of Nietzsche and Heidegger. As we have seen, what such theoretical scientists as Einstein, Schrödinger, Heisenberg, Monod, Eigen, Winkler, Thom, and others value in a new theory is its "beauty," by which they mean its unity, consistency, neatness, symmetry, simplicity, and so on—these are all *rational* aesthetic criteria, imposed by metaphysics on fine art. The preference for a rational aesthetics is equally shared by such "extraordinary" philosophers and historians of science as Hanson, Kuhn, Holton, and to some extent Feyerabend, as well as by a number of recent studies on "aesthetics in science." These studies recognize only what has already been stressed by Schiller and such Neo-Kantians as Lange and Vaihinger: the *secondary* role of the imagination-intuition and aesthetics-play in the scientific process of cognition. In such works as Holton's *The Scientific Imagination* and Judith Wechsler's *On Aesthetics in Science*, the emphasis is on a *thematic* approach to the history of science (reminiscent of the thematic approaches to the history of fine art), which usually involves a study of theoretical "sources and influences," or the formal features of a scientific theory and the various changes they undergo through the ages. Thus, Wechsler (an art historian by profession) points out that in her collective volume aesthetics appears as a "mode of cognition which focuses on forms and metaphors used in scientific conceptualizing and modelling," concerning itself with "the metaphorical and analogical relationship between reality and concepts, theories and models." In addition, her version of aesthetics in science examines the role "played by paradigms (Kuhn) and personal style in discovery and invention."[92] (See not only Kuhn but also Schrödinger, Heisenberg, and Holton.) This thematic approach, although admittedly more

92. Judith Wechsler, *On Aesthetics in Science*, introduction, pp. 6–7.

complex than the ahistorical approaches of the traditional philosophy of science, never questions the rational nature of scientific values or, for that matter, the rational bias of the various aesthetic theories from which the thematic approach itself draws its sources and which have been forced upon fine art by rationalist philosophers (often disguised as art critics and literary theorists) at least since Plato and Aristotle.

Even those scholars who recognize the "essential tension" between the rational and the "irrational" in science (including Kuhn and Holton) never really question "law and order" as a sine qua non of the scientific enterprise.[93] For example, Julian H. Shelley, one of the editors (with Peter Medawar) of *Structure in Science and Art*, defends the appropriateness of the title of their collective volume as follows: "Perhaps the choice of title is yet another case in point, demonstrating the universality of an *a priori* expectation of order and our reluctance in accepting chaos. Maynard Smith pinpoints the difficulties: 'both in ordinary everyday life and in the formation of scientific hypotheses, we find it remarkably difficult to use the concept of randomness.' "[94]

Moreover, at the end of his introduction (commenting on John Wheeler's unorthodox contribution, significantly entitled "Law without Law," where Wheeler proposes an "order out of chaos" cosmological model based on recent astrophysical studies of the so-called black holes), Shelley strikes a long-familiar note of rationalist optimism: "Towards the end of the book the reader might dismally agree with Wheeler's claim that 'the greater the island of knowledge grows, the greater becomes the shoreline of the unknown'. . . ; however, it is hoped that he will also be left with a belief in the basic structuralist tenet,

93. A good example here is Holton's essay "Dionysians, Apollonians and the Scientific Imagination," especially the postscript, where Holton proposes a Schillerian synthesis, beyond what he perceives as the "Dionysian" and the "Apollonian" views of science, which would reconcile Reason and Imagination in the scientific enterprise: "Possibly the worst service the new Dionysians and the new Apollonians render is that their antithetical attacks continue to discredit the accommodation of the classically rationalistic with the sensualistic components of knowledge. We should, rather, strive to acquire a clearer notion of how actual mortal beings, with all their frailties, have managed to use both these faculties to grasp the outlines of a unique and fundamentally simple universe, characterized by necessity and harmony" (*The Scientific Imagination*, pp. 109–110). *Unicity, simplicity, necessity*, and *harmony* have been obvious code words for rationalist world views at least since Plato.

94. Maynard Smith, *Structure in Science and Art* (Amsterdam/Oxford/Princeton, N.J., 1980), Introd., p. xii.

namely, the interconnectedness of facts about the world and, hence, of our knowledge" (p. xii).

In view of the nearly unanimous call for law and order on the part of the contemporary scientists and their public representatives (the philosophers and the historians of science), one can safely conclude that Feyerabend's anarchistic epistemology and free society have little chance of becoming reality in the foreseeable future. Even during its periods of "aestheticism," scientific discourse remains the most faithful ally of the rational mentality, and the few dissenting voices that advocate (however confusedly) prerational values in science are mostly ignored. In this regard, the advocates of a prerational mentality in philosophy and art have been more successful than their scientific allies. From the point of view of our history, however, the agon between rational and prerational mentality (and between rational and prerational play) remains as fierce today as it was almost two and a half millennia ago when, in the Athenian agora, Socrates challenged, and was in turn challenged by, the Sophists. Yet despite its fierceness, this agon will remain forever undecided, because it is its very perpetuation that allows the power-oriented values of our culture to return, generation after generation, like Cadmian warriors sprouting out of the dragon's teeth.

# Index

*Library of Congress Cataloging-in-Publication Data*
Spariosu, Mihai.
  Dionysus reborn : play and the aesthetic dimension in modern philosophical and scientific discourse/Mihai I. Spariosu.
      p. cm.
  Includes index.
  ISBN 0–8014–2327–9 (alk. paper)
  1. Play (Philosophy)—History. 2. Aesthetics, Modern.
3. Science—Philosophy—History. I. Title.
B105.P54S65   1989
128—dc19                                                                      89–923